Harold Evans was editor of the *Sunday Times* and *The Times* (and earlier of the *Northern Echo* and assistant editor of the *Manchester Evening News*). A graduate of Durham University, he has written a number of bestselling histories. He followed the late Alastair Cooke in commentaries on America for the BBC. He holds a British Press Awards' Gold Award for Lifetime Achievement and the European Gold Medal of the Institute of Journalists. In 2001 British journalists voted him the all-time greatest British newspaper editor. He was knighted in 2004.

'"Inspiring" is an overused word. This truly is. Anyone who feels cynical about public life in general, and journalists in particular, should drink down this wonderful book in a single gulp. Harry Evans was the great crusader of the twentieth-century British press. His memoir, which is also a jaw-dropping social history, is the best education possible in what true journalism's all about' ANDREW MARR

'Reading these evocative and enjoyable memoirs, one feels the warmth of his sunny personality even as the lights seem to be going out in much of print journalism. He saw the best of it – o, lucky man!' ROBERT HARRIS, **Sunday Times**

'Illuminating and entertaining . . . The important reason to read it is that it tells you how good newspapers were once made and why they still matter' **Guardian**

'One of the great figures of modern journalism . . . *My Paper Chase* is both gripping and timely . . . His story is one of relentless ambition and determination' **Economist**

'Journalists' memoirs tend to be as transitory as the great stories they lovingly recall. Few of them impart much of value, except perhaps for a fleeting sense of nostalgia. Harold Evans must surely be counted an exception' **Spectator**

'Crisp, amusing and highly readable . . . What struck me about the writing was not just the fizzing energy and the exactitude of recall, but the tone' **Observer**

'*My Paper Chase* elega   TLS

'An absorbing book' In

'The story of one of   e twentieth-century . . . Nearly eve

ALSO BY HAROLD EVANS

MY PAPER CHASE

True Stories of Vanished Times

an autobiography

HAROLD EVANS

ABACUS

First published in Great Britain in 2009 by Little, Brown
This paperback edition published in 2010 by Abacus

The author gratefully acknowledges permission to quote from the following:
'For the Fallen', The Society of Authors as the Literary Representative of the
Estate of Laurence Binyon; Excerpt from 'Annus Mirabilis' from *Collected Poems*
by Philip Larkin. Copyright © 1988, 2003 by the Estate of Philip Larkin.
Reprinted by permission of Faber and Faber Limited; 'The Northern Ireland
Question', Desmond Egan from *Elegies, Selected Poems*, the Goldsmith Press Ltd.,
Ireland; Anthony Taylor Dunn for an excerpt from 'The Dinosaur'.

A CIP catalogue record for this book
is available from the British Library.

ISBN 978-0-349-12245-8

Typeset in Sabon by M Rules
Printed and bound in Great Britain by Clays Ltd, St Ives plc

Papers used by Abacus are natural, renewable and
recyclable products sourced from well-managed forests and certified
in accordance with the rules of the Forest Stewardship Council.

Mixed Sources
Product group from well-managed
forests and other controlled sources
www.fsc.org   Cert no. SGS-COC-004081
FSC   © 1996 Forest Stewardship Council

Abacus
An imprint of
Little, Brown Book Group
100 Victoria Embankment
London EC4Y 0DY

An Hachette UK Company
www.hachette.co.uk

www.littlebrown.co.uk

Dedicated to my granddaughters, Emily and Anna

Contents

Knowledge will forever govern ignorance and a people who mean to be their own governors must arm themselves with the power which knowledge gives.

James Madison, Letter to W. T. Barry, August 1822

BOOK ONE

True Stories of Vanished Times

1

GRAINS OF TRUTH

The most exciting sound in the world for me as a boy was the slow whoosh-whoosh of the big steam engine leaving Manchester Exchange Station for Rhyl in North Wales. Every year as summer neared I counted the days to when the whole family – six of us then – would escape the bleakness of Northern winters and take the train for a week at the seaside, buckets and spades in hand.

I was nearly twelve the summer I saw the bodies of the soldiers scattered about the sands.

The soldiers were so still, their clothing so torn, their faces so pale, they looked as if they had died where they fell. And yet they had escaped death, unlike thousands of their comrades left on the battle-grounds of northern France; thousands more were on their way to years in German internment camps. The men I saw were the lucky ones, a few hundred of the 198,229 of the British Expeditionary Force (BEF) who just days before in May–June 1940 had fought their way to Dunkirk. Twenty-four hours earlier, these men had been on that other beach, being hammered from the air by Stuka dive bombers, strafed by the machine guns of Messerschmitts, rescue ships ablaze offshore, and every hour the German Panzers closing the ring. They were a forlorn group, unshaven, some in remnants of uniform, some in makeshift outfits of pyjamas and sweaters, not a hat between them, lying apart from the rows of deckchairs and the Punch and Judy show and the pier and the ice-cream stands. Most of the men who were evacuated had been sent to bases and hospitals in the south of England, but several thousand had been put on trains to seaside resorts in North Wales, where there were Army camps and spare beds in the boarding houses. The bulk of the men sprawled on the Rhyl beach were members of the Royal Corps of Signals attached to artillery regiments; some sixty-four officers and 2,500 other ranks had been sent to the 2nd Signal Training Centre at Prestatyn, which shared six miles of sand with Rhyl.

When we set out for the family holiday, we had no idea that survivors of Dunkirk had just arrived in Rhyl. Nobody in Mrs McCann's redbrick boarding house on the front said anything about the arrivals; they didn't know and wartime censorship didn't encourage people to talk anyway. Our first day on the beach I bullied my younger brothers – ten, four and going on two – into helping me build a huge wall of sand to keep out the advancing Irish Sea while Mum sat in a deckchair knitting and Dad read the newspaper. My father, a steam train driver, had worn himself out taking munitions trains through the blackness of wartime Britain, but he could never sit in a deckchair for long. He would inhale the salt air for ten minutes, then declare we should swim, kick a soccer ball or join an impromptu beach cricket match.

The next bright morning when I hoped to build a bigger, better sand wall, Dad was restive again. He suggested we should all go for a brisk walk along the sands to work up an appetite for Mrs McCann's lunch. My mother and three brothers preferred to idle by the paddling pool, so with ill grace I fell in beside him. Not only could he not sit still for long, he was compulsively gregarious. Everyone else on the beach was getting on with their seaside relief from factory shifts and holding a family together in the stress of war. To my frustration, when we had gone beyond the pier Dad saw these sprawling clumps of men, isolated from the holiday crowds, and he walked along to find out who they were. I can see him now squatting among them, offering a cigarette here and there. At thirty-nine, he must have been several years older than most of them, but you would never have known, so weary and haggard were they. I was always embarrassed by Dad's readiness to strike up a conversation with strangers, but he moved among groups of the soldiers most of the morning and I tagged along.

We had been encouraged to celebrate Dunkirk as some kind of victory. A *Daily Mirror* front page I'd seen pinned up in our boarding house had the headline 'Bloody Marvellous!' How was it then Dad found nothing marvellous, only dejection, as he moved among them?

Only two years later, when my ambitions to be a newspaper reporter flowered, did I understand that Dad was doing what a good reporter would do. Asking questions. Listening. It never occurred to me to take a note, and write it up in my diary, but to this day I remember the sadness of the soldiers who had seen such havoc on that other beach and who knew, too, that they owed their lives to the countless acts of heroism of the rearguard who fought to the last man to keep open the escape corridor.

'They said they had nothing to fight with,' Dad told everyone back in the dining room that lunchtime. The men were not triumphant, he explained, as they were said to be – they were bewildered, bitter that the Maginot Line had proved useless because the Germans bypassed it by coming through Belgium, bitter with the French Army, bitter with the Royal Air Force they felt had left them so exposed to the Luftwaffe as they lined up on the beach and scrambled for the shallow-draft little boats that would take them to the bigger ships. (The histories suggest the French and the RAF both performed better than it seemed at the time, but misperceptions are the common currency of war.) The newspapers we'd seen had given the impression that the survivors couldn't wait to get back into battle to avenge our defeat. Maybe thousands were, but not those prostrate on the Rhyl sands. Nor the dispirited men who, according to the historian Richard Collier in his 1961 history of Dunkirk, flung their rifles away after landing at Dover.

Dad's account of the mood of the men compared well with the national archives records I checked years later. 'We didn't deserve the cheers,' said Albert Powell, a truck driver, of their reception after landing in Ramsgate before entraining for Rhyl. Bert Meakin, a gunner with the 51st Medium Regiment, was critical of the weapons they'd been given to hold back the Germans: 'First World War six-inch howitzers on iron wheels, pretty useless really!' His group fought south of the Somme, then were told it was every man for himself; they abandoned the howitzers in the woods. He arrived in Rhyl with a seven-day leave warrant but without a penny. Powell, a Royal Signals truck driver attached to 3rd Corps, Medium Artillery, got to La Panne on foot. 'On the beaches we huddled together in the sand dunes for protection from the constant bombing and machine-gunning from the air. The bombing was ineffectual, just blowing up loads of sand, but the machine-gunning was another matter.' Once Powell reached a boat, it was swamped by a dive bomber's near miss and he was flung into the sea. He swam 50 yards, 'arrived at the ship completely knackered and found myself hauled aboard'.

Looking back on my boyhood snapshot memory of the difference between what I read and what I saw, I often wondered if Dad and I were overly impressed with a first-hand experience, and hadn't seen the woods for the trees. Dad talked, after all, to a tiny fraction of the evacuated soldiers (and surely newspaper reporters would have talked to hundreds?). So it was interesting to learn later that Winston Churchill got so worried at the presentation of the retreat as a triumph that he felt it necessary to remind everyone 'wars are not won by evacuations'. Even more illuminating on the role of the press was Phillip Knightley's authoritative account of war reporting in his book *The First Casualty*, first published in 1975. Of Dunkirk, he wrote: 'Above all, the stories stressed the high morale of the evacuated troops, itching to get back to France and into the fight again. It was not until the late 1950s and early 1960s – nearly twenty years after the event – that a fuller, truer picture of Dunkirk began to emerge.' Alexander Werth, the *Manchester Guardian* correspondent, confessed that after the fall of France he felt guilty at the 'soft soap' he had been giving his readers.

The discordance between the waterfront and the front pages was bewildering, the first vague stirring of doubt about my untutored trust in newspapers. As a kid in short trousers, I had hardly followed the events of the 1930s with the avidity with which I later read the histories, but I remember how troubled my father was on 3 September 1939 – Chamberlain's declaration of war on Germany that morning was so contrary to what we had been insistently told by the *Daily Express*, the newspaper my parents took at home. The paper had reassured its millions of readers there would be no war, its front-page campaign slogan: 'The *Daily Express* declares that Britain will not be involved in a European War this year, next year either'. Everyone believed it. And why not? The *Express* was then a brilliant broadsheet with a circulation of 3 million and a huge secondary readership. Most British homes were reached by one of the bigger newspapers: some 13 million read the *Express* newspapers, the *Daily Mirror*, *News of the World* and *People* in 1939 and 22 million by 1948. Newspapers played a crucial role in shaping public perceptions. As the social historian Richard Hoggart noted in his study of the working class at this time, people often used to say as evidence of disputed truth: 'Oh, but it was in the papers.'

But what if you couldn't trust a newspaper to tell the truth, and nothing but the truth? Which institution was more trustworthy, the state or the press? Later in adulthood, it was easier to understand how predictive headlines could turn out to be wrong than to reconcile what we experienced in Rhyl with the emphasis in what we read as fact. How did newspapers come to conclusions? Were they acting at the request of government? Was there a deliberate and widespread gloss on Dunkirk? Would that have been justified as a means of sustaining the nation's morale at a crucial time? Should newspapers take account of such imperatives or just report things as they see them? How does a newspaper decide these things?

After a lifetime in newspapers, the same questions resonate with me. There were to be many times when I found that what was presented as a truth did not square with what I discovered as a reporter or, as an editor, learned from good shoe-leather reporters. This was not so much that deliberate lies were told (though they sometimes were) and not always to conceal a villainy: 'In wartime,' Churchill remarked, 'truth is so precious that she should be attended by a bodyguard of lies.' We all understand in an age of terrorism that refraining from exposing a lie may be necessary for the protection of innocents. But 'national interest' is an elastic concept that if stretched can snap with a sting. When, in the early 1970s, the *Sunday Times* began reporting the anger building among the Catholic minority in Northern Ireland, a group of Conservative MPs invoked the national interest to demand that we stop. They came to tell me, as the paper's editor, that it was 'treasonable' to continue. Actually, the real offence was failing to give Northern Ireland full attention in the early 1960s when the violence was incubated.

A commoner issue than outright lying is that people of good faith resent facts that run contrary to their beliefs and assumptions. The nineteenth-century American humorist Josh Billings said it best: 'It ain't ignorance that causes all the trouble in this world. It's the things people know that ain't so.' No institution has a monopoly of vice in these matters – not governments, not trade unions, not company heads, not lawyers, not academia, nor the press for that matter. In what came to be known as the thalidomide affair in Britain, children were born with deformities – a shortened arm, or no arm at all, or no leg, or completely limbless – because the mother had taken a prenatal drug prescribed by the National Health Service. They were left to endure their ordeal without help or compensation, a shocking situation that persisted for a decade because the government and the lawyers representing the families alike assumed the children had been the victims of an unforeseeable disaster. The lawyers sincerely believed they were making the best of a bad case; but the argument for adequate compensation, properly investigated by the *Sunday Times*, was overwhelming. Revealing it brought furious lawsuits, led by the government of the day, with the Attorney General accusing me and the newspaper of contempt of court, punishable by a jail sentence.

Independent reporting has a history of provoking denunciation. Take the legend that 'unpatriotic' reporters lost Vietnam. It doesn't stand up to serious examination. Print and TV supportively reported the war in the context of Cold War ideology; they wanted the US to win. What maddened them were the little deceptions of the US, the hubris of its generals, the corrupt incompetence of the South

Vietnamese establishment, and the way the political military bureaucracy deceived itself into telling Washington what it wanted to hear. The corrective correspondents did a real service; and too many of them were killed doing it. Similarly, early in the Iraq war the Bush administration charged that the reporters on the ground were being lazy, foolish, cowardly and unpatriotic for reporting that the country was on a vicious downward spiral. It was. The administration deceived itself and no good came of that. Indeed, a more accurate charge against the press on Iraq would not be that it was unpatriotic after the war began but that it wasn't patriotic enough before. Faced with a secretive administration bent on war come what may, and a popular clamour for post-9/11 revenge, the press forsook its true function. The real national interest required the most searching examination of the reasons for sending thousands to their deaths, and it did not get it.

The epiphany on Rhyl beach shook my faith in the printed word, but it did not make me averse to newspapers. On the contrary, as I entered my teens I grew ever more eager to involve myself in their mysteries. Newspapers were clearly more important and more fascinating than I had imagined, reporting more than a matter of stenography. But how was I to become a reporter and learn the newspaper trade? I was a working-class boy who had already been branded a failure, having failed to qualify for grammar school. Was I reaching too far? Was I really fit for the work? What were the pitfalls, the ethical dilemmas and the traps I could barely imagine? How could I equip myself to decode the complex, ever-changing, thrillingly dynamic mosaic of live news, and bring it to the public with the raw integrity of truth?

So began my paper chase.

2

GETTING UP STEAM

When I was three years old I was expected to die of pneumonia. My first fevered memory of life is staring at the coloured counting beads of an abacus at the side of the narrow bed where I was confined in a room with the curtains drawn.

I was born in the summer of 1928 in one of the long rows of two-up, two-down terraced houses off the Liverpool Road, Patricroft, Eccles, part of the sprawl of the cities of Salford and Greater Manchester, and raised in the L. S. Lowry landscape of bent stick figures scurrying past sooty monuments of the industrial revolution. The Renshaw Street houses were so narrow that people shook their heads about how hard it was to get a coffin down the staircase.

Until antibiotics became widely available in England at the end of the 1930s, one in twenty infants died – mostly from pneumonia, meningitis, diphtheria and tuberculosis. TB was always referred to in a whisper as 'the consumption, you know. They'll never rear him'; indeed, it carried off my cousin Freddy around the time I had pneumonia.

During that family crisis, my mother was up half the night nursing my brother, who had whooping cough; my father was working nights. I was mostly nursed by a neighbour, Mrs Amy Roberts, who lived opposite us, had some nursing experience, and volunteered to sit with me through the nights of fever. In 1978, after I'd become known as a journalist, Amy told the *Eccles Journal* that when she visited my distraught mother she found: 'Harold had been put to bed with whooping cough he had caught from his brother, but was lying on his back, which is dangerous for a sick child.' She added: 'Harold was a very tiny child with a small peaky face and was too weak to be bothered with anything. He did perk up towards the end of the week but even then he was very shy.'

The shyness is at odds with family folklore from when I was two. My mother, on a walk through a local park, parked my baby carriage behind a bench at the duck pond while she chatted with other young mothers. When she turned to go, my carriage was empty. The consensus among the calmest of the young women consoling my mother was that her blue-eyed son had been seized by an international gang of baby smugglers and was even then on his way across the Channel. In fact, the guilty party was happily ensconced in another baby carriage. I had undone my harness and climbed unseen from my own pram into another where eventually I was found cuddling a baby girl.

My brother Fred, who became the keeper of the family history, told me I was actually nursed through the pneumonia by another good neighbour, Mrs 'Matt' (Matthew) Newstead, the wife of my father's best friend, which is how my second name came to be Matthew. Perhaps the two women took turns at my bedside. In any event, there are people who feel they both have a lot to answer for.

My grandfather, John Evans, was born in 1854 at Llanrhaeadr-ym-Mochnant in Montgomeryshire, a little village in mid-Wales, where the Bible was first translated into Welsh. He left school when he was nine years old to run errands for platelayers mending railway tracks around Crewe railway junction, the gateway to the North of England. (Compulsory schooling to fourteen was enacted only in 1918.) He later married Sarah Jane Collins, a girl eleven years his junior from Church Minshull, Cheshire, who gave birth to my father on 1 August 1900. She failed to register his birth within the six weeks required and so, fearful of prosecution, she registered

Frederick Evans as having been born fifteen days later, on 21 August. In this manner, my father acquired a distinction shared with the Queen – two birthdays, and we never knew which to celebrate.

Grandfather John sustained his family in a rented cottage in the village of Coppenhall, Cheshire, in North-West England by repairing shoes and cutting hair at the end of his day's work on the railway. My father told me: 'He saved halfpennies so that we'd have Christmas stockings. Mine always had a twopenny mouth organ, an apple, a nut, and a shiny new penny. Nobody had a radio. It hadn't been invented. On Christmas night, we blew out the candles and sat around telling ghost stories.' Every Christmas in my own childhood, whatever else was in our stockings, there was always an apple, a nut and a shiny new penny.

My father had little formal education. His father had none: a family secret we didn't learn for fifty years. In 1981, when I was editing *The Times* of London, the paper was delivered to a cottage I had in Shoreham, Kent, where Dad and Mum were taking a break; Dad was recovering from a heart attack he'd had while visiting us. 'You know, Harold, it's a rum thing,' he said, opening the paper. 'What would people say if they knew the man editing this newspaper is the grandson of a man who couldn't read a word of it?'

I had six very different aunts and uncles from Dad's brothers and sisters. One of them, Wild Jack, was a gambler who lost everything betting on horses. The other older brother, Albert, was a railway chief detective superintendent who slept in freight cars to catch thieves. Dick was a house painter and Len a very quiet fisherman who didn't seem to have any work. Dad's two sisters were opposites in temperament. Aunt Beattie, the toughest of all my father's family, married a younger widowed farmer in Oswestry near the Welsh border and ruled him and the kids with a rod of iron. Mild Aunt Maggie, the youngest and plumpest in the family, helped in a shop in a back street in Crewe, and always fed me sweets when we visited; my first sexual thrill at the age of ten was when her teenage daughter, and her giggling friend in another bed in the same room, teased me about what might happen to 'little Harold' if they came in with me. In retrospect, I regret they lost their nerve, but at the time I was terrified. They seemed like fully grown women to me, though they were probably around fourteen.

My mother, Mary Hannah (known to all as Polly), was one of thirteen children of whom, so far as I could discover, only three survived to adulthood. She was born in Stockport, Cheshire, in 1904, the daughter of Lucy Haselum (née Murray), which gave us a tinge of Irish blood to mix with the Welsh: the Murrays were connected to the Collinses. Grandmother Lucy's father captained ferry boats making the run from Merseyside to Ireland. My mother left school at the age of twelve, and helped the family budget by chopping firewood in Eccles. At thirteen, she was clattering down the street in clogs on the way to the card room of the local cotton mill. Her older sister, named 'Big' Eva to distinguish her from her daughter and my cousin 'Little' Eva, married a cobbler who had lost a leg in the First World War; her younger brother, Arnold, was a dashing engineer and a Merchant Navy officer in the Second World War.

My mother always had ambitions for a better life. Childhood measles and scarlet fever left her without a sense of smell and her hearing deteriorated in her thirties, but she never complained. Not only did she manage to bring up four boys with equal affection – five if you include Dad, who was lost without her – in time she started a business that thrived on their relationship.

My father was the optimist, my mother was the worrier. She had a habit, when sitting in an armchair, of repeatedly running her hand along the fabric, smoothing it out in a rhythmic manner that Richard Hoggart perceived (rightly I think) as an effort by working-class women of that generation to smooth out their anxieties. Unlike my gregarious father, she never struck up a conversation with strangers, never talked politics. She reserved her energies for figuring out a future for everyone in the family. She hugged us and cared for us – all of us, including Dad – through accidents and sicknesses; even when I had tonsils removed at eighteen, she busied herself bringing to the sickbed every day some concoction of egg and brandy with a mystery ingredient I thought might be brown beef-sauce. It seemed to work.

Dad had not much of a better start in life than his father, punished like so many bright boys for being born poor. He was a good all-round student, top of his class in arithmetic, and picked for advancement to high school in Crewe, but the family needed him to become a wage earner, so schooling ended when he was eleven. At thirteen he stoked the furnaces making steel at Crewe Works. 'It was a rotten time,' he remembered. 'We had no electricity in the countryside at Coppenhall; in winter we got up at four-thirty to light the fire, thaw the taps. I ran the mile or two to Crewe to get there for six, just in time for a cup of sweet tea and a bun.'

In 1916, he volunteered for the Royal Flying Corps, passed some tests and was downcast when they found out he was sixteen, not the seventeen he claimed, and therefore too young. The war ended before he could be sent to the trenches, but he joined the Territorial Army. For a time, he trained as a boxer, modelling his footwork on a legendary flyweight world champion hardened in a Welsh coal mine, the skinny, 5-foot-2 Jimmy Wilde. Dad put boxing gloves on all his four boys, one at a time encouraging us to take a swing at him and to learn to dodge and weave. 'A good little 'un will always beat a big 'un,' Dad assured us. It was one of his aphorisms I preferred not to test on the back streets of Newton Heath where I collected enough bloody noses simply protecting my marbles from predators.

My father was a bit of a puzzle about martial matters. He was the least belligerent of men but he loved military ceremonies like the changing of the guard at Buckingham Palace and spoke of John Philip Sousa's marching music with almost the same reverence as he accorded a run down the wing by his idol on the football field, Stanley Matthews, the wizard of dribble. In his spick and span time in the Territorial Army, he learned to beat out an impressive tattoo on a kettledrum; he practised it for years on the panel of our bedroom doors when we were slow to get up for school.

My mother was nineteen and my father twenty-three when they met at the 'monkey run', as everyone called the Saturday evening dance at a social club on Liverpool Road. The stylish wedding picture of the slim, elegant couple at Patricroft Parish Church in September

1924 belies the bleakness from which they emerged. The newlyweds
had to squeeze into a tiny house at 39 Renshaw Street with Granny
Haselum and her dying husband Adam, a labourer in a chemical factory.

My mother and father were lucky in a way. They had jobs when
they married. Three million Britons did not. My father had been
taken on by the London, Midland and Scottish Railway (LMS) to
clean steam engines and my mother had the cotton mill job until I
was born. They were then wholly dependent on my father not being
sacked. The fear that they might have to go down to the labour
exchange to register for unemployment money from the government
filled them both with horror; they had a prideful revulsion at taking
'dole money' that was still vivid in their minds when I was a teenager
and they were secure. They radiated a quiet confidence that they
were giving us a better start than they had. 'I'll see you never wear
clogs,' Mum said often – and always with uncharacteristic fierceness.
They both took it for granted their boys would climb Everest. 'The
railway's not for you,' Dad told each of his four boys.

They saved every penny in Renshaw Street, and with the birth of
a second child (my brother Fred in October 1929) they rented an
airier, better-built house, one of a row at 14 May Street, Munton.

It was just across Liverpool Road, but it was a different world. On
Renshaw Street you were in the living room as soon as you crossed
the doorstep, so much so that families were judged by how freshly
sanded they kept that front doorstep. On May Street, Mum didn't
have to kneel every morning at the front door with a bucket of hot
water and a pumice stone: now we had a gate, we had a tiny front
garden, we had leaves. In fact, after the abacus my earliest memory is
of the leaves on privets. To my young eye, being wheeled to a nursery
school where we all had cots for afternoon naps, the neighbourhood of May Street was a corridor of privet hedges – moats to the
semi-detached castles of the English lower orders. Horticulturists
value *Ligustrum ovalifolium* for its ability to survive industrial
pollution; the self-consciously respectable working class in which
I grew up cared more about preserving privacy than combating
the then little-appreciated effects of pollution. How sedulously they

tended their *Ligustra* defences against prying eyes! Such was the prevalence of the question, 'What will the neighbours think?' that I got the idea God had planted busybodies as prolifically as privets.

My father was a genius with numbers. If you named a date five, twenty, thirty-seven years ahead, in a flash he'd tell you what day of the week it would be. Or tell him the date of your birth and he'd name the day you were born. I never knew him to get it wrong and I never knew how he did it.

At work on the railway, he became a legend among workmates – 'a ruddy marvel' – for being able to calculate in his head what any one of them was due in his pay packet at the end of a string of complexly different wage rates and irregular hours. The first railwayman who took him at his word got a brusque reception at the 'gaffer's' office until they discovered they had indeed short-changed him. This happened so often that when a worker took the pay slip back to the cashier and said: 'Freddie Evans says it is five pennies out,' they'd pay it without argument. Ken Law, a Manchester steam fireman, recalls encountering my father at the Newton Heath rail depot's large glass casement that displayed all the assignments of some thirty or more Links (groups of drivers, firemen, cleaners), each Link with twelve weeks' work in it. 'If you stopped for a word, he would suddenly amaze you by telling you that Number 3 Link had four hours' more night rate in twelve weeks' work than Number 5 Link, or that Number 2 Link had more Sundays than Number 7 Link and so on. It was no effort. Freddie could work out these statistics just in his head while he waited to be given his engine number. Few could do it today even with the aid of a pocket calculator. Of course nobody had those then. We had Freddie Evans.'

In his middle years Dad experimented with the laws of chance. 'Gambling is a mug's game' was his mantra, derived from the experiences of his crazy older brother Jack. Among working men, all sorts of foolproof betting 'systems' enjoyed brief vogues, all ending in disaster, so Mum was fearful when Dad said he had devised a mathematical system for betting on greyhounds. Off he went to the track in Salford with four pounds. He lost it all.

He was depressed, but he knew why his scheme had failed. 'I'm sorry, Polly, I got greedy,' he told my mother. Henceforth it was his iron rule that once he had won a pound he walked off the track. His railway hours did not allow him to go as often as he would have liked, but month after month, year after year, he won his pound and came home, eventually accumulating enough to pay for every family summer holiday.

He didn't impose any kind of regimentation on his boys, so I didn't associate him with discipline. But he was disciplined with himself, apart from being unable to control an appetite for conversation. In his mid-forties he suddenly decided to give up smoking because prices went up. 'That's my last cigarette,' he said one day, and it was. I'd tried a few cigarettes with our street band of boys. We collected discarded ends called 'dimps' and rolled the tobacco into hand-made cigarettes for secret group smokes. A few puffs made me cough and I never touched cigarettes again.

My father's phenomenal numeracy was of no interest to the railway company then, nor in the 1950s and 1960s to nationalized British Railways which had swallowed the LMS. However conscientiously a cleaner, fireman or driver performed, however well they did in tests, whatever ideas on efficiency they put forward, however long they served with distinction, however much they were esteemed by their peers, they could never hope to achieve advancement into the officer class of supervisors and above. That was ordained by the hierarchies of class.

The question I asked myself often about my parents was what they might have done if they'd had a real chance. Like millions of others, they'd been held back from birth by the belief among the ruling elites that education could do nothing for the working class – nor should it. The Liberal party in power after the First World War set about introducing universal secondary education to the age of sixteen, reducing classroom sizes below sixty and opening a door to universities, but the Tories dominant after 1922 – the hardliners, not all of them – abruptly reversed the progress. Growing up, I got bored when Dad went on and on about 'the Geddes axe', not realizing then how frontal an assault it had been on any hope of equality of opportunity.

Sir Eric Geddes (Lord Inchcape), a Tory grandee and Minister of the Crown and a former manager of the North-East Railway Company, had a predictable contempt for the working class. It expressed itself most nakedly in his advice to Parliament not to waste money giving poor children a secondary education – 'children whose mental capabilities do not justify it' was the way he put it in the report of his committee examining public expenditure. This was unappealing as rhetoric; it was appalling as policy. It was exactly the wrong prescription when Britain was suffering from chronic over-reliance on unskilled labour in declining industries. Naturally it was greeted with applause in the press, just as was Winston Churchill's disastrous return to the gold standard in 1925 which priced British exports out of world markets. The conviction of the conventional wisdom in press and politics was that if it hurt, it must be good for you. Those who were most hurt, of course, were not the advocates of salvation by masochism. They were the coal miners, factory hands and shipbuilders who endured wage cuts, longer hours and lockouts.

Recollection of my father's dim view of Churchill pains me, since like millions of others I came to see Churchill as a hero for his wartime leadership. From the perspective of the 1920s, however, my father's attitude was justified. It was hard to forgive the consequences of Churchill's gold standard blunder, his ill-fated assault on Gallipoli, nor his virulence in the General Strike of 1926, a failed attempt to stop a reduction in coal miners' wages. He edited the government newspaper the *British Gazette*, which attacked the miners and persistently printed foolish fabrications, assuring Londoners, for instance, that buses and trains were running near to normal when, having to walk to work, they knew they weren't. When later in my career I took a look at the record, I was shocked at the distortions coated in hysteria and shoved down the throat of the public. (The fledgling BBC also was hardly a beacon, suppressing anything that might help the strikers, including a conciliatory appeal from the Archbishop of Canterbury.) Even the Prime Minister Stanley Baldwin and the government's commissioner in charge of information, L. C. Davidson, were alarmed at Churchill's reckless conduct. Davidson wrote later that Churchill and his ally Lord Birkenhead were 'absolutely mad . . . he [Winston] had it firmly in his mind that everyone who was out of work was a Bolshevik; he was most extraordinary and never have I listened to such poppycock and rot.' Churchill simply allowed political passion to swamp journalistic principle.

The distrust carried over into the darkening 1930s, when Churchill was so valiant in his efforts to awaken Britain to the menace of Nazi Germany. Dad called him a 'warmonger', a common perception among his mates. They were quietly patriotic but disillusioned by the First World War, the heady parades through the streets, the senseless slaughter that hit every family, the slow realization, as the histories filtered down, that the men marching off so proudly had been sacrificed by stupidity and that the war itself was just a terrible accident. Daily at work Dad passed a memorial to the twenty-seven local railwaymen who did not come back from Gallipoli and the Somme:

> *Forget us O Land for which we fell*
> *May it go well for England, still go well?*
> *Keep her proud banner without blot or stain*
> *Lest we may dream that we have died in vain.*

The wretched years of appeasement have to be understood in that context; men like my father had no faith in 'that talking matchstick' Neville Chamberlain, but nor did they have any enthusiasm for a rerun of 1914–18. Dad was by no means a pacifist, though the Labour party lessons in history and geography he had taken had made him otherwise a disciple of Jimmy Maxton, a militant Scottish socialist and pacifist who was elected to Parliament in 1922 – an admiration later shared by Maxton's biographer, Prime Minister Gordon Brown. What really inspired my father was faith in the brotherhood of man, a characteristic he shared with the giant who walked the full length of 'the world's longest platform' at Manchester Exchange Station to shake hands with the footplate crew who had brought him safely to his destination. The passenger was Paul Robeson, who was finally free to tour outside America after eight years of being denied a renewal of his passport. In the Cold War hysteria of the time, it had been judged treasonable for Robeson to have said: 'Our will to peace is strong. We shall not make war on anyone. We shall not make war on the Soviet Union.' The egalitarianism of Robeson's handshake appealed to my father; certainly it was something no British political leader of the era would have dreamed of doing.

Robeson, like my father, had a romantic view of the Soviet Union. Dad believed that it exemplified Karl Marx's slogan 'From each according to his abilities, to each according to his needs', an illusion fostered by Sidney and Beatrice Webb's 1935 book *Soviet Communism: a New Civilization?* read by my father in Labour party and trade union courses. Dad was as unaware as millions of others of Stalin's mass murders. Nor was Dad of revolutionary disposition. When I got him to talk about his part in the General Strike of 1926, I said he must have felt bitter when it was broken. 'No,' he said, 'I didn't feel bitter. I just felt sorry for the way the miners were let down.'

The job my father had when I was born, Engine Cleaner, was a bigger deal than it sounds. It was the first rung on a very long but very coveted ladder to becoming a locomotive driver.

Train drivers were an aristocracy among the working classes. They had a job for life, the social esteem that came with security, and better-than-average pay. The downside was that the job was brutally hard in its physical and mental demands. The hours of work were horrible – 2 a.m. one week, 3 p.m. the next, then 5 a.m. another week. It was a matter of pride to my father that he never needed the knocker-up to rap on the window with his long pole (a long-gone profession from the days when alarm clocks were uncommon). But the shifts meant that week to week we were asleep when he was up and he was asleep when we were up.

The railway historian Frank McKenna observed that 'the eyes of a footplateman appear to be a decade younger than the rest of his physique'. Dad's were striking, deep in his sockets. Perfect eyesight and physical fitness were demanded of an Engine Cleaner as of the driver. A slight fall-off in the eyesight test, a hint of colour blindness or physical limitation, and a driver would be demoted to sweeping the sheds, or shunting wagons in a freight yard or cleaning lavatories, or dismissed altogether. Dad was so sensitive about his fine vision that he would not hear of it when as a teenager I thought I was becoming short-sighted. I was, but he was in a state of denial I didn't understand at the time. Now I see that the eye-rolling exercises I picked up from a book by an Indian doctor would have alarmed anyone.

Every schoolboy then might have wanted to be an engine driver, but there was no glamour in the first step. On his night shift, among other dirty jobs, Dad as an Engine Cleaner had to go under the engine and climb into the dark belly of the beast to oil the big ends of the pistons, fearfully trusting that nobody would move the engine (as occasionally some lunatic did). It was several years of this before he was tested for work on the footplate (that is in the open cab), first qualifying as a Passed Cleaner, which carried the prospect of some turns as a fireman. What back-breaking work! I have a mental picture of my father coming home, exhausted from an all-night firing job on a goods train, keeping a foothold on the rocking engine while hour after hour shovelling coal from the tender, maybe six tons of it, and hurling it through the small firehole into the right places in the firebox to raise the necessary steam pressure. 'Where's my steam?' was the yell no fireman wanted to hear from the driver.

In time, the Passed Cleaner could hope to become a Red Ink Fireman, on the footplate for a few months; then, all being well, a Black Ink Fireman, on the rosters for regular firing; and finally Passed Fireman, tested to drive any train in his depot. As a Red Ink Driver he would be on the roster for driving in holiday periods, and then, eventually, a Black Ink Driver, the top of the ladder. No other craft or profession exacted such a lengthy 'apprenticeship'. Dad carefully annotated the details of every driving turn he acquired. It typically took at least twenty years to get there. 'Dead man's shoes,' said Dad.

A driver could not take a train on a route until he knew its every particularity – the siting of every signal, the sounds and shadows that might guide him in fog and snowstorm when visibility was near zero, the shape of every curve in the track, the length and darkness of every tunnel, the trickiness of every ascent where extra steam and sand might be needed, the location of every set of points where they might be switched to a different line. They called this familiarization 'learning the road' and Dad learned many roads, rattling most happily along the North Wales coast where many years later at Bluebell Wood cemetery at Coed Bell in Prestatyn he was to find his final resting place.

Drivers and firemen were subject to strict military discipline and it was easy to see why. A railwayman who did not read, memorize and follow the hundreds of regulations in the precious Rule Book risked his own life, his workmates' and the lives of several hundred passengers. Dad knew the Rule Book back to front. In the kitchen, testing himself, he'd ask questions rhetorically: What do you do with a runaway train on a hill or a train slipping back? How in an emergency do you signal to the guard at the back of the train? If you pass through facing points on to a curve what is the safe speed? What if you have to run backwards? What's the right thing to do if there's an obstruction on the line, an uprooted sleeper, a snowdrift? If you run out of steam, what lights do you lay down on the track and where? The work ethic was puritanical – clean overalls, no drink, no swearing, no smoking on duty, and no tolerance for misdemeanours. If he was ten minutes late at the sheds, he risked being sent home with the warning that next time he'd be fired. I remember a railway inspector coming to our house to see if Dad had taken home one of the high-quality hand rags issued to footplate crews for oiling work. He hadn't. He knew better.

We worried about my father's daily risks. Usually, he came home chuckling over some incident. It was ominous when he didn't:

'What's the matter, Dad?'

'*Something terrible.*'

'But what?'

'*Bad accident.*'

'What kind of accident?'

'*Finish your tea.*'

We'd eventually discover that a platelayer had lost a leg, a shunter had been crushed between wagons, a fireman had been scalded, a driver had been killed walking across a track to check a frozen signal. His own most common affliction was grit in the eye, looking out of his open cab at speed: there was no protective eye shield for footplatemen.

He tried to educate his union, the Associated Society of Locomotive Engineers and Firemen, not always to campaign for wage increases but to aim for medical benefits and for decent pensions, pointing out that an extra shilling or two now would be better invested for retirement. But he could never persuade them, so when he did retire his pension after fifty years was seven shillings a week (about £3 at today's values).

In the early 1930s, the composition of the manpower at the LMS Newton Heath sheds, way across the other side of Manchester, offered a better prospect of graduating from Passed Cleaner to Red Ink Fireman. Newton Heath was a very big depot with more than 200 locomotives. Also of some relevance was Dad's passion for football; he never saw a ball he didn't want to dribble around an imaginary fullback, and scorning players who could not shoot with both feet, drilled us hard on that. Naturally, he liked the idea that Newton Heath loco sheds were the birthplace of a football team – not any old team but The Heathens, a bunch of railwaymen who managed to get into the Football League, nearly went bankrupt, then did rather better after 1902 when they changed their name to Manchester United.

Dad at once applied for a transfer to Newton Heath. He and my mother took the plunge of putting down all their savings as a deposit on a £300 house a few miles from the railway sheds, their first time out of rented accommodation. It was a barely finished, semi-detached place at 54 Ashworth Street, a new estate close to Manchester City's wooded Brookdale Park, famed for its birds, grasslands and Victorian bandstand; many were the times irate park-keepers chased Fred and me for getting into the park by climbing the iron railings instead of walking ten minutes to the park entrance.

Our new house was right on the edge of open countryside and farms. In the days before the war, a farmer in pony and trap came round early in the morning selling milk he ladled out of a big churn strapped to the trap; in the summer everyone joined in haymaking.

This was the place where for more than twenty years my three brothers and I, sleeping two to a bed, grew up. All our fun was very much home-made – marbles, yo-yos, hopscotch, tag, whipping a spinning top along the street. Fred and I would go out to the big paved space at the three-way junction where our house stood to stage a cricket match with a rival street, using a tennis ball and a gas lamppost for a wicket. In winter, we made long ice-slides, and when it snowed Dad hammered together crude sleds, lining the runners with metal from discarded tins of Heinz beans. I collected scrap lead, boiled it on the kitchen stove and used clay impressions of tin soldiers to create armies for battles with cannons firing matchsticks. From a smelly works along the Rochdale Canal we 'lifted' bits of ebonite tubing for pea-shooter contests. We were manic competitors in everything with all the kids in the street, but most of all in completing cigarette-card series of soccer teams, cricketers, kings, aircraft, cars, wars and film stars.

Very occasionally we'd test our parents' good temper by venturing into enemy territory to engage in running stone-throwing battles with kids from other streets in Newton Heath, everyone scattering at the sight of the angry red face of the pot-bellied Police Constable Robinson; he had a truncheon and lived opposite our school, Brookdale Park Elementary.

Communal good will prevailed, though, every November 5th, when Guy Fawkes brought our neighbourhood together. After 300 years there wasn't any lingering resentment of Captain Fawkes for trying to blow up Parliament in 1605 – quite a few in 1936 thought it was a great idea – but the passage of time hardly lessened the appetite for a bonfire feast of baked potatoes, boiled ham and cheese, treacle tart, toffee apples and parkin accompanied by fireworks and sing-song. Fred and I enthroned a stuffed, bearded effigy of the conspirator in a cart made from old carriage wheels and begged around for 'a penny for the Guy' to be spent on fireworks.

Every household made a contribution to the blaze, which lasted past midnight fuelled by logs from the fields, broken-down settees and chairs, and our 'Guy Fawkes' on top, exploding with firecrackers. I can still smell the cordite.

Mum and Dad gave their four sons warm encouragement at every stage. They were devoted to each other, too, but they didn't let it show. None of my brothers can recall any cross words between them – nor any show of open affection. I don't think I ever saw them embrace or kiss. But if Dad was there to help Mum with the dishes after supper, sometimes we'd hear him attempt the lilting lyric of the music hall song 'If you were the only girl in the world, and I was the only boy'.

He was moved by music from America. My nostalgic ear catches now the innocence of the refrain of 'Home on the Range' which Dad puff-cheeked out of his mouth organ. He wished he had been born in Wyoming, not Crewe, so he would sit at our kitchen fireplace imagining he was playing it by a prairie campfire under the stars before rolling up in his horse blanket, his saddle for a pillow. Sometimes he sang it to us: 'Oh give me a home where the buffalo roam, where the deer and the antelope play, where seldom is heard a discouraging word, and the skies are not cloudy all day.'

He wanted us to appreciate the harmony of Nelson Eddy and Jeanette MacDonald singing 'Rose Marie' in the film about Canadian Mounties, the majesty of Paul Robeson's 'Ol' Man River', the romance of Stephen Foster's 'Camptown Races'. When we were toddlers, he would us hold on his knee and give an unsteady version of Al Jolson from the movie *The Singing Fool*, which came out the year I was born: 'Climb upon my knee, sonny boy. You've no way of knowing, there's no way of showing, what you mean to me, sonny boy.' He took the words to heart. I grew up when boys were regularly beaten by their fathers. There was only one occasion when he took a strap to my backside – for playing with matches.

My parents were affectionate, but they were reticent – no, down-right obscure – about anything to do with sex. My worldlier younger brother claimed superior knowledge, but until I was about ten I sincerely believed that babies were delivered in the little black

Gladstone bags that doctors carried. That doesn't say much for my powers of observation, since my mother had by then carried another brother to term.

The only hint that my parents were aware of the hormonal turmoil of teenage life was a book – from the Boy Scouts I think – on the awful consequences of masturbation, which just happened to be left lying around and of course caused immediate and unmentionable panic among us boys. We subsequently struggled between the Boy Scout reign of terror and a *Naturist* magazine featuring sepia nudes that was slipped to me in an exercise book at school.

Nowadays my father would be considered a prude. Mother's brother Arnold, who looked like Clark Gable and rode a fast motorcycle, once began to tell Dad a risqué joke, and then had the sense to stop when Dad's face dropped. He liked the kind of riddles stuffed in Christmas crackers, music hall impersonations and idiomatic radio sketches of Northerners coping with the frustrations of their lives. Ken Law told me: 'If you met your Dad in the very early hours of a cold damp frosty morning or in the middle of a rain-lashed railway shed yard, he'd always come up with something funny.'

Never would it require the prop of a profanity. He'd 'damn' and 'blast it' but I can't recall him saying 'bloody' and indeed the effing and blinding that is the vernacular today was not then a feature of respectable working-class speech in the North.

Most of all, my father liked telling daft stories about himself and the family loved to have him act them out. One night, he told us, he went to a rough working men's club to collect a small debt. He climbed to the top of the stairs. 'When I got to the top there was no light and I could just make out the shadowy figure standing there. I said: "Hello, I've come to see a friend of mine." He didn't reply so I told him again. And he stood there saying nothing, so I took another step forward and so did he! I thought – he's coming for me.'

And at this point Dad, who was no more than 5′ 6″ but muscled from all that coal-shovelling, would hunch into a boxing stance.

'I was such a fool!' he explained. 'There was a big mirror at the top of the stairs. I was talking to myself! I'd been misled because I'd done something I don't normally do – wear a hat!'

He was indeed a creature of habit; we knew the ending, but we hooted with laughter every time he told the story in exactly the same way. We were part of the performance and his performance, like good theatre, always seemed fresh, as if he was discovering it for himself for the first time.

Rituals were a big part of our happy family life. Mum tossed pancakes on Shrove Tuesday, baked treacle toffee for the bonfires on Guy Fawkes Night, hid eggs at Easter, and made sure that the first person to enter the house after midnight on 31 December carried a piece of coal for good luck.

Most of all, on occasional Saturday nights Mum and Dad enjoyed opening the house to relatives and neighbours for cold meat and pie suppers and games pitting teams of adults and kids in musical chairs, charades, bobbing for toffee apples, blind man's bluff, scavenger hunts, memory games, and on and on through a repertoire filled with excitement and laughter.

My father was enthusiastic about his quaint ceremonial rituals at club nights in the working men's fraternal association, the Royal Antediluvian Order of Buffaloes, the 'Buffs'. (Dad would have joined the Freemasons if anyone had asked him.) In my adolescence I dreaded occasions when we moved into the company of strangers. He would always open a conversation while I curled up in embarrassment and affected not to be with him. For me, Dad on holiday at breakfast in the dining room of a seaside boarding house was a recipe for importing anxiety by the bucketful. He would make the opening sally to the family at the next table and vistas opened on an infinity of world controversies while we fretted to get out to the beach before it rained. Without Mum's giving him a kick under the table, we'd have been stuck for the day.

Writing about my parents and their role, I realize how easy it is, just as it was in her lifetime, to allow Mum's more contained personality to become subsumed under memories of Dad's magical ebullience. But it was Mum's down-to-earth practicality and native intelligence that were key to a rise in the family fortunes. The girl who had started in a mill in clogs developed an entrepreneurial streak.

Our house at 54 Ashworth Street was on the edge of open fields and farmland stretching for miles in the direction of Daisy Nook, a sweet valley of woods and water, and hills dominated by Hartshead Pike, where the druids, we were told, made sacrifices and the Romans lit beacons to warn local garrisons of heathens on the prowl. At Easter, more pacific modern hordes made the trek to Daisy Nook for a big annual fair, but every weekend there was a steady flow of ramblers passing our door for picnics at Daisy Nook and boating on the adjacent Crime Lake. Often they'd knock on our door and ask if we could give them a glass of water. My mother obliged. There were so many knocks at the door she came up with the idea that she would make lemonade and sell it for a halfpenny a glass. She sold it all and ambitions soared.

My parents walked two miles to Rothwell Street and asked to see Antonio and Fred Sivori, who owned a little ice cream factory. The Sivori brothers had their own horse-drawn 'ice cream parlour travelling the streets of Newton Heath', but Dad persuaded them to deliver to Ashworth Street on Sunday morning a big tub of ice cream at wholesale price, packed around with ice (we had no refrigerator), and a scoop for making cornets and a wafer maker. That first Sunday as nascent capitalists, my parents were apprehensive. Dad painted 'ice cream here' on a big piece of cardboard and they stood by the garden gate. If it rained, they'd lose the investment.

By late afternoon, they'd sold out, and Dad went cheerfully off to the night shift. They tried it again the following Sunday: another sellout. In the third week, the ice cream had all gone by lunchtime. It was a long way to Rothwell Street for a refill and the container was so heavy they carried it between them along the streets. They were almost at the Sivoris, and exhausted, when one of them – neither would ever take the credit – realized that the weight was mainly melted ice that could be poured away. The Sivori brothers ferried the refilled tub back to Ashworth Street. It was empty by teatime.

Soon there was a growing parade of Sunday and then Saturday customers at number 54. They'd ask if Mum had sweets, or pop, or cigarettes, or a bun, and her answer was always the same: 'Sorry, no, but we'll have it next week.' She got Dad to take down the garden gate and build shelves in the hallway. The litany of promissories led to stock spilling out from the hall into our front room, so she removed all the furniture, installed a big counter, started stocking groceries and haberdasheries for neighbours and in time installed a plate-glass window and a refrigerator – wonders in the Ashworth Street neighbourhood. Within a year, a full-scale corner shop flowered in our old parlour, managed, staffed and maintained by Mum. Under her canny eye it became really successful. While she could not match the virtuoso calculations of my father, in the blink of an eye she could add up a long column of pounds, shillings, pence and half-pence – twelve pence to a shilling, twenty shillings to a pound – and get it right first time. Out of one pound of the takings, she'd make two shillings, a nice 10 per cent profit that she stored in an old Oxo tin.

Sometimes she allowed Fred or me to help in serving. This was a great treat. I put on a white apron, scrubbed my hands and slicked back my hair with a helping of butter. Boys and girls I played with in the street outside incredulously pressed their noses against the plate-glass window and the array of sweets displayed. My stock rose. I served customers simple items, cigarettes, bread, milk, tinned food. Bacon came in a big roll that had to be sliced. I was not allowed anywhere near the horrendous slicing machine; seeing Mum with her hand feeding the bacon so close to the swift-circling sharp blade gave me nightmares. The most glamorous job was filing the colourful dust jackets and re-jacketing the returns of the lending library Mum started. Fred and I came to blows over this privilege, wrestling furiously in the backroom until one of us got the other in a headlock and won a concession.

When his shifts worked out, Dad liked nothing better than coming home, discarding his overalls and putting on a clean white apron to serve in the shop – such a contrast from what he had been doing all day. This was sometimes to my mother's exasperation when the shop filled with people. Dad listened to every tale from a customer, whereas Mum knew who was a gasbag to be deftly cut off at second breath. His style was altogether free and easy: asked for half a pound of boiled ham, he'd sacrifice his passion for precision in numbers and let the Avery scale ride over the 8-ounce mark. He redeemed this liberality, though, on one occasion when a woman came in and asked for a back stud for her husband's shirt. Dad rifled in the haberdashery drawer, and presented it to her. 'That's one penny.' The woman responded sharply. 'No, I want a good one, it's for a wedding.' Dad took the back stud from her, rummaged around in the drawer, and pulled out the same stud. 'Twopence,' he said. She beamed and went off happy that she had a good-quality back stud.

I still marvel at how my mother managed to give birth to two new boys – Peter was born in January 1936, John in December 1938 – look after Fred and me and Dad, run the shop six days a week, which meant ordering supplies, pricing them for retail, and dealing with customers, and never lose her temper.

When she closed the shop her working day wasn't over. She'd sit at her Singer sewing machine doggedly making clothes for us, a billowing nightgown for Dad (the cause of much hilarity) and white satin blouses for us to wear in the All Saints' Whitsun Procession: the family didn't go to church but we were regulars at Sunday school. Mum darned all our socks, knitted pullovers, ironed shirts, washed all our laundry by hand and ironed it, too, and saw my Dad off on night shift with his can of loose tea, sugar and milk to be brewed up on the engine, sandwiches and playing cards in an old tobacco tin. If something bothered her, she retreated into silence, her lips tightening.

And then came bad news.

As more of the fields filled with housing, two neighbours copied Mum, turning over their parlours to groceries, and the Co-operative Society chain announced it would open one of its big stores and butchers in Miriam Street, a few hundred yards down Ashworth Street. The Co-op was a business which had the appealing message of being in theory owned by its customers. Buying in bulk for many branches allowed it to cut prices, and thrift-minded customers who shopped became 'members' who could accumulate a cash dividend on purchases. George Orwell, in *The Road to Wigan Pier* in 1937, observed that the arrival of a Co-op was a disaster for the independent shopkeeper. Local authorities that built housing estates rigidly limited the number of shops in the area and gave preference to the Co-op: 'Many a small shopkeeper is utterly ruined, their whole clientele taken away from them at a single swoop.'

Mum and Dad debated whether they should keep going. While they worried, an inspector came round from our controlling local authority, Failsworth Council. 'I have the power to shut you down forthwith,' he told all three front-parlour entrepreneurs. 'Not one of you has a licence and you don't stand a chance of getting one if I'm not satisfied with the way you store food.' Having inspected ours first – Dad was at work – he went off to look at the others, then came back in the afternoon and told Mum: 'I must speak to the man of the house.' In the 1930s women were presumed not to have any competence at business of any kind; very few worked. The inspector waited around until my father came home and took him aside.

'Mr Evans, I take it that Mrs Evans is in charge?' My Dad said yes, she was. 'In that case,' said the inspector, 'I have to tell you, Mr Evans, you are a lucky man. I have never seen a better-run grocery in all my years as an inspector. I am giving you a licence. I am closing down the others.'

The day after the Co-op opened its doors, Mum went in to check its prices. Employees didn't know who she was so they indulged a slightly deaf lady who asked for prices on a lot of items. Only a few of the Co-op prices were cheaper, and Mum immediately marked down ours. We lost a few customers in the first week, but most drifted back, probably because my mother identified with her customers in a way the Co-op staff, conscious of their elevated position, could not match. As the semis expanded further into the countryside, we stopped worrying; it was plain there was room for both ventures, and indeed our shop was still flourishing under Korean management in 2007.

The Evanses were moving up! By the time I was nine my parents were doing well enough to buy a second-hand red Hillman Minx, an unheard-of acquisition in our area. A car outside a house had always meant bad news: only doctors had cars. I heard years later from my schoolmate at Brookdale Park, Alf Morris, that I was known behind my back as 'Posh' Evans on account of the purchase; another version of the nickname was attributed to the fact that my trousers had no holes, as my Dad always had work and could afford to properly clothe me. In truth, I did not enjoy the car. The smell of leather inside made me sick, so when the family went on weekend drives into Cheshire on Sundays I stayed at home, moping around and looking at terrifying representations of hell in an illustrated bible, where the Boy Scouts' helpful literature on the perils of masturbation assured me I was undoubtedly headed.

Much more exciting to me than any car was the day Dad became a king of the iron road.

He had washed and had his supper before he told us he had at last been promoted to Black Ink Driver. It must have been an effort for such a talkative man to say nothing, but he waited until Mum had closed the shop. There were handshakes at the sheds, but no ceremony. He would still be doing the same work, rising at all hours, taking out a train in all weathers, but as a full driver he had acquired a certain majesty, meriting respect and deference all along the line as a reflection of the responsibility he bore.

He had taken his licks as a fireman working with cantankerous drivers, and as a part-time driver he'd had to tolerate a few lazy or careless firemen. Now he was indisputably in charge. Nobody could tell him to take out a fireman he thought incompetent or an engine he considered defective. He could insist on a replacement. Railway management rarely authorized any visits to the footplate, not least when it was moving, but nobody could mount on his footplate without his permission, and while he was in charge of the big engine he was answerable to no one.

I longed to see my father at work, but the hours were unhelpful. As a driver, he often set off, in his new glossy peaked cap and serge jacket, just when I was spreading out homework on the living-room table. I had to wait for the privilege and it came by chance when I was sixteen. One summer evening when I arrived by train at Manchester Victoria station, Dad was on the opposite platform about to drive a few hundred passengers home to Oldham. 'Hop on quick,' he said. I seized the moment.

Sitting in the comfort of a railway carriage, as I had been on the way in, gave no idea of the ferocious goings on up there in front on the open footplate as the train gathered speed out of the station and up the line – of the heat and noise that made speech impossible, the roar and flames of the firebox, the sweat of the fireman with a long-handled shovel feeding the red-hot maw, the noise of iron meeting iron on the swaying footplate, the intensity of Dad's concentration looking up the line for pinprick signals of red and green, checking boiler pressure, opening and closing the steam regulator arm according to gradient and track. And then at the end, at the station platform, the slamming of the carriage doors as the passengers got off the train, their voices drifting into the night, oblivious of what we had been through.

I was astounded and bursting with pride.

3

FIRST, KNOW YOUR ENEMY

I was eleven when Prime Minister Neville Chamberlain told 47 million Britons: 'this country is at war with Germany'. That Sunday morning at 11 a.m. on 3 September 1939, I listened to his broadcast with the rest of the family, all of us huddled round the vibrating fabric of our brown-enamel wireless set.

Dad was unusually silent, but Mum unusually commented, saying of Chamberlain: 'He seems to be more sorry for himself than the rest of us.' Reading the speech today I can see what she meant: 'You can imagine what a bitter blow it is to me that all my long struggle for peace has failed. Yet I cannot believe that there is anything more or anything different I could have done and that would have been more successful.'

Mum was right. It was all about him.

No sooner had Chamberlain finished speaking than the air raid sirens howled. Fred and I rushed into the street. It was a crazy thing to do. But it was a false alarm. We were disappointed not to see Stuka dive bombers tangling with the big fat blue barrage balloons in the blue sky. We were even more upset when, the same day, the government shut down all the cinemas. What would we do for the rest of our lives?

The echo of Chamberlain's plaintive voice has stayed with me all

these years. At the time I could not get out of my head the posh way
he talked about our '*embessador*' in Berlin and the '*plens*' we would
all have to make. The plummy announcers on the BBC had made me
acutely conscious of accents as an indicator of class, of ineluctable
superiority. Just turning on the radio made me ashamed. Nobody in
my universe spoke like that; therefore we must be outcasts, belong-
ing to some inarticulate barbarian tribe. These were the years when
the announcers and news readers all spoke so-called Standard
English, meaning the soft tones of the alien South; harmonious
Oxbridge voices of long vowels, distinct p's and t's, and effortless
aspirates. The BBC tolerated J. B. Priestley's Yorkshire accent for a
few months from June to October 1940 in his 'Postscripts' series of
morale-boosting talks, but not his political opinions: seen by the
Tories as too socialist, the programme was axed. In 1941 it was
front-page news when Wilfred Pickles brought a Yorkshire accent to
BBC news-reading – one would have thought a cathedral or two had
been sacked – but he too was soon removed from the national air-
waves and Standard English prevailed for the next thirty years.

Our teacher at Brookdale Park elementary school interposed her
good soul between civilization and us aural barbarians, struggling
against centuries of cultural history to get us to 'speak nicely', which
meant mimicking the BBC. Chastised early in reading class for referring to an ''ospital', I approached every 'aitch' as a pole vaulter
running at a high bar. (Of course, educated youth now affect a
slovenly 'mockney' which is more affected than ever were we BBC
imitators in the Brookdale English lessons.)

Chamberlain's announcement created hardly a ripple in our
neighbourhood compared with the excitements of the night before
he spoke. Every Saturday, a half-hour between 5 and 6 p.m. was
sacrosanct. We could count on being undisturbed by the shop bell
because every household was poised by the radio for the BBC's
pip-pip-pip prelude to the day's football scores. Seeing match results
on television or the Web today doesn't begin to compare to the
effect of hearing one calm authoritative voice announce the end of
the world: 'Manchester United 1, Charlton Athletic 7.'

The scores were of paramount importance because predicting the results could take you from the hard grind and dreary back streets to a fantasy life of ease and luxury. The Football Pools were not quite a lottery; there was a certain skill in assessing the clubs and their key players. Fortunes were made overnight; getting all but a few matches right might win hundreds of thousands of pounds, zillions more than anyone could earn in a lifetime. Before mailing in the coupon with his sixpenny bets, Dad spent hours studying the form, then used his little stubby pencil to mark the match lists with the numeral 1 for a team's home win, x for a draw and 2 for a win away from home. If he'd bet that the star team of Blackpool, playing at home, would beat Leeds, the radio announcer's pause after 'Blackpool 1' was excruciating. The disembodied voice of fate seemed to extend every syllable in 'L-e-e-d-s' before ruining everything by declaring that Leeds had scored 2. Crueller still was 'Middlesbrough 4', Dad's prediction for a home win, followed by 'Everton . . . 4'. The house rule against breathing a word couldn't stand such freak results.

Fearing that British stoicism could not bear the strain of the Saturday pools and at the same time win a war, the Football League suspended its matches 'for the duration'. It was a phrase we were to hate hearing, along with 'Don't you know there's a war on?' Knowing now of the years of convulsions that were to follow Chamberlain's declaration of war, it is weird how calm and confident the people were sitting down to roast lamb and mint sauce after his speech.

Perhaps that was partly because we were under the illusion that we were ready. We had already collected our identity cards and gas masks. Fred and I paraded around in the masks parodying 'Heil Hitler' salutes, but the smell of the rubber made us gag and after that we wore ours only for the drill at school, when on the command we assumed foetal positions under desks.

We helped Mum and Dad stick tape all over our windows to hold the fragments in a bomb blast, put up blackout blinds and double curtains and hated it when a bossy Air Raid Warden knocked on the door to say a chink of light was showing: he was just a neighbour in a tin hat. Riding the electric tramcar along Oldham Road, we could see sandbags heaped around Failsworth's ceremonial flagpole, and at

supposedly key points in the straggling communities of small terraced houses served by clusters of fish-and-chip shops, haberdashers,
pubs, hairdressers, newsagents, bookies, savings banks, pawnbro-
kers, butchers and the occasional cinema and church. Iron railings
round the churches and graveyards and everywhere else had already
been taken away, to make tanks we were told. The flowers in
Manchester's Piccadilly Gardens had been dug up for trenches and
air raid shelters. The more active householders had dug deep holes in
their gardens and roofed them with six sheets of curved corrugated
iron supplied by the local council. The finished bunker was called an
Anderson shelter after its progenitor.

Dad thought the Anderson useless. Many in our street filled with
water. Some people did not bother to prepare at all. Everybody knew
the war would be over by Christmas. The mass of people had no
idea of just how ill-prepared our military was; they were betrayed by
the newspapers, led by the *Times*, *Express* and *Daily Mail*, and even
the BBC, who had shamefully soft-pedalled and suppressed the years
of alarms from a small band of Chamberlain's critics in his own
party (including future Prime Ministers Churchill and Harold
Macmillan, but not a vain and timid Sir Anthony Eden). 'Germany's
tanks are made of cardboard,' a know-all boomingly reassured a
shop full of our customers. 'Joe, that can't be right,' said my father,
who was helping out that day. Then he delivered a numbing recital
of figures of German steel production, recalled from constant read-
ings of his well-thumbed *World Almanac and Book of Facts*. (This
didn't go down at all well. My mother had to remind him that never
mind his blessed almanac, the customer was always right.)

Dad's irregular shifts at the railway meant we often didn't see him
for two or three weeks. He'd be in bed when we were up and we'd
be in bed when he was up. He drove trains carrying thousands of
children out of Manchester, their schools closed and relocated miles
away from industrial areas considered prime targets for bombing.
Schoolmates from Brookdale and Briscoe Lane Junior, with their
nametags and mandatory gas masks, were put on a train to
Ramsbottom, a village on the West Pennine moors where the local
families could pick and choose who to welcome into their homes for

the duration. By all accounts, most of the evacuees, even the scruffiest, were kindly received in foster homes more comfortable than the dwellings they'd left behind, in the process happily finding out about the mysterious 'countryside'. Schoolmate Alf Morris, who in the fullness of time became a Labour minister and later Lord Morris, was one of the unlucky ones. Separated from his brother and sister, who were taken in by a well-to-do family, Alf was billeted with a mean old couple who sent him out hawking firewood they chopped for a living, and half-starved him on suppers from the fish-and-chip shop.

As the city emptied, my parents kept us in Ashworth Street. They wrote to my father's mother, Sarah Jane, to ask if Fred and I could stay with her on the Welsh border. She was now Granny Jones, having married a gravedigger called Jack. Anything remotely to do with death upset me, but I was not wild about the prospect of going to Ramsbottom either. I'd heard too many comics on Rhyl pier mouthing the syllables as if the name was a joke in itself: my inclination to stay away if I could was clinched when a postcard came back from a Brookdale classmate saying that it was once known as Tup's Arse which was bound to produce giggles; I didn't know a tup was a ram, the monarch of the herd and revered alike by shepherd and ewe. Anyway, Alf Morris was back home in a month or two.

Once or twice a week a Brookdale teacher came to the house and gave us homework, but Mum and Dad worried we were falling behind. While we waited for Granny Jones to write back, a neighbour told Mum about another possible sanctuary. It excited me most of all: Somerford Hall, which was an old manor house in the countryside near Congleton in Cheshire where the Manchester education committee had set up a boarding school.

To appreciate the attraction of Somerford Hall, you have to know about the *Magnet*. Of all the comic books we bought at the newsagents every week – *Beano*, *Wizard*, *Dandy*, *Hotspur* – the *Magnet* most insinuated itself into my imagination. This is where 'Frank Richards' (Charles Hamilton) recorded the adventures of the Fifth Form at Greyfriars, the ancient ivy-covered public school like Eton, secure in its gentlemanly traditions. The setting represented some of the lyrical features of English life evoked by Rupert Brooke's

Grantchester poem – 'Stands the Church clock at ten to three? And is there honey still for tea?' The class overtones should have grated on me, I suppose, but they didn't. After the asphalt playgrounds of Newton Heath, I liked the idea of surviving the war with toffs on the lawns of Greyfriars, and I relished the *Magnet* stories where every week beastly cads got their comeuppance and good eggs and goodness triumphed. Here were Harry Wharton, Bob Cherry, Frank Nugent, Johnny Bull, the Indian cricketer Hurree Jamset Ram Singh, the Form Master Mr Quelch, too ready with the cane; and the crafty Billy Bunter, the 'fat owl of the Remove', plotting to steal someone else's tuck. I identified most with Harry Wharton, captain of the Remove and editor of the *Greyfriars Herald*. I saw myself seeing out the war at Somerford Hall, toasting crumpets for tea with Bob Cherry after hitting one of Ram Singh's googlies for six to acclaim from the whole of Greyfriars.

One glorious morning we heard that Fred and I had been accepted for Somerford Hall. Arriving a week later, we found no gracious hall and no ivy. The school was a collection of six or seven wooden sheds in soggy fields, an encampment in the grounds of the shut-up old country house. None of the city evacuees had time to acknowledge my resemblance to Harry Wharton; they were too busy jostling for sheets and blankets and fighting for jam sandwiches from the makeshift kitchen. At bedtime, I was assigned the upper berth of an iron bunk in a bare board hut with about thirty others. The first night, as the wind howled, homesick and disillusioned, I sobbed my heart out. 'Shut up, crybaby!' yelled everyone. The protesters hurled shoes at my bunk; even Fred told me to put a sock in it. Cripes! I was Billy Bunter, the object of execration. The next day we had lessons. In the English class we were told to write home and present our letters to the teacher, who would check the grammar before putting them in the post. I wrote two pages about my disappointments and handed them in. I was called to the teacher's high desk up front. 'This just won't do,' he snarled, screwing up my effort into a small ball he lobbed into the wastepaper basket to giggles behind me. 'Go back to your desk and write something cheerful.'

That night, with a thumping heart, I sneaked out of the back of

Somerford Hall after lights out, and found a postbox for a letter to Ashworth Street pleading to be rescued. I had no stamp for it, but at the weekend both my parents arrived at the camp and took me home. The hut was glad to see the back of me. Fred, less infected by the Greyfriars fantasy, elected to stay and had a great time for six months. Down the years, he developed a number of different theories concerning my lack of moral fibre, none of which bears scrutiny.

Brookdale was still closed when I came home. Within days I was bound for the Welsh hills, more precisely for the hamlet of Hengoed in the county of Shropshire but a slingshot east of Offa's Dyke. Dad had no petrol ration for his car, so we took two trains to Gobowen, the railhead for Oswestry, then walked four miles in fading sunshine along winding densely hedged lanes, through tunnels of overhanging trees, trying to find the Old Vicarage before dark. To baffle German parachutists all the signposts had been taken down, but eventually we were directed to St Barnabas Church, where Grandfather Jones plied his trade. Down the hill from the church we opened a door in a high wall of mellow stone to find Granny Jones scattering grain among scores of chickens.

She was a pale wraith of a woman in her mid-seventies, inherently graceful and affectionate and very attentive to the needs of her new husband, who must have been fifteen years younger. She scurried around in her flowered pinafore to take off Gravedigger Jack's boots when he clumped into the stone-floored kitchen and dropped into a high-backed wooden chair by the fireplace: his chair, his hearth, and his house. He was a red-faced man in corduroy trousers hoisted by a fat leather belt he said he would apply to my backside if I didn't behave. I convinced myself he had a twinkle in his eye. It was good to hear he had spent the day cutting hedges and clearing ditches in the next hamlet, there being a shortage at St Barnabas of candidates for the next world.

Gravedigger Jack rarely spoke and he had an iron routine. If supper was not on the table sharp at six he wouldn't eat it. For hours after eating, he'd sit silently smoking his pipe while I read *The Count of Monte Cristo* by the light of an oil lamp, and Granny filled the kitchen with the warm smell of homemade bread. Her secluded old house, set in meadows with an apple orchard and a brook at the back, had no electricity, no gas, no radio, and we drew water from a pump in the yard. On Sundays we sang in the Hengoed church's little choir, smug in our white surplices. Not a whisper of the war percolated. It was paradise.

Finding short cuts across fields to the village school in Gobowen was a daily adventure: seeing the flash of a fox in a copse, leaping brooks, slashing a path through banks of nettles and bramble with a sword fashioned from a stripped elderberry branch; it was 1066 and I was on Senlac Hill with my namesake king, driving the bastard Normans back into the sea. I was romantic and reckless. When a route skirted a wasp's nest, I set fire to it and was stung on the eye for my folly; so much for acting King Harold. Still, the hazard that gave regular pause to my impetuosity was the cow pasture where there might be a possessive bull. Every boy at school had a fanciful story of racing death against thudding hoofs and sharp horns. I had been the fastest runner at Brookdale and fancied myself to beat any bull. After I saw one on the loose, I decided against putting my speed to the test. I checked every beast for balls and every pasture I crossed for an exit.

At school, there were some sixty boys and girls from eight to about fourteen, scrunched up at little desks, all learning the same things. I could not concentrate much on what was going on because I soon fell madly in love with a poised thirteen-year-old evacuee from London called Gwyneth. A Southern beauty! I wooed her in the conker season, making her a gift of my prized niner. I forbore to tell her that to make it harder I had peed on it. This was no perversion. It was common practice to urinate on the conker, soak it in vinegar, and expose it to heat. Big juicy conkers often succumbed to a blow from a hard little conker. Blissfully unaware, she appreciated the gift.

My next gambit, proof of manhood, was to announce that while Gwyneth ate her sandwiches in the midday break I was going to climb to the top of a spectacular tree in the playground. I did. The effect of my bravado was rather ruined because I couldn't get down before the bell went for classes. I never saw her again. Lovesick, I hung around the cottage where she stayed for days until someone told me she'd been called back to London, where her school had reopened.

Eventually, I was summoned home, too. I'd had four happy months with Granny Jones, followed by a spartan two months under the thumb of Aunt Beattie on Uncle Ted's little farm at Old Stone House – he had six fields, twelve cows, a couple of horses and countless pigs, to which he fed swill from the Oswestry army camp. To Aunt Beattie, stomping through the mud in big rubber boots, I was a city sissy: I failed miserably at milking a cow.

In the absence of German warplanes, classes had resumed at Brookdale, but my return was required anyway because I had reached the age to take part in the all-important national '11-plus' examinations, tests administered to eleven- and twelve-year-olds. Sitting in a draughty classroom for four hours with forty others, I didn't appreciate that the curious questions, some of which seemed easy and some of which were incomprehensible to me, would decide my future. The aim of the examinations was to identify a handful of really bright boys and girls who would be offered a superior 'grammar school' education to the age of sixteen, and with that the opportunity to win a Joint Matriculation Board certificate, the passport to a good job. There were places at grammar schools for no more than 10 per cent of the eleven-year-olds. The other 90 per cent were destined to remain at elementary school and leave for work at the age of fourteen, trade apprenticeships if they were lucky, menial work if not. Put another way, the results of the 11-plus would decide the course of the rest of my life as surely as a switch in the railway points would decide whether Dad's train went east or west.

My fate was contained in a buff envelope Mum brought up the stairs to the bathroom one morning when I was washing my face. I opened it with soapy fingers. 'Harold Evans has been selected for St Mary's Road Central School.'

I was at once bothered and bewildered. I had not been selected for a cherished grammar school place. But neither had it been decreed I should stay in the elementary school. St Mary's Road Central School,

I discovered, was one step up from elementary school, a co-ed inter-mediary school where you could stay to fifteen, and a few pupils might have a chance to sit the crucial Joint Matriculation Board examinations along with the grammar school boys. I fretted that I had been held back by evacuation and country school; on the other hand, Fred came home later from the Congleton camp and sailed into a grammar school. Alf Morris, too, was selected for grammar school, but his family could not afford the uniform and he stayed at Brookdale until he was fourteen.

I was excited all the same. It was not so much the education – there was a rumour that St Mary's expected its pupils to learn French – as the blue cap, school tie with lion rampant, and crested blazer I would be entitled to wear, and the leather satchel for my exercise books.

Fearful that sporting this lot risked jeers and jostles from the lads who were staying on at Brookdale, as I passed my old playground I sprinted up Albert Street to the No. 7 bus stop at the entrance to Brookdale Park. Fifteen minutes later I was looking up at the gaunt Victorian redbrick edifice of St Mary's Road Central School, across a street from the coal heaps and rusting ironmongery of Newton Heath rail yard and the great sheds which housed the steam loco-motives Dad drove. Not a single blade of grass was in sight; the playground was tarmac running into brick walls.

Looking down from the schoolrooms we could see a railway line leading from the locomotive sheds to a turntable at the foot of our red cliff. I always hoped I would catch a glimpse of my father in command of a steam locomotive, but I never did. Gazing out of the high win-dows ran the risk of being discovered doing nothing by the school's dominating person, the headmaster Mr W. L. Marsland. He appeared to us as a sinister figure. He glided through the school without appar-ently moving his legs, and had his head held well back so he appeared to be looking down on you. I was in a high state of nervous tension. I'd just discovered Dickens and the cruel schoolmaster Wackford Squeers was fresh in my mind. For a few weeks I avoided stepping on cracks in the pavement and obsessively touched every third lamppost just to be sure the gods were on my side. Going up the road from school to the bus stop for home, we always ran past a spooky derelict building that was once an inn called the Duke of York; the body of a young woman killed crossing the railway line in the nineteenth century had been brought there, and we believed it when we were told her footsteps could still be heard around the shattered old bar.

But if the exterior of St Mary's was workhouse grim, its environs bleak, and the headmaster forbidding, I soon discovered the school was infused with an appealing spirit, a nurturing combination of respect for traditional values and zestful competition created by Marsland. (I was spurred on by the brilliance of Betty Ogden who, as Mrs Peter Horton, became Lady Mayoress of Sheffield in 1987–8 and the mother of three daughters, all academic stars at Oxford, Cambridge and Harvard.) We were all attached to one of four houses honouring British heroes of empire, industry and exploration. I was in Scott, others were in Livingstone, Gordon and Stephenson. Various privileges, whose nature I've forgotten, were awarded to members of the house that had accumulated the most 'good house points' in the class and on our infrequent visits to a sports field where we wore our house colours (I regretted Scott was yellow).

Marsland's disconcerting way of looking at us, I discovered, was not an expression of contempt. It was physiological; his eyelids were stuck because he'd been gassed in the First World War. I never heard him talk about his experiences, but he wanted us to remember the price of freedom: St Mary's Road Central School 'adopted' Czechoslovakia, sacrificed at Munich. And each day in assembly, while a flower was placed on the school war memorial plaque, a boy or girl read out the lines of Laurence Binyon's memorial poem:

> They shall grow not old, as we that are left grow old;
> Age shall not weary them, nor the years condemn.
> At the going down of the sun and in the morning
> We will remember them.

Marsland had pride in his school. He expected us to behave like grammar school boys, and we – all grammar school rejects – strove to justify his faith – and ourselves.

Six decades later I can still see all the teachers, recall their names and mannerisms. For the first few lessons with the science teacher Eddie Whipp (a precise representation of his name), we focused only on the *dees* and *doze* of his nasal speech, but he was a masterly choreographer of chemicals. Every time I passed the sombre Philips gas works at the end of Briscoe Lane, I thought of Mr Whipp's magically enriching hydrocarbons dancing within. There was the (still tangible) first-time thrill of seeing litmus paper turn red, proving the substance in the beaker was an acid, and the excitement of summoning up hills and valleys after the angular, testy John Bateman had shown how the contour lines on maps could be converted into shapes. I was enthused enough by the suave Joe Abbott describing the day Cromwell had King Charles I beheaded to spend hours at home memorizing the dates and events leading to that dreadful sequel.

Early on I picked up the journalist's habit of never throwing anything away, and still have the school reports of those years. It is nothing less than saintly of me to acknowledge that in the first year I scored a disgraceful 2 per cent in the music exam set by the ample Miss Polly Wardle, whom I couldn't help but think of as Miss Warble. This 'terrible result', as she described it, puzzled the good Miss Polly because she certified I had indeed 'worked in class'. But this may have been a reference to my countertenor rendering of Handel's 'Where'er You Walk', a promising diversion from reading scores until I fell out of favour when my voice broke mid-song.

Meanwhile, in geometry and algebra I was damned as 'often careless', 'erratic', and 'disappointing', and my efforts in physical education were dismissed as 'tries hard but has no sense of rhythm'.

I had such a dim start for all my efforts that I thought the 11-plus examiners had me right. As the terms went by, however, I began doing well ('promising'), then very well ('excellent worker'). I was always top of the class in history exams, high in French and English Composition, Language and Literature, and battled the brainy brunette Betty Ogden for top place in science and geography. Even the demon physical training instructor in the third year was moved to dub me 'nimble, a very good performer'. My surviving little blue English composition exercise books reflect my romantic addiction to the adventurous historical novels of Jeffery Farnol (*The Amateur Gentleman*), H. Rider Haggard (*King Solomon's Mines*), Arthur Conan Doyle (*The White Company*), P. C. Wren (*Beau Geste*), Walter Scott (*Guy Mannering*) – all borrowed from my beloved Failsworth Public Library. But a degenerate streak soon shows itself. I had the idea I would grow up to write enthralling fiction. I had no talent for it. No subject was safe from the pestilential prose I inflicted on S. J. Pawley, a gentle English teacher with a withered arm. He set us a composition innocuously entitled 'Village Shop'. I submitted one beginning: 'I looked up from the bare uncarpeted floor. There she stood, no longer young, but a huge mass of fat. Wiping her bare red arms on her dirty apron she waddles towards me.'

In the fourth year I was elected school captain by some combination of staff nominations and school votes. A blue shield was ceremoniously pinned on the lapel of my blazer and I kept it on at home. My brother Fred, who was rebelling at Chadderton Grammar, said I was a goody-goody, and while the badge was supposed to confer authority over all my schoolmates, Fred made it clear my writ did not run at home. My main school duties were to organize the prefects to watch out for bullies and troublemakers in the playground and, when the bell went for classes to resume, keep order in the long lines on the stairs and in the corridors. There were many bigger stronger boys in the school. I'd been terrified of one brute who liked to grip smaller boys in a rib-cracking bear hug. The blue shield was like invisible armour; I was no longer singled out for his embraces.

I fretted a lot in these adolescent years about being skinny and flat-chested. There weren't anything like as many muscle men on the beach as there are these days, but I felt I was exactly the pale 7-stone weakling featured in a comic-strip advertisement for the body-building system of Charles Atlas. The ads we saw featured a sand-kicking bully on a beach humiliating a scrawny boy walking with his girlfriend. Weeks later, rebuilt by Charles Atlas, the weakling sees off the bully and wins the admiration of the girl. It was my first experience of the power of advertising. Brother Fred was stronger than I was, but the ads got to him, too, so we persuaded Dad that he should invest in our taking the correspondence course. With all that heavy work on the footplate, Dad didn't need the course, but when he was home he joined us in our bare-chested nightly efforts to look like the glistening Mr Atlas. The sight of the three tensed-up men in her life straining to pit muscle against muscle in their own bodies in the system called 'dynamic tension' was tolerated by Mum so long as efforts did not delay our arrival at the supper table.

As school captain I was supposed to set an example to the whole school. This was complicated by the fact that the school captain had fallen in with bad company. Howard Davies, a youth who lived nearby, was so slick he had a toothbrush moustache at seventeen, Brylcreemed his hair and claimed to have had carnal knowledge of several Wren ratings, promising that he would initiate me too. He was the Stromboli to my Pinocchio.

Among other things, Davies taught me magic tricks. Of course, I hated him at first, not just for his sexual prowess but because in my Christmas stocking I received a velvet bag that could make an egg disappear – but he had one, too, and was better at the trick than I was. He became a good enough conjuror to be engaged by Uncle Mac's amateur concert party, and later by the semi-official body for entertaining the troops. Uncle Mac, though, was on a lower plane than many of the stars he toured with. His main gig was putting on shows at night for the service men and women in the North-West bored out of their minds when they weren't operating the search-lights and ack-ack batteries. He also organized summer shows in the parks for the Stay-At-Home Holiday campaign (which encouraged people not to travel in their holidays) for which I was drafted as the rear half of a costume donkey.

Mum and Dad didn't like Howard, but I quickly became stage-struck. The world of Leichner make-up, footlights and frenzied changes backstage between acts was even more exciting than banging the school gong, but one night offered an experience that was unnerv-ing for an adolescent. A pretty young actress in a sketch had just rushed offstage while I awaited my cue. I looked back and through a gap in one of the changing-room curtains my eye lingered on her beautiful white bottom wriggling out of a pair of tights. I had no psychological mechanism for the shock when moments later the curtains parted to reveal that the favoured backside belonged to a boy.

I was haunted by the ambiguity and regarded as condign punishment the subsequent drama of the red ball. After the Peeping Tom trauma I re-dedicated my spare time to practising Howard's sleight-of-hand card tricks. He taught me how to acquire dexterity by rolling a little red ball from finger to finger, and I did it furtively at all times of the day in school. Classes would stop when I lost the grip and the ball rolled to the front. I would retrieve it with a 'Sorry, sir.' One day I was practising in the washroom next to the teachers' recreation room, and the ball fell down the plughole drain. I did not see it again until a week later. Mr Marsland held it up before the whole school in assembly. 'Who is the boy who owns this little red ball? Who is the boy who has blocked the washrooms with it? Who is the boy who flooded the teachers' staff room? Let him have the decency to own up and see me in my room after assembly.'

I was punished with three strikes of a leather strap on my open hand. Hand-strapping was commonplace in the classrooms, but the pain here was in letting down Mr Marsland.

Marsland was something of a mystery, for though he wasn't a graduate he was a more cultivated man than the Manchester Council required or expected. St Mary's had no playing field, so he taught us the refinements of cricket on expeditions to a city park.

In this final year, five of us were thought to have a chance of passing the Joint Matriculation examinations normally reserved for the grammar schools. Marsland organized after-hours coaching on Shakespeare. When everyone else went home at four o'clock, we five, three girls and two boys, stayed behind in his study. The school's emptiness echoed around us as he took us through *As You Like It* and *A Midsummer Night's Dream*. We were hard put not to giggle when he acted out Pyramus on tiptoe talking to Thisbe through Wall's chink, but we soon became entranced ourselves, listening to his gentle voice teasing out the significance of every syllable. He showed another side of his histrionic gifts, directing us gorily in the school performance of *Sweeney Todd, the Demon Barber of Fleet Street*. It has always been a sadness to me to think how little we were able to respond to his graciousness and learning, and his courage in trying to raise the academic and athletic standards of his school. He died some years later from the effects of his First World War service, and St Mary's Road Central School was demolished by an education committee which can have known nothing of the magic the Forest of Arden summoned up as dusk fell over the railway yards.

In 1940, when Hitler smashed Norway in April and then the Low Countries and France in May, I was more concerned that the end of the phony war marked the demise of the *Magnet* comic book, closed by paper rationing. The fictional Greyfriars vanished along with the universal illusion that the war would soon be won. My days of careless youth ebbed away, too, after the morning on the beach at Rhyl with the Dunkirk survivors. I resented the time Dad spent with them instead of with me, but I came to see the encounter as cathartic. And while I didn't suddenly grow up, I read more and more about the war. I was already intoxicated by the *Express* and by newspapers altogether as a manifestation of a more potent magic than Howard Davies's. The *Daily Surprise*, as I came to think of the newspaper, simply amazed me. How did they do it not once, but differently every day? How was all this information gathered? How was everything fitted in with nothing over? How did the photograph get taken on the battlefield and how was it reproduced? Who were these dazzling figures with notebooks sitting at the feet of Churchill and Roosevelt? How were the newspaper's strong opinions determined? Little opinion seeped out of the radio. (On political questions, the august governors of the BBC would rather be caught naked in Whitehall than be seen trying to influence people.)

Oh, yes, and who was the mysterious anonymous columnist in the *Daily Express* who signed himself Beachcomber and wrote a few hundred words headed 'By the Way'? They convulsed me with insane laughter I could never explain to Fred or anyone else. 'Sixty Horses Wedged in Chimney' was a typical Beachcomber headline, followed by: 'The story to fit this sensational headline has not turned up yet.' Beachcomber was nonsense on stilts, but comically perfect in his parodies of newspaper style: 'Erratum. In my article on the

Price of Milk, "Horses" should have read "Cows" throughout.' As a toddler, I'd been hooked on a comic strip in the *Express*, the adventures of Rupert Bear; the incentive to finish my porridge in the morning was to see his antic figure painted on the bottom of the bowl. But Beachcomber was a lifetime's addiction even after I soured on his host newspaper for its vendettas and political distortions. For thirty-very-odd years, I was to follow his surreal daily reports from an asylum populated by Dr Strabismus (whom God Preserve) of Utrecht (inventor of Bracerot juice, designed to make Hitler's trousers fall down); Mr Justice Cocklecarrot at the Court of Uncommon Pleas (adjudicating the right of Mrs Renton continually to ring the doorbell of Mrs Tasker for the purpose of depositing twelve red-bearded dwarfs); Great White Carstairs (the over-patriotic ambassador who could not talk on the telephone to the Foreign Office without saluting); the celebrated Russian ballet dancer Serge Trousier; and Narkover School's cunningly villainous headmaster, the light-fingered Dr Smart-Allick, all of them in a funny-mirrors gallery of grotesques similar to the daily procession of frauds and fools who, happily for us, provoked Beachcomber, alias John Cameron Andrieu Bingham Michael Morton, to put on his countryman's boots and scale mountains of absurdity. No word or phrase was safe from his mischief. A clue, he wrote, 'is what the police find when they fail to arrest a criminal'. And again: 'One disadvantage of being a hog is that any minute some blundering fool will try to make a silk purse out of your wife's ear.' Morton's ink flowed into the veins of Spike Milligan, Peter Sellers and Harry Secombe (the *Goon Show*), John Cleese, Michael Palin and Eric Idle (*Monty Python*), and Richard Ingrams (*Private Eye*). He had a place in my pantheon with Evelyn Waugh, P. G. Wodehouse, Stephen Leacock, Jerome K. Jerome and S. J. Perelman.

Hollywood reinforced my infatuation with newspapers from the pre-teens into young adulthood. Our local cinemas, the Magnet, the Pavilion, the Picture Palace, the Ceylon and the Grand, reopened in the autumn of 1939. Every Saturday at the Magnet matinee Fred and I jostled other kids lining up to get in and then scrambled for the sweets the manager threw into the mob. The run of movies in those years still seems remarkable: Clark Gable in *Gone with the Wind*; Orson Welles' *Citizen Kane*; Billy Wilder's *Ace in the Hole*; Chaplin's *Gold Rush*; John Ford's *Stagecoach*; Humphrey Bogart in *Casablanca*; Alfred Hitchcock's *Foreign Correspondent*; Michael Powell's *49th Parallel*; Gary Cooper in *Beau Geste*, Ben Hecht's *Front Page*; George Stevens' *Gunga Din*; the Marx brothers' *The Big Store*, Noël Coward and David Lean's *In Which We Serve*; and Bob Hope and Bing Crosby on the road some-mad-where with Dorothy Lamour. Heroes – and hilarity – aplenty. I loved them all, but it was the movies about newspapers I tried to see over and over again. Charles Foster Kane begins as a tribune of the people, the immigrants and the unions, against the 'Octopus' of the Southern Pacific Railroad, the bosses of Tammany Hall, and the banks and Wall Street, and ends up manipulating the news as a crypto-fascist crusader for capitalism. Was that a true portrait of William Randolph Hearst? I learned in due course that it was a distortion of Hearst, but I relished the moment when Citizen Kane's managing editor Mr Bernstein pulled up the proofs of two front pages made up in advance, one announcing Mr Charles Foster Kane had won New York's gubernatorial election and the other announcing he had lost, one banner-headlined 'Kane Elected', the other 'Fraud at Polls!' What fun! I identified with the small-town editors standing up to crooks, and snap-brimmed reporters winning the story and the girl, and the foreign correspondent outwitting enemy agents. That was the easy part, cops and robbers in different dress, but some of the newspaper movies stayed in my mind when the adrenalin rush had gone. How could *Ace in the Hole* reporter Kirk Douglas (1951) be so greedy for a scoop on a man trapped in a mine that he delayed the rescue just to keep the story alive for the media circus he created?

The war became intensely personal when bombing of the Manchester area began in August 1940. It was only sporadic at first, but Dad was much at risk out there in the blackness in some godforsaken tangle of railway lines. Schoolgirl Enid Parker, who was to enter my life ten years later, saw an exploding ammunition train light up the sky near her home on Queens Drive, Liverpool. Much more was to come. The full-scale blitzes began on 7 September 1940, with heavy bombers pounding London for fifty-seven nights in succession. People in Manchester kept saying jocularly. 'Well, we're bound to get it next.'

We did. The awesome two-day Christmas blitz of Manchester began at dusk on Sunday, 22 December. After the bombing of Liverpool, Mum made up camp beds in the brick shelter that the Failsworth council had built to replace the waterlogged Anderson shelter dug into the back garden. As soon as the sirens sounded on the Sunday, she shut the shop and hustled baby John, four-year-old Peter and me out of the house and into the shelter with a big basket of sandwiches, hot water bottles, Thermos flasks and a torch. Two of the family were missing. On Saturday, 21 December, Dad, on a day off work, had taken my ten-year-old brother Fred with him to Gobowen, the village near Oswestry, to see if Granny Jones had a turkey she could spare for Christmas. Without a telephone, we had not expected to hear anything from them, but sitting in the brick shelter in the cold candlelight without the perennially cheerful head of the family, we were lonely and very afraid, our shelter isolated in a vast cavern of echoing noise, the drone of more than a hundred bombers, the crump of our ack-ack guns, the blast of the bombs.

We'd no idea we were smack in the bombers' sights, our very street clearly to be seen on the high-level aerial reconnaissance photographs of targets made by German planes on 5 October 1940. I came across the dated and marked photographs only when I started to write this memoir and visited Peter Charlton, a school friend from Brookdale Park and St Mary's Road. He had become the historian of Newton Heath, and in German archives had unearthed one headed:

Manchester-Newton Heath
Flugzeugzellenfabrik A.V. Roe & Co Ltd.

Superimposed on the image were black rectangles of areas to be bombed. The perimeter of the principal target, the aircraft factory of A. V. Roe, was just down the road from us. The aeronautical genius Alliott Verdon-Roe, born, as I was, in Patricroft, designed the RAF's most successful bomber, the Lancaster, which flew 156,000 operations from 1942 to 1945. Lancasters delivered the bouncing bombs that broke the dams of the Ruhr valley in 1943, and the 12,000lb Tallboy bombs, also designed by Dr Barnes Wallis, that finally sank the mighty German battleship *Tirpitz* in November 1946. Three other targets in our neighbourhood are marked on the Luftwaffe map: Gaswerk am Philips Park (which featured in my science lessons), the Mather and Platt gun factory, and the Crossley Brothers diesel works.

Apart from starting a fire in one building of Crossley Motors, the 270 bombers missed all the targets so meticulously pinpointed. Instead, their 272 tons of high explosives and 1,032 canisters of incendiaries fell three miles to the south-west of the war factories, blowing up and burning the area from Manchester's city centre of Piccadilly Gardens to Victoria Station, the cathedral and into Salford and Stretford. Had the bombers erred in the opposite direction, missing A. V. Roe as much to the north-east as they did to the south-west, they'd have obliterated our Brookdale area and 54 Ashworth Street and all of us with it. As it was, around the devastated city centre 700 people were dead.

We could smell the smoke and fires were still raging when we came out of the shelter the next morning. My uncle Arnold and his wife Gertie emerged from their garden shelter near Trafford Park to find their home was gone, burned to the ground. And by lunchtime Dad and Fred had still not reappeared. We worried all day. Mum refused to go down to Newton Heath police station to ask if they had heard anything about bombs falling on Welsh border villages: 'We can't bother them, they have enough on their hands and Dad can look after himself.' She reopened the shop and I helped to look after baby John and infant Peter, while popping out from time to time to stand watch at the street corner. At dusk, when nobody was about, I saw figures coming up Farm Street, but moving very slowly. I ran down the street and it was Dad and Fred, laden with turkey and other good country things. (Throughout the war, rationing restricted everyone to tiny quantities of everything – bacon, butter, meat, tea, sugar, jam, cereals, eggs, milk, sweets, clothing, biscuits, canned fruit – but the country people somehow managed to have more than one egg a week and were altogether not as reliant as city people on the fish and chip shop.)

They'd caught a morning train from Gobowen to Crewe and another to Manchester, but a bomb had torn up the track from Eccles, so they had to walk, jumping on any bus that was still running in the hope it was heading in the right direction: all of the destination markers were blanked out. They arrived just in time for the second full night of bombing. It was just as bad as the first night, but with them back with us the fear evaporated.

The only consolation for all the bad news on the evening radio in the early years of the war was that the steadiness of the ice-clear baritone voice of the BBC announcer Alvar Lidell suggested there would always be an England. In these radio years, voices were so important to us, the anchors of our hopes as much by tone and inflection as by the words. Churchill had no better news for us than Chamberlain, but his voice evoked the spirit of St Crispin's Day; Chamberlain's would not have scared a sparrow hawk. We suffered a sense of isolation until the marvellous moment in December 1941 when Mr Lidell at last had something good to relate. America had entered the war. Fighting spirits rose hearing Churchill growl his epic phrases; FDR's voice soothed. Having just learned about the Gulf Stream from Mr Bateman, I thought of FDR's words as a powerful warm current crossing the ocean to keep us calm and cheerful. His words were uplifting – 'we will gain the inevitable triumph, so help us God' – but the almost languid calm of his rolling articulation was essential to the reassurance.

The words became gloriously manifest when in Manchester's bomb-gutted Piccadilly I first saw a leather-jacketed lanky American airman on a weekend pass from the Flying Fortresses at Burtonwood, Warrington. Soon after that I saw my very first black man. The British Empire had dominion over millions of black and brown people, but before the war we were still a homogeneous race of pale whites living insular lives, never hearing a foreign accent in the provinces or venturing across our narrow moat into Europe: when Dad, in 1938, took us all on a day ferry from

Ramsgate for a few hours in Boulogne it was the talk of our neighbourhood for weeks.

What colour and dash the smiling Americans brought to our
bleak grey world! We saw them all as film stars, so sleek and well-
tailored in their smooth uniforms. Any one of the big-boned
American servicemen sighted in the city drew a flock of kids asking
'Any gum, chum?' and they always got something. Women, we
heard, were given gifts of nylon stockings and cigarettes, arousing
some resentments. My widowed cousin Little Eva was the happy
recipient of this generosity from one of the black servicemen she
brought home to tea in Eccles, to some spiteful gossip according to
my mother; later she had a lovely baby daughter by another
airman. The odd sourpuss in our shop might recycle the crack by
the comedian Tommy Trinder that the Yanks were 'overpaid,
overfed, oversexed, and over here', but as far as I could see the
Americans were warmly welcome. Most English people were just
too inhibited to express much emotion beyond an occasional
thumbs-up gesture.

The war dragged on. It was a strain for Mum the shopkeeper. The
histories I've read about the home front highlight how hard
rationing was on the public – but nobody bothers much with what
it was like for the shopkeeper, the hub of the system. The administration of it was complex. Some foods were rationed by weight,
some by quantity, some by groups, so a customer could opt for jam
rather than marmalade or swap the jam for extra sugar; early in the
war holders of ration books were also given sixteen points they
could spend on unrationed foods like a tin of Fray Bentos corned
beef, a packet of Kellogg's corn flakes, a box of Peek Freans assorted
biscuits, or the tin of Tate & Lyle golden syrup – a defunct lion
plagued by bees on the label – that made such a difference to the
morning porridge. But supplies of such luxuries were erratic. Mum
was so scrupulously honest that when there was a lucky break – one
month the arrival of six unrationed tins of salmon – she agonized
about whose need was greatest among the several hundred registered customers, and had to distribute it by stealth to avoid jealous
fights.

The unseen burden was counting the coupons from the ration books. The number of coupons in various categories returned to the Ministry of Food offices in Failsworth determined what supplies the shop would get the following week. No coupons, no food. It was an awful chore counting and recounting these fiddly bits of paper; the coupons for sweets and chocolate were tiny and easily lost. Some shops had to close. Everyone in the family had to help out at the end of the week, all of us kneeling on the carpet for four or five hours on a Sunday night. It was the burden of rationing, which continued after the war, that induced Mum to sell the business.

I'd no ambitions to be a shopkeeper. By the time I was thirteen, I had grand ideas of myself as a journalist-historian of the war. In the fourth and last year at St Mary's there was an election to choose an editor for a new school magazine. The English teachers nominated a handful of candidates and I was utterly shameless in campaigning to win the editorship.

The magazine I produced was a limp little thing. My incipient journalistic juices must have gone into my pet project at home. I scoured the *Daily Express*, *Daily Dispatch*, *Manchester Evening News* and any magazines I could get my hands on for maps, drawings and pictures. I pasted them into Manchester City education committee exercise books from night bookkeeping classes I took in the summer, so that the tumult of the war overlay neat balance sheets of assets and liabilities of fictional companies. I still have these war books with my copperplate captions and their headlines:

'First, Know Your Enemy: Silhouettes of New Luftwaffe war-planes'
'Achtung! Britain's Perfect Bomber-Buster Comes Off the Secret List'
'German tanks burn on a Tunisia Battlefield – British six pounders hold the position'
'Iron Crosses for seven but look at their boots'
'Over mountains, through steaming jungle, to smash the Jap Toe-Hold at Buna'
'These Italians are happy to be out of the struggle'

'Gurkha rescued under fire at Mareth'
'RAF aimed well – factory is hit; the homes are spared'

The pictures that most excited me were panoramas of our invincible armies on the march in the Western desert, cutaway drawings of our deadly fighter planes and flying boats dominating the skies, and gallant destroyers on heaving seas sinking U-boats. The British nationalism was intense, but the Free French cavalry in the desert was allowed to gallop into the pages in sepia; I gave a page to bearded Cossack guerrillas in the snow, and one to a portrait of Lenin. Any number of my classmates were superior in identifying aircraft silhouettes; I was in for the drama.

The impression the pages give is of a 'Boy's Own' jingo paper: we were winning gloriously. Of course, all of us of that generation had grown up with an exaggerated idea of Britain's prowess. The schoolroom maps of our world were mostly coloured red for the two-fifths of the globe that was the British Empire and its dominions; half the traffic through the Suez Canal was British. How lustily we belted out 'Rule Britannia, Britannia rule the waves/Britons never, never, never shall be slaves!' In the end it was assumed a given that the nation of Wellington and Nelson would triumph. My selections were loaded for optimism, because they were, again, a reflection of what was in the newspapers, though leafing through the two crammed books today, I rather scent the mephitic vapours of the time. The scrapbook was a comforter, something to hold on to in a depressing yearning for certainty. Just look at that Mosquito, the world's fastest reconnaissance bomber, on its way to attack Gestapo headquarters in Oslo!

My little war book was something I kept to myself. I didn't show it to Dad. I glowed with his constant encouragement, but about the war I feared his scepticism. He still had reservations about Churchill. He admired Franklin Roosevelt, but as the war ground on, he talked most about the Russians. 'That Marshal Zhukov!' he'd chuckle, gripping me in an imitation of a grizzly bear's squeeze. 'He'll get them in a pincer movement. Just watch.' Only years later, writing history myself, did I think Dad may have been doing more than indulging his romantic view of Russia; he may have divined from the numbers what most people did not at the time, that the bulk of the fighting against Germany was being done by the Russians, so the European War would be won or lost on the Eastern Front.

I don't think any of us St Mary's graduates thought at all about the distant future that summer of 1943 as we stood in the last assembly belting out 'Forty years on, when afar and asunder, Parted are those who are singing today.' The war was too much in the way. There was no future, there were only black lines and arrows on newspaper maps marking the clash of armies and navies in the infinities of Russia and the Pacific Ocean.

I had done well in the examinations for the Central School Certificate (distinctions in literature, French, science, geography and history), but what really counted were the results of the Joint Matriculation Board examinations the select five of us had sat.

I was on edge that summer. Most of the boys in my class had within days of graduation signed on as apprentice merchants of death, the cleverest working on blueprints, others in the Avro factory riveting the fuselages of Lancaster four-engine bombers destined to do to the Germans what they had done to Manchester in the blitz. I'd see these boys on the streets in blue overalls, school kids who had been kicking a tennis ball round the playground a few weeks earlier, joining the droves of men and women headed for the factories around the time the milkman was leaving bottles on our doorsteps. Other classmates vanished behind the long camouflaged walls of Mather and Platt as trainee draughtsmen, making drawings for parts of big guns. These factories were just round the corner on Briscoe Lane in Newton Heath. A few others trekked across Manchester's suburbs to Metro-Vickers in the great sprawling Trafford Park, the misnomer for the world's first industrial estate, a prime target for the Heinkels. When I bumped into former classmates, they'd pull out a pay slip. 'Take a look at that! Two quid! Two quid! I got to keep ten bob.'

My own pocket money was a fraction of that, two shillings and sixpence, the satisfyingly heavy silver 'half a crown'. I was not envious, but glad the war effort depended on their skills, not mine. These

were the boys who had made perfect dovetail joints in the dark basement at St Mary's Road where we were taught woodwork. The
carpentry teacher, the bristling, red-faced Joe Hall, had been so disgusted by my efforts he threw the finished joint the length of the
room, yelling: 'You one-eyed kaffir!' The joint's disintegration in
flight proved his point: I was not good with my hands. I would not
get an apprenticeship even if I'd wanted one.

Partly as an insurance against academic failure, my parents had
been saving pennies and shillings in those little boxes around the
house. In that summer of 1943, they told me they'd accumulated
£70 – about £6,000 at today's values – and starting right away
they were ready to pay for me to acquire the tools of the reporter's
trade by taking full-time classes at Loreburn Business College in
the city for shorthand and touch typing, plus a little German to
add to my so-so French. I was as much impressed by their fore-
sight as by their sacrifice. I'd talked about shorthand and typing
but hadn't worked out how I would get the skill. Now I had the
opportunity.

The Loreburn classes were all girls learning to be secretaries, giggling about having two sissy boys do what they were doing. Dick
Walton, the other boy, as thin, pale and nervy as I was, aspired to
be a writer, too. I found Pitman's shorthand as exciting as a spy
code and took to it, as did Dick, so that we beat the girls for speed
and transcription. We reached 180 words a minute (and examination diplomas for 120 wpm). But not all was triumph: thump our
Underwood machines hard as we might, the keyboard covered by
a shield, we never outmatched the nimblest of the girls in touch
typing.

With some vague idea that if ever I became a reporter I'd have to
unmask embezzlers and fraudsters, I enrolled in night classes at
Brookdale for double-entry book-keeping. I wouldn't say I shone. I
was distracted a lot by a ping-pong table in the hall and became so
obsessed by the game that I played every night – no, off and on I
played for the rest of my life. I teamed up as a doubles partner with
a neighbourhood friend, a much better player, Ron Allcock; we
entered all the tournaments and he played for England.

I was still high from a winning match at Manchester YMCA when I returned home to find a buff envelope reminiscent of the one from Manchester Education Committee telling me I'd failed the 11-plus. This one was marked Joint Matriculation Board. I wasn't eager to open it. I took it into the back room to read it alone before Dad came home. Mum was in the shop serving a crotchety customer, but I broke into the transactions exclaiming: 'I've passed! I've passed!' I'd done more. I'd passed in all six subjects with credits in five of them.

I was forgiven the interruption. It was a huge moment, bigger even than I realized at the time.

I had a chance in life.

4

HOT METAL

In 1944, when I was sixteen, I applied for my first job in news-papers. I raided my mother's box of Basildon Bond notepaper, calculating the fine blue sheets would make an impression of refine-ment. I had to clean up after the family supper before I could sit down at the kitchen table with a steel pen and a bottle of ink. I succeeded in ruining several drafts with blots, so it was dark when I went out with my stamped letter to the little red postbox at the end of the street. By then the wartime blackout had been relaxed a little. People were allowed to use a flashlight provided the glass was covered in cardboard with a tiny hole in the middle.

From Failsworth Public Library, my home away from home, I had culled the addresses of eight or nine daily newspapers in the city where I was born, Manchester. I wrote a letter a night for a week. With each letter I enclosed a stamped, self-addressed envelope 'for courtesy of a reply'. I didn't get many, and wondered if some mis-creant had steamed off my precious stamp; the replies that did come more or less said get lost.

In three weeks or so, I was stuck, like the British Army at Caen following the D-Day landings in Normandy that month. So I aban-doned the big city newspapers and scouted more obscure titles in the urban wastes of Lancashire, and then the posher towns of Cheshire,

trying to outpace the rejections and silences with bolder advertisements for myself. Captain of the school! Editor of the school
magazine! School certificate! Shorthand and typing! I had also
included a testimonial from the headmaster of my school. What
more could they want?

In fact, I hadn't expected much of a testimonial from headmaster
Marsland. His end-of-school testimonial, at first reading, didn't suggest I had been a disappointment, so I had a copy typed to send with
each application. I still have it after all these years:

> Harold Evans, who has been a conscientious and successful
> School Captain, is a boy with very lively intelligence, possessing
> powers of original thought along with a very retentive memory.
> He is perhaps too impetuous at present, but will outgrow that.
> He has won his success, both as a Captain and in the classroom,
> because he never spares himself, and seldom flags in his interest.
> His success in the athletic life of the school is largely due to his
> determined energy. We shall miss his integrity and willing service,
> and we wish him all the success he deserves.

When none of my letters had any effect, I had the dark thought
that the testimonial was not foolproof, in fact might be a hostage to
fortune. Wouldn't an editor contemplating a risky hiring be quite put
off by 'too impetuous'? Not just impetuous – that was bad enough –
but '*too* impetuous'. Clearly this was an alert that the applicant was
foaming at the mouth. 'Seldom' flags in his interest? Could that be
read as a hint that he flaked out when the going got tough? And
that reference to energy in athletics suggested brute force rather than
exquisite skill. As for being wished 'all the success he deserves', it
could be a back-hander; perhaps this youth deserved only a tiny
bit of success – or none at all! For one mad moment, I impetuously
drafted a letter asking Mr Marsland to withdraw this reference to
impetuosity and conclude with something like 'we wish him the
glittering success he so thoroughly deserves'. Fortunately, the paranoid parsing was pre-empted. One of my scatter-shot applications
produced a returned envelope with a peremptory command beneath

the magnificent blue Gothic title *Ashton-under-Lyne Weekly Reporter* series: Come to Ashton at 10 a.m. the following Wednesday and ask for me. (Signed) John W. Middlehurst, News Editor.

I knew nothing of Ashton except that it was one of a cluster of cotton and coal towns east of Manchester with odd names like Stalybridge and Dukinfield. It proved to be an initiative test in itself just finding a way there. Manchester was crisscrossed with rail and bus lines, but every bus and train anywhere accessible from our house in Failsworth shied away from Ashton-under-Lyne.

It was a miserable wet day that Wednesday. My father had been on the footplate all night but insisted on giving my shoes 'a special railwayman's shine' before he went to bed, and Mum ironed a fresh white shirt between serving customers in our corner shop. It took three bus rides before I was deposited outside the sooty Town Hall of Ashton-under-Lyne. Across the cobbled market square, asserting equality in its authority, rose the Victorian redbrick headquarters of the *Ashton-under-Lyne Reporter*. It was market day. Vendors in the square huddled from the drizzle beneath their canvases, and there was hardly anybody about. I took shelter by a stall selling teapots until two minutes to the hour, and then ran across the street through the revolving front door of the *Reporter*. In the front office, I asked to see Mr Middlehurst, speaking in my best BBC voice to disguise my flat North Country accent. A sniffy clerk told me I'd have to use the back entrance. Where was that? 'Just round the corner. Use your eyes!'

He didn't say which corner, but an unmarked side door opened onto a narrow flight of worn stone steps. I ran up them to the second floor and discovered another world: the floor was filled with long lines of iron monsters, each seven feet high, five feet wide, decked out with an incomprehensible array of moving parts – gears, pulleys, camshafts, levers and bars. A man crouched in communion at the foot of each contraption. This was my first sight of the Linotype machine, at whose 90-character keyboard a deft operator could automatically render words into metal slugs at the rate of five column lines a minute. There was an exciting smell to which I would become addicted. It was hot news. Lead, antimony and tin bubbled in each Linotype's melting pot, kept at 300 degrees centigrade by a petrol burner. Digital typesetting at a computer has consigned the Linotype to the museum, but the speeding electron has none of the aromatic urgency of hot metal marinated with printer's ink.

I interrupted one of the Linotype operators at his devotions, 'I'm here to see Mr Middlehurst.'

'Jack or Dennis? They're both in there!'

Behind a flimsy wooden partition at the side of the big room were a number of desks piled high with papers, telephone directories, pots of glue, spikes, and a full-sized glass kiosk with a candlestick telephone inside. One gingery-haired middle-aged reporter with a pipe clenched in his teeth sat bolt upright at a typewriter in the corner, and another wizened walnut of a man was hunched over a desk writing with a pen in front of a window overlooking the market square. Neither acknowledged that the saviour of British journalism had arrived.

At the end of the room stood a big dishevelled man in thick glasses, running his hands through thinning hair, and steaming at a stolid man in a printer's apron who had his hands on his hips in what looked like a posture of defiance. The big man broke off in midstream. This was clearly my quarry, Mr Middlehurst.

'Evans?' Without any more ado, without even looking at me, he scooped up bunches of paper from the turmoil of his desk and thrust them into my hand.

'Asparagus,' he mumbled in a rapid monotone. 'Asparagus – four copies, an' quick about 'em laddie!'

He went back to his confrontation with the printer. Asparagus? It was a delicacy unknown to Lancashire dinner tables; I'd barely heard of it. The little old man at the window desk gave me a wad of coarse newsprint copy paper, about six inches wide by three inches deep, and gestured to an empty chair by an Underwood typewriter.

I skimmed the papers Middlehurst had given me, mostly handwritten scrawl on letters, postcards and sheets torn from an exercise book. There were names of winners of a women's whist drive in Audenshaw; a note about a gift day at a Rotary club; a typed sheet from an undertaker naming a list of mourners; a rambling report on 'Christianity in action' at the Welbeck Street Baptist Church; a letter about a clergyman back from China 'after thrilling adventures', maddeningly unspecified; and a handwritten page about a burst pipe at a Methodist church that doused the choir in steam and drenched the conductor. The correspondent testified that 'Mr Joseph Thornrey carried on unperturbed.'

I was at a loss. No mention of asparagus in any of these disconnected vignettes of local life, not even a flower show. The hunched figure at the window radiated: 'You're on your own.' The ramrod ginger-haired typist was on automatic pilot, pounding away without pause. The sight of Mr Middlehurst frothing at his desk behind a big spike impaled with paper and a gallery of column proofs deterred me from going back to enquire what I was supposed to be doing.

I typed *asparagus 1* at the top of the copy sheet, and prayed for inspiration, whereupon there appeared at my elbow a fairy godmother in the shape of a handsome, slight youth my age with dark wavy hair. As he spoke, he kept washing hands together Uriah Heep style. 'You're new. I'm Laurence Taylor, let me show you the ropes. Yes, yes,' he chuckled, 'just write up these submissions separately as paragraphs.'

Asparagraphs! As paragraphs. Paragraphs!

He had decoded the sibilant Middlehurst mumble and saved my life. I rendered each of the submissions neatly into six-line typed paragraphs, removed the messy carbon paper required to make four copies and took the lot to Mr Middlehurst, his head down as he fertilized another heap of asparagus. He ran a stubby black pencil over my first efforts in professional journalism, slashed out some words, and put the top sheets in an out-tray. Glory, could it really be that my first words were truly bound for print? That they were is evident in the files I consulted in Stalybridge Public Library years later.

Middlehurst spoke again, raising his bushy eyebrows several times. 'Spitman, eh?' He wanted to test my ability to take down a note in Pitman's shorthand. My Pitman was easily up to the pace of his brief dictation about some council committee or other. It was the way he spoke that made it hard, first decoding the mumble into intelligible words, then coding the words into the Pitman's phonetic code of loops, hooks and dots and then decoding the squiggles back at the Underwood.

The transcription passed muster. I was rewarded with a wedding: four folded sheets of blue paper bearing the pre-printed blanks for names of bride and groom, their addresses, occupations, what they wore, what the bride's mother wore, who played the organ, who performed the ceremony and where, who arranged the flowers, who were the bridesmaids and the best man and their relationships to the happy couple, where the reception was held, who spoke, and what the bride wore as she headed off on honeymoon. Only at that point did the *Reporter* restrain its curiosity. Laurence took me over to the bound files of previous editions so that I could learn how to render the bullets of information into imperishable prose that would support the headline 'Stalybridge Man Marries Ashton Woman', or 'Ashton Woman Marries Stalybridge Man', or with any luck something more graphic like 'War Workers Marry'. Even then flights of fancy were clearly not an option. I could type up 'the marriage was solemnized of . . .' or 'Ada Briscoe and John Tomlinson were married' or 'the wedding took place on Friday of . . .'

My effort was rewarded by another rapid elevation of Middlehurst's eyebrows. I was to learn that if they were elevated three times in rapid succession, it was a sign of benevolence.

He offered me three months' trial. 'Pound a week. Righty, laddie?'

A pound a week was about half what my classmates were now earning in factories. I didn't care. I might have to be on trial, but I had my first job in newspapers.

The offices of the *Ashton-under-Lyne Reporter* were too difficult to get to by bus from our home in Newton Heath, so I cycled fourteen miles every morning.

The *Reporter* had thirteen editions serving 80,000 readers living in the dreary back streets and industrial sprawl of Gorton and Openshaw, as well as the beautiful vales and villages of Derbyshire's High Peak district. Correspondents who walked the hills around Mossley, Saddleworth and New Mills put their copy into envelopes stamped 'News Urgent' and gave them to bus drivers. One of my first tasks as a junior reporter was to hang around at the bus stop in Ashton waiting to identify the right bus to collect those stories and feed them into the Middlehurst mowing machine. To miss the bus was a capital crime; not only was the flow of news imperilled but vital advertising revenue. Every weekly newspaper in the *Reporter* group gave up its front page to classified ads, as they had since 1855, and the inside pages were packed with news with no bylines. The only personal credit allowed was initials for a reviewer's critique, thereby bowing to the arts. Much of the news was collected by what was termed 'parring' or 'paragraphing' – forays to gather the news on foot. None of us had desk telephones; they were regarded as an extravagance. Very few homes, including mine, had the luxury of a telephone.

The kindly Laurence Taylor, whose hand-washing turned out to be exercises for his advanced piano lessons, initiated me into the labour of 'parring'. He paid the bus fare to Droylsden, then we walked the streets for hours making house calls, scavenging for names of the recently dead and the lucky.

I was very self-conscious. I hated going into the undertakers. They were unforgivably cheery when they had a lot to report. I was glad Laurence was with me though he, too, was of a morbid temperament. We roused grumpy caretakers in innumerable working men's clubs rancid with stale beer and sawdust, we drank tea in vicarage and rectory, dropped in on union secretaries and Catholic priests, youth centres and party political offices. We wrote down the names of winners of whist drives, cribbage contests and darts championships, of speakers and candidates for office and cake-makers and soup-servers in the Meals on Wheels service for those confined to their homes. Names, names, names! In search of scoops, we asked everyone if they had any news and drew blanks. In time I learned that people didn't recognize 'news' the way journalists defined it; you just had to get them talking freely and then fish out the bits and pieces that might add up to something significant. The police stations, promising drama, invariably delivered nothing at all, and we meekly accepted a duty sergeant's brush-off. No doubt we were thought not grown up enough to be exposed to crime stories. The county coroner's office was more forthcoming. We were invited to view a body ready for an inquest, someone who in the blackout had fallen in a canal. I couldn't face it.

We schoolboy reporters were filling in for men who were fighting the war. The senior newspapermen at work, like my teachers at school, were among the walking wounded. The robot at the type-writer I encountered on my first day had a wheezing chest complaint; he was Dennis Middlehurst, the taciturn son of the news editor Mr Middlehurst. The other man, a reporter by the name of Billy Mee, who lived to be ninety-eight, looked as if he was beyond recruiting age for the Boer War. When I first encountered the third senior reporter, he was lying inert and silent on the newsroom floor with his hat on. He was a plump man with a club foot. His nose was bleed-ing. 'Just step over him,' said Middlehurst junior, without looking up from his typing. 'Raphie has these attacks from time to time.'

When not prone, Raphie (Ralph Alder) was the most considerate of men who encouraged us juniors. We were all very circumspect, never referring to his disability – a sensitivity not respected by the chief photographer, a ball of energy in his late thirties, Charlie Sutcliffe, who would burst into the newsroom and say with a big grin: 'Come on, Raphie, don't drag your bloody feet.'

Charlie had his own problem. His right hand had been severed at the wrist during factory war work. His leather glove concealed a prosthetic hand, but he nonetheless wielded the blinding flashlight of his big Speed Graphic camera like a tomahawk. He was our very own Weegee in a rakish trilby hat, and a cynic. 'You're Boy Scouts,' he'd needle us. 'We're all in it for the money, right?' But he was very professional about getting his exposures right. (His bullied young assistant, a thin youth with a squeaky voice, got his revenge by win-ning £250,000 on the football pools and quit newspapers.)

We novice reporters were nervous of Charlie's vulgar energy – and we all loved going on assignment with him. He had petrol coupons for essential war work so we got to ride in his car, Charlie laughing his way past any resistance. 'Give the lad the bloody story!' he'd yell at some stick-in-the-mud official or difficult cop. None of us dared hang back from persisting when Charlie was present.

The tumult of the war was represented in the newsroom by Charlie's polar opposite, a scholarly young reporter with a prolonged brainy forehead, rimless glasses and the elaborately courteous manners of a diplomat at the court of Louis XIV. He sported a brown beret and a shoulder patch that proclaimed him a member of the Royal Army Pay Corps. This was Private John David Michael Hides, doing a little journalism as an arts reviewer. His initials, JDMH, at the end of his music and theatre reviews were regarded as a royal seal.

Michael was destined to be chief sub-editor of the *Manchester Guardian*, a key man on its perilous 1961 transition to London printing, and then the editor of Sheffield's *Morning Telegraph* who against all the odds got his paper out during a strike. I learned later that even when I first met him he had assumed a high responsibility, charged with seeing that money got through to Popski's Private Army, 'Popski' being Vladmir Reniakoff, a Belgian of Russian parentage who worked behind enemy lines in North Africa and Italy blowing up fuel dumps and aircraft on the ground. Of these adventures, JDMH said nothing. He was more concerned to tell us that we should catch Gustav Mahler. I'd never heard of Gustav Mahler. 'I'll alert the Droylsden police on my calls,' I told him. He seemed pleased.

The most striking figure among the younger reporters resembled Franz Kafka on the back of my Penguin copy of *The Castle*. This was Frank Keeble, who had a habit of clenching his jaw and promising to thump people who put obstacles in the path of truth and justice. I was at once in awe of him. He radiated glory, his friends including famous reporters like Tommie Thomson and Walter Terry, both of whom had graduated from Ashton into the big time of political reporting with bylines in the *Daily Mail*. Frank wasn't a man to be intimidated by anyone – even the august directors of the Stalybridge and Hyde Transport Board. They thought it was unconscionable that he should have reported a complaint about a bus driver who had got stuck on a hill in the snow. According to the intrepid Keeble, the driver had ordered all the passengers off the bus with the command: 'If tha' wants to get home tonight, tha'll have to get out and push.'

Such an order, protested the directors of the Transport Board, would have been contrary to the best traditions of the bus company. Keeble stuck to his story, and Middlehurst stood by his man. To us juniors, all this was stirring stuff.

At the end of my first week as a reporter I was beside myself. Bundles of newspapers came up from the printing presses in the basement. Incandescent on a number of pages were those paragraphs I'd written on the first day and others, and a couple of wedding reports of mine to the tune of about two full columns of paragraphs. Nobody acknowledged the glow these contributions shed over the whole paper. The room had become crowded with strangers – pipe-smokers in tweedy jackets from hill country talking among themselves – and my new pals, the junior reporters who were too busy rushing about with brooms and shovels. They swept the floor of the week's wadded-up balls of discarded copy paper, they cleared the desks of incriminating cups, they straightened up the newspaper files, emptied the ashtrays, extinguished cigarettes. Soon the place looked like a bank.

All this labour was performed for one singular man: 'Mr Will', namely William Hobson Andrew, Justice of the Peace, Captain of the 3rd Volunteer Brigade of the Manchester Regiment, and governing director of the entire *Reporter* series, i.e. our employer. Each Friday he appeared in the newsroom carrying a quart-sized metal canister of milk which he deposited on Mr Middlehurst's desk, specially cleared of papers for the occasion. We were a pale, fidgety bunch in off-the-peg suits. Mr Will was from another planet, silver-haired, slim in his hand-tailored suit and suntanned from daily hours on the golf course. He stood erectly among us, bracing his shoulders and gleaming with purpose.

'Good paper this week,' he said, exposing several gold teeth.

He made a few more comments, then after an awkward silence Mr Middlehurst indicated I was the new boy. 'He cycled all the way from Failsworth,' he added.

'Very good,' said Mr Will. 'Now, Evans, how many spokes are there in a bicycle wheel?'

'I don't know, sir.'

'Find out! Curiosity is the thing in journalism. Curiosity. Ask questions, Evans.'

Then he nodded to us all and was gone, taking his milk can with him.

A clerk in the front office often met Mr Will at the entrance of the building and carried the milk can for him. He told me he was rewarded for this task with an apple fished from Mr Will's pocket and polished on his very own sleeve. (The clerk, Derek Rigby, became a reporter with a world scoop to his credit: he was the first to report the discovery on Saddleworth Moor of the bodies of two child victims of the so-called Monsters of the Moors, Myra Hindley and Ian Brady.)

That Friday after Mr Will had gone to his office, Mr Middlehurst wasn't finished with me. He beckoned me over, his head down, avoiding eye contact.

'You're expensive,' he said.

I felt tempted to retort a pound a week wasn't a lot for the long hours I worked, but I'd misheard him again.

'Your expenses! Your expenses! Where's your expense report, laddie?'

'I haven't spent anything,' I explained.

'You must have. You must have taken bus rides.'

'No, sir, I walked.'

He glowered. 'Downstairs will think you're not working.' Then he scribbled on a slip of paper. 'Take that to the cashier.' I read it on the way down the stone steps to the front office:

'Harold Evans, Bus fares, Droylsden calls, 3 pence. Approved, J. W. Middlehurst, News Editor.'

I took every penny.

Everyone was a little scared of Mr Will, including Mr Middlehurst, who wore his jacket for these Friday encounters with him. The irreverent Keeble was the only one of us who dared to risk the wrath of the owner by entering the office at the main entrance like management. This meant surviving the glaring disapproval of the clerks and junior managers as he ascended the stairs and passed Mr Will's office. One day, Mr Will sprang out at him: 'Well, young man!' he said indignantly. '*Well!*'

But Frank had an inspired response. He duly explained that he'd come to thank the governing director for his leadership and guidance – and was it not time he was rewarded for his own dedication? A week later, he found an additional shilling in his pay packet.

Mr Will was represented every week in the paper by six asterisks at the foot of his own column called 'Golf Causerie'. He wrote anecdotes about personalities and course records and ordered that not a syllable of his copy should ever be changed. Thus it was that one of his columns informed us: 'There is no greater thrill than to drop your balls on a damp green.'

Golf Causerie was Mr Will's arcane indulgence, perhaps, but I see now it was a nice, chatty little enrichment even for those who didn't know the difference between a birdie and bogey. Mr Will was a shrewd owner-manager. He had worked in every department of the business since taking over twenty-six years before; he'd helped to push the transition from hand-setting to Linotypes, set up branch offices; and he'd committed the *Reporter* to solid non-partisan community news reporting at a time when even weeklies tended to be conspicuously Conservative or Liberal (never Labour). We juniors had little appreciation of these matters; we were more concerned with the vast areas of human activity about which he required information. One week his parting shot to one of us was: 'Do bones make good soup?' He left another junior slack-jawed with the parting question: 'How long, young man, does it take a banana to ripen?'

A junior named Bob Sands who became deputy northern editor of the *Daily Mirror* had laboured hard on a detailed report of a Stalybridge council meeting, and Mr Will, who lived in that town, challenged him with: 'Well, Sands, how many steps on Stalybridge Town Hall?'

'A lot,' said Bob.

'Count them, count them! Look about you. Good day to you all.'

We juniors were lucky to be on a weekly newspaper during the war. Chronicling darts winners and blushing brides might have palled after a while but for the adrenalin of being by proxy on the battle-fronts.

War Office service bulletins about local men in action came into the office regularly and Middlehurst doled them out selectively like lollipops. Sometimes we arrived on the doorstep with information the family did not have. A woman whose husband was killed in Holland had no idea why the army sent her a ribbon in an envelope, but we had details of the action. We were allowed into the front office when readers came in with letters from war fronts, and when we heard someone was on leave we could go round and see if they had a story: a sailor rescued after an hour in icy water following the torpedoing of his cargo ship; an airman who had disposed of a live bomb just before it exploded; a navy telegraphist on how he managed to keep in touch with all the ships in a convoy to Murmansk beset by seven days of blizzards and U-boat packs; a prisoner of war in a German camp with a surprisingly cheerful take on life in the Stalag.

I arrived one morning to find I had been taken prisoner myself. Mr Middlehurst fluttered his hand like a priest sprinkling water and waved me over to a young man in a double-breasted suit tightly buttoned over an incongruous sweater. I had not seen him around. He had a lordly air, but he looked like a bouncer; he was squarely built with a boxer's nose and a strangely hooded left eye. The bad news was that he would 'keep watch' on me for the remainder of my three-month trial as a reporter. This sinister figure, name of Eric Marsden, was not enthusiastic about his new charge. I learned years later that the ancient warrior Billy Mee had taken him aside to say: 'That boy Evans will never make the grade.'

Marsden plucked from my desk a piece of copy I'd written and barely glanced at it. 'I don't know what I'm supposed to do with you,' he said disdainfully, only to add: 'We may as well make a start with film reviews.' This was promising.

'Gary Cooper's on round the corner at the Pavilion in *Casanova Brown*,' explained Marsden, 'David Niven's at the Roxy in *The Way Ahead* and Tyrone Power is in *Old Chicago* at the Palace. See what you make of them. Make it snappy.'

I leapt up.

'Where are you going?'

'I see the matinee starts at two at the Pavilion, I can just make it.'

'Control yourself. All you need, Harold, is here in the files. And no more than thirty words a film.' With a wave of his hand he left me a few dog-eared publications published by the cinema trades whose cryptic phrases, like 'bodice-ripper', 'good thick ear', 'great smoocher', I had to translate along with their breathless plot summaries.

Marsden was smart: he'd been a star scholarship student at grammar school and won a prize for an essay on Thomas Hardy's *Mayor of Casterbridge* – and dammit, he'd seen war action. As a junior fireman in the Auxiliary Fire Service, he'd manned a stirrup pump to put out incendiaries dropped on Manchester roofs in German night raids, and at seventeen he was an officer cadet, training to be a pilot in the Fleet Air Arm. I felt inadequate. I didn't have a double-breasted suit and wouldn't have filled it so impressively; I'd not dowsed a single incendiary in the blitz, and I was the only one of the juniors who had failed the 11-plus to get into grammar school.

At the end of the week, though, I was invited to join Marsden, Taylor and Keeble for the lunch they had regularly at the Co-op Café. I was flattered. They were all grammar school boys, though my shorthand and typing were better than theirs. The routine was for the ace reporters to swagger into the upstairs café with a copy of the paper to give to a pretty waitress. After baked beans on toast, Marsden pulled out a pocket chess set, soon checkmated Laurence, and challenged me to a game. He beat me with ease. That night I took a chess book out of Failsworth library and spent the weekend memorizing openings for the next Friday encounter.

I was convinced that Marsden was a complication to my hopes of being taken on the staff. As it was, I already lived in constant apprehension that I might mishear the mumbling Mr Middlehurst and be fired. He was all detonator and no fuse. He blew up when I blundered in the worst task in the office, transcribing the eye-straining, interminable and complex results from marked-up dog show catalogues. It took a second to mix up the results of the Border Collie with those of the Border Terrier class. In these days of 'recovered memory', I could have blamed the error on the black mongrel which sank its teeth in my leg when, at the age of ten, I was innocently cycling in the street; truth was I couldn't tell one dog from another. As punishment, I was assigned to be Middlehurst's runner for Mossley United's Saturday football match in the Cheshire League. I sat with him in the stands while he wrote up the game in longhand and every fifteen minutes was sent off to a telephone booth to read it to the *Sunday Empire News*, for which he was paid by the line.

Another form of torture was to be sent into the readers' department adjacent to the newsroom. It was like a cave with little pools of light from desk lamps, and in the shadows two or three murmuring men curled like commas over galley proofs. I was assigned as the copyholder to a reader, a retired headmaster of vinous complexion by the name of J. R. Hall, who practised his pedagogy in the margins of text in type as I slowly and quietly gave voice to the reporter's original words. But I did at least learn to be on the alert for the curious interloper in newspapers known as 'Etaoin Shrdlu'.

He sounded half Irish, half Indian. I'd seen him make random appearances in the pages of all kinds of newspapers, sometimes in the byline position but most often and bafflingly in the middle of a story, so it read like this:

> Several demonstrators had
> minor injuries and one of
> tawk Etaoin Shrdlu
> the leaders was taken to
> hospital. Thirty-two were

The start of the incomprehensible third line represented the operator's mistake in trying to key 'the leaders' of the correct fourth line. Operators who erred in casting a line of type (called a slug) quickly strummed down the first vertical keys in the letter section of the board. These were E-t-a-o-i-n S-h-r-d-l-u and represented an alert to copy readers and compositors to discard that line. (These digital days, Shrdlu no longer haunts newspaper pages.) Hall explained that

Etaoin was a saboteur and it was our duty to apprehend him before
he made print anywhere in the *Reporter* series of newspapers. Never
on his watch had the fellow slipped through as he did in newspapers
conducted more carelessly than ours. Mr Hall let me know every
time he made an arrest and scrawled a large 'must delete' mark in the
margin of the galley.

The experience in the readers' room also yielded an insight into
how Mr Middlehurst wrung water out of copy. His speaking manner
might be woolly, but he brought a very sharp mind to the editing of
text. He had no time to instruct juniors directly, still less for small
talk, since he edited every line in the entire series of newspapers,
wrote the headlines, made all the assignments, wrote the (anodyne)
editorial comment, and also contrived to contribute a chatty column
of notes under the byline 'Pilgrim' called 'Round and About'. ('One
wonders how much time is spent by those who take a delight in
obliterating the red labels on the windows of non-smoking railway
compartments?') Mr Middlehurst never made a comment on copy;
he talked with his black pencil. He had been on the job since 1930
and was to die at his desk with his pencil in his hand.

Soon after his triumph on the chess board, Eric Marsden picked
up a review I'd written of a Droylsden comedy, and held it like
he held a pawn, between thumb and forefinger. 'Nice intro,' he said,
and seemed to mean it. To my surprise, he now wanted me to review
theatre. It was a break: we could use adjectives, we could make
judgements. We could imagine being the James Agate – the legendary
Sunday Times theatre critic – of our generation. I kept a note of
Agate's critical shafts ('Theatre director: a person engaged by the
management to conceal the fact that the players cannot act') with the
hope of somehow matching him when taking on local community
theatre productions.

When I was used to being a drama critic, I had the cheek to review
a new church company, the Clayton Players, whose performers
included Marsden. My review of their debut in *Doctor's Orders*, a
two-act farce, was proudly signed with my initials, H.M.E., and I
wrote: 'Eric Marsden as Banks gave a good impersonation of the

legendary butler, Jeeves. His chief fault, like that of most of the cast, was a tendency to lower his voice in his longer speeches.' The amazing thing is that Marsden did not raise a voice of protest the next day in the office when he saw my copy. I decided he was a man of discernment.

I was right, for the wrong reason. In fact, I had misread him altogether. Marsden looked twenty-five, but was only nineteen. Fixating on the menacing eye, I'd missed his tolerant humour. And the prosperity suggested by his new double-breasted did not exist: the suit was a farewell gift from the Navy. Gradually I learned that his imperious air masked privation. His family was really poor, living in a mean terraced house amid factories. His father was a drunk who had abandoned his sick wife, so Eric had been forced to leave grammar school to be the breadwinner, working as a clerk in the Manchester textile company of Tootal Broadhurst Lee. This meant giving up a near-certainty of a university scholarship: only a handful of working-class boys had any hope of college then, however brilliant they were. At seventeen, he'd volunteered for the Fleet Air Arm but his billet in Skegness, Yorkshire, while he waited to leave for flying training in Canada, was a thin plywood shack cursed with a coke stove leaking toxic fumes. Endless winter rain coursed down the inside walls and onto his bed and he shivered the nights away. The pleurisy he developed, which ended his flying career, was to dog him all his life.

It was a cruel outcome for such a brave spirit. I discovered he was a sturdy romantic who did his own thinking. His gods were Beethoven and Shakespeare and he made them mine. At sixteen, I had not heard a note of classical music. Eric, while clerking at Tootals, had got into the habit of relieving the drudgery by walking over to Manchester Central Library for its lunchtime recitals by pianists and violinists, then he'd saved up to go to the classical concerts by Manchester's famous Hallé orchestra. He studied the composers by playing second-hand records on a wind-up gramophone.

That was the way he introduced me to an enduring joy of my life. He lent me a tiny 45-rpm record of 'Dance of the Hours', the ballet music by Amilcare Ponchielli. To the family's amusement, then irritation, I played it dementedly on a portable wind-up in Ashworth Street. It's a trifling sugary piece, lampooned in Walt Disney's *Fantasia* as a dance for hippos.

Eric taught me the etiquette of concert-going and how it had changed since the nineteenth century, when people talked and sometimes played cards and clapped at anything they liked. I was not to talk, not to cough, not to sniff, not to tap a foot, not to rustle paper, not to breathe, in fact, unless absolutely necessary; and, for Pete's sake, not to clap when they stopped playing but wait till I was absolutely sure from the programme notes that they really had finished what they were about. The first time I heard Beethoven's Third Symphony, the Eroica, I was exalted. I read all I could on Beethoven in Failsworth Public Library, learning most from J. W. N. Sullivan's Pelican paperback *Beethoven: His Spiritual Development*. Who could not be moved by the drama of the composer's struggle against deafness and depression: 'I will take fate by the throat; it shall not overcome me!' I found myself reflecting, albeit immaturely, on the dissonance between physical appearance and character. Ludwig – and Eric – were both ill-favoured, so clearly the face was not a window on the soul.

Thereafter I begged to write stories about the Hallé; I couldn't afford to pay for a regular ticket.

It was no reward for Eric's beneficence that on the following Friday at the Co-op Café I tried out one of the chess openings I'd learned, the queen's pawn gambit, and about which I had breathed not a word. It enabled me to control the centre of the board against both Laurence and Eric. 'Once more unto the breach, dear friends,' cried Eric, but I was merciless. Thereafter every Friday for two years, when all the other customers had fled, we tussled from lunch to teatime in the empty café as I matched my book learning against his originality. Eric probably still had the edge but latterly became careless in his crusading style, his mating mind divided between the tiny chess board and the vivacious Co-op waitress with a frilly lace apron. She had a curious accent – flat Lancastrian with some extra zing in it that made her seem snooty. This was a contradiction. Ever acute to the nuances of class, I couldn't work out how someone with a working-class accent could manage to be haughty as the upper class.

It transpired that she was a Belgian aristocrat, Jacqueline Henriette Alphonsine Marie Dirix de Kessel, who had risked her life in the Belgian Resistance. She'd been interrogated by the Gestapo and let go. In 1945 she married a handsome British soldier who brought her home to Ashton. It must have been a terrible shock – a disillusion suffered by thousands – to come from war dramas to the rainy vicissitudes of a cotton town and find that the dashing liberator was a bully who regarded a wife as a chattel.

She had divorced him, and everyone lusted after her. We knew 'Ereek', as she called Marsden, had no chance. The unstoppable Charlie Sutcliffe was in hot pursuit. It was obvious that, unversed in the nuances of the English class and educational system, Jackie would see the dashing photographer as the war-wounded Cavalier and the much cleverer Eric as the plodding Roundhead. Charlie had a car, and a Fleet Street career beckoned. He would sweep her off her feet and she would be glamorously at his side in a Hemingway-style life of adventure in the world's capitals. My asthmatic hero would be left to grow old on the *Ashton Reporter*, like the wrinkled walnut Billy Mee I'd encountered on my first day.

You can't script someone else's life, let alone your own. Jackie and Eric were married in 1947. And while Charlie stayed rooted to the same spot for the rest of his life, it was Eric who became a brave and accomplished foreign correspondent. When night work subbing in the Manchester office of the *Daily Telegraph* became too much of a strain on his health, he moved to Kenya in 1957 to work twelve years for Nairobi's *East African Standard*. He reported war and civil strife in Africa and the Middle East. He risked exposing abuses that governments preferred to cover up – in 1969, supposedly a guest of the Arab League, he was marched at bayonet point through Cairo as a suspected spy. The League apologized. Later the same year, now deputy editor of the *East African Standard*, he was deported from Kenya for displeasing Jomo Kenyatta by publishing reports of machete attacks – and was then invited back after protests by the African journalists. When he and Jackie started receiving death threats in Kenya, I invited him to join the *Sunday Times*, where I was the editor, as our correspondent in Israel, and later South Africa.

Whatever doubts there may have been about my fitness to join the staff, they were put to the test by the Red Wharf Bay murder, in which the victim was a local army sergeant's wife. Mr Middlehurst dispatched his son, Dennis, to report the sergeant's trial in Anglesey. But there was a problem. The court hearing opened on a Thursday and the paper went to press that night. The only way Dennis could get his long report back in time was to phone it through to the office, and the only person with sufficient touch-typing speed to take his dictation was me.

At 4 p.m., I was locked in the newsroom telephone booth, with its candlestick telephone. The Underwood was lifted onto the little ledge inside. I was given dodgy earphones, and Dennis dictated his story at top speed. Everyone crowded round outside the booth looking in on me, the typing fish in the aquarium. It was hot inside – so hot that the windows misted up. I could see Mr Middlehurst pacing urgently outside. Every time I finished a page his paw came into the booth and took it out to the Linotype operators. I was three hours in the aquarium, we made the edition, and Mr Middlehurst never said another word about my being on trial at the paper. The following Friday I had an extra shilling in my pay packet.

I soon got better assignments. A gaunt suave senior named Jameson, just medically discharged out of combat missions for the Royal Air Force, initiated me into the art of reporting the dispensation of justice. He had once worked on a Manchester daily and policemen nodded to him as we crossed the icy cobbled square and climbed the many steps into the Town Hall where the magistrates decided local cases.

This was March 1945, when the Allied armies had crossed the Rhine and we were winning the war in Europe. None of this made any difference to our life in Ashton. It was 20 degrees below freezing and coal, already rationed by the bag, was not to be had. (Coal fires were the only form of heating in draughty homes where the wind rattled the windows; nobody could afford electric heat and nobody had heard of central heating, except in the American wonderland.) Hot and cold water pipes froze all over town as did my fingers trying to write shorthand in the Arctic courtroom to which I was now assigned.

Disconcertingly, one morning Mr Will, bristling with good purpose, appeared high up on the bench as one of the presiding magistrates (mental resolve: count the Town Hall steps on the way out), but even he for all his milk vitamins was not immune to the cold. The court adjourned after fining one publican for embezzling the brewer and acquitting another man accused of being 'absent from essential war work without reasonable excuse'. Ten minutes later the magistrates came back in overcoats and scarves, four men and a woman, banging their feet and rubbing their hands, not in the proper mood to deal with a wretch accused of stealing coal. Jameson, languid on the wooden benches, left these cases to me. He perked up when a police sergeant took to the witness box and solemnly described what he had seen when he entered a house of ill repute. Mr Will looked flushed. Jameson whispered it was too big a case for town magistrates and I should take down the depositions verbatim. Back at the office, he edited my notes into a short report, sanitized for our Methodist readers, then carefully put the longest version in an envelope addressed to the *News of the World*, the seamiest of the Sunday papers. 'We'll make a pretty penny out of this,' he confided, and so we did. The splash on Sunday in the *News of the World* was 'Girl of Fourteen Wanted to be Taken for Sixteen'. I received 3 shillings as my share of those wages of sin.

These many years later, I had forgotten what a slog it was on the *Reporter* until I looked at the pocket diaries I've saved and deciphered the shorthand, a ridiculous subterfuge for a blameless life. The night work, when I thought it advisable to abandon the bike and go by bus, was onerous:

6 Feb: Manchester after work in freezing fog for NUJ lectures at Young Journalists' Club on interviewing. John Beavan of

Manchester Evening News talked on importance of college education for journalists

7 Feb 45: Hard day. Court in morning, then two inquests back to
back and stuffy old Englishe night at Rotarian dinner. Home
about 11.

9 Feb: Worked like hell. Long Ashton Council meeting. Missed
10 pm bus.

Some weeks I filled ten columns of the paper. My fingers ached
from all the typing on a heavy keyboard, but the personal demands
were the hardest. I was given the name of a parachutist who had died
in action in Italy. 'Make sure,' I was told, 'you bring back a good photograph and a few lines on his life.' I was to call on his parents; he was
their only son. I walked towards the door of the terraced house, spiral-
bound notebook in my raincoat pocket, and walked away again.

I felt a terrible intruder, a teenager not long out of short trousers
sent on a man's mission. I imagined a reporter calling on my own
mother announcing my death. I canvassed my conscience with the
idea of going back to the office to say sorry, nobody was in. I had to
keep telling myself, this was it; this was the real test, and picturing
what it would be like returning to the office empty-handed with a
lame excuse.

When I finally knocked on the door, praying nobody would come
after all, I was quite drained. 'Sit down lad and have a cup of tea,'
said the mother, while the father extracted a photograph from its
frame.

They were sorrowful but proud, ready to talk about their son for
hours to someone from the *Reporter*. I found time and again we
were regarded not as nosy intruders but as friends of the family. That
was not because of any magic we reporters had. It was a reflection of
respect for the paper; it bothered with the little things in people's
lives, the whist drives and flower shows, so it was trusted to be part
of the big things. An Army Signals sergeant, in a letter describing
their month's long advance down the Railway Corridor in the
Burmese jungle, wrote: 'In spite of the rain, mud, sticky heat, insects,
we are quite a happy crowd. I must give thanks to the American Air

Force for the splendid way they supplied us with the necessary things of life, including little luxuries such as canteen supplies, etc. and most of all that great morale booster mail from home – along with a few welcome *Reporters*.'

For all the respect the *Reporter* enjoyed, encounters of this kind never came easy to me. I developed a little mental trick I played on myself many times in rough waters in later years, of imagining the shame I'd feel if I surrendered to embarrassment or shyness: if I failed to knock, shirked a tough question, accepted an obvious lie, retreated from the glare of a VIP. What I most of all took away from these years going into so many homes was identification with the people of the back streets and appreciation of their fortitude, too often in the face of a vast official carelessness. I got worked up about the way they were used and tossed aside.

The *Reporter* style was deadpan, without hint of comment in the news, but I couldn't contain myself after I knocked on a door in Abbey Hey, Gorton, and was welcomed in by Mr William Henry Adams and his widowed father. William, a skeleton of thirty-seven, had volunteered for the Army within days of the outbreak of war. He had been ill for two months with double pneumonia and though somewhat groggy he enlisted and rushed to the front in France. Conditions at Cherbourg with the Royal Engineers were grim. Bivouacked in heavy rain, he was diagnosed with tuberculosis in both lungs. He was discharged, unfit for active duty, unable ever to work again yet denied any form of war service pension. He had been appealing for four years when I met him, and had just been rescued by the local MP, Alderman Will Oldfield, who had taken up his case. Rescued? The pension was all of two pounds and five shillings a week.

I wrote: 'This is the story of a man who sacrificed his health to serve his country and was all but forgotten when he was no longer needed. He is grateful for the pension but those years of waiting are no credit to England.'

Mr Middlehurst let it through and even gave me a personal reference, inserting, 'writes a *Reporter* representative'.

*

I got to be very proud announcing 'I'm press.' It went to my head. In the bitterly cold February of 1945, just after the Allied armies had finally blocked Hitler's Panzers thrusting from their Ardennes lair towards the English Channel, Mr Middlehurst murmured that I was to go and see General Carpenter, who was in town for a night. He gave me a scrap of copy paper with the name Major Bagworth, who would introduce me to the General, and the address where they were to be found. It was a hall packed with uniformed men and women. I could not find the Major. It was hard to ask questions because the uniformed ones were banging tambourines, clapping hands and singing a hymn to a brass band. The headgear of the women revealed that they were Salvation Army bonnets, and General Carpenter was their general – in fact, the leading general of the Salvation Army. The Salvationists kindly made room for me to squeeze in on the front row when I mentioned 'the *Reporter*' and I took out my notebook, ready to report his speech.

The General had other priorities. Instead of mounting the plat-form, he walked into the body of the hall and asked every individual to stand so that one by one he could commend their souls to the Lord's care. He started on my row, at the far right, speaking to every individual. I remained seated as he advanced towards me.

'Won't you stand for Jesus, son?' the General asked.

'I'm press.'

He looked at me and smiled: 'You can still be saved.'

5

HOW I WON THE WAR

The record of my war years need not detain us long, particularly as the war was over.

I answered the nation's call on Monday, 12 August 1946. His Majesty's Royal Air Force needed me and would brook no delay. It didn't seem to have remembered its urgent need when I reported for duty at the RAF station at Padgate, near Warrington: I was one of hundreds of pale young men sitting on the floor of a big hut, waiting for something to happen. For days we were in a no man's land between civilian and service life.

Among us somewhere, though I didn't know it at the time, was another numberless man whose words would shake governments, Aircraftman William Rees-Mogg, later the distinguished editor of *The Times*. He was going through his own culture shock, mystified by the frequency of the 'f' word, applied to almost every noun: 'I had not previously come across an effing knife and an effing fork on my effing plate. Nor oddly did I often come across it much later in the RAF.' Someone in the Air Ministry must have had a premonition that this numberless one would become an august member of the establishment because, on emergence from limbo, he was compensated with one of the cushiest of billets as a sergeant in the Education Corps.

When I was given a number, 2318611, I clung to the seven digits of my new identity as a baby to a mother. I'd have been no good under interrogation by an enemy. Just the word 'number' would trigger a reflex response.

The transmutation from reporter to recruit was complete when I went through one door in a sports jacket and came out the other in a uniform and an improbable forage cap badged with the even more implausible motto *Per Ardua Ad Astra* (Through hardship to the stars). We were all given effing haircuts and effing kitbags, huge sausages designed to dislocate shoulders and impose hours of ironing time for everything stuffed inside. Then as numbered freight we were dispatched in groups to Compton Bassett, Wiltshire, for six weeks of square bashing to make men of us. Opinion is divided to this day on whether they succeeded.

I found it a relief to be turned into a robot for six weeks; no need to plan, worry and think for oneself, just do what the man said when he shouted a number. It gave me a glimpse of how a fighting unit that didn't happen to have me in it could perform acts of incredible bravery. The challenge set for me on passing out of the drill squad as an AC2 (Aircraftman second class) was how to escape from the clerical Colditz to which I was immediately sent, the dreaded RAF Records Office at Innsworth. There grown men recently trained in warfare went on paper chases into the endless rows of filing cabinets and were never seen again. Redundant aircrew flew metal desks.

I was pretty miserable myself; collecting the names of whist drive winners was thrilling by comparison with my duties at Records. I was in a division responsible for compiling and filing movement orders that sent airmen to their new stations. I tried hard to get the RAF to realize it had a wasting asset. I filled in lots of forms for reassignment. I volunteered for aptitude tests whose results suggested I had no aptitude for anything. I never heard another word.

When, resigned, I'd all but forgotten these escape attempts, I received one of the movement orders we sent to others. With effect immediately, 2318611 was posted to RAF Hullavington in Wiltshire, home of the Empire Flying School (EFS), and headquarters of No. 23 Group in the Flying Training Command. There was no hint what 2318611 would be doing there. I didn't care. It was such a relief to exchange the claustrophobia of Innsworth for the vicarious excitements of an active airfield. Flying School! It was as if I had stepped through the pages of my wartime scrapbook.

Hullavington was in countryside not far from the charming old town of Chippenham, but the fumes of the war lingered. Bombers and fighter planes lined the runways, fitters and armourers sweated in the hangars, the aroma of combat was as strong at the base canteen as the tea was weak.

The military police at the guard room directed me away from the airfield, but I found myself in the stratosphere entering the offices of an Air Commodore on his way to being an Air Vice Marshal, Claude McClean Vincent. He was the Air Commandant in charge of the whole station, home of the crack pilots in the All-Weather Squadron which specialized in flying on instruments into electric storms just to see what the hell happened. He'd asked the station adjutant to get him a shorthand typist. If he was expecting a comely Women's Air Force officer to brighten the all-male station of 800 officers and enlisted men he kept a stiff upper lip, as you'd expect of a pilot with a Distinguished Flying Cross who'd flown in the First World War and most recently commanded a group of Spitfires in the Middle East.

'Dog's dinner, I'm afraid,' he said, asking me to type a manuscript of crabbed handwriting and convoluted revisions. It didn't take much imagination to see why he reminded me that I was bound by the Official Secrets Act. The terse reports I sent to the Air Ministry could have been turned into news leads: BRAVE TEST PILOT'S ORDEAL IN STORM: EXCLUSIVE FULL DETAILS by our air correspondent somewhere in Wiltshire. Unfortunately, I also saw the effects of the flying errors I recorded, being several times ordered to lead a guard crew when one of our planes crashed.

I had a lot of dog's dinners from the Air Commodore and from his successors over the next two and a half years. They were all apologetic, as if asking me to undertake some dangerous mission. In addition to being the secretary to the Air Commandant I had paperwork to do for all the five RAF stations in 23 Group, but here too my boss, Squadron Leader Papworth, was so courteous I forgot I was the lowest of the low in RAF ranks. He was intrigued that I had been a newspaper reporter and took me home for tea with his wife in his cottage in Bourton-on-the-Water, the lovely village called the 'Venice of the Cotswolds'.

Nothing remarkable about that, you may say, but the RAF was my first realization that my mental map of class boundaries was a stereotype. I'd not before been in close contact with the officer class. I was disarmed by the lack of pretence among the majority on the station, who'd been through the war. Being shot up over Düsseldorf and seeing your mates die night after night didn't leave any taste for affectation. Commissioned and non-commissioned officers shared the same risks on bombing missions.

Visiting the airfield and the hangars, I noticed the ease of exchanges between officer pilots and other ranks working as airframe fitters, armourers and maintenance technicians. A sergeant bomb aimer I got to know playing table tennis introduced me to a flight lieutenant whose North Country accent was so much more marked than mine that I got called 'educated Evans'. This officer took a Lancaster bomber on 'training flights' and one weekend invited me to go along for a flight that ended very conveniently at Ringway Airport near Manchester, his hometown and mine. It just happened that his bride lived there and a few mechanics who came along also happened to be from Manchester. In this way, qualified by geography and accent, I had my first-ever flight in any aircraft – and subsequently as many as I could contrive in all sorts of RAF planes. Getting from Wiltshire to Manchester by the worn-out and indirect train service used up most of a 48-hour pass, and always risked running foul of some officious military policeman at the station intent on finding your brass buttons and badge not bright enough to blind passersby. Airborne, the weekends at home were blissfully extended.

This is how, when I am describing how I won the war, I can discourse on what it was like freezing at 20,000 feet in the rear gun turret of a Lancaster. If I have the right captive audience I can also describe my first German prisoner of war, Oberschütze Walter Greis, a tall, good-looking blond Aryan of Hitler's fevered dreams. Actually, he was an eighteen-year-old bank clerk who'd surrendered to the American Army at the end of the war and been sent to

Hullavington to work. He was not an enemy but an ally of mine against the endless flow of 'bumf' – RAF slang for useless paper – flowing into my office as the headquarters of 23 Group.

Nobody had any idea why we had to fill in and dispatch so many forms, so after a year of this I invented a form of my own. I circulated an official note to all stations saying that in accordance with the No. 23 Group medical officer's determination to limit fly-borne infections, commanding officers were henceforth required to make sure there was a weekly examination of the sticky fly paper hung up in various locations and a record submitted of the number of flies caught. 'Group expects,' I wrote, 'that the numbers of intruders brought down should increase if careful study is made of the optimum placement of the traps.'

The compliance was gratifying, though I never got round to visiting the stations to check the accuracy of the reports. No doubt they are still being submitted.

Desperate to get on while my career in journalism was stalled. I applied for every promotion, every examination. One examination to do with RAF regulations that I passed with a 100 per cent score was so obscure that nobody on the station had ever taken it before and so important I cannot remember a single thing about it.

Within a year I had moved up from AC2 to AC1, then to Leading Aircraftman (entitled to a propeller on my sleeve), then Corporal. All that the Corporal's two chevrons did was put me in charge of my barrack room, theoretically responsible for the good conduct of forty airmen and their performance on the hated kit and rifle inspections. Let us say my writ was lightly applied and more lightly accepted. The biggest call on my authority was who should next have the room's ironing board and iron to get a razor-edge crease in trousers. I considered drawing up a waiting list, then thought better of it. Was I an ace reporter or was I Corporal Jeeves?

Papworth encouraged me to apply for a commission. I could tell you the idea appealed for the extra money, the greater freedom, the uniform smoother than my blue serge, the snob appeal to women in town, the equality of status, the privilege of easier weekend passes, the pleasure it would give my parents. It was all those things, but it was also a question of grub. The food in what was called the Other Ranks Mess (as if we were an afterthought) was notoriously inferior to the Officers and Sergeants Messes. Every night, though, an officer moved along our crowded mess tables, asking us to approve of what we had just consumed, i.e., to lie. The duty officer was preceded a few yards by a Sergeant calling out: 'Orderly officer, any complaints? Any complaints?' We might have gagged on the greasy lamb, but nobody ever said a word. The officer might be amiable enough, but the menacing demeanour of the Sergeant, a stiff-backed soldier from the RAF Regiment, made it clear that there would be a penalty. On an historic occasion in our Mess, much celebrated thereafter, I heard that a Leading Aircraftman from Air Traffic Control had broken ranks. When the Sergeant bellowed his 'any complaints?' question, Traffic stood up:

'Yes, sir, it's shit!'

Everyone froze. Officer and Sergeant stopped dead in their tracks.

'What did you say, Airman?'

'It's shit, sir,' said Traffic in the silence. 'But it's beautifully cooked.'

I had a better idea than trying to become an officer, which would have meant signing on for three years. In the summer of 1947, a full year into service, I finally realized what I should be doing. There were 800 men, plus some favoured ones with families in married quarters. What they needed was what I needed – a station newspaper. I got permission provided I did the work in my spare time. Officers and sergeants volunteered to be reporters and printers. There was a wartime can-do spirit about the whole enterprise.

A local printing company said they'd let us have several sacks of old type they didn't need, but warned the sizes and letters were all mixed up. From a mountain of metal deposited in the hut, we had to pick up thin slivers of characters by fingertip, guess the size, read the single character on the surface and dispose of it in the correct little box in a composing tray so we could pick out t-h-e to form *the* in a composing stick. There were 90 little boxes, the size varying according to how often the letter was likely to be needed.

We all joined in at night after the day's duties. It was eye-straining work under a single light bulb. It was cold, too, with just one fire. I tried Tom Sawyer's trick of telling friends what a fascinating time we were having exploring the mysteries of print. A clerk called Jock McPhee joined with a few others to sort type as we neared Christmas and the closure of the camp. Then another difficulty pressed. In my mad whirl to stay occupied, before the newspaper was approved, I'd been cast in a station production of a play, *Men in Shadow*, about the French Resistance. I was 'Polly', a downed flyer hiding out in the roof of a barn. The nights I had reserved for editing copy and writing headlines were the nights I was supposed to be dropping out of a trapdoor to link up with the lead player 'Kenny' (none other than our own printer, Sergeant Mott).

Lacking the gift of being in two places at the same time, our days through November were morning parade, a full day's work followed by rehearsal or play performance, and then print shop duties until midnight. This was so fraught an enterprise that I took in my stride the first blemish in the editorial content I'd ordered up: a review of *Men in Shadow* concluded: 'It would have been better if Corporal Evans as Polly had been more consistent with the Lancashire accent and left the Shakespearean gestures to John Gielgud.'

The night before the camp was due to break for Christmas we still had to finish setting the final page to run off the *Empire Flying School Review* on our flat-bed press. We worked through the night. By nine o'clock we were all drooping around the setting table and still we had not set enough. Out of time and material, we slapped the words STOP PRESS on four inches of blank space at the foot of the page, as if we were a regular newspaper expecting to insert late news there at any minute.

As the pages came off the press, still wet with the ink, Jock ran out of the shop to the camp gate with the first 100 *Review*s to sell at threepence a copy. Following with the second batch, I met him on his way back to the print shop – he was empty-handed. We sold all we could print in time.

After Christmas, the station welfare committee voted to float the cost of professional printing if we would commit to repaying their grant from advertising income and sales. This mighty enterprise would cost £25. If we sold 600 at sixpence – double our initial rate – we'd have £15 and could make up the rest from advertising.

Sixpence? In order to justify that price, we'd have to concoct a magazine whose price and quality of paper might draw more advertisers. This meant devising a cover each month, an art that was not part of the Middlehurst Ashton-under-Lyne curriculum. I had the idea of having small silhouettes of six of the station's most celebrated planes fitted into the spaces of the letters 'EFS' for Empire Flying School. The concept was a disaster. Our customers recoiled from being reminded of work. 'We've enough of kites [planes] all day. Give us a break!' Sales were off target on two issues. This much of a failure with a third issue would kill us.

What to do?

Our first newspaper had included a photograph of Veronica Lake's thighs and I had flash recall of it pinned up in a barrack room. Would I pander to these baser instincts?

Ask me another. The third glossy cover design featured the lovely red-head actress Hazel Court. Sales shot up. One of the civilian workers suggested we feature a blonde bombshell of a girl from his hometown of Swindon. It sounded unpromising; Diana Fluck, as he knew her, was a little-known film actress, but I liked the sound of how she had responded to a studio's request to change her name: 'I suppose they were afraid that if my real name was in lights, and one of the lights blew . . .' She changed it to Diana Dors, and eventually became known as Britain's answer to Marilyn Monroe. I guess we were the first magazine to make her a cover girl; soon after we featured her naked, sitting on a snowy stile with a strategically placed fur muff, she was cast in *Oliver Twist* and made into a star by Pinewood Studios.

Just when the August 1948 date neared for my demobilization, Joe Stalin intervened. He stopped all road, rail and water traffic crossing the Soviet zone in Germany at the end of June, threatening 2.5 million people in the western sector of Berlin with starvation. The Royal Air Force and the US Air Force immediately joined in the great Berlin Airlift, carrying coal and food round the clock. It was good news for the Berliners – among them the repatriated Walter

Greis – but it was bad news for me. The Airlift required selectively postponing the release of thousands of airmen, and I was one of them.

I was kept back eight more months – but the time flew. The day's paperwork assumed an air of relevance and urgency, the *Review* had its deadlines, and in every spare minute, now that I had been snared by the big world outside camp, I tried to understand what was behind some of the more worrisome headlines in the newspapers. Dollar Drain! Payments Crisis! Austerity Budget! Bank of England Row! In my barrack room were two airmen, junior to me in rank but way ahead in being able to follow the ups and downs of the economic trials of the new Labour government. They'd been called up during their first year at university, one at Oxford, one at Cambridge, and had made a nodding acquaintance with people I'd never heard of like John Maynard Keynes and Alfred Marshall. With the encouragement of my clever new friends I wrote away to 'Wolsey Hall' in Oxford, which was offering to teach economics by correspondence course. Wolsey Hall was not an Oxford college (as I'd imagined), but a commercial enterprise. Still, it was a first step into what they called the dismal science. 'Why is a pound of diamonds valued more than a pound of bread?' Wolsey Hall asked. I couldn't for the life of me see how to apply the lessons to Mum's grocery, which is just as well, but I conscientiously wrote up the short answers in the station library and waited anxiously for the red ink marks from Oxford.

In the library one day, a typed note crammed among many on the bulletin board announced that Manchester University was offering servicemen a two-week residential course of lectures and discussions entitled 'The Rights of Man'.

I raced down to the education department to apply. Happily nobody else did and a few weeks later, with the permission of the Air Commodore, I was installed in civvies in the University's Holly Royde House in Didsbury, Manchester, cerebrating with men and women of all ranks from all the armed forces. Here I met Thomas Paine and Edmund Burke, John Locke and Thomas Jefferson, Jean-Jacques Rousseau and Thomas Hobbes. I made no more than a nodding acquaintance with these strangers, but I got the idea that somewhere in their writings they might, in the urgent clamour of postwar politics, furnish a better compass than the newspapers.

I re-entered civilian life in March 1949 in a shiny demob suit, returning to Ashton-under-Lyne and weekly newspaper reporting. I'd been promoted and was now chief reporter of the edition called the *Gorton and Openshaw Reporter*, but I carried around the cold streets a fever incubated at the Empire Flying School. I burned to learn more about politics and economics.

I just had to find a way to get to university. My new ambition marked me out as some kind of freak. When I was unwise enough to express it in the Ashton head office the general refrain was: 'You've lost three years in the RAF, now another three for university? You can say goodbye to Fleet Street!' Even my old colleague the erudite Michael Hides was sceptical. He wrote me a long letter explaining why academic studies would not only be a diversion from acquiring the skills for journalism but would distort them. He'd been taken on by the *Manchester Guardian* and was deep into the mysteries of his new craft as a sub-editor, the first of our batch of Ashton juniors to make the big time. But the flicker of envy I felt was expunged by the prospect of exploring mysteries of my own.

6

NON NOBIS SOLUM

It must seem an unexceptional ambition today, but in the 1940s for a working-class boy to say he was going to university was like announcing he was about to marry Betty Grable. Our only idea of a university was through films like *A Yank at Oxford*, which was less about book-learning than rowing boats, forcible debagging, and heavy breathing over Vivien Leigh. College just never occurred to the brightest of my schoolmates nor to any of the newspaper people I met. I knew of nobody in Newton Heath who had gone to a cap-and-gown university, as distinct from a few wizards who went to a technical college.

There were very few places open anyway in the handful of universities and nationally only a tiny fraction of those qualified could hope for admittance. I continued to post short essays to Wolsey Hall, but tried to keep up with my education in journalism. Every Thursday night, after handing in the last Gorton story, I'd take the bus into Manchester for a series of talks by leading daily newspapermen organized by the National Union of Journalists. I learned some tricks of the trade, but the major impression was made by the writer-editor John Beavan (later Lord Ardwick) descending from the clouds, which is how I then regarded the *Manchester Guardian*. Beavan informed us in his silky way that we were all ignoramuses.

How could we explain what was really going on, Beavan scolded, if we'd not read Macaulay and Tawney? His barbs were resented by the group. The bitterness of postwar politics made imperative some understanding of economics and political history, however I acquired it.

The country, led by the coalition government with Winston Churchill as prime minister, had been united through five years of war. The press had more or less reflected that spirit of common striving, and the impeccable BBC radio news had reinforced it. I'd been too young to see how newspapers crucified the Labour party in the 1930s, so I wasn't prepared for the scaremongering and character assassination that followed the dissolution of the coalition government and the run-up to the general election in July 1945.

The experience at Rhyl beach of encountering the men from Dunkirk had been only a taster of how a clever newspaper could deal with situations it didn't like. Facts were most malleable in the biggest-selling newspaper of the day, Lord Beaverbrook's flagship *Daily Express* (3.3 million). The banner headline 'Gestapo In Britain If Socialists Win' was an extrapolation from a near-hysterical broadcast by Churchill, in hours allotted to each party, but the *Express* banner four days before polling, 'Socialists Decide They Have Lost', was original craftsmanship.

We had the *Express* at home and Dad just brushed aside its political coverage. 'It's all a stunt,' he said, 'just like the Zinoviev Letter.' This was the political scandal of the 1924 election when the Labour party was smeared as the tool of communist revolutionaries. The *Daily Mail*, four days before polling, carried the sensational report that Grigori Zinoviev, head of the Communist International, had written a letter to 'sympathetic forces' in the Labour party calling on everyone to mobilize for revolution. The letter did exist, but it was a forgery concocted by British intelligence agents and White Russians to scuttle an unratified Anglo-Soviet treaty. Proof of the plot came forty years later, rather too late for Labour. It lost the 'Red Letter' election in a landslide.

In 1945, it was hard work for the Conservative press trying to make the blood run cold about Labour leader Clement Attlee. If he was indeed, as they asserted, a tiger disguised as a mouse it had made him seem more interesting than he looked and sounded. People who had grown used to Attlee as deputy prime minister working quietly alongside Churchill, with Labour's giants Ernie Bevin and Herbert Morrison, were not easily persuaded that overnight he'd turned into a raving Red or Fascist dictator or Gauleiter – the Tory papers could never make up their mind which sounded the most sinister. They had more traction with Sir Stafford Cripps, who was to become Minister for Economic Affairs and Chancellor in 1947. His lean and hungry look, his then cranky vegetarianism and the iron discipline he imposed on consumers and unions exposed him to savage caricatures. A BBC news announcer referred to him as Sir Stifford Craps. It was a Spoonerism, a slip of the tongue – perhaps one should say tip of the slung, for it reflected the vitriol the Conservative newspapers hurled at him every day. The attacks were grossly unfair to Cripps, who squeezed inflation and took Labour through the economic storms I'd read about without fully understanding.

Given my family background, I resented the manipulation by the Conservative press, but had to note that the *Daily Herald* (2 million) was six pages of what seemed to me pure Labour propaganda and the *Daily Mirror* (2.3 million) worked on class emotions: the VOTE FOR HIM theme it ran for weeks, with an illustration of a soldier holding out a bandaged hand, drawn by Zec, suggested that a vote for the Conservatives betrayed the sacrifices of the men and women who had fought the war.

Unfortunately for the Tories, Churchill's partisan hectoring not only clouded his image as a leader uniting a nation but it also obscured how much the party had changed for the better. It was committed to Rab Butler's progressive 1944 Education Act, the 1944 Employment White Paper and most of the proposals for attacking poverty in Lord Beveridge's famous paper. The judgements of the voters in 1945, however, were probably less about this or that domestic or foreign affairs programme or even the personalities of the Left and Right. After five years of war, most people had been in the mood for a giant shake-up. It was the playing out of a folk memory. Voters were raising a fist against the 1930s, irredeemably associated in most minds with social ills and with limp-wristed Tories who had run the country for so long ('upper-class twits' said one of the Holly Royde group). And somehow the Tories didn't seem to have their heart in reform – the Tory press reviled the idea and ideals of the National Health Service.

It was still unusual for anyone to reveal their political feelings – returning servicemen were more outspoken – but walking the streets and riding the buses on my endless rounds of reporting before I was called up I'd sensed the mood. The passion for a new start had been evident among my mother's customers, but I'd no idea it would turn out so dramatically. The press as a whole so expected a Conservative victory that a contrary trend detected in several Gallup Polls had been pretty well ignored.

Most of our very mixed group of servicemen at Holly Royde in 1949 were highly critical of the role of the press in 1945 and its continuance during the first postwar Labour government. Provoked into airy debates on whether socialism was incompatible with liberty, most of us thought we saw a New Jerusalem in the welfare state being created by Attlee's Labour government. With one hand, it had set up free medical care, unemployment and family allowances, and taken into public ownership the coal mines, railways, the Bank of England, steelworks and airways; with the other hand, it liquidated the British Empire, giving independence to India, the major step in converting the British Empire into the Commonwealth. I recall how surprised I was when a couple of Army officers in the group revealed they had voted for Labour. Later analysis showed that Labour, while attracting more working-class votes than ever before, had indeed also taken an unprecedented slice of the middle-class vote, one manager in three voting for Attlee.

How much effect any of the newspapers had one way or another is a guess. Anti-Labour daily and Sunday newspapers did not prevail, though they reached nearly twice as many people as the pro-Labour papers. State intervention must not have seemed such a threat to liberty as the Tory press made out it would be with Labour. In the popular mind, the role of the state in winning the war, defending the population and organizing a fair system of rationing associated the state with measures for the common good. I have to add, however, that by 1949 my father was less enthused by nationalization. He had brimmed with hope about a people's railway, but when I came home from the RAF he observed that in four years the only change for him had been the badge on his cap.

In training for the attempt to enter a university, I abandoned cycling to the office through Daisy Nook in favour of three bus rides, because they gave me a chance to catch up with a few centuries of political philosophy. I have an aptitude for losing things, so it is quite astonishing to me that I still have the tiny blue hardback book I carried everywhere in my jacket pocket: *The History of the Peloponnesian War*, written by Thucydides and edited in translation by R. W. Livingstone.

Sitting with Thucydides on the top deck of the Oldham to Ashton bus, rain spattering the windows, I was not carried back to the fifth century BC in Athens but rather into the middle of the twentieth century – and beyond, since the Athenians' arguments about democracy and equality, power and patriotism, war and imperialism, so lucidly reported, will be with us for some time. Of course, the Athenian democracy had no role for women and was dependent on slave labour, but I was moved – then and now – by Pericles' evocation of the spirit of the idealists striving for a liberal democracy: a society which honours excellence and beauty but gives equal chances to all its citizens; where individuals give the state due service of their own free will and without compulsion; where they are free within the law to lead their private lives their own way without black looks and angry words:

Wealth to us is not mere material for vainglory but an opportunity for achievement; and poverty we think it no disgrace to acknowledge but a real degradation to make no effort to overcome. Our citizens attend both to public and private duties, and do not allow absorption in their own various affairs to interfere with their knowledge of the city's. We differ from other states in regarding the man who holds aloof from public life not as 'quiet' but as useless.

The useless man is with us still. He does not vote, he dodges taxes, he volunteers for nothing, he does not speak up for any cause, he turns a blind eye to the propagation of hatred, he 'minds his own business'. For any social ill, he deals in the coinage of cowardice: 'They should do something about it.'

I marked another passage where the historian of 400 BC spoke directly to the reporter of AD 1949:

> With reference to the narrative of events, far from permitting myself to derive it from the first source that came to hand, I did not even trust my own first impressions, but it rests partly on what I saw myself, partly on what others saw for me, the accuracy of the report being always tried by the most severe and detailed tests possible.

I wrote to every one of the fourteen English universities, offering to study there for a Bachelor of Arts degree. None of them was impressed. While I had those precious five school certificate credits, not one of them was in Latin, and Latin, I now learned, was required to read for an Arts degree. It was readily apparent that I had got myself into an H. M. Bateman cartoon: The Man Who Had No Latin and Thought He Could Get Into a Cloistered Hall of Learning. I wondered if I could take a crash course but was told that adequate preparation to sit the examination would entail three years of evening classes, not very feasible with so many night reporting jobs. There was also even more daunting arithmetic: I could not conjure up anything like enough money to pay for college accommodation and teaching; nor could Mum and Dad. They had four sons to prepare for the big world. There was no organized system comparable to the American one of working one's way through college.

I can't remember who told me that the wartime coalition government had passed Further Education and Training provisions in the Butler Education Act whereby the Ministry of Education was empowered to give grants to men and women who had served in the war. Well, I had almost done that, hadn't I? Wasn't the Berlin Airlift a key conflict in the Cold War? The Act was much more circumscribed

than the GI Bill in the United States, but I wrote to the Ministry. The
answer was swift. Sorry, mate, you must have a place in a college
before we can even begin to consider whether you qualify for an ex-
serviceman's grant. No Latin, no college. No college, no money.
Catch-22.

I'd been through all the brochures for degrees in politics and
economics, but I started again, this time looking at everything universities had to offer. Amidst some small print, I discovered there
was a three-year course called Social Studies leading to a Bachelor
of Arts degree. I'd skipped past it, but now I noticed Latin was not
mentioned in its entry requirements, only 'matriculation'. Was it an
oversight? And what were Social Studies? There was a brief reference to political theory, industrial history, economics – and
psychology. What was the catch? Would I emerge adept in the
social skill of settling disputes in a soup kitchen when the under-
paid chef ran amok with a cleaver? Or divining at close quarters
the emotional impulses of depraved juveniles? Further research was
needed but time was running out for entry in the autumn.

I wrote to Durham, the university offering this degree, and asked
them if they really could admit someone without Latin. Durham
promptly wrote back, informing me that I could apply to enrol for
social studies unconjugated by Latin – but I could not be admitted to
the degree course unless I had also been admitted to one of the five
men's residential colleges in Durham City or St Cuthbert's Society,
whose members lived at home or lodged in town. They kindly
attached the fees. And any residential college would want first to be
assured I was acceptable to the Durham Colleges' academic authorities. Catch-22 redux.

Nevertheless, in the leaflet from University College, Durham,
one of the residential colleges, there was a tiny picture of an undergraduate's room in Durham Castle complete with a fireplace and
mantelpiece and I could not resist imagining myself there. I wrote to
University College and was told I could put in an appearance for
interview on 13 September, provided I had satisfied the Registrar I
had matriculated. Clutching my five credits I took a train – and the
chance they would not spring a Latin trap on me.

I'd imagined Durham city to be one vast coal heap with social studies graduates toiling somewhere in the dust. Instead, an incomparable vista opened up when the train steamed through the last obscuring hedges and over the spectacular viaduct. The magnificent Romanesque cathedral the Normans built on the rocky wooded peninsula high over a loop of the River Wear was the most inspiring single scene of my life, then and ever after. If men could build that prayer in granite in the service of God, what could they not do? Across from the cathedral, where lay the bones of St Cuthbert and the Venerable Bede, stood the redoubtable Norman castle: 'Half church of God, half castle 'gainst the Scot' proclaimed Sir Walter Scott's ode to Durham, those words cut in the stonework of the graceful Prebends Bridge (1777), where Turner planted his easel to paint the peninsula.

I found the Registrar in a dainty pastel-washed little house in a cobbled side street by the cathedral. I presented my School Certificate parchment. In the blink of an eye a 'W. W. Angus' signed a valuable document: 'I certify that Harold Matthew Evans is qualified without further examination to matriculate in the University of Durham, to read for the degree of B.A. in Social Studies.' It meant I was admissible to the university, provided a college . . . yes, yes, I knew the refrain by heart. Now to gain a college place I first had to scale the ramparts of the castle. It stood across from the cathedral, separated by the immaculate lawn of Palace Green.

Founded soon after the Norman Conquest, the castle had for eight centuries been the palace of the immensely rich Prince Bishops of Durham. It is the oldest inhabited university building in the world and surely the most grandly housed college in the universe.

The moat had been cobbled over, but the castle had defences in depth against pretentious interlopers. First of these was the dragon lady who popped out from a crevice in the wall to bar my way when I dared open a little door in the great iron-studded castle gate beneath the embattlements of the crenellated keep.

'Castle is closed,' she was pleased to inform me.

'I'm here to see the Master of the College.'

It made no difference.

'No visitors.'

I protested:

'But I have an appointment!'

'Are you a university student?'

'No, but I will be.'

She paused to consider the impertinence, then vanished back into the crevice. I was left to contemplate the University College arms, a shield of four lions rampant and two bishops' mitres with the scrolled inscription. It was Latin: *Non Nobis Solum*.

What did it mean? I thought better of asking the dragon lady when at length she reappeared to admit me into the courtyard. But what would I say when the Master asked me to discuss the inscription's relevance to college life? It was humbling enough just to be in the presence of the Master of University College, Lt. Colonel Angus Alexander MacFarlane Grieve, MC, MA. I stood in the doorway to his room. He looked at me without saying anything. I calculated that through his thick bottle glasses I must be much diminished in size. I wasn't much to start with – five foot, seven inches according to the RAF – but I shrank with every passing second. I was probably about twelve inches high by the time I advanced, braced to babble about Thucydides if he broached the importance of a classical education. He offered a gentle smile.

'Do you row, Evans?'

I'd been in a paddle boat in Rhyl amusement park, but I didn't go into that. I said there had not been much chance of rowing in the RAF, but what a strenuous and exciting sport it was, relying on what I'd seen of oarsmen sweating it out along the Isis in *A Yank at Oxford*. It was as well not to claim knowledge. The Master had been Captain of Boats when he was at University College as an undergraduate and he was the author of a history of rowing in Durham. As he discoursed on how well College's oarsmen had been doing in races on the River Wear, I noticed he wore no socks. I found the incongruity of the formal demeanour and this manifestation of individuality strangely relaxing for all of the five minutes before he ended the meeting. He sent me to see the Senior Tutor, a physicist and doctor of philosophy. 'You will find him on the Norman Gallery. Good morning, Evans. And close the door on your way out.'

To reach the Norman Gallery I had to re-engage the dragon lady and ask her to point the way. There was a door off the courtyard, then beyond that an obscure crack in an ancient wall leading to the steep spiral of a very narrow stone staircase. As I climbed, I came upon a tiny panelled doorway in the rock. I knocked. No answer. I waited, and knocked again and waited. So I eased the door open, coughed politely and fell on my knees. It was not a prayerful posture. There were several steps immediately behind the door, catapulting one forward, no doubt some crude Norman's idea of a practical joke. Beyond the steps, there was no Head Tutor. I had stumbled into a toilet.

I returned to the ascent, and the staircase finally opened out on a beautiful gallery of fretted Norman arches and pillars, its windows looking out over the courtyard and gatehouse to the cathedral. I found the Head Tutor secreted off the Gallery behind a big black door with black iron bolts. He was running his hands through his hair, a work of supererogation since he had none that I could discern in the dim filtered light. He sat reeking cleverness in a wood-panelled room. There was the deliciously musty smell of books and of the dust of centuries of crumbling stone. The cathedral bells tolled the hour and the crucial interview began.

Why did I want to be in Castle [as University College was known]? Why not in St Cuthbert's Society? What about King's College, Newcastle, then part of Durham University? I extrapolated about residential college life from those weeks at Holly Royde. Why spend three years away from the headlines? Did I realize how long three years was? What did I think I would get out of Social Studies? Why not an Honours course? 'Mmm, no Latin, no Latin, eh, well never mind. You'd learn something I suppose.' What did I learn in the RAF? What books had impressed me? What was I reading now? What did I think of the literary quality of English newspapers? What did a reporter do? What did I consider good writing? I emerged about an hour later and flew over the cathedral:

I had been offered a place in Castle for the Michaelmas term, just a month away.

Now all I had to do was find the money. I told the Ministry the good news. They were equal to the challenge. To qualify for a grant, they now informed me that as well as winning a college place I would have to satisfy them that I was 'ex-service' enough, and asked me to confirm that RAF service had disrupted an original intention to go to university. They couldn't have hordes of ex-National Servicemen suddenly deciding they wanted three years at a university, could they?

It was going to be hard for me to prove my intentions of 1943, especially since I didn't have any then. In a rush, I entreated supporting letters from St Mary's headmaster Marsland; the head of Brookdale Night School; Loreburn Business College; and the lordly Beavan. The best they could do for me was to testify I had always wanted to be a journalist, that the RAF had stopped my rise, and they believed a university education would make me a better man. It was not quite what the Ministry had demanded, but I posted these letters and spent hours in Manchester's landmark Central Library collecting any book references on leading editors who had been to college and how Western civilization would collapse if too few numbers of newspapermen had college educations.

There were not many, but I sent these, too, and waited.

And waited.

Castle invited me to a freshman's dinner on 10 October, the day before formal registration was required in Durham. I gave notice on the paper. I did my rounds in Gorton. Mum optimistically began knitting a pullover in the Castle colours of maroon and white. I found a translation of Castle's motto. *Non Nobis Solum* meant 'not for ourselves alone'. I sent another letter to the Ministry.

With only four days to go to registration, I reminded the Ministry of Oblivion that Durham was expecting me and my trunk was on its way by British Railways. Again, silence. On the day before I was due to leave home, I sent the Ministry a telegram in desperation. The next morning, Mum finished the pullover. The household was depressed. Nobody knew what to say. The train to Durham was leaving Manchester just after noon. Two suitcases stood in the hall. We fretted on the doorstep. A Post Office boy cycled up the street and stopped at our door asking me to sign for a telegram. It was from the Ministry and had the oracular tone of a communiqué from Dumbledore to Harry Potter:

PROCEED TO DURHAM

7

THE STING OF DISRAELI'S GIBE

I proceeded to Durham and my higher education Hogwarts with three pounds in my pocket – and Dumbledore's telegram. It said nothing about a Ministry grant for university and college fees, but I presumed the college bursar wouldn't be so ill-mannered as to ask for cash on the nail as soon as I climbed the hill to Castle that night for the first college dinner in Great Hall.

I mingled with the other freshmen, all of us wearing black academic gowns as we stood on the steps of the Hall, looking on the courtyard, clock tower and the splendid Norman Gallery. I was convinced that half of them must be baronets. I heard a few ask the defining question of the English class system: 'What was your school?' meaning one of the all-male public schools.

At the gong, we trooped in to stand by long tables, awaiting the arrival of the top table of dignitaries and dons. I noticed the Master among them; I was to learn he might look forbidding, but he was shy, less happy mingling with the dons than with his Dumfriesshire sheep. It was exalting just standing there, looking up at the fraying battle flags left by the Duke of Wellington when he dined in the college after the battle of Waterloo. By this stage I would have been disappointed if the grace, read that night by the college chaplain after a bow to the Master, had been in anything other than Latin.

Until I knew it off by heart, I learned to listen for the ending '*per Christum Dominum nostrum*' and say Amen. More challenging was the array of knives, forks, spoons and glasses at my place. I worked out the etiquette by sly observation of my fellow diners.

Gradually, we all thawed out into recognizable human beings, shedding diffidence and self-consciousness. There was not a baronet at our table and it turned out that a goodly proportion were ex-servicemen. Scholars were on a rota to read grace, and one of them from a distinctly unprivileged background, John (Lofty) Moreland, struck a blow for regional pride by reading the Latin in a different regional accent each night for two weeks. It caused offence to a handful of purists who thought the scattered peoples of the Roman Empire all had spoken like BBC announcers.

There were about a dozen bright sparks on scholarships like Moreland, straight from grammar schools, and a contingent from public schools. We were an eclectic mix of ambitious undergraduates hoping to become business managers, explorers, schoolteachers, composers, research scientists, industrial chemists, translators of French literature and, in my case, a newspaper editor. A few were on the way to being vicars, though most of the future parsons were on their knees in St John's and St Chad's colleges located in the shadow of the cathedral. Perhaps the best thing about us was how biologist talked to geographer, music scholar to mathematician, geologist to theologian, chemist to historian. On one side, Phil from the Army and Manchester Grammar School treated us to a ribald rendering of Chaucer in old English pronunciation, and on the other John, a balding physicist, drew an outline of the innards of a nuclear reactor. By the time the carafe of port – vintage port! – was passed along the table we felt we had become Castlemen. The college, and indeed Durham itself, was small and concentrated enough – no more than 2,000 students – for the sense of community to be real.

After such a heady first evening I sweated my two suitcases down the cobbled streets all the way through town, past the arches of the spectacular Victorian railway viaduct, and up steep Western Hill to a terrace house where I had been allocated lodgings with six other Castlemen. There were no rooms for freshmen in college that first year. My trunk occupied most of the tiny room I was to share with a music scholar and his cello. Here, too, we brave six had our first encounter with a landlady who liked to catch one of us on the stairs and pin us to the wall with her outsize bosom.

My first lectures on Palace Green took place in old almshouses under the shadow of the cathedral. The alms location seemed more appropriate the more days passed and I heard nothing about my grant. It was some ten days into college life, when I was down to my last pound, that I found in my mailbox at the Castle Gatehouse a buff envelope marked 'On His Majesty's Service'. Imagination worked overtime as I opened it amid the Castlemen jostling to unload books and shed their gowns for lunch in Hall. Conceivably the letter might say 'Unproceed from Durham. You have been unmasked.'

I read it twice before the wonderful news sank in: Ex-Corporal Evans had been awarded an ex-serviceman's grant of £315 a year for three years – on condition he survived the first-year examinations. With the Ministry paying university teaching fees directly, it was enough for living, as well as travel to and from home, though not for all the books on the extensive reading list – but those gaps could be filled in the rambling library on Palace Green.

I took happily to the routine of college life – the lectures, the one-on-one tutorials, the inter-collegiate sporting rivalries, the Parliamentary-style debates in the oak-beamed Union Hall, the ritual and ceremony, the black academic gowns billowing in the breeze as we rushed about, the ponderous hum of the still incomprehensible grace in Latin, the solemn processions of dignitaries into cathedral and castle. The agreeably disputatious political radicals on campus, anticipating the 1960s rebels by a decade, saw college rituals as symbols of reaction and wanted to abolish all ceremony. In the show-off arguments at coffee breaks they explained that if we all turned up for lectures without gowns or refused to stand for Grace or boycotted Union Society debates in favour of political agitation, it would be a blow for the depressed proletariat. And where was I at this historic moment in British history?

I'd thought of myself as a radical eager for reform. To my surprise I recoiled from their brave new world where everything 'unnecessary' was to be swept away in favour of a rational new order without ornament or ritual. The best I could muster against the rationalists were naïve incantations about how much families enjoyed Easter eggs and Guy Fawkes Night. Why, I argued defensively, 'you'll be saying get rid of Christmas next.' They hooted with derision: 'Commercial exploitation of religious myth!'

I aspired to be a journalist partly because I thought good journalism could identify the consequences of the use of power or the failure to use it for the common good. In 1950, having just read E. S. Turner's polemic *The Road to Ruin: The Shocking History of Social Reform*, I steamed about how 'tradition' had been repeatedly invoked to defend the indefensible as it had been in slavery, denying votes to women, sending children into the coal mines and so on. ('Don't talk to me about naval tradition,' Winston Churchill said. 'It's nothing but rum, sodomy and the lash.') But what was to distinguish between the customs and traditions I thought benign and those I thought repressive? Had I taken Edmund Burke to heart as well as E. S. Turner, I'd have been better equipped to argue that we should espouse those uses of power that reaffirmed traditional values and resist those that eroded our heritage of a liberal, humanistic society. I'd have cited Burke's remark that the individual is foolish but the species wise, that our common law, the majority's tolerance of minorities, our respect for private property, and even my tolerance in listening to them spout nonsense, had all come to us as customs in the trial-and-error evolution of civilization. But I'd yet to hear any lectures on Burke, so such ammunition was not at my disposal.

The vehemence of my sparring partners made me wary of the warriors of cold reason. Years later, I think the Durham encounters gave me a framework of sorts for deciding when we were defending a precious custom and when legal theory was being used to sanctify injustice. The sardonic remark of a French diplomat in a negotiation has stayed with me: 'Yes, we agree it will work well in practice but how will it work in theory?'

My grant dependent on getting through the first-year examinations, I immured myself in the past. In the silent solitude of the library I absorbed the notion of the sanctity of property from John Locke, of free opinion from John Stuart Mill, of free will and the immorality of treating others as a means to one's selfish ends from Immanuel Kant. I recoiled from the mob-rule totalitarianism, as I saw it, of Jean-Jacques Rousseau, and found myself at one with Burke again in loathing the mob in the French Terror – my favourite Dickens was *A Tale of Two Cities* – while sympathizing with the revolutionaries in America. It was thrilling to read how the abstractions of Enlightenment philosophies became muscle in the American Declaration of Independence. I got so carried away by that dangerous thing, a little learning, that I offered to give a paper to the pipe-sucking intellectuals in University College's 'Read and Weed Club' on the modern relevance of absolutism and determinism in Thomas Hobbes's *Leviathan*. It served me right that my effort reached print in the college's newspaper as 'Harold Evans talked on hobbies today'.

Later, practical experience in journalism made me question and qualify the philosophies I had absorbed like a sponge. I could have questioned them when I sat in my tutorials with the professors of politics and economics. There was Francis Hood, the gaunt head of the department of politics, who was so short-sighted his nose literally swept along the undulating contours of the handwriting in the essay he was judging; his utterances in a deep bass voice with a refined Scottish burr fell like mortar shells among one's assumptions. He dealt kindly, though, with my fellow Castleman John Perkins, who could never quite finish an essay because he was studying Arabic (which he could never quite master because he was studying Aristotle). Hood would go from one to another of the five of us – 'Mr Evans, Mr Gilbertson . . . will you read your essay,' and so on – until he got to Perkins, whereupon he said: 'Mr Perkins, would you give us the benefit of your notes?'

There was the diminutive bow-tied Edgar Allen, who created arches with his fingertips while analysing elaborate economic models, always prefaced with the Latin *ceteris paribus* (meaning he was assuming other elements remained the same). There was the darkly handsome Viennese psychologist Dr Wolfgang von Leyden, the heart-throb of the women undergraduates, who schooled us in the ambiguities of perception. And Dr Peter Bromhead, the owlish authority on political constitutions, who challenged me to stay awake long enough to track all the legislative processes of Labour's Parliamentary Bill nationalizing the gas industry. He returned my report and its laboured tabulation with a lot of J's pencilled in the margins: 'J equals journalese. You can take this as a compliment or not, as you prefer.'

Whatever it was that did the trick, after I sat the first-year examinations the professors promoted me to the second year of the Honours course in Politics and Economics, though *ceteris paribus* was my only working Latin.

The Ministry renewed its grant. I'd taken the precaution of working in all the vacations, at Christmas ensuring the Royal Mail got through hail, sleet and snow, and at other times writing shorthand instructions to relay to the engineers at Mather and Platt, and drivers at British Road Services. I saved to afford a second-hand Triumph motorcycle – Dad taught me how to handle the beast. It was as well I had wheels, since in the second year the college authorities decreed I was to be rescued from Western Hill and afforded sanctuary in a fourteenth-century fortress at Lumley Castle, Chester-le-Street, fifteen miles from Durham City. Others given rooms at Lumley, after spending the day in lectures at Palace Green, had to suffer a long bus ride while I raced up the A1 into Lumley's thickly wooded parklands in time for tea.

I threw myself into college life that second year. I joined the Boat Club as a gesture to the Master, I participated in Union debates, I ran the half-mile for Castle, played squash, and started a Durham University table tennis club. Some of the heavies from the Rugby and Boat Clubs derided ping-pong as about the level of tiddlywinks, a weakling's sport not worthy of the sporting honour of the Colours we coveted. It made no impression on them at all when I bragged that I'd played in the 1948 English Open championships, the Wimbledon of the sport. I didn't stress that I'd been put out in the first round, nor offer my lame excuse that the ball was a bit of a blur because I was near-sighted and too vain to wear spectacles.

This weakness of mine was cruelly exploited in the men's singles by the French national champion, Maurice Bordrez, who then went all the way to the semi-finals, but the issue of whether ping-pong qualified as athletic was satisfactorily resolved in Durham by inviting the loudest objectors to play a game where a mix of angled long and short shots had them running round the table until they dropped.

Not surprisingly, in that hectic second year I succumbed to the imperatives of journalism. There was competition among the colleges for one of their own to have the distinction of editing the university's bi-weekly *Palatinate*, though nobody was rushing to do any of the slog of collecting enough news and putting the newspaper together. At one point, there had been a Union Society debate on the proposition that 'The journalist is a man who has sold his soul.' It had been carried overwhelmingly. From the masthead only three people seemed to be engaged in this activity. I volunteered and was sucked in. It was so time-consuming going round all the colleges, I gave up coxing a Castle racing four, which was a relief to the crew; during one training session, fiddling for glasses in my pocket as we headed back to the boathouse, I saw my driving licence fall in the river and retrieved it only by frantic commands as we drifted into the weir.

I was rewarded for my *Palatinate* industry with the masthead title of assistant editor. This was an inflation of my role, which was sitting in a cold room in the Union proffering the gluepot to the editor, pasting up his columns into pages and reading proofs. Nobody could hope to edit *Palatinate* for long given all the lectures, tutorials, examinations, but when the editor resigned I let my name go forward to the owners of the paper, the Student Representative Council (SRC), an elected group of the most active undergraduates and graduates. I was summoned to a meeting to learn that I'd been elected, then promptly sandbagged: I inherited a newspaper practically bankrupted by the cost of paper and the zinc used to reproduce photographs. What, asked the President of SRC, did the wizard of Ashton-under-Lyne propose to do about it? Was I going to ask for a bigger subsidy? Hand on heart, I recklessly declared that no journalist worth his salt would ever take a penny in any subsidy from anyone because it would compromise his independence. Rhetoric wouldn't pay our bills, so I proposed that we be allowed to increase the price and maybe the advertising rates. Some jibbed at this, urging that it was preferable to reduce the number of pages to eight from ten. 'You'll have a job filling them anyway.'

It was a proposition I was to hear many times in my newspaper life. Believing then, as I do now, that the way to kill a newspaper is to ask more for less, I pleaded that we should be allowed to charge 33 per cent more but go up two pages to twelve. This was rash. I didn't know a thing about newspaper management, but I boasted of my RAF experience in doubling the price of the *Empire Flying School Review*.

The Council was persuaded to give us a trial, which meant that the three of us committed to the paper had to think very fast to justify the extra pages and the higher price. We concerted our plan of attack: more sport, more news, of course, but we'd introduce features, which meant recruiting more help. We wooed widely among second-year students, varying the pitch a little according to our judgement of the tastes of the quarry. 'Look what a spell on *Palatinate* can do for you,' we'd say. 'Do you realize who's the chief sub-editor of *The Times*?' If that glazed the eye, we'd try: 'And do you know who edits Britain's largest-selling daily newspaper, the *Daily Mirror*? Both Durham men!' We weren't sure that either Reginald Easthope at *The Times* or Silvester Bolam at the *Mirror* had actually worked on *Palatinate*, but why cloud the issue that Durham men were stars in journalism? There seemed no point, either, in mentioning that Bolam, a fervent defender of the virtue of tabloid journalism, was currently in prison for documenting the crimes of a vampire murderer before the courts had decided the killer's guilt.

Among our undergraduate recruits was a gregarious and ebulliently eloquent literary star, Trevor Johnson, who displayed an encyclopedic knowledge of the books of Evelyn Waugh. He wrote to the famous author, and thereby secured an interview on Waugh's Gloucestershire estate. Trevor took trains all the way from Durham to King's Cross and then into the West Country from Paddington. After alighting at Stinchcombe station he paused to ask directions, and by way of thanks explained to the station master the influence of T. S. Eliot on John Betjeman's railway poems. When he arrived at the Georgian mansion, Piers Court, an upstairs sash window opened and Waugh's angry red face appeared. 'You are five minutes late. I will not tolerate rudeness! Good day to you, sir!'

Without our literary scoop, we fell back on a loquacious member of Hatfield College, Ian Rodger, an irreverent gadfly poet who proposed that he should visit all the Durham pubs within staggering distance of Palace Green to report on how far the natives were friendly and whether their beer was drinkable. To support this enterprise he required expenses. In justification, he wrote: 'Around the peninsula lies a permanent challenge to wit and conversation and beneath in its black earth, lies the constant reminder of laughter, bright cups and tinkling glass.' We were moved. We gave him a pound of SRC money. Our undercover pub reporter wasn't seen on Palace Green for two whole weeks, but bang on deadline he came into our office bursting with intelligence: Did we know there was a pub over Framwellgate Bridge where you could debate capitalism with Marxist miners? Did we know the one where a leading lecturer suitably primed could be guaranteed to lose all sense of discretion in a vivid dissection of his fellow dons? He confided this intelligence with a flourish: 'Amid the smoke-filled air, to the strange sound of one of the most fascinating English dialects and the monotonous clink of the dominoes, the student can indeed say in after years that this is where memory both begins and ends.'

I was less moved by the prospect of dominoes than by his identification of a hideaway upriver ideally placed for cool refreshment after a long summer punt beneath the willow trees. I made a note of it for a personal campaign. I'd lately been taken with the grace and vivacity of Enid Parker, a biology undergraduate in St Aidan's Society. I liked the way an apparently gentle question from her punctured hot-air balloons in the gabfests of Union coffee breaks. Though she had been seen on campus with a college tennis star, I got in early with a fast service. The moment I learned the date of the elegant garden party Castle staged in the Fellows' Garden in the spring, I passed her a note in the Union. She accepted. Fifteen–love to me. I next discovered we had a bond in both being from the North, albeit she was from Liverpool, Manchester's rival. Thirty–love. And she liked the ride on the Triumph I gave her – in those days it was hugely impressive for anyone to have wheels. Forty–love. The punting expedition recommended by our intrepid pub reporter might in due course be game, set and match. She erred only once in her impeccable judgement that I know of, which was a year later in agreeing to be my wife.

Here are a few extracts from my college diary of these momentous days:

Monday, January 29, 1951: Lots of *Palatinate* copy to edit and an essay to do for tomorrow. Couldn't get out of table tennis match with miners, took bus, still editing copy, then came back to late night at Lumley and finished the essay such as it is.

Tuesday, January 30: Ethics tutorial in Harrison's cat-infested room. He pads about in slippers and flannel bags talking in an Oxford voice about the concept of good. Took notes at evening emergency meeting SRC. Late back Lumley. Copied economics notes before bed.

Wednesday, January 31: Windy bike ride in from Lumley, very tricky. Dashed to Hood tutorial on Hobbes. Did headlines. Noisy college meeting made me captain of athletics. I'm taking on too much! Girl in Union is Enid, Edgar Jones says she goes with Danny F, so forget it.

Thursday, February 1: Missed lecture in the morning, but it was only by the odious man from Cambridge so I didn't miss anything. A little late, too, for tutorial. Page makeup in the afternoon and evening. Hectic. At one point we seemed a page down. Went for a drink. Late at night John Nettleton helped me decide we did have enough for 12 pages. Doors locked, so went down a fire escape with a torch and ran to the printers with page proofs.

The final acquisition for the new *Palatinate* was to find someone to write a gossip column under the pen name Argus. We knew we had found the right man when he sent in a little note about one of the prominent communists on campus, a tough former shop steward called Michael McVeigh of St Cuthbert's Society, who was constantly recruiting comrades:

Mr McVeigh I understand has changed his lodging due to a disagreement with his landlady about the proportion of water in the milk supplied with his porridge each morning. Obviously no Scotsman could be fooled on a matter connected with porridge, and for her pains the good lady is now no doubt blacklisted by the Cominform. However, even a clash on so fundamental an issue hardly explains why he left so quietly as he did, and at midnight.

I think it's safe now to say Argus was the pseudonym for Derek Holbrook, a close friend (and so he remains). He was a brilliant and angelic-looking English scholar, who after Durham abandoned a promising career in journalism to solve all sorts of intractable problems with the trade unions as a labour officer with Imperial Chemical Industries on Teesside. No doubt he did this in his lunch hour, for he was the epitome of the saying that if you want to get something done, look for the busiest person around. Even the Soviet Stakhanovites would never have guessed that he could find time for social espionage. He was a runner for Union Society presidency, a leading speaker in its debates, a member of SRC, editor of the literary magazine *New Durham*, a national governor of the United Federation for Animal Welfare, and treasurer of the Liberal Club. He was also highly visible at all the social functions in an eyepatch and beard, escorting some of the most attractive women in Durham – relationships whose fulfilment required a great deal of cunning, since his room was right in the Master's house.

*

My first issue was published on Friday, 2 February 1951. '*Palatinate* came into the Union coffee bar earlier than I thought it would. I was in a funk,' I learn from my diary. 'Had to find somewhere to hide. I bolted to obscure corner of the library, had lunch in Lyons in town instead of Castle and read the paper. Such sensitivity!'

When I summoned up the nerve to venture back on Palace Green I found we were fast selling out.

The new features were popular, especially the Palace Green Notes by Argus, and on page 1 we had a hot news break. University campuses in the 1950s were riven by discord about just how serious a menace was international communism. Mao's communists had taken over China, Stalin had tried to starve out West Berlin, communist North Korea had invaded the South, but even so our Union Society in 1951 seriously debated the motion 'That the United States is as much a menace to world peace as the Soviet Union,' and another time voted 2:1 that 'We could not conscientiously take part in any future war.' America was seen as provocative and dumb for backing Chiang Kai-shek's corrupt Kuomintang regime; Senator Joe McCarthy and the House Un-American Activities Committee were derided and despised for the witch hunts for secret 'Reds' in Washington and Hollywood. Alger Hiss, we now know, was indeed a Soviet spy, but at Durham then he was the campus hero, not the courageous Whittaker Chambers who exposed his betrayal.

It was in this fevered period that Durham's ice hockey team accepted an invitation to take part in the Ninth World University Games. The Warden of the Durham Colleges, Sir James Duff, and the Academic Council of professors banned them from going. The official explanation was that the four-day interruption of studies in term time was too much. This was regarded as whitewash. Everyone believed that the real reason was the anti-communist hysteria of the time. The Games were in Poiana, Rumania, behind the Iron Curtain. Memory tells me I accompanied our front-page report with a brave and stinging editorial rebuking the Academic Council for its paranoid worry that Durham men could be suborned or bullied into pro-communist 'peace statements': I had tried out for the ice hockey team and had the bruises to testify that they were not deeply interested in peace with anyone. But finding the editorial again now I see that the roar I imagined was all weasel: 'Whatever views may be taken of the attitude of the authorities on this subject,' I wrote, 'all will welcome a better indication of the extent of undergraduate liberty during term, for we cannot but notice certain inconsistencies in this matter.'

In fact, read today almost all my editorials for *Palatinate* were lamentable. They were affected, studded with quotations I'd looked up. A reasonable critique of a Student Council vote concluded: 'Perhaps this sounds too much like a homily on democracy or "that fatal drollery called a representative government . . ." Can we, though, make ours work a little better and escape the sting of Disraeli's gibe?'

I cringe.

The only editorial I wrote that was any good came out of my baptism of fire in political journalism. The members of the Durham Colleges Conservative and Unionist Association were always complaining that they did not get enough space in the paper. They were wrong, but the assaults made me acutely aware that an editor had to be like Caesar's wife, above suspicion. I'd been invited to join the Conservative, the Liberal, the Labour and the Socialist societies. A sixth sense held me back from allegiance to any political party. Two years after graduating I was invited by the Liberal party in Altrincham, Cheshire, to be their Parliamentary candidate in the next General Election against the sitting Conservative MP. I felt flattered – and ran a mile in the opposite direction. After my Durham experience, I knew that pinning a party badge on my lapel would make it harder to be seen as unbiased, which by this time I was. (I have to say, though, that I've known many leading journalists who've been party men in both Britain and the US without it in any way making their work suspect or hindering their rise.)

These were somewhat discomfiting years in terms of class consciousness. When our table tennis team travelled to play against clubs in the mining villages in south Durham, we were disconcertingly regarded as toffs. In town the shopkeepers were deferential to 'gentlemen of college', which made me feel fraudulent, and then in the third year living in the Castle itself I had the privilege of a college servant known as a 'scout'. I was gloriously accommodated in two rooms on the Norman Gallery where I'd taken the crucial entrance interview. My rooms looked over the town and down on the terrace where I could admire the sockless Master doing callisthenics at the crack of dawn. Returning from lectures, I was happy to find my scattered books and papers neatly stacked on my desk, my coal fire ready, and a tray laid for tea with jam and crumpets for toasting. I remained uneasy that the scout was a woman of my mother's age.

I had a precious privacy. From my quarters the door opened not directly on the Gallery but on a second outer door, this one being an inviolable 'oak' that could never be opened by anyone else from outside, so that the scholar within would not be disturbed while reading. Closing the outer of the two doors was called Sporting the Oak: a ritual signalling private study – or a woman visitor arriving for tea. Visitors to our rooms were all clocked in and out by the vigilant dragon lady who had met me at the lodge when I first arrived.

I'd resigned my editorship in good time for the third-year purgatory of Finals. I frequently resit those examinations, mad recurring dreams of staring at the blank paper wondering who on earth is this David Ricardo to demand rent and what did he have to do with the categorical imperative and Question Time in the House of Commons and marginal utility and anyway how can it serve the greatest good of the greatest number of people if someone has taken the lovingly long-preserved head of Jeremy Bentham out of his cabinet at University College London? My fellow Castleman John Perkins didn't seem to worry at all about getting ready for Finals. He continued to row on the Wear. When faced in a horrible economics paper with questions that left him cold, he sat there calmly translating all the questions into French, Italian and German and went back to the river. Failure didn't do him any harm. He had a dazzling career as a detective, first in the Special Branch of Scotland Yard, then investigating insurance rackets in Canada and doing valiant work for the Mounties, and finally prospering as a manufacturer of ballpoint pens. Lacking his imagination and linguistic skills, I was very happy to get through and qualify for the graduation ceremonies in the stately Great Hall in Castle.

Mum and Dad came early for the graduation, looking long and proudly at the degree notice board on Palace Green to see I headed the Honours Politics and Economics list. Their pride was tempered by calculation. My brother Peter recently came across a picture postcard of the cathedral that Mum sent home with just these words: 'Harold has had a lot of expense. See if there are any pounds or such like in my club moneybox. Bring it along and the pound out of the brass box in the living room.'

I had already started looking for work, writing applications this time on the Castle's red-crested letter paper. At the end of that idyllic summer of 1952, I left Durham with a telegram in my pocket as peremptory as the one from the Ministry of Education that had sent me there three years before:

REPORT HERE MONDAY MORNING
Manchester Evening News, Manchester

8

STOP PRESS

There had been no individual signature on the telegram summoning me to the *Manchester Evening News*. I landed in the office of T. E. Henry, the editor in chief, an imposing, beefy presence with forbidding spectacles, a military moustache and slicked-back hair. He barked into an intercom and passed me like a hot coal to his assistant editor next door, a soft-spoken man who smiled and immediately got on his intercom to summon a tiny man bristling with urgency who grimaced and hurried me out of the inner sanctum and into the hands of a dapper, bow-tied No. 4.

The pass-the-new-boy game came to a halt in a big room, starkly lit by fluorescent tubes. One end of the room was hectic with reporters lassoed by telephone wires hanging from the ceiling, hot-foot messengers and banks of copy-takers, girls wearing headsets clacking away on sit-up-and-beg Underwood typewriters. The noise of the newsroom then! Today's tippity-tap at computers like mice dancing on a keyboard can never set pulses racing in the same way. At the other end of the floor, there was silence. Cigarette smoke drifted from a score of men in shirtsleeves, curled up in prayerful postures before the dominant feature of the room: a schoolhouse clock with big Roman numerals.

These were the paper's sub-editors. I had applied for a job

outlining my reporting experience. The net result of the morning's lightning transactions was that I was to be given a trial – not as a reporter, but as a sub. Everyone knows what reporters do, collecting information and writing it up in 'a story', whereupon it becomes 'copy'. But nothing reporters write gets into a newspaper without passing through the hands of the subs, the hidden impresarios of news. Subs take pride in translating the complex into the comprehensible, in making sense of conflicting information from divergent sources, in making sure the story fits the space allotted to it, in writing read-this-or-die headlines. In the first stage in the process, text goes to a sub designated to assess the worth of every story from everywhere – from staff reporters, freelance reporters, and above all, the news agencies, notably the Associated Press in the US and the Press Association in Britain. I'd bet that only a handful of the millions then and now who get their news from the newspapers know how much they depend on the sub as the human filter of the torrent of words and pictures from reporters and the wire services. The 32-page *Evening News* got enough information every day to fill 500 pages. (Today with the Internet it would be many thousands of pages.)

In British parlance, the sub who filters the copy is called a 'copy taster', for he must have a palate sensitive enough to differentiate at once between the fresh and the stale. He will skim maybe 100,000 words in an hour to make the preliminary selection of the best stories. In those days, he impaled the discards on a basic tool of his trade, a sharp metal spike; nowadays the term 'spiked' means a story has gone into electronic trash.

The copy taster passes his selected stories to the chief sub-editor, a Chinese tailor of page design who fashions page layouts to express a range of priorities and distributes the copy to his gang of sub-editors for editing with instructions as to story length and headline size and style.

Subs never know one minute to the next whether the packet of copy coming their way will be a shout or a murmur: a short story requiring a small headline (SMALL EARTHQUAKE IN CHILE; NOT MANY DEAD) or a story calling for a front-page thunderbolt:

EVEREST CONQUERED/AT LAST THE FOUR MINUTE MILE. The packet may contain only a few paragraphs, dispatched in a few minutes, or two thousand words to be carefully trimmed to five hundred. The good sub is an artist in economy. The news feed unedited that would make a full column is often enough rendered in half that space without losing a single relevant fact or sacrificing good writing. These skills have been but poorly developed in the United States and Canada, where the copy editors have been accustomed to grazing on acres of newsprint; in Britain, the effect of wartime newsprint rationing put a premium on conciseness. To be described as a 'tight sub' in Britain is a high compliment. (The practice I've wearily observed on too many American news desks of simply lopping off the end of an over-long story is an abomination. It assumes that the reporter has assembled the essence of the story in the first paragraphs, and that the portion on the spike is impossible to condense.)

Saving space is a necessity in itself, given the cost of newsprint and the prodigious flow of information; but clarity, as much as economy, is at stake. Meaning is fogged when sentences are freighted with unnecessary words – whether in print, broadcasting, or on the Internet. A good sub would no more hesitate to remove unnecessary words than an engineer would to remove unnecessary parts of a machine. Excess words and abstractions impose on the receiver's time and attention. This morning as I took a walk along the beach at my house in Quogue on Long Island, I checked the weather report on my cell phone. By the time I heard 'Abnormal weather conditions resulting in bursts of heavy precipitation are a likely eventuality for the North-east,' it was already raining.

Not surprisingly, reporters everywhere have a lexicon of rude words for the sub. The colour and detail on which the reporter laboured have to be reconciled with the imperatives of time and space, and the subs have to be merciless. They struggle to retain all the details relevant to the central idea of a story, changing the woolly into the concrete: 'provision for increased retail opportunities' becomes 'more shops'. In addition to all this, the sub also does a score of checks – for grammatical barbarisms, for inner consistency and coherence, for apparent errors of fact, for fairness, for double meanings, for propaganda, for libel, for nonsense: 'The truck driver said he was going north when he saw the deceased walk into the road.'

All this editing and checking has to be done with an eye on the clock. Kipling biographer and essayist Edward Shanks put it well: 'Sub editors, when I meet them, seem to have only two eyes just like other people; where they keep the other two I cannot say, but I know they must have them.' These unlikely supermen may not be very good writers; they may have been undistinguished as reporters. The skills are just different. When I arrived at the *Manchester Evening News*, they were still talking about a young man before me who flopped as a reporter. He was too shy to go out into the city and ask questions of people he had never met before. I knew the feeling. He pleaded that instead of being fired he should be given a chance in the subs room, and from there his rise was meteoric – copy taster; chief sub-editor; editor in chief; joint managing director of the whole company; wartime editor in chief of the BBC; then director general, and finally he was Sir William Haley, the much-feared editor of *The Times* who thundered about moral issues – and replaced the classic first page of classified advertising with front-page news.

His attitude to life was manifest in what he did at the *Evening News* when he had finished seeing the main edition to press. He would come quietly into the reporters' room, not to chat – he never wasted breath on mere conversation – but to tap the Manchester United reporter Tom Jackson on the shoulder. It was a signal to stop typing and come down the corridor for a game of table tennis with the boss. 'I always won, but one day I did lose to him,' Tom told me. 'He never invited me again.' Tom died five years later with eight of United's star players – the Busby Babes – and seven other bylined reporters when their plane crashed trying to take off at Munich on 6 February 1958.

While plodding round for paragraphs in Droylsden, I'd gorged on the 1944 edition of F. J. Mansfield's *Complete Journalist* and the anecdotage in Fleet Street's *Inky Way* annuals. I loved the photographs of hunched men in cardigans reducing cataclysms to column inches. So I knew what daily newspaper subs were supposed to do, but my only practical knowledge of a sub's role had come from seeing scissor-hands Middlehurst at work in Ashton. I did not know then how much the British subs are a breed apart, their work more intense and more highly specialized than their apparent counterparts on American newspapers, the copy editors, who are expected to do so much less and rise to the challenge. It remained a question of whether Harold Evans, BA (Hons. Politics, Economics and Moral Philosophy), could do it well enough as a greenhorn to survive with the gunslingers on the biggest, fastest, slickest, most profitable and humdingiest popular regional daily, with a million-plus readers.

The subs' end of the room seemed tranquil compared with the reporters' end. It wasn't. The turmoil was psychic. All the subs, in tight balls of concentration, were too preoccupied to raise so much as an eyelid as Mr Bow Tie, who turned out to be the day's copy taster, indicated an empty chair at the long table and equipped me with the tools of the trade: spike, gluepot, two pencils, scissors, a galley listing deadline times for every page of the day's editions, a pad of copy paper, and an office book of type faces. I had no time to open it. The tiny man I'd met in the final sequence of my arrival turned out to be the chief sub-editor, Norman F. Thornton, known to all as Nifty; except to the man himself, who froze the room on any suggestion of familiarity. We were all 'Mister'. Having lost ninety seconds in meeting me, he was now emitting steam.

'Boy!' he called. 'Boy! Boy!'

The summons was addressed not to me but one of six teenage copy boys, usually a dead-end job then.

'Mr Evans, and sharp about it.'

I received four folios of teleprinter copy about a mother of five who had won £50,000 on the football pools on her first attempt. Nifty's headline instructions were written on top: '24 xi xi, p.4 Home.'

The sub next to me uncoiled long enough to whisper: 'Two lines 24 point round here is three pars, no more.' From reading the paper I knew its paragraphs were short, two or three sentences at most.

From Mansfield, I remembered the vital little rules devised for fast newspaper production. Head printers shared the typesetting among scores of Linotype operators. A sub who failed to number and mark every folio would create chaos, so I identified my little story with the catchline Mother, then I numbered every folio – Mother 1 for the headline, Mother 2, 3 and 4 for the text. I marked every folio 'xi' for single-column setting, double-ticked the capital letters, circled the full stops; indented for new paragraphs, defined the destination and edition on every folio, wrote 'mf' (for 'more follows') at the end of each folio, and made a double-gated pound sign at the end, so that the printers assembling the story would know not to wait for more. Routine clerical stuff really, but as important as a bank teller being able to count.

More time-consuming was that the story I had been given to edit ran ten paragraphs and had to be contained in three. Clearly if I couldn't do that by now I should seek another line of work. But according to the time sheet I had only twelve minutes for text and headlines. I had almost no experience writing headlines. The type book, each line measured off against column widths, told me that at the size of 24 point Century Bold – the standard headline face of the paper – no more than 12 letters, including word spaces, would fit in a single column. Having squeezed the text, I turned to the headline. I tried:

Mother of five
has big pools win

No good. 'Mother of five' counted out at 14 characters and M was a wide letter. I fiddled and fiddled. Five minutes left:

Mother hits
jackpot . . .

It fitted but it was rather vague.

Five lucky children . . .

Even more vague.

With three minutes to go I had a brain wave. I wrote:

Mum wins big
first time

and self-consciously shouted 'Boy!' He scooped the folios and dumped them in the chief sub's wire basket.

Other subs sent their text straight up to the composing room, but mine had to be scrutinized. It was a relief to hear the 'plop!' as Nifty made it vanish up a vacuum tube, but he held back the single folio with my headline written on it.

'Mum isn't style,' he rapped. 'Mum! We're not the *Daily Mirror*.'

He might as well have told the room I had syphilis. How the hell was I to know what the office style was? They hadn't given me the house stylebook. In a blink, Nifty scribbled his own headline. When the galley proofs came down, I saw he had written:

Mother's big
pools win

By now I was deep into copy bundles piling up in front of me for the next edition. Help! It was only fifty minutes away. My desk was right under the schoolhouse clock. Out of the corner of my eye, I caught the blur of a moustache in motion. It adorned the upper lip of the editor in chief – Mr T. E. Henry, Mr Tom Henry, aka Big Tom. As razored moustaches go, it was not exceptional, but it was spotlighted by two patches of high colour in his complexion, the whole ensemble lending urgency and authority to the words issuing forth as he strode without pause through the subs' room, his slipstream buffeting a retinue of assistant editor and copy boy, and often the excitable photo editor trying to get him to glance at a print. A herd of wild elephants could not have caused more commotion.

A few minutes later the intercom buzzed. Nifty sprang to it. Everyone sat up. 'Who the hell,' asked the harsh voice, reverberating through the squawk box, 'who the hell subbed this twenty-four-point that's as long as Cross Street?' It was Big Tom speaking from the stone – the composing room where all the type was assembled in iron frames (chases) laid out on flat stone tables. It wasn't my 24-point, it was someone else's whose text had run to five paragraphs and would not therefore fit the three-paragraph space Nifty had allocated for it on his neat page plan. The excess paragraphs were a double waste of time – of the Linotype operator's, and of the editor's overseeing the page to press. Simply discarding those lines in hot metal might also discard a key point, even the basis for the headline, yet there might not be time to have the galley reset. Nifty choked on his anger. The erring sub shrivelled in his chair.

You could feel the room stiffen every morning when Big Tom swept through on his way to the stone for the first edition, catapulting commands and lobbing questions, answers to which were shouted back as if they were grenades about to explode. We all of us dreaded the sound of Darth Vader on the squawk box. His wrath fell on anyone who wrote a politically slanted headline, a commonplace on other dailies, left and right. He was insistent on the unbiased presentation of news – so long as it did not concern Manchester United football club, which occupied a different universe of gods and supermen. (When they lost 5–1 one Saturday, Big Tom was inspired to write: 'United in Six Goal Thriller'.)

The tendency in the newsroom, cowed by the intercom blasts, was to regard Big Tom as a vulgarian. He'd risen through subbing sport, for Pete's sake. He chomped on a cigar. He wore red braces and spotted bow ties. His voice was hoarse. The two editors before him, ice-cold Haley and the glossy John Beavan, were accomplished writers with the air of university dons. 'Had an excellent weekend, thank you,' Haley would say. 'Read eight books and reviewed three of them.' Tom gave himself no intellectual airs, but he was an organizer of genius. For the big scheduled events like the presentation of the national budget, six or seven foolscap sheets from his office would tell forty individual subs and reporters precisely what they were to do at 3.10 p.m, at 3.15 p.m, and at 3.50 p.m. Subs assigned to the stone with him hated to admit it, but they were in awe of his speed and skill, his relentless drive to get the paper out on time. He had no equal. Printers loved his decisiveness and expertise. Gothic heads emerged from the Ludlow machine seconds after he had scrawled a banner that fitted perfectly. Like all good stone men, he would read the story in mirror image, cut it, change a weak headline and issue boil-in-oil curses on its writer.

At the end of a week of Nifty and Darth Vader, I was shaking. I made myself invisible in the turmoil of the Saturday sports edition, calculating to forestall the suggestion that I wouldn't be needed the following week. On Monday morning I got in bright and early, catching a train virtually from the back door of the house in Failsworth where the family now lived after the sale of the shop in Ashworth Street. Bow Tie was already at his desk, spruce in a white shirt, sleeves rolled up, two shiny spikes ready for the day's torrent of copy. 'It's hard for you as a novice from a weekly,' he reflected, between satisfying puffs of Churchman's on his pipe. 'Not to worry. A lot of subs from the dailies who come just can't take the pressure here, no sir, just can't hack it.'

Nifty, he kindly informed me, kept a book of the comings and goings which showed that in four years ninety-four subs had joined and left the paper, some sacked on the spot, most running for the exit. That's close to one departure every two weeks, which meant that by the law of averages another head was due to roll; mine, I feared.

Nothing before, and nothing I have experienced since, working for newspapers, radio, television and websites in London and New York and Washington, matches the speed demanded of everyone on the *Evening News*. Newspapers were the way millions got their first inkling we had been invaded by men from Mars; there was no Internet, no cell phones, and cheap transistor radios awaited the 1960s. In those anxious analogue days, you had to reckon on at least half an hour for a photograph to become an engraving. I understood why the needle-thin picture editor, Owen French, whom I came to call Volcano, was in permanent eruption. Nifty was apt to call over for the picture for a Manchester story as soon as he saw the returning photographer taking off his raincoat. Volcano would swear loudly and profusely about last straws and impossible chief subs, grab his hat and storm out of the room, glad to see the back of us all.

Who would do his work? He would. His anger was genuine enough but it was cathartic. After the pantomime, he always came back five minutes later, radiating benevolence for his fellow slaves to the clock.

Reporters and subs had to operate like a souped-up Internet news service, producing eight editions in six hours – more if big news broke – and without the crutch of desktop computers. We had trains to catch, and vans to race into the suburbs; in the words commonly (but mistakenly) attributed to the Confederate lieutenant general Nathan Bedford Forrest in the American Civil War, we were desperate to be 'fustest with the mostest'. The crowds on the city streets had to carry home an *Evening News* rather than the hated *Manchester Evening Chronicle*, our direct challenger. Both papers wrote 'contents bills' – news placards designed to titillate but not satisfy: SEX TRIAL SHOCKS.

As the two evening newspapers slugged it out, hundreds of other reporters, critics, feature writers, subs and photographers were competing like mad to beat us and everyone else. Manchester was Newspaper City. Six million people in the north of England got their news through Manchester. Daily and Sunday, no fewer than twenty-six newspapers were written, edited and published within a couple of square miles of the four central railway stations.

The twenty-four-hour inner city simply throbbed with news day and night, in the newsrooms and in all the smoky watering holes where journalists and comps loved to gossip, keep an ear open for any clue to what rivals were up to, and uniformly agree that the gritty northern editions of their newspapers were much superior to those put out by their effete bosses in Fleet Street.

Every day on the way to work I had to walk by the entrenchments of the enemy in Withy Grove, a rabbit warren a few yards from Victoria Station where 3,000 people in Europe's biggest printing plant produced twelve papers, including the *Evening Chronicle*, the *Daily Telegraph*, the *Daily Mirror*, the *Daily Dispatch*, the *Sporting Chronicle* and three Sunday papers; from Deansgate, out rushed the delivery vans of the *Daily Mail* and *People*; the trade unions' *Daily Herald* was tucked away the other side of the railway tracks in Chester Street; and to the west rose the glass Black Lubyanka, where the slickest of the slick produced the *Daily* and *Sunday Express* for Lord Beaverbrook, the press baron for whom the phrase 'whim of iron' was invented.

Men who survived Manchester went on to great things – Hugh Cudlipp, cutting his teeth at the *Evening Chronicle*, said of it: 'In Manchester I really learned what journalism was about. I met most of the operators who were later to fill the editor's chairs.' Editors of exotic reputation flowered in the glass Lubyanka: Arthur Christiansen, Tim Hewat (whom I mistakenly referred to as 'Strangler Hewat' – that appellation more properly belongs to his predecessor, Dick Lewis – 'Strangler Lewis') and Derek Jameson. Brian Hitchen, who came to us a hotshot reporter, had started as a fifteen-year-old copy boy at the *Daily Despatch*, and via the *Daily Mirror* and assorted wars became editor of the *Daily Star* and then editor in chief of the *Sunday Express*. Hunter Davies, a future Atticus columnist on the *Sunday Times* and biographer of the Beatles, was on the *Evening Chronicle*; Michael Kennedy was at the *Telegraph*; Bernard Shrimsley, later the first editor of the *Mail on Sunday*, was on the *Daily Mirror*; Harold Pendlebury and Vincent Mulchrone were at the *Daily Mail*, and so was Paul Dacre, one of the new influx of university men into newspapers after the 1960s, who in 1992 became a vital force in British journalism on becoming the *Mail*'s editor.

At the *Guardian*, then proudly named the *Manchester Guardian*, A. P. Wadsworth was about to hand the paper, and the Suez Crisis, to the scholarly Scot Alastair Hetherington, who made the bravest of stands against British intervention. In 1963 he saved the paper from closure. Manchester was the base for his witty successor Peter Preston and the team that covered the Irish Troubles so well (Simon Winchester, Simon Hoggart and Harry Jackson).

The *Guardian* and *Evening News* were both owned by the Scott Trust; we had offices on different floors and separate composing rooms, but we shared the presses and the cafeteria – with a nod to liberal principles, company chairman Laurence and his brother Charles shared the same meat-and-potatoes menus. At the lunch table where the *Guardian* editorial people tended to assemble, you'd find the provocatively droll Harry Whewell, who became the editor in Manchester, providing northern backbone when the paper moved to London in 1961; the gentle Bill Weatherby, who became the most sensitive interpreter of black America; the ardent Mary Stott, who revolutionized women's pages; Brian Redhead, a newly arrived, cocky and very clever Cambridge graduate, destined for the editorship of the *Evening News*, and a popular BBC talk show; the stylist Norman Shrapnel, whose prose, like his moustache, had no dangling participles; Bob Ackerman, an American intern from Brown University who decided he would rather dissect the brains of chimpanzees as a neurologist in Boston; and a pale, emaciated new reporter with a devilish smile, who amazed us by saying how entertaining that morning's proceedings of the North-West Gas Board had been. The gas moguls were not amused by his report in the *Guardian*, but the experience was great training for becoming Michael Frayn, playwright and novelist. I was entranced to hear that Frayn, another Cambridge graduate, had learned Russian so as to better appreciate its literature, a linguistic accomplishment that catapulted him into journalism. He was approached to become a spy and made up his mind on a newspaper career instead when Control – or whoever, maybe Alec Guinness as Smiley – laid a venturesome hand on his thigh. The North-West Gas Board paid for the indiscretion.

At the *MEN*, we always liked to show Newspaper City how we could turn on a dime. In delivery, of course, hot metal news takes far longer to reach the reader, but it was the rush of the raw editing time of text and photographs that was so taxing. It was not uncommon for our subs to be physically sick from the tension. In the second week, I felt so queasy I made lunch a boring glass of milk, forsaking the corned beef sandwiches Mum had put in my raincoat pocket. Nifty gave us only twenty minutes for lunch anyway; if during the day we got up to go to the toilet, more copy would be piled up for our return as punishment for indulging human weakness.

The survivors around me were all used to the sound of gunfire. The artist who drew our maps had been a lieutenant in the Royal Naval Volunteer Reserve. His Japanese captors had him kneel for a beheading, then changed their minds and chopped off an arm instead. Bob Gibbens, the soft-spoken sub who had rescued me from letting that first story run too long, had been a tank commander, decorated with a Military Cross for battlefield bravery: a fact only discovered when a buff envelope crested 'On His Majesty's Service' was left on his desk on his day off. A sub who came and went every day without saying a word to anyone had been a bomber pilot, badly shot up over Düsseldorf. A vehement blond man with a black eyepatch, Derek Maude had lost his eye in the Army, but was still a quicksilver sub. The amiable Bow Tie, who looked such a dandy – he came to work every day in yellow gloves, and for the 1956 Suez invasion turned up in a pith helmet – had for four years been Quartermaster Duncan Measor on the destroyer *Hotspur*, dropping depth charges on U-boats in the Atlantic. The only man who regularly ignited laughs in the tense room, clowning if there was a chance between editions, was a Royal Naval Reserve officer with a Distinguished Service Medal, name of Bob Ashton: when he was given the agricultural notes to edit, he tied boxing string round his trouser legs in bowyangs: 'If I'm going to work like a navvy, I'd better look like one.'

Nifty was the fastest and best sub and layout man in the room, and I dare say on the planet; his instructions on copy, written at speed, could be read by a man on a galloping horse. He was also a tight-lipped disciplinarian. No banter, no jokes, gentlemen; keep your heads down, get the copy out. He had a watertight memory. When a story ran through two or three news cycles, he knew precisely which elements were fresh. A sub would be rebuked: 'Wake up! That headline was the page four lead in the *Express* this morning.' The subs took these chastisements quietly. He was always right.

The only sub I ever saw openly rebel was John Morgan, a genial giant with long hair and a leather jacket who sprawled over two desks, elbows out, hoovering up the copy. 'Mr Morgan, that's a morning paper headline, don't you read the dailies on your way to work?' Nifty called out across the room, shooting a first-edition headline back to him. No 'Mr Thornton, yes sir,' from Morgan. Gruffly he volleyed: 'I'd like to see you read the dailies on a bloody motorbike!' Morgan, who emigrated to Melbourne and eventually became editor of the *Sun* and then executive editor of the *Herald* and

Weekly Times, did indeed ride heroically over the moors in blizzard and fog. Everyone in the room sat up for a scene. But then Darth Vader came on the squawk box wanting to know what the hell had happened to the picture for page 3. We went back to being troglodytes.

We might as well have been on a spaceship, receiving signals from all over the world but stuck in our chairs, hermetically sealed off from the daily life of a vibrant city. In the mornings, having memorized all the headlines I could from half a dozen dailies on the train from Failsworth, I walked with the city crowds, inhaling the aromas of French cheese and Latin American coffee seeping out of the cellars of the wholesale houses along the damp streets near the cathedral. It was the nearest I'd get to foreign parts for some time. At the blackened Victorian building in Cross Street near the corner of bustling Market Street where the tram cars stopped, there'd always be a gaggle of people pausing to look at our news pictures in the display windows of the front office, a matter of pride when I'd edited the captions. I'd pause to savour a little romance. Here was where the legendary *Manchester Guardian* editor C. P. Scott ('facts are sacred, comment is free') jumped off his bicycle every day, having ridden the three miles from his home at The Firs, Fallowfield, and back again at night, a practice he continued until he was past eighty. Here, in January 1932, the crowds stood ten deep for his funeral cortege. Here too is where Neville Cardus, a bastard son of a prostitute from a Rusholme slum, came to gaze up at the *Guardian*'s lighted windows, dreaming he might one day write for the paper, and eventually he did, gloriously, as the doyen of cricket and music critics.

In the first weeks I was happy to take home a paper to show off the stories I had edited. But they weren't much, little single-column efforts. Mum, Dad and my brother Fred were nice about it, but clearly baffled by my sense of achievement. No, I hadn't written anything really, I'd say, not like the *Ashton Reporter*, but you see this story and this one, well, I edited them and they all caught the page in time, and you should have seen what they were like before I did the editing . . .

Two months into the work, I was being trusted with inside page leads and was officially taken on the staff, but I became jealous of the aristocracy at the subs' table, the three or four 'top-table' subs who were given the really big stories and made it seem effortless. One of them, the unflappable Bill Lloyd, edited while he lay back in his chair like a nonchalant Battle of Britain pilot awaiting the siren, his pencil, with a life of its own, gliding over the copy and oozing headlines. If only I could take home a front-page splash I had edited! When there was a loud bang on the shutter between the subs and the wireroom, indicating the arrival of a 'rush', some kind of sensation, I'd sit up like a puppy dog, tongue out for a juicy bone. Nifty would look round and invariably award the prize – 'Rush this, please, ninety-four-point Gothic caps' – to Mr Lloyd, Mr Finnegan, Mr Futrell, Mr Batchelor. He might as well have announced: 'To anyone but Mr Evans.'

He was correct in that judgement. I was in the right place as a down-table sub. I still made mistakes in the endless rush, sending up two folios numbered four, writing a headline that didn't fit, one day taking three minutes too long on squeezing the best juice out of a complicated court case. Big Tom had to rewrite one of my Saturday sports headlines when the Port Vale soccer team beat Chester. My headline was a succinct summary of the play but the comps fell about with laughter when they set it in metal for Big Tom: 'Port Vale Thrusts Bottle up Chester'. Nifty's punishment for infractions was a rain of 'K's' – the three-line fillers at the end of columns which required a headline in small bold caps, meaning there were too few letters to do more than grunt.

It was Chinese water torture all day: drip, drip, drip. Someone recognized my soul was in torment. Every week two or three of the editorial staff were handed books for review. The others got histories and novels. Not me. The first one on my desk was *The Eclipse of God* by Martin Buber. ('All journeys have secret destinations of which the traveller is unaware.') The following weekend I had to devote myself to studying Paul Tillich's *Systematic Theology*, and the third was consumed by two sledgehammer volumes on the philosophies of the East and West. I was a marked man.

When the big day came it was more than I bargained for. At 8.25 a.m. the wireroom shutter banged, signalling a rush story. Nifty shouted 'Boy! Mr Evans!' I was sharpening a pencil. A single Press Association folio landed on my desk.

RUSH 1
Train
TRAIN CRASH 8.19 XXXXX IN FOG XXX PASSENGER TRAIN IN STATION XXX

Oh, no, please not Dad! But I'd no time to fret. 'Rejigging page one,' Nifty called to the room, giving instructions for new displays. And to me: 'Crash for lead replate at nine.'

A boy gave me Nifty's folio of instructions for head and text setting.

8.38: Another folio:

RUSH: TWO TRAINS LONDON MIDLAND REGION COLLIDE HARROW WEALDSTONE STATION. COACHES PILED UP. WRECKAGE BLOCKS LINE. FOG. AMBULANCES. FIRE BRIGADES POLICE RUSH TO SITE.

Not Dad's region . . . More folios followed, in summary:

8.40: *Express from Perth with four sleeping cars ran into back of local on fast line. Est sixty miles an hour.*

8.41: *Local Tring–Euston train nine coaches stopped at Harrow-Wealdstone station for minute-plus, running seven minutes late in fog . . . Rear coaches telescoped by impact of Perth express. People still on platform scythed down. Unknown numbers trapped inside wreck . . .*

8.46: RUSH RUSH
One minute after primary crash, wreckage hurled across adjacent tracks derails two engines pulling Euston-

*Manchester-Liverpool express approaching at 60 mph. No word
of casualties . . .*

So now we had three trains in a wreck – two express trains and
one local in which an unknown number were trapped in smashed
coaches.

8.54: Four minutes to deadline. I'd translated the cryptic rushes
into sentences and sent the story to the printer. The banner was easy:
THREE TRAINS IN HIGH SPEED COLLISION. Second deck:
Many feared trapped in coaches.

8.58: I'd made the edition, but now an important nugget came
two minutes to deadline: *Police: Casualties bound to be heavy on
Tring train. Twenty bodies on stretchers . . .*

'Boy!' I yelled at the same instant as I marked the folio for a bold
flash intro and wrote a new substitute head that Nifty accepted:
TWENTY DEAD IN EXPRESS PILE-UP.

I was feeling pleased that I was keeping up with the pace of the in-
flow, but suffered remorse the instant the page had gone to press. I'd
presumed 'bodies' meant people who were no longer alive, but . . .

9.02: *Twenty bodies unconfirmed dead. Repeat unconfirmed
dead.*

Nifty brushed aside my concern. He was already calling instructions for the next edition in 58 minutes. 'Streamer cross 8 twice 94
point. Second deck 36 point cross 4. Close ten o'clock. Let it run.'

9.05: I killed all the type from the first edition and started to com-
pose a new story from all the fragments.

9.06: *The station foreman assXXXX assigned to count passengers
for rail census says, 'I counted 332 passengers coming down the
stair from the footbridge. God knows what's happened. I heard
terrific noise and screams.'*

9:06: RUSHFULL
*Twenty now confirmed dead. Police say total likely higher.
Names withheld pending notification of next of kin.*

9.07: Rescuers trying to reach Driver of Perth express R.S. Jones and Fireman C. Turnock of Crewe North Sheds. Buried somewhere under mountain of twisted iron. Rescue crane due 9.40

9.09: Loudspeakers command quiet so rescuers can listen for cries from the trapped passengers under the mountains of twisted iron.

The separate folios, a sentence on each, were falling like snowflakes in a blizzard, mixing the urgently important, the relevant, the repetitive and the disposable:

9.09: Harrow-Wealdstone 11 miles from Euston. Six tracks for 17 miles . . .

9.12: Witness: 'We came up on the local line, then crossed to the express line. Our train was packed. We hadn't shut the door of our coach. There was one hell of a crash. Our train leaped off the ground. We were hurled against one side of the compartment. Then another engine flashed by in the opposite direction. It was a nightmare.'

9.16: Guard J. Kent in rear Perth Express survived. Linked up with Perth express Driver Jones at Crewe. Jones told him had difficulty backing new engine onto train in fog. Express running 32 minutes late, would do best to make up times.

9.17: Minister of Transport heading to scene.

9.17: Driver Perkins Manchester-Liverpool Express killed in derailment.

9.18: Worst train crash 22 May 1915. Troop train collided with passenger train at Gretna Green, Scotland. 227 killed.

9.20: RUSH: Electric train from Watford headed into wreckage scattered across electric line but stopped by alert signalman switching off current. British Rail keeping him secluded. Said to be shaken.

9.21: *Tring train passenger in ambulance: 'The most terrible thing is the screams coming out of the middle of the great heap of the wreckage from the poor devils trapped inside.'*

9.25: *Injured Perth express survivor in hospital: driver must have run through signals. Must have been drunk.*

9.30–9.40: Half an hour to deadline. I edited the first half dozen folios into a sequence, trying to make the story flow and writing cross-headings every four or five paragraphs, taking note of my numbered folios, holding back the intro for the hardest and latest news. I set aside the allegation about the driver. Not because of family ties. How did the survivor know? The driver was still in the wreckage.

9.40: *Lucky escape Guard W. H. Merritt of Tring train along train to his van at rear said heard express approaching at speed and dived under coping of platform, then ran to signal box to sound alarm to close all lines.*

9.43: *Express sleeping car attendant says brakes went on hard seconds before crash. None of sleeping car passengers hurt.*

9.44: *All the station clocks stopped at 8.19*

9.45: *Firemen climbing 40 ft into piled-high twisted debris. Score of stretchers laid across tracks. Coach and wreckage jammed under station footbridge.*

9.50: 'Five minutes to close,' called Nifty. 'Banner please.'
I'd now written a lead paragraph on twenty confirmed dead in a three-train collision. No sooner has it left my hand, than a new flash landed:

9.51: *Total thirty-one bodies pulled out of Tring train wreckage.*

I wrote a new intro, marked it as substitute for the intro just sent ('substitute' meant the earlier one had to be thrown away) and warned the stone.

9.59: A minute before deadline I gave Nifty the banner: THIRTY-ONE DEAD IN EXPRESS CRASH.

Nifty had replanned the page for noon. A crude diagram showed the paths of the three trains on two lines. There were picture captions to write, new headlines for a jump to the back page to report names of the dead – including a Manchester QC – miracle rescues, interviews with the hundred plus in hospitals, the arrival of bigger cranes, and now, if I wanted, I could use a new PA lead reconstructing the crash with descriptive writing: Hundreds six deep, chatting and reading newspapers as they waited for the tube across from the doomed Tring platform, 'suddenly heard the roaring and vibration of an approaching express, the shriek of a whistle, the hiss of steam. Before horror could shape itself upon the faces of the crowd, they saw the express from Perth smash into the rear of the waiting train and in that that eerie frozen moment of horror there came from the direction of Manchester the thunderous pounding of the express from Manchester gathering speed into the wreckage.'

I subbed the best of the new material into yet another version of the story for the noon edition. So it went all day: edit this, spike that, change this, number that, check the number, insert a paragraph here, delete a paragraph overtaken, shout for a proof, mark it and send it back . . . and watch the clock. I was oblivious to all the activity in the subs' room, utterly immersed in a story changing every minute, writing and rewriting the narrative, waiting for the last seconds for the final headline, heart pounding, praying that what I was rushing into metal read well. By final edition the news was much bigger than it had begun. At 4 p.m. I wrote the Late Night Final edition banner:

75 KNOWN, 110 FEARED DEAD IN RAIL DISASTER
Full platform 'scythed': Children trapped hours

The Harrow-Wealdstone disaster, my baptism of fire, was the

worst crash since 1915: 112 people died. The official inquiry concluded that express Driver Jones had died on impact and so had his
fireman. The signalmen were exonerated, so the explanation offered
was that Jones, a healthy experienced driver of forty-three who knew
the road, had almost certainly not reduced speed when taking the train
past a distant signal coloured yellow for caution, meaning he should
be ready to stop at the next one if it was red for danger. He passed two
'not very conspicuous' semaphore signals at danger running through 'a
deceptive patch of denser fog'.

Even with a computer today, that kind of fast-changing, multi-
sourced news report is tricky to handle; with hot metal, it is the
supreme test of a news sub. My anxiety was whether I had passed.
The next morning, I opened an envelope on my desk. It was from Big
Tom. 'To mark your excellent work yesterday I am putting you
down for one pound special work bonus.' My euphoria was such I
have kept the note all these years.

Thereafter, I got a fair share as a top-table retailer of disaster and
triumph. Floods, a ship drifting packed with explosives, another rail
crash, a building collapse, a Royal visit (for which Dad drove the
Royal train to a few Lancashire towns and Bow Tie announced to
the room that Driver Evans had pulled into the station precisely at
the scheduled hour, as the clock struck eleven). I told myself that,
four months into the job, I was almost up there with the aristos.
Then I was pitchforked into page design and thought again. Late
every afternoon, when everyone was putting on their coats to head
for home or pub, one sub stayed late as editor of the 'Star' edition.
This was the first edition next day. The Star editor had to lay out
and sub five or six inside news pages ready for the early shift of the
printers. The first edition, with a newsy front page and runners at
various horse races, could then be on the street before noon. 'Here
you are then, Mr Editor,' said Bow Tie, depositing a bundle of
timeless agency copy, photographs and layout sheets. 'Make the
pages sing! Goodnight.'

The reporters' room was empty. The tea trolley was cold. Within
an hour, the cleaners had coped with the day's debris and I was alone

with a lubricious library girl. She swayed over for a chat, but quickly decided that filing old clippings was more exciting than my impromptu exegesis on the challenges of page design. I laid out pyramids of headlines on top of one large photograph and one small with a boxed panel and text starting at three columns, descending into two columns for one inch deep and then into single-column. It was an arresting new look for the *Evening News*. It was also utterly unworkable, a jigsaw that would not fit together unless the relevant words in text and headline once cast in hot metal matched exactly the number of lines the layouts required. I also discovered how little I really knew about scaling a photograph for the engravers so that when reduced to fit my page, it would occupy exactly the space I'd allotted on the layout. As for a fancy enlargement in the second photograph, I hadn't a clue how to work out the scale for that. (It seems very unfair that today the calculation is done by the computer before you can say George Eastman.)

I was in the middle of exasperated fiddling with the photograph, hunched over a light box, when a lovely soft voice said: 'Still here? Like to come to the Opera House when you're done?' Ah! The library girl, a second chance! No, it was a perfect entry, stage left, by Denys Futrell, a sunny plump sub obsessed with the theatre and Yorkshire cricket, who had come back on his day off to pick up tickets from the news editor's desk. In his evening away from Nifty's lash, he directed amateur theatricals and wrote innumerable reviews. I showed him my comic opera of a page. 'Trying too hard, old lad, trying too hard,' he sighed. 'Till you get the hang of it, just copy some layouts from other days. Nobody in Ancoats is going to complain that they've seen that layout before.' He showed me how to measure the enlargement, then headed off to the more satisfying drama of Ibsen's *A Doll's House*. 'You should be through in an hour. I'll leave your ticket at the box office.'

Denys needed plenty of time to get there, handicapped by a club foot from a childhood accident after which his leg had been badly reset, but I had no chance of catching up with him. I did as he suggested, subordinating originality to sanity, but I still had to sub all the copy, write all the headlines, all the captions, and do it all over again for four more pages. They were just about ringing down the curtain at the Opera House when I crawled up to the composing room with the copy and layouts for the Star edition. Next day nobody complained that the layouts had been seen before.

Eventually, I became a fast page designer. A few months later, when I was the Star editor, my diary affirms I was home at 7.30 p.m., in time for the Third Programme's broadcast of Mozart's 'Coronation Mass', and a week later 'a furious attack' on the Star pages had me out of the office at 6 p.m., impelled to catch a 6.30 train to Leeds with a big backpack loaded with tent, blankets, ground sheet and Primus stove. I had inveigled Enid Parker, then teaching at a progressive school in the Yorkshire village of Wennington, to realize that her biology teaching would be much enhanced if she camped with me in the Yorkshire Dales. (We were married a year later.) Beyond that attraction, I also took any chance I could to get out of the city, walking the vales of Derbyshire and climbing the moorlands to Kinder Scout with other subs gasping for clean air.

The first year of subbing on the *Manchester Evening News* was a companionable roller-coaster ride. In the second, I was restive. I more and more lived for the big days. In the summer of 1953, we were all keyed up for the coronation of Queen Elizabeth II. Everybody was. The *Guardian* got in trouble for publishing a cartoon by David Low which mildly questioned the millions of pounds' cost of the proceedings, while its historian, David Ayerst, noted the 'quasi-religious fervour' sweeping the country. Certainly the community spirit was infectious. Across the city and into the suburbs, streets were outdoing each other in profusions of Union Jacks and red-white-and-blue bunting; mothers and grandmothers in pinafores with buckets and soap were on their knees scrubbing the very pavements so they'd glisten for the street parties on Tuesday, June 2nd. Everybody in these streets, like ours, knew each other: 'Flo is good for sausage rolls, Jill will ice the cake.'

The excitement at the *MEN* was in preparing to outdo the *Chronicle* and the dailies with a souvenir issue. (The excitement would have been even more intense if we had known the British conquest of Everest would be achieved the same day.) Nifty took me aside the weekend before the Tuesday. He confided: 'You have been hand-picked for our special edition.' He said no more about my anointment, but I knew at once I was going to be asked to comment on the significance of the crowning; at home that weekend, I read Bagehot's essay on monarchy, and made notes on the role of religion and the history behind each ceremonial act in the crowning. Big Tom's multi-paged battle plan, circulated on the Monday, described other intents. Photo-captions: H. Evans.

I was deflated. It was actually an important job on a coronation edition filled with pictures, but I had already begun to wonder if Michael Hides had been right in our Ashton-under-Lyne days that reading Hobbes and Keynes was all very well, but irrelevant to getting on in newspapers. There was a common feeling, too, that the painstaking act of subbing to save words ruined the fluency for writing. 'Show me a good sub and I will show you a dead writer,' was Bob Ashton's jaunty challenge, not so much directed at me as at the subs who kept threatening to write novels. On the day there was a surprise cut in the Bank Rate, everybody had an opinion about what it meant for the average man in Manchester. I sulked that nobody asked me. When I finally volunteered a paragraph I'd written, it was brushed aside as too late, too complex. Doubtless it was both those things. Another day, I fretted at the London political correspondent's analysis of the annual economic survey. I thought we could do better and said so. A diary entry records the fall-out: 'It was a mistake to speak of Bank Rate, etc. to colleagues. They will only think of me now as a know-all.' When I was given the splash that the new Tory government was going to break the BBC monopoly by permitting commercial television, Bill Lloyd ribbed my pretensions, calling out: 'What's Aristotle got to do with it?'

The frustrations came to a head when my newspaper – which is how I thought of it – joined the chorus endorsing the death sentence for an illiterate youth for a murder he did not commit. Sydney Silverman, the tiny leftist Labour member of Parliament, a passionate abolitionist, was leading the protests; my old Brookdale school chum, Alf Morris, newly elected for Wythenshawe, Manchester, was his teller. 'Silverman is only doing this for personal publicity,' declared Big Tom out loud on his quick way through the subs' room.

He was not inviting a discussion; he was venting. The sub opposite me protested by repeatedly jabbing his cigarette stub in the ashtray. I shared his feeling.

Derek Bentley, the condemned youth in the cell, was a weak-willed nineteen-year-old who had suffered a head injury from V1 rocket debris, and was judged to have a mental age of eleven. His pal Christopher Craig was sixteen, but he was brighter – and he carried a gun the night the pair tried to burgle a warehouse. Four policemen cornered them on the roof. One policeman caught Bentley. He made no attempt to escape, though the policeman had been shot in the shoulder by Craig who, still free, kept firing and shot Constable Miles dead. Craig was undoubtedly guilty of murder, but he was spared the death sentence on account of his age. Lord Chief Justice Goddard – 'the hanging judge' to his critics – ignored the jury's recommendation of mercy for Bentley. Parliament was not allowed to debate whether Bentley deserved to hang until he had been. Silverman urged the Home Secretary, Sir David Maxwell Fyfe, to make a recommendation of mercy to the Queen. Silverman had the support of 200 MPs, but the Home Secretary turned them down.

Though my Mum and Dad were not opposed to capital punishment, as I was, they just could not understand why Bentley should be the one to die. I was empowered to go to the public phone booth at the end of the street and dictate a family telegram to the Home Secretary. I followed up with a letter in the *Guardian*, which did not meet with universal approval around the subs' table. 'Why do you think you know better than the people in authority?' asked Jimmy Entwistle, one of the most capable and charming men on the newspaper. Bentley went to the gallows on 28 January 1953. Forty-five years later, three Court of Appeal judges quashed the conviction on the grounds of misdirections to the jury by the 'intemperate' and 'blatantly prejudiced' Goddard. Lord Chief Justice Thomas Bingham said Bentley had been denied 'that fair trial that is the birthright of every British citizen'. Craig, sixty-two and long out of jail, having served ten years, said: 'I am truly sorry that my actions on 2 November 1952 caused so much pain and misery for the family of PC Miles, who died that night doing his duty. A day does not go by when I don't think about Derek and now his innocence has been proved with this judgement.'

Six months after my family telegram of protest, my diary tells me I abandoned my scruples about the death penalty. 'John Reginald Halliday Christie,' I wrote, 'forfeited the right to be treated as a human being. Seven murders and an innocent man executed!' The innocent man was Timothy Evans [no relation], who a decade later was to haunt my first editorship.

Fortunately for everyone's peace of mind on the paper, I found an outlet for the didactic impulses I never knew I had: I volunteered to be an evening tutor on politics and economics for the Workers' Educational Association, founded in 1903 to help adults who had missed out on education. Twice a week that October, after the day's subbing, I took bus rides into Tyldesley, near Bolton in Greater Manchester, crossing a darkened playground to a schoolhouse where a gallant group sat at children's desks: retired coal miners, clerks, a watchman, a sprinkling of housewives and a couple of shopkeepers. There were never more than sixteen of them; I had an idea that the room would soon be packed when word got around that I was lighting the sky. It didn't happen. Two dropped out in the second week and another in the third week. If this went on, I'd have no class.

The survivors were embarrassed by the defections. They were so nice, trying to put me at my ease, but I'd missed a trick. I'd not engaged them. They'd lived much of the interwar political and economic history I proposed to teach. They'd seen the thuggish behaviour of the blackshirts of Oswald Mosley, the incitements in the Jewish area of Cheetham Hill. Mosley was a Manchester man; one of the main thoroughfares was Mosley Street. He'd had his second wedding in Goebbels' house in Berlin and Hitler had been the best man. So I made the evenings more of a discussion than a lecture. It took more preparation, not less, to plot a kind of sub-Socratic question-and-answer dialogue that led somewhere, but the classes got livelier. Short-changed by the educational system, just like my father, the group was touchingly eager to explore – but not uncritical. One of the housewives and a storekeeper, in alliance, were not convinced (nor was Mrs Thatcher years later!) that in the Great

Depression they'd lived through, the government should have increased spending instead of sticking to balanced budgets: they had to stay in the black in their household accounts, why shouldn't government? They attended the twice-weekly classes in all weathers – one dropout even came back – and they all signed up, with newcomers, too, for a second year. At the end of the course, they took up a collection to buy me a going-away present of an Oxford English Dictionary that I cherish fifty years later.

In truth, I was in their debt. Face to face, I'd been made to appreciate what schoolteachers learn painfully, but journalists behind a shield of print rarely do: that transmitting information is easier than creating understanding. For me, it was a step towards grasping the art of popular explanatory journalism.

I was not able to teach a third year. Big Tom had a better idea.

9

'WHY AREN'T THEIR WOMEN WEARING OUR FROCKS?'

Late on Friday, 18 December 1953, just as I was putting the lid on the messy gluepot to head home, the editor's secretary dropped an envelope on my desk. I'd seen Big Tom stride out of the office in his cashmere overcoat, cigar between his teeth, and a copy boy trailing behind with an armful of books. I sliced open the envelope. The letter was headed Private and Confidential, underscored in red.

It was good news. 'My dear Evans,' the three-page letter began, 'I feel quite sure in my own mind that you are qualified to have a shot at the job of Evening News Leader Writer, and I want you to take up duties for a trial period of three months. In the first place your salary will be increased to £14.10.0 per week plus Cost of Living bonus.'

My paranoid instinct fastened on the phrase 'in my own mind'. Did it imply everyone else thought he was off his head? But he went on: 'I will now develop one or two matters arising from this appointment.'

I'll say.

He acknowledged there would be 'a great deal of political and economic reading' – no more novels at the weekend, only *The Economist*, *Hansard Parliamentary Debates* and Chatham House Reports. I was also to get out of the office and interview Labour,

Conservative and Liberal organizers, MPs in their constituency clinics, councillors, and anyone who might lead me to a story. 'Do not forget the political leaders outside Manchester, say in Altrincham, Knutsford, and other divisions. Never let up on them. Follow and probe indefatigably; keep stories flowing and watch for good tips for Mr Manchester's Diary. I think this could be very rewarding and I am keen to have it done thoroughly. The test is how many stories and how many tips you can produce. Let me see them all.'

He hadn't finished: 'Afternoons at 2.30 p.m. (except Friday), I want you to go into the subs' room and lead the parliamentary subbing team.' What this meant was that I could select who would stand with me to protect the sanity of Mancunians from the tsunami of verbiage. I selected Bow Tie. He was fast and genial, and not someone who would blow cigarette smoke in my face. I was even authorized to become a Nifty in training, giving work to other subs if we could not cope.

To be acknowledged as a top-table sub would have been promotion enough, but writing the editorials was the big deal. They had struck me as sensible and lucid for the most part, and the phlegmatic man who had been writing them, Sidney Cursley, certainly fitted the role. He would emerge from his inner sanctum next to the editor, and stand stock-still sucking on his briar pipe, incubating great thoughts as he looked on our bowed heads. Happily for me, he was sailing to New York to become the UK chief information officer responsible for explaining to Americans what the British were up to.

I was thrilled to accept the trial, but with the Bentley hanging still in my mind I fretted about what I would do when asked to write against my conscience. This was a preposterous exercise in self-regard. The editorial column was not my prerogative. I was there to express the viewpoint of the paper for which the editor was responsible, and if faced with an impossible demand I could take my conscience with me back to the subs' room.

There were, moreover, new perplexities to humble my pretensions. Britain was in transition from a Labour government headed by Clement Attlee to a Conservative government headed by Winston Churchill. Attlee's ministry had nationalized major industries, established the welfare state – of which the jewel was Aneurin Bevan's National Health Service – and emphasized the planned collectivist economy. Collectivism and planning were incendiary words to Churchill. He announced that 'at the head of our mainmast we, like the United States, fly the flag of free enterprise.' How should the two philosophies be reconciled? And while Attlee's government had begun shedding the Empire that Churchill loved, giving India independence in 1947 over his vehement objections, it had not pulled up the drawbridge. It had vigorously fought an insurgency in Malaya (where Britain had rubber and tin interests). It had committed itself to NATO, and the development of an independent nuclear deterrent. Churchill, an unashamed imperialist, was even more determined to maintain Britain as a big power. But could Britain afford the military means to protect her overseas interests, especially in the Middle East, maintain the welfare state and meet the rising expectations of the trade unions? The Second World War had cost Britain a quarter of its wealth. Fully 10 per cent of the gross national product was spent on defence during the Korean War, just ended. The pound sterling was vulnerable.

How could they expect a boy from Failsworth to solve all this, even with his precious degree?

On the Monday, wearing a bow tie as Big Tom did, I walked through the subs' room into the office of the Assistant Editor I'd met briefly on turning up in Cross Street, Bill Pepper, the meditative consigliere to Tom's brusque Corleone. I was given a small desk there, looking out on the newsprint trucks.

At 8.30 a.m. I was alone at the typewriter Cursley had abandoned for Manhattan. At 8.31 a.m. Big Tom's frame filled the doorway. 'First leader, the Queen of Tonga, second the Canberra jet-bomber.' Then he was gone. Over the weekend, I'd read myself ragged on all the economic and political news. In these preparations, Queen Salote, the South Sea Islands, and indeed the whole southern hemisphere, had not figured at all. I was abandoned on a coral reef without a clue how to get off.

I sent for the clips, and then remembered the caption I'd written on our Coronation special in June when Queen Salote had enchanted the crowds by sitting in the rain in her open carriage. Now the young

Queen Elizabeth and the Duke of Edinburgh were her guests in
Tonga, and luckily it was raining in paradise, too, so I was able to
say how pleasing it was that the Queen of the world's largest kingdom and the Queen of the smallest shared an umbrella – and they
shared certain ideals, etc. (My first editorial was not the place to
recycle Noel Coward's wicked response when asked who was the
little man sitting with Queen Salote in the London celebration. He
replied: 'Her lunch.')

The new Canberra jet-bomber was easy. Flying London to
Capetown in record time, it had beaten every major long-distance
world record, but the chief engineer of British European Airways, a
Mr Shenstone, had chosen that moment to condemn the quality of
the work on British aircraft, and vaguely at that. We took him to
task for this damaging generalization. (Note the editorial 'we'. And
as a former RAF corporal hiding behind the royal 'we', I'm relieved
all these years later that 'our' vigorous defence of the Canberra was
vindicated by its versatile life of fifty-five years. Not until 31 July
2006 did it go out of service.)

I could never guess what bee buzzing in Big Tom's head would fly
out to sting. Every morning at the paper was a lottery. The space was
usually half a column, but he would sometimes ask for double the
normal length for a major foreign affairs subject – our role in
Europe, say, or what we had to do in the Middle East to make
friends with Arab nationalism without sacrificing Israel. It served me
right, having felt frustrated in expressing the occasional opinion on
something I knew about, that I should now be called upon to express
an opinion on *everything*. There was no Google or Ask.com, no
Aladdin's lamp I could rub to bring me facts from the vasty deep of
cyberspace. I was reliant instead on the snip-snip of the library girls'
press clippings, and the prayer that whatever reading I had been able
to do was pertinent to the editor's impulses. Should we arm
Germany? Should the Church of England remarry divorced people?
How much of a menace was Egypt's Colonel Neguib? Was the government right to impose a fourteen-day ban on television discussing
anything down for debate in Parliament? What should be in the
Chancellor's upcoming Budget? Did women over thirty-two become

unattractive, querulous and antisocial, as an American airline maintained in rejecting them as 'air hostesses'? Guerrilla strikes! Income tax! Delays in court! The Common Market! Nationalization! Cricket manners! Algeria! Cotton exports! The slums! Neighbourliness! Joe McCarthy! Food prices! Immigration! I became a rag and bone man of the opinion trade.

Big Tom himself edited the copy on all these efforts. He did not fiddle with the wording, apart from a startling 'For why?' he wrote into sentences of mine that he thought needed more pep. I'd spend the first fifteen minutes of the precious writing time throwing crunched-up balls of paper in the waste basket. If the editorial was a tiny bit long for the space, most often because an advertisement had invaded the space, he'd invariably just lop off my precious first paragraph. He didn't say anything, but I got the message: No throat clearing.

Working closely with Tom, I gradually came to know a more sensitive – and prudent – man than the fairground barker I'd seen from the subs' table. At the end of a day scuffling with news he would go home to his violin and wrestle with Bach. In circumstances he never explained, he had played with the Berlin Philharmonic after the Second World War. The evening he was due to collect an award at a city banquet, having been named Mancunian of the Year, he came into the office with a heavy suitcase. 'All the family silver,' he said, index finger tapping nose. With a touch of pride, he explained: 'Burglars read our paper, too, you know.' He had an uncanny instinct for news. In 1945, by elaborate preparation and shrewd interpretation of a stray message from Rheims, this same Tom Henry secured a world scoop and had his prepared 'WAR IS OVER' edition on the streets well ahead of the official announcement, every other newspaper and the BBC.

Big Tom bristled with certainties, but the secret of his success was the way he identified with his diverse Manchester readers, though he was born in the East Midlands and had an Irish background. The sacred hour in his day was when his secretary carried in the day's 'Postbag', letters to the editor. He fell on them, licking his lips, read every one, then gave over huge amounts of space in the next day's

paper to these missives. He enabled citizen journalism long before
the blogging era. Later one of my jobs was to edit the letters for publication. On many papers this was regarded as the ultimate ignominy
for a sub. Not on the *Manchester Evening News*. Indeed, the editors
whom I later heard boast that they didn't ever bother to look at
readers' letters invariably ran second-rate papers.

Big Tom's attachment to Manchester, its needs and its achievements no doubt came with the job like his black Jaguar Mark VII –
but it was heartfelt and justified. He was the reason for the soaring
success of the paper, reaching peaks of circulation and influence no
provincial evening newspaper is likely ever again to reach. The profits generated under his leadership, nurturing a near-monopoly of job
and house classified advertising, kept the *Manchester Guardian* alive
when it edged into loss in 1961, and plunged ever deeper thereafter
to the brink of shutting down for good in 1966. Some of my friends
on the *News* in the 1950s felt that the *Guardian* staff patronized
them as being from a lower universe. I didn't sense that, but stories
of *Guardian* eccentrics had a ready currency. 'One of their leader
writers came up in the lift with me carrying six umbrellas – on a dry
day. Can you believe it?' said Bow Tie. It was later alleged that the
Guardian editor, lacking the editorial from the leader writer, had sent
a messenger along to retrieve it and found he had passed out, his
head resting on the typewriter on which the only written word was
'Notwithstanding'.

Big Tom was on the board of directors of the *Manchester
Guardian* but rather relished his different point of view on
Manchester, most notably over the city's plan to build new towns in
the green belt of the Cheshire plain which the *Guardian* supported
and we didn't. The *Guardian*'s housing specialist was outraged by
Tom's conviction that the city was chasing moonbeams in applying
for compulsory purchase orders to build two little Manchesters in
Mobberley and Lymm. It took eight years for the government to say
No. In the meantime, Manchester had 20,000 homeless and 68,000
houses unfit for habitation. We argued that given the land famine –
sites available for only a tenth of the housing needed – we should
immediately build upwards, not outwards. We envisaged six-storey

housing in attractive landscaping, emphasizing that they must not be designed as soulless barrack blocks. I had my doubts whether the city had the imagination to achieve that, but it was a better bet than waiting for unfit homes to collapse: they were falling down at the rate of two a day.

The slums were a legacy of Manchester's leadership of the industrial revolution. Benjamin Disraeli, prime minister and novelist, had said in 1844, in his novel *Coningsby*, 'What art was to the ancient world, Science is to the modern. Rightly understood, Manchester is as great a human exploit as Athens.' It was true. The invention of the world's textile industry in and around Cottonopolis was only part of it. Whitworth, Fairbairn, Nasmyth, A. V. Roe and Royce developed revolutionary discoveries in engineering; Ferranti in electronics; John Dalton in chemistry. The first pilots to fly the Atlantic Ocean non-stop were two former Manchester Central High School students, J. W. Alcock and A. W. Brown. It was at Manchester University that Ernest Rutherford knowingly split the nucleus of the atom, Hans Geiger invented his Geiger counter, and William Jevons devised his 'Logic Piano', the proto-computer that was the first machine which enabled a problem to be solved faster with the machine rather than without.

We paid a price for industrial pioneering. Too often we lived the opening page of *Bleak House*: fog everywhere. No, it was worse. This was not grey fog rolling down the river, misty clouds creeping in from marshes. This was black fog hanging over us day after day, still and suffocating. We went to bed breathing fog and we got up breathing fog and we worked breathing fog. People coughed themselves to death; the black spots spoiling the washing hanging to dry in backyards were the stuff being breathed into lungs.

We called it smog – fog enveloped by coal smoke from a million chimney pots like ours at home, from thousands of factories and coal-fired steam trains. On clear days, just from our house in Hale Lane, Failsworth, adjacent to the rail line, we could count scores of belchers, tall redbrick cotton mill chimneys. It was a double nightmare for Dad; hundreds of passenger lives were dependent on him seeing the signals. The smog was so dense that in January you could not see them; in fact you could not see a yard ahead. It was not unknown for men walking home from work to fall in canals and drown. The only warning you were about to collide with some other struggler was the cough, mysteriously disembodied.

London newspapers had chosen to call their five days of fog in December 1952 'Pea Soupers'. In the subs' room we had favoured *Darkness at Noon* banners until Nifty said: 'Enough literary allusion, stick to the facts.' (We had our own smog-makers. While I was at the paper, I was about the only non-smoker.) Everyone seemed to accept the smog as an Act of God. I'd recognized the fatalism of the working-class communities. 'Where there's muck, there's money, Harold,' wheezed a bronchitic neighbour. But it was the same among my more or less middle-class colleagues – 'Price of progress.' Perhaps I'd been reading too much Dickens. I didn't just want to record the smog. I wanted to get rid of it. It pained me to hear Dad coughing all night in the next bedroom on the occasions he came down with bronchitis. One morning, before Big Tom could issue his command, I ventured to suggest I press for control of both industrial and domestic smoke. 'Go to it,' he said.

Manchester City Council had some years before decreed that in the heart of the city nobody could burn coal, only specially treated smokeless briquettes. This had created one of the first smokeless zones in the country and we had applauded it, but the order was still confined to the limited area around the Town Hall, leaving most of the city as smoky as ever. National measures lagged, had done for decades, until the 'great smog' in London in December led to the premature deaths of at least 4,000 people. Why did it take deaths in the capital city to spur action when people in the North had been suffering for years? Three years after London's smog, a national Clean Air Bill was making its way through Parliament, ostensibly banning the burning of coal in domestic chimneys, but it had lots of loopholes, exemptions and long delays before enforcement. It had too few teeth, and Tom let me say so, time and again.

For this campaigning, we got bitten on the ankle by *The*

Economist – until that moment more or less my bible. We did not understand what we were talking about, they pronounced. Mustn't rush things, you know, think of industry. I got steamed up imagining them in their ventilated London offices. Of course, London had had its smog, but day in and day out the workers of the industrial North breathed the most polluted air in the world. They were five times more liable to die of bronchitis than people in country areas. Since the founding doctrine of *The Economist* in 1843, laissez-faire economics and free trade, had been borrowed in the early nineteenth century from our own 'Manchester School', I felt entitled to correct their interpretation. You couldn't go to a concert at the splendid Free Trade Hall without thinking of how, from a temporary wooden hut here in Peter Street, just over a hundred years ago Richard Cobden and John Bright had stirred the whole country to win the repeal of the Corn Laws, taxes on food imports which fattened the farmers at the expense of the millworkers. Cobden and Bright fought for cheap food for the workers, not for poisoning them.

Looking back, it is shocking that the clean air advocates had to face so much resistance. In the end we got significant improvements in the Clean Air Act passed in 1956. An empirical investigation into the effects of the Act published in 1994 concluded it markedly improved the quality of the air: average urban concentrations of smoke down by 80 per cent, and sulphates down by 70 per cent since 1960. So we won that battle in the end, but the war goes on into the age of global warming where new interests put up a familiar resistance.

Even before we were criticized for the campaign for clean air, I already shared a primitively biased North v. South complex: we all thought Southerners, apart from Cockneys, were 'stuck up' folk who wore stiff white collars and never got their hands dirty with real work. They were 'Them', not 'Us'. They were 'the beastly bourgeois' of D. H. Lawrence's savage little poem. It was a silly prejudice, but the condescension of *The Economist* and the torpor of the Tory ministers responsible stirred embers of resentment fired by my reading histories of social reform.

St Peter's Square, in the centre of Manchester, where I frequented its grand circular library, stirred my over-active imagination. Back in the nineteenth century, all the industrial cities – Manchester, Birmingham, Liverpool, Leeds – were denied representation in Parliament. On the hot summer's day of 16 August 1819, middle-class families and workpeople in their Sunday best assembled in St Peter's Square to hear speeches calling for universal suffrage (for men). The people were peaceful, and the speakers did not incite violence, but the crowd was so big – 50,000 crammed the square – that the magistrates panicked. They ordered the arrest of the platform; several hundred ill-trained amateur cavalrymen of the Yeomanry rode into the crowd, slashing their sabres. Eleven citizens were killed, eight died later and more than 650 were wounded, a quarter of them women. When Richard Carlile published a first-hand account in his newspaper, *Sherwin's Political Register*, his complete stock of newspapers and pamphlets was seized and he was thrown in jail. So was James Wroe, who documented the attack in his *Manchester Observer* and gave it the name 'the Peterloo Massacre'. Years later in editing I took inspiration from the greatest editor of *The Times*, Thomas Barnes, who defied the authorities and published an account of the massacre by his reporter John Tyas who'd been arrested and jailed just for being there taking notes.

For all its heroic history in political and industrial innovation, for all the renown of its Hallé orchestra, and its Gaiety Theatre where British repertory was born, its great university, its art galleries and its standing as Newspaper City, Manchester was neglectful of its heritage. After my years in proud Durham City, I was dismayed that the brass chamber in which Rutherford first split the nucleus of the atom ended up in the Cavendish Laboratory in Cambridge; that William Jevons's logic machine, made in Manchester at Ferranti, went to Oxford. I'd grown up in the city, I'd seen it come through the bombings, and I felt it should make more of itself. Perversely, the German bombing had given us a chance to create something special, but typically the great centre of Piccadilly Gardens remained nothing but a big ugly traffic roundabout.

One day, dodging cars in St Ann's Square, which was quite near the office, I had an idea. What a jewel it would be if the geographical heart of the city wasn't so lacerated by traffic, so noisy, so defaced by ugly street clutter! My thought was to return the spacious square to its Georgian tranquillity – a pedestrian area like St Mark's in Venice. There was a splendid focal point at the King Street end in the towered neoclassical St Ann's Church, a Grade I building in pink sandstone, probably built by a pupil of Christopher Wren in 1712. There was J. E. Gregan's graceful corner palazzo (Grade II), with its arches and Venetian windows; and the terraces of Edwardian and Victorian buildings were well mannered and genially grouped. There were fashionable shops and a bronze statue of Richard Cobden. But one could almost see Cobden shrinking from the racket of heavy trucks, buses and cars, holding his nose from the exhaust fumes; the Boer War soldiers featured in another statue seemed on the point of surrender.

Back at the office, I sought out Bert Hackett. He was a pale young man in the art department who had difficulty in swallowing, the residue of some accident. He was confined to drawing maps and little sketches, but I was to discover he had an unexploited imagination for larger tasks. Presented with my vague idea he swiftly completed a fine sketch of how St Ann's Square would look without traffic, with silver birch trees, fountains and ornamental pool and pavement cafés, where Mancunians could pause to admire the view and gossip. I presented it to Big Tom. I told him there was a rear service road where shops could be supplied, and, hand on heart, that there would be as many days in Manchester when people could sit outside as there were in Northern France.

Tom was so enthusiastic for Manchester that he'd long ago decided it *never* rained, just as Manchester United never lost a match. He embraced the new St Ann's Square as an *Evening News* campaign, giving it a page in the paper headlined 'This Could be Manchester. Picture a Peaceful Plaza in the Sun'.

I called on the Civic Trust in London, a voluntary partnership to help regenerate decaying urban areas. The deputy director, a town planner, came north and enthused. Laurence Scott, the chairman of the *Guardian*, and Bill Mather, head of the great engineering firm of Mather and Platt, rallied round, and so did St Ann's Canon Eric Saxon. We called a public meeting in the Town Hall of city officials, property owners and businessmen. The buzz was good. I had high hopes when the chairman of the city's planning committee reported that the city surveyor found it 'an attractive scheme'. Then he added: 'But the surveyor thinks it should wait until the ring road is finished.' Bill Mather argued that the world's biggest industrial area of Greater Manchester should have such a showpiece without delay. The objections were fewer than I expected; most of the traders said they would happily cope, but a Mr R. R. Stoker argued that to deprive people of a place to park their cars threatened life, liberty and the pursuit of happiness. Instead of a plaza, he advocated 'flower baskets, trees with coloured lights and taxis painted pink and green'.

St Ann's is now a pedestrian square. My idea was not exactly an overnight success. It took twenty years. But more came out of the initiative. With Scott and Mather doing the heavy financial lifting, we formed a Civic Trust for the North-West to work for a cleaner, more agreeable city. I went around with a photographer identifying areas of remediable squalor. My old stamping ground of Ashton-under-Lyne reversed the slogan that 'What Manchester does today, the rest of the world does tomorrow.' Two months after the St Ann's meeting, Ashton adopted an attractive design for the Market Square where I had sheltered from the rain opposite the *Reporter* office. With guidance from the Civic Trust, the borough adopted a plan to turn the area into a traffic-free shopping and social centre – and to do it that year.

Long before anyone had heard the phrase 'green revolution', the initiatives of the Civic Trust caught on. Within a few years, citizens in no fewer than 300 places gave their time and money to conserving what was beautiful and pitching out the unsightly. The cause united Rottingdean with Wigan, craggy folk with snow on their boots in Inveresk with villagers on the Downs, burghers of Bristol with potters of Burslem, men and women in Godalming with Glasgow. In Stepney a group turned blitzed sites into gardens. In Lincolnshire and Staffordshire volunteers cleared away from the countryside the debris of pillboxes, Nissen huts and concrete left over ten years by the biggest litter louts of all – the Air Ministry and War Office.

I was proud to have played a part in all this. When Enid and I moved from our flat in Altrincham to a house in the village of Disley on the edge of the wildly beautiful High Peak national park, we formed a society to lead volunteers in the weekend clearing of woods and fields and ghastly waterholes filled with three-piece suites, mattresses, broken television sets, prams and other throwaways of civilization.

I was on the opinion treadmill for nearly three years, then (after an interlude I will describe in the next chapter) Big Tom promoted me to feature writing. One day he lingered in my office for a record five minutes. 'Where did you get the shirt you're wearing?' he asked to my surprise.

'Lewis's. My mother . . .'

'Why don't the Swedes wear shirts like that?'

'No taste?'

'And why aren't their women wearing our frocks from Manchester?'

'Look what's happening, my boy,' Big Tom went on with indignation mounting. 'Lancashire cotton exports way down, mills closed. I want you to go to the Continent and find out why. Leave right away.'

'Of course,' I replied, praying my passport was in order. Those were the days when going to 'the Continent', as we called Europe, was a vast mystery; beyond a day trip by ferry from Ramsgate to Boulogne as a schoolboy, I'd only been out of the country once.

Tom hadn't finished. 'And what about the Norwegians, eh? Whose pyjamas do they wear? They could be wearing German pyjamas! Think of it, the Germans!'

He seemed ready to fight World War Three over pyjamas, but exploring the bedroom attire of the Vikings struck me as chancy. 'You want me to go to Norway as well as Sweden?' I ventured. 'Yes, yes, Oslo. And while you're about it, swing down through Denmark, and come back through Germany and Holland.'

By night trains and planes, I was soon deposited in snow-etched Oslo. I called on various offices, starting with the Handelskammer, the city's chamber of commerce. Everyone seemed to speak English, which was fortunate since the phrase books didn't have anything like

'I am an Englishman from Manchester. Kindly help us understand why you don't wear our shirts.'

The officials I spoke with were very helpful in explaining import and export rules and custom duties, but had no more idea than I had myself why Lancashire cottons were no longer as popular as they used to be. On my bewildered first night, I nursed a beer at a table looking out on the Volkswagens scudding round the city square. Where on earth was I to begin the next day? This was my first big overseas assignment. All I had now were the names of a few import agents, none in Oslo. A talkative old Norwegian materialized, putting his beer down next to mine and gesturing to the VW going by, remarked, 'See we buy from our enemies and not from Britain, our old friend,' he mused. He became uneasy and moved away when I asked him if he would mind turning back the collar of his shirt to see where it was made.

The waitress was more obliging; I asked her where she bought her clothes, tablecloths and curtains. Next morning, I trudged through the snow to the department store she mentioned. It was advertising a clearance sale. I found a rack of poplin raincoats at the bargain price of £2. 2s. shillings (around £25 today). I checked the label – a Manchester manufacturer. I tried it on. 'Anything wrong with this?' I asked a salesman. 'Nothing wrong. It's good quality and it looks good on you.' Flattered, I bought the coat, but asked why they were selling our poplin raincoats for so little. 'The English style never changes,' he explained. 'It's out of date.'

I went to another store and watched various women choose curtain material. It was all German, French, Swiss, Italian, Norwegian – except for two languishing pieces from Lancashire with designs as cheerful as cold porridge: on one a network of the old familiar pallid rosebuds, on another what looked like a sickly green bird in a turquoise ocean. An import wholesaler explained the popularity of German pyjamas. 'Your people offer me five colours, the Germans fifty. And on piece goods you fob us off with gaudy leftovers from the colonial trade. You're stuck in the Victorian era.'

The refrain became depressingly familiar from agents and store buyers throughout Norway, Sweden and Denmark: design and service were more important than price. The décor in the homes of Scandinavians I was invited to was so different from the oak sideboards, floral curtains and stuffed sofas of the pre-Conran and Habitat English homes. My hosts' style of richer woods, ornamental glassware, trailing plants, angled spotlights, demanded fabrics as striking. At twenty-eight, I was feeling out of date myself.

It was when I stopped off in Malmö, Sweden, that I solved the mystery of the unsold Cottonopolis shirts that had sent me on the journey in the first place. A kindly and effusively pro-British director of two leading men's stores told me how for years he'd asked a quality British shirt company to pack its merchandise more attractively. He'd been told it wasn't necessary. 'Just recently,' he told me, 'the Swiss have come in with shirts in an attractive transparent wrapping, folded with a broad front. Just look at them.' Seen side by side, I had to admit, I would have bought the Swiss even though it was a little more expensive. 'See,' said my new friend, 'that's why I have 200 English shirts I can't sell. Take one, take two. Help yourself.'

In Düsseldorf, soon rebuilt after the RAF devastations, I scoured one huge department store after another and discovered something extraordinary: not a stitch of Lancashire cloth anywhere. And I noticed something just as odd: the same German fabrics I'd seen in Copenhagen were more costly here in the home market – and that despite the Danish tariff. The plump export manager of a large German textile company invited me to dinner because his wife, a dazzling beauty, was grateful for being treated kindly by British troops at the end of the war. He sketched a confusing system of high German tariffs and turnover tax relief that basically enabled the German manufacturers to charge high prices in their protected market while sending below-cost fabrics abroad. 'Dumping,' I called it in the third article I wrote.

By this time, two of the three Cotton in Crisis articles had been published under the rubric 'How Not to Sell Cotton'. Big Tom was pleased; the cotton kings were not. But a few months later the President of the Board of Trade intervened. He announced that his department and the Cotton Board would send a special commission in my footsteps to investigate all I had reported about design, selling and after-sales service, prices, and dumping, to be followed by a 'hell for leather drive to take Lancashire cotton out of the doldrums'. Big Tom made it a page one splash:

'COTTON AWAKES!'

Big Tom's next idea was to send me back to Germany to ask how lads from the Greater Manchester district in the Guards divisions of the British Army of the Rhine liked life over there. It looked like a boring assignment – until I stumbled on real news, rather as my father had done that morning he came across the Dunkirk survivors on Rhyl beach. I just happened to arrive at the barracks when the officers and grenadiers were boiling over about their obsolete weaponry. They were stuck with old-fashioned bolt-action Lee-Enfield Mark IV rifles while other NATO armies had the automatic self-loading FN; the far too heavy Vickers medium machine gun from the First and Second World Wars; radios that did not work; and the Sten, the emergency submachine gun that had been introduced to me in my RAF training as having killed as many of our soldiers as the enemy because of a defective safety catch. A tank commander said his radio equipment for keeping track of his squadron was nothing like as good as the Germans' in the Second World War, who'd been able to keep in speaking contact at night over a distance of fifteen miles. 'On one recent night manoeuvre I had to sit on top of a haystack to speak to artillery 100 yards away. Amazing we won the war, you know. God knows how we'd cope with the Red Army.'

The stir created in Lancashire by the cotton articles was nothing to the outcry about the Army report. It was cited in a full-scale debate in the Commons and the Lords and the Minister promised swift action, as he put it 'a concentrated phase of renovation and re-equipment such as has never been seen before'.

Subsequently, Tom piled on the assignments. Go into the baleful and bleak Communist zone of East Berlin (I did: when I pointed my camera at a Red Guard he summoned me over because he wanted to pose properly); examine the case for equal pay for women; go and check on whether the new West German Army is something to be scared of; see what's cooking at our major science research institution, the National Physical Laboratory (the birth-place of radar and much else was starved of resources); examine technical education; explain atomic energy and look at solar power ... I was split three ways: foreign correspondent, science correspondent, northern political correspondent. They were all rewarding assignments. In West Berlin, it was joyful to call on my liberated prisoner, Walter Greis, back at work in a bank and happy with his wife Alice in their new apartment. I had only one com-plaint: could they please explain the strange customs in their bathhouses? On the first night, exhausted by the difficult journey, I had gone into a public facility for a massage, wearing a swim suit and over it a fur and leather astrakhan coat I'd invested in for the Scandinavian travels, intending to use it as a blanket for a little sleep afterwards. Inside the bathhouse, the Berliners stared and laughed at me. I was the only one dressed, they were all naked, men and women. I re-entered fearlessly, bravely unclad: even the Royal Air Force unarmed combat course hadn't prepared me for this. The massage was so good, I went back the next night for a swim, disrobed and walked in. Cries rang out on every side. Everyone was wearing bathing suits or dressing gowns. Walter explained my German would have to cope with tricky little notices the bathhouses changed every night. The first night I'd missed a sign *Entkleiden Sie sich bitte vor Eingehen* (please undress before entering), and the second night *Badeanzuge erforderlich vor dem Zugang heute Abend* (bathing suits required before entry tonight).

The job of northern political correspondent gave me a front seat at the seaside spectaculars at Blackpool where the Labour party dele-gates – political leaders, humble constituency workers, and trade union rank and file – wrestled for the party's soul in the annual party conference. The Labour government had just been turfed out by the Conservative party and the vociferous Marxist Left claimed this was because voters had been so bamboozled by the press they'd failed to understand the issues. This was akin, said the party leader Hugh Gaitskell, quoting Oscar Wilde, to saying that the play was a success but the audience was a failure. I admired the way Gaitskell stood up to the catcalls of abuse he got for defending the wisdom of the voters and the virtues of the Atlantic alliance and a mixed economy. I thought he represented Labour's best hope (though it took four decades for Tony Blair to convince the party), but for me the revelation at Blackpool came from Gaitskell's leading critic within the party, Aneurin Bevan.

I saw for the first time how conviction can be suborned by a particular kind of eloquence. The resonant generalities and voices of, say, Winston Churchill and Barack Obama inspire, but that is different from the gifted debater's ability to take an opponent's case apart piece by piece and substitute a glittering alternative. I'd known Bevan could do this from reading his dazzling attacks on the Suez intervention: 'Sir Anthony Eden has been pretending that he is now invading Egypt in order to strengthen the United Nations. Every burglar of course could say the same thing, he could argue that he was entering the house in order to train the police.' But to see and hear Bevan in full flow was a singular experience. Nobody in party or press ever risked missing a minute of him. He'd take the expectant crowd through the labyrinth of a policy argument with wit and passion, his index finger quivering in admonition, his silver forelock flopping, his lilting Welsh cadences beautifully calculated between mocking vituperation, intellectual analysis and beseechment, his face flushed (I learned he always took a very hot bath before he spoke).

Big Tom was relentless. Now he suggested that I combine political and Parliamentary reporting with organizing our book reviews, cover activities at Manchester University, and, as an afterthought, he dropped me a note: 'I am told you are keen on table tennis. I'd like you to cover the sport for us.'

Will that be all, sir? 'No, now you ask,' said Big Tom. 'I want you to write a column. Every Thursday. Make it snappy. It will pay a guinea.' (A guinea always sounded grander than the one pound one shilling it represented.) He told the features department that this new assignment should be presented as 'The Column of a Manchester Man who Speaks his Mind' and headed with my name in bold type. In the guise of modesty, I told him I preferred to write under the pen name of Mark Antony (ambition is made of sterner stuff). He agreed but told the features editor to have a sketch of me at the top of the column, and artist Bert Hackett drew a tight-lipped, jaw-jutting profile of someone with the kind of steel-rimmed glasses that went out of favour with Heinrich Himmler. But about the column that was supposed to follow the feature dressing, I was given not a clue. It surely had to be personal, but being personal cut across the grain of my training. I'd been schooled in the anonymity of neutral reporting, to eschew any personal note except in theatre and book reviews or features. 'Never,' said J. W. Middlehurst, 'let me see the word "I" in anything you write for the *Ashton-under-Lyne Reporter*.'

One found the new cloak hard to wear. My first column was passable, with three or four shorter items, but it was not personal and it could have been written by a man on the Clapham omnibus. I was rescued by the antic behaviour of the nationalized Electricity Board responsible for serving the whole of the North-West. During my lunch hour, I walked into their showroom in Manchester to buy an electric cooker they had in their window. It was an older model at a knock-down price; I was newly married with furniture bought on credit and we couldn't afford a new model. I paid and gave the salesman the address for delivery to our flat in Altrincham, a suburb of Manchester. He revoked the sale. In no circumstances would he deliver to Altrincham, he explained. It was in the rules. Not giving up, I went to the Altrincham showroom of the same Board. They didn't have a cheap model. Would they kindly order it from their colleagues in Manchester? 'Oh dear me, no. We're not on speaking terms with Manchester.' I went back to Electricity HQ. I said I'd buy it and arrange my own pick-up and delivery. 'We're a state enterprise,' said the salesman triumphantly. 'We can't deal with a private trucker.' They didn't thank me for my apology for thinking I was in Manchester, not Moscow.

Recalling the farce, I found a voice – and my grand alias Mark Antony found an audience. It led to a newlywed couple inviting Mark Antony to their brand-new home where they handed over a bag filled with tiny brown pellets. Crushed between thumb and finger, the pellets formed a sandy deposit on my desk. They were the remnants of defective mortar supposed to be holding the bricks of their house in place; it was already shifting on its foundations. It turned out to be just one example of a wave of jerry-building. Newspapers and the BBC followed up. Mark Antony would survive. Indeed, he was even invited to speak.

I was admittedly only one of a hundred eager Manchester newspaper writers auditioned for the role of broadcaster. After furious debates, the Conservative government had deemed that the BBC monopoly of television, paid for by the licence fees of viewers, should be challenged by a handful of independent companies in the regions who would finance their programmes on the 'dreadful' American model of carrying paid-for advertising. In the North, only just recently reached by the BBC's flickering blue signal, the commercial franchise was won by the irrepressible Sidney Bernstein, a smooth silver-haired talker of creative vitality, who looked like a cross between a Roman emperor and a beaten-up boxer. On his father's beginnings in cinema, Bernstein had built a huge chain of splendid cinemas inspired by what he'd seen in America in the 1920s. He sought the Northern franchise in preference to London, he said, because he preferred to get away from the London metropolitan atmosphere to a more distinctive closely knit culture. With his brother Cecil he set out to make his Granada Television synonymous with the North – he called it Granadaland. His soap *Coronation Street* introduced Northern life to the South, and became the longest-running drama on British television – still running fifty years after its launch.

Granada's flair for innovation left the BBC looking very much the aunty. Bernstein was clever to suborn two *Daily Express* staffers – its Northern editor Tim Hewat, creator of the investigative programme *World in Action* that was revolutionary for television, and Barrie Heads, its acerbically witty television critic. Heads became the first producer of the long-running newsreel show *All Our Yesterdays* (anchor Brian Inglis), *University Challenge* (anchor Bamber Gascoigne), and *Discovery*, featuring eminent scientists such as Bernard Lovell of Jodrell Bank and the Nobel prize winner Sir Edward Appleton, who'd used BBC radio to discover a dependable reflector of radio waves in the ionosphere thereafter known as the 'Appleton layer'. Denis Forman, who'd lost a leg in Second World War combat, became the presiding genius. He created the incomparable *Brideshead Revisited* and *Jewel in the Crown*. He had the impudent idea of Granada making a documentary about the BBC. I wrote the script but he came up with the entertaining notion of enlivening our production by popping in theme tunes from the more popular BBC shows. Wherever Forman's spark landed, fireworks blazed.

Granada didn't have a news operation, so it made a deal with the *Manchester Evening News* to cut and paste our stories and present them as its own Granada news bulletin. None of us yet knew anything about television, including the Granada executives who'd come from print, marketing and the Bernstein brothers' interests. I presumed their inexperience explained why when I'd said all of twenty words to the camera, they invited me to undertake one of their first outside broadcast interviews – in time I might take off from the *Manchester Evening News*. Later, the producer Barrie Heads (also fresh from newspapers) explained to me that I'd just been lucky. Sidney Bernstein had a list of characteristics of performers he loathed – anyone who was bald or bearded or had a foreign accent or wore a metal watch strap, suede shoes or a bow tie. In a hurry that morning I'd not bothered tying the bow tie I often wore, hence my selection. Barrie told me it was the ambition of several frustrated producers, hoping to end their careers on a high note, to find a middle-aged, bow-tied and bearded Bulgarian in sandals they could put under a lengthy cast-iron contract.

The laconic Barrie Heads was the supervising producer of my first interview with L. S. Lowry, the reclusive eccentric whose paintings capture the fortitude of the Manchester working class in the toils of the North's urban decay. Lowry was in his seventies when I went to see him in his remote moorland stone house at Mottram in Longdendale. His modest home – which had no telephone – was his studio, too, with paintings piled up. I was in awe of him. Not Barrie. As if directing a scene in a TV studio, he had the nerve to tell the great man that a finished painting of moorland hills and valleys lacked something – the familiar Lowry skeletons in drab suits perhaps. A few days later Lowry told Barrie he was quite right. 'It needed some folk in it. I've put in a picnic party.'

The show itself went surprisingly well for a first effort, mainly because the unassuming Lowry made it easy to ask questions. I did a couple more shows, with Big Tom's agreement, then someone had the bright idea that Granada would do a public service if it introduced travelling gypsies to a wider audience. A gypsy encampment was selected in a siding just below the busy East Lancashire Road linking Manchester and Liverpool. As a programme idea, it was hardly earth-shattering, but viewers then were known to switch on just to watch the signal for an idle hour.

The extrovert director assigned for the gypsy show, H. K. Lewenhak, was said to have come from making movies in Hollywood. For a couple of hours of television in the afternoon, he directed me to wander among the caravans with a microphone earnestly asking various gypsies about their lives. There was no script. We made it up as we went along. I was on camera, but basically rehearsing set positions for the shorter main evening show. One grouping around a caravan steps, seen by Lewenhak as the climax, was aesthetically unpleasing to him in the run-through. He didn't like the way I'd had to lean over with the microphone to catch what the gypsy chief was saying. 'Harold, on the show,' Lewenhak advised, 'give him the mike with your left hand then when he gives it back turn full face to camera two, wrap up with a four-minute summary, smile, count three, then smile and say "Goodnight viewers from all of us at Granada."'

This was Hollywood talking! I'd be ready for my close-up. The gypsy chief had stars in his eyes, too. Under the blaze of the spotlights, he answered the question. I proffered my hand for the mike. He kept it and segued expertly into a litany of grievances. He named one town for its intolerance, then another and another – a gazette of local councils and cruelty the width and breadth of the land. Starting in the South in Surrey, he was working his way north to the Outer Hebrides. Lewenhak's alarmed floor manager was holding up two fingers. As a rude gesture, it was appropriate. I had two minutes to close. I leaned over to retrieve the mike from the chief: he leaned back. I moved forward; he moved further back. He was clinging to the mike. We struggled for possession. He was still talking as I managed to get a hand on it. These politically correct days I would be denounced for oppressing a minority. I didn't see it that way. It was *my* mike. But the chief wouldn't stop talking. Police sirens were now blaring. Trucks and cars, drawn like moths to the spotlights, had stopped to see what was going on. One car ran into the back of another. It was chaos. Lewenhak rolled the credits over the unstoppable talking gypsy and doused the lights. I had no close-up.

It was time to get back to print.

10

ADVENTURES IN THE
LAND OF OPPORTUNITY

I am addicted to print. That is different from being addicted to reading. An addiction to print means you get your fix by looking at the shapes of letters in type even when the words don't make any sense. I savour the design of letters, the ascenders piercing the skyline, the fugues created by the descenders. On those assignments in Europe for the *Evening News*, I felt compelled every day to scour the Norwegian, Swedish and Danish newspapers without understanding a word. It was a guilty pleasure to be relieved of the burden of comprehension. I scan newspaper pages of classified advertisements even when I'm not looking for anything.

Today I waste emotional energy nursing grievances about the migraine-inducing type on medicine bottles, and the ridiculously emaciated compressed capital letters of credits on DVD boxes. What are they trying to hide?

Early in 1956, in the midst of my quick scan of the first pages of *The Economist*, I found myself mesmerized by five lines of small type. The longer I looked, the larger they got, expanding into a new world: *the* new world. British and Commonwealth graduates, the advertisement announced, were offered the opportunity to travel and study in the United States at the expense of a body called the Commonwealth Fund.

So many millions now visit America every year, it's hard to appreciate how magical those few lines were in 1956. Even crossing the Atlantic was an adventure then; non-stop flights and mass air travel were years away. The everyday material pleasures of Americans – their hamburgers and hot dogs, their jeans and gadgets for everything – are now a commonplace in every community in the world, but they were curiosities then. America was at once a vast mystery and an inspiration.

Its universal lustre was dimmed in the years of the George W. Bush presidency, but as a schoolboy who'd shivered in an air raid shelter during the Nazi bombing blitz in 1940 when England seemed unlikely to survive, I can never forget the America that came to the rescue: Franklin Roosevelt was as large in our imaginations as Winston Churchill. Then, when the war had been won in the West and in the East, I'd seen this same America sustain Western civilization by acts of courage, generosity and vision. They didn't occupy the freed lands as Stalin did; they created a new world liberal order.

What kind of people were they? In 1933 in the Great Depression they sang 'We're in the money' when all they had to live on was hope. In America, it seemed, it was permissible to dream. How had they survived so many crises, achieved so much abundance, fostered so many innovations, translated so many immigrants arriving at Ellis Island with their pathetic bundles into American citizens making a mark in the world? See, there in the line on Ellis Island – Albert Einstein, Bob Hope, Cary Grant and Alexander Graham Bell, and there's Irving Berlin and Charlie Chaplin and Frank Capra and Enrico Fermi. There's a more nuanced image of America today than mine in 1956 formed by films and novels. But who with an atom of romance in his soul could not feel the pull of the mythic America? To walk into a small-town diner in a Norman Rockwell painting, to follow Raymond Chandler in a roadster up Sunset Boulevard, to steam down Huck Finn and Jim's Mississippi, to see Faulkner's Yoknapatawpha County and Gatsby's Great Egg, and Zane Grey's Wild West, and Damon Runyon's Broadway. Yes, there was the heartache in the history and in the literature, in the Okies of Steinbeck's *Grapes of Wrath* fleeing the dustbowl and finding California not such a promised land, and most of all in Gunnar Myrdal's *An American*

Dilemma on discrimination against black people. But how were things now in the 1950s? Were these Americans as open, as breezily uninhibited and welcoming as their GIs? And were their newspapers anything like as exciting as they were in the films?

I responded to the advertisement in *The Economist* as soon as I got into my office at the *Evening News*. It transpired that the Commonwealth Fund had nothing to do with our far-flung British Commonwealth. It was an American foundation established in 1918 by Anna Harkness with 10 million dollars of the fortune left her by her husband Stephen Harkness, who'd discovered a more profitable business than making harnesses in Cleveland, Ohio: he got together with John D. Rockefeller to co-found Standard Oil. Anna had made her Anglophile son Edward president of her foundation, and he saw the Commonwealth Fund Fellowships (later called Harkness Fellowships) as reciprocating the Rhodes scholarships. The idea was that returning home after seeing the country first-hand would promote 'mutual amity and understanding between Great Britain and the United States'.

The Fund seemed mostly to have been seeking genius scientists who would further their researches on the cosmos, but three Harkness Fellowships were open to 'graduate opinion-forming journalists' who would be required to commit to a research project and promise that when finished they'd not linger in Hollywood.

My heart sank when the Harkness application forms arrived. The British selection committee included none other than Sir James Fitzgerald Duff, the fierce Warden of the Durham Colleges, whom I had criticized in the student newspaper *Palatinate* for banning Durham's ice hockey team from playing in matches behind the Iron Curtain. Could he have taken offence? Could he even have read it, heaven forbid, as an indication I was soft on communism? I wasn't – after all, it was the Soviet attempt to snuff out West Berlin that had prolonged my time in the RAF – but any suggestion of deviant socialist tendencies was a sure disqualifier then for entering the United States.

The Fund stipulated that an application had to be accompanied by a substantive proposal for study in the United States, identifying the university and a programme of travel. It would be a lot of work. Given the presence of Sir James, I doubted it was worth the effort. I put the forms aside – yet as the deadline approached, every story I read about the United States revived my initial excitement. If I succeeded, I'd be in America for the 1956 presidential election!

I dug out the *Palatinate* editorial; it was much less forthright than I'd thought. Nevertheless, I'd have to overcome any residual hostility from Sir James by presenting the Harkness selectors with a proposal so reeking of responsibility, so central to the future of mankind, that my previous acts of rebellion would be forgiven.

The study idea I hoped would take me across the Atlantic came in a circuitous way from Big Tom. When he vanished for two weeks in my first year on the *Evening News*, everyone presumed he was following Manchester United in Europe. In fact, he was more cerebrally engaged at a conference in Delhi called by the International Press Institute (IPI), an association of daily news-paper editors from around the world that was to play a critical role in my career. Formed in the early postwar years, with support from the Ford and Rockefeller foundations, the IPI had become concerned at distortions in the flow of news that complicated relations between nations and sometimes led to conflict. The Institute had commissioned twenty-two foreign correspondents in ten countries to assess the way their native countries were portrayed. I sent off to Zurich for the two reports, 'The Flow of News' (1953) and 'As Others See Us' (1954). The stereotypes were startling. The IPI had supplied Alex H. Faulkner, US corre-spondent for the *Daily Telegraph*, with a four-month collection of reports on Britain in 105 American newspapers. Americans, he found, were being presented with a Britain that was 'an inefficient, old-world, rundown country at the end of her tether, a twentieth-century anachronism with no part to play in the world of atom bombs and jet planes . . . a chronic panhandler always trying to touch Uncle Sam for an extra dollar'.

It didn't sound like home, but that was the point. We had no idea how we looked to others. Surely, I wrote to Harkness, we ought to analyse how those impressions were formed and fixed, how justified

they were, and what influence they might have in the making of foreign policy. I trusted the Harkness selectors would see valour in my
intention to choose Chicago as my headquarters. The *Chicago
Tribune* under Col. Robert 'Bertie' McCormick was the citadel of
Midwest isolationism, rivalled in the pungency of its expression only
by the city's Anglophobic three-time mayor, William Hale 'Big Bill'
Thompson, once a pal of Al Capone. He, too, had claimed to be
speaking for the Midwest when he said, in the 1930s, that if ever the
king of England came to Chicago, he'd punch him on the nose.

I wasn't just being quixotic in choosing Chicago. Its university,
founded by Stephen Harkness's workmate, had an entire department
concerned with the influence of reading and media and its chancellor,
Robert Hutchins, had raised the sights of journalism, I thought, when
he had chaired a commission on the responsibilities of a free press.

It was a nice surprise to be summoned to an interview at Harkness
House in London, but the selection committee presented a terrifying spectacle. The florid Sir James Duff, bushy eyebrows twitching,
sat with a convocation of university vice chancellors, Oxbridge
college heads, a professor of physics, the managing director of *The
Economist* Geoffrey Crowther, and a man justly described as one
of the founders of the postwar world, Oliver Franks, former ambassador to the US and then chairman of Lloyds Bank. I got the
impression that they did not go to bed at night worrying about
stereotypes of other countries. Sir James asked me hardly anything;
if that *Palatinate* had made any mark on his consciousness, he didn't
show it.

Years later, when I met him at a function in Durham, he told me
what happened. 'You were up against some very formidable competitors – there were long odds against you. I need hardly say I
myself had almost to lean over backwards against any semblance of
favouring a candidate from my own university.'

Apparently, a key question in my interview had nothing to do
with foreign reporting. It was whether I had met any American professors. I could recall only a visitor from Chicago who'd talked on
society and crime and I told the selectors: 'I think he called himself
a criminologist.' The idea that crime should merit a whole 'ology' to

itself, and by a professor from Al Capone's city, tickled the selectors, according to Sir James, as if I had deftly epitomized the eccentricities of American academia. So the British committee of Harkness recommended me for a fellowship on the strength of a witticism I didn't know I'd made.

It is intriguing the way unreflective, transitory moments like this can change the trajectory of a life. It changed mine for good, as a similar one changed the life of the Blackpool boy Alistair Cooke, who applied for a Harkness before me. At his interview, straight out of Cambridge in 1932, he happened to look Lord Halifax in the eye. Halifax took this as a sign of self-confidence, and recommended him to the other selectors, adding: 'What's more he's from the North Country and they're always the best types.' I wasn't going to cavil at advertisements for northerners, but I did object when the sponsors in New York sent a document I had to sign as a condition of their accepting the British committee's nomination. The 'Conditions of Tenure' were explicit: if I were to become a Harkness Fellow I would have to be celibate. 'Fellowships are vacated by marriage,' the rules announced.

Wasn't it, I suggested, carrying New England Puritanism too far? New York Harkness stood fast. Wives diverted a Fellow from the pursuit of knowledge. Also, they had no budget for them. The other two 'opinion formers' who got through the eye of the needle that year were Brian Beedham of *The Economist* and Alastair Burnet from the *Glasgow Herald*, later editor of *The Economist* from 1965 to 1974, editor of the *Daily Express* 1974–6, and the anchor for Independent Television News for many years. Both bachelors, they had no Harkness dilemmas. (When Burnet married nine months into his two-year tenure, he vacated his fellowship.)

At the *Manchester Evening News*, newsroom mates thought I should just forfeit the Harkness. They were aghast, not so much that I should cavalierly abandon a new wife for the ivory tower, but should even think of losing my grip on the greasy pole of newspapers. I didn't intend to do that; I thought I might learn a thing or two from American journalism. But they had a point. Two years was a long time to be absent from an industry where reputations were made or lost in minutes. Indeed, there were moments when I flirted with the idea that a Harkness Fellowship was an open door to a change of career. I was tempted by beguiling images of myself as a history don delving into dusty diaries in a university library, relieved of the clamour of scoops and deadlines. I must have been deranged. In any event I was not prepared to leave Enid teaching biology in a rough Liverpool school while I swanned around the cloisters pretending to be a monk.

The Harkness man in London, Gorley Putt, encouraged me to attempt a transatlantic negotiation. The deadlock was resolved when New York finally said if I would go to America as a bachelor for the first six months, they would waive celibacy as a condition of tenure for the rest of the Fellowship. This was on the understanding I would be responsible for my wife's upkeep when she arrived. Enid accepted the six months of purdah with customary good grace, and on 8 September 1956 she joined Mum and Dad and my youngest brother John in waving me off with a simulation of cheerfulness as Cunard's RMS *Franconia* steamed out of Liverpool harbour.

On board, I shared a tiny cabin with a white-haired Welshman going back to California for the sun after trying to retire in the rain-sodden Welsh hills of his birth, and a Merseysider youth leaving his seaside town to be a mate on a dredger. We learned to avoid the bearded artist next door, returning to Philadelphia from a scholarship, who was keen to explain the sexual maladjustments leading him to contemplate divorce. We were nine days at sea, most of which, one gale excepting, I spent crouched on deck over a chess board, combating Carl, a German soldier who had become a naturalized Englishman; it was a rerun of the ebb and flow of the Second World War until the liner picked up a pilot for the tricky navigation of entry into New York and we all rushed to the foredeck. We couldn't see a thing for the fog.

This, though, is the only way to arrive in America, as the first Virginians and Pilgrims did. The millions who now come by air every year to JFK or Newark miss the euphoria of landfall as the sea mists dissolve into Lady Liberty and syncopating skyscrapers, and soon enough you are tasting the cosmopolitan street life of the city. P. G. Wodehouse said that arriving in New York was like going to heaven without the bother and expense of dying. I woke the next morning floating on a cumulonimbus cloud, my soul borne up by the glorious sound of Bach's *St Matthew Passion.*

The prosaic explanation for this was that I was in a high-rise apartment on West 23rd Street, the guest of a friend of a friend, who'd installed loudspeakers under the beds, each wired to the perpetual loop of a tape recorder. Herb Erthein could not live without round-the-clock music, therapy for his days spent manufacturing metal coat hangers for the Seventh Avenue garment trade.

When I wandered round Herb's apartment, I had a measure of how we'd fallen behind America. Herb's high-tech kitchen had a dishwasher, four-slice toaster, deep freeze, washing machine and spin dryer: everyone I knew back home was still washing clothes by hand in the sink and making toast with a fork held over the fire. I'd seen nothing like the giant supermarket in Herb's block, a single warehouse serving everything you could possibly think of to more than 1,200 families. Back home, you shopped for the family at four or five corner shops like my mother's. Years of doing without everything had dulled my appetite for acquisition: Britain's food rationing had only just ended, nine years after the war, with the liberation of the banana. Here I felt like a Visigoth in Imperial Rome. Thirty varieties of ice cream! Tectonic layers of steaks! Gallons of orange juice!

All of this, of course, had to be sustained by salesmanship. Away from the supermarket, one had to appease news vendors, diner counter cooks, waiters, department store salesmen, hotel staff. Every purchase I made provoked the same challenge: 'What else?' There was no escaping the hard sell. A newlywed friend of Herb's took an apartment high up above the Hudson River, cosily safe, he thought, from the hustle of the marketplace. No way. Sign writers for a church got to work on a facing wall across from the apartment and every night the couple found themselves staring at a spotlit warning: 'The wages of sin are death.'

It would take more than doomsayers to shake America's satisfaction with itself in the mid-1950s. I'd arrived in the middle of the presidential election campaign in which the eloquent Adlai Stevenson was again challenging Dwight Eisenhower, running for a second term. America was at peace. The Suez crisis had not yet erupted, the cloud of McCarthy's anti-communist hysteria was lifting; there seemed to be a thaw in the Cold War with the new Soviet leader, Khrushchev, denouncing Stalin's crimes; and Eisenhower himself had ended the Korean War with a veiled nuclear threat.

I could see why the mass of people liked Ike. He was a reassuring figure; Stevenson exuded erudition, Ike good will. I saw the effect at a small airport I went to with some friends of Herb's, all wearing 'All the way with Adlai' pins. When Ike stepped out of a light plane and waved to us, he was so presidential but so friendly, the most powerful man in the world waving to us, his supposed critics, that we all cheered him.

They were no doubt mindful of the good times. Americans were enjoying a level of prosperity never before seen in the history of the world, splurging their three- and fourfold increases in purchasing power on new homes with kitchens like Herb's, and longer and longer automobiles with ever more extravagant tail fins. The majority of people in Britain did not have cars or telephones. In America between 1951 and 1956 the number of *two-car* families doubled. Most homes had a television set, not yet in colour, but they had more programmes: *The $64,000 Question, Gunsmoke, Wagon Train, I Love Lucy* and Alice and Ralph Kramden in Bensonhurst (*The Honeymooners* did not reach Britain until 1989).

I found the brighter western light buoyed the spirits, and the pace of New York was exhilarating to someone from a grey Britain that had yet to boom. The sense of impermanence in Gotham was pervasive – in the helter-skelter erection of new skyscrapers taking the place of the ones built in the previous generation; the number of going-out-of-business sales (all bogus, I learned); the Brooklyn Dodgers deserting Brooklyn for Los Angeles. Something new was invented every minute. It was the decade for the debut of novelties that are still with us – Kentucky Fried Chicken and McDonald's – and others that are not. I miss the carhop – the waitress in roller skates ferrying hamburgers to your car – and the iconic images of Monroe

and Brando framed against the night sky as I passed drive-in movie the-
atres. I miss the diners where the juke boxes offered Elvis and 'Hound
Dog' and The Five Satins doo-wopping 'In the Still of the Night'.

Of course, there was a darker side. I had the familiar angst in
New York of trying to reconcile the plenty with the beggars and
vagrants: there were 10,000 of them sleeping in the parks, in the
screeching subways, in the flophouses, gutters and sheltered door-
ways. Alarmed by the gap between those who had and those who
did not, Herb's friends met weekly to discuss questions such as what
an intellectual should do for a cause he believed in, like the relieving of poverty. They were all anxious for me to know that New York
wasn't the real America. Wherever I went in the next two years,
all over the country, I would be told the real America was somewhere else.

I loved it all the same, but I could not linger scrounging off
friends. The agreeable folk at the Commonwealth Fund's splendid
headquarters at 75th and Fifth wished me Godspeed with a $100 bill
put in my hand and I set out for Chicago University. Downtown
there at the kiosk at the elevated railway I bought a ticket. As the
transaction completed, I said, in the English manner: 'Thank you
very much.' And the man behind the grille snarled at me: 'Did ya say
sumfin' wise guy?'

Was this the real America? No, I was assured by Professor
Douglas Waples, my academic adviser at the university. The real
America was Gary, Indiana.

Chicago University itself was a study in dissonance – the pseudo-
Gothic architecture copied from Oxbridge; the students in sandals
and T-shirts sipping Coke together through sweetheart straws; one of
the wealthiest institutions in the country set down in the middle of a
slum called Hyde Park. The whole area was in flux, every day receiving hundreds of blacks escaping from the South.

It was from this Chicago's South Side that fourteen-year-old
Emmett 'Bobo' Till set out in August 1955 for a summer break to
visit family in the Mississippi Delta, and it was to this Chicago he
came home in a pine box, a disfigured corpse, his face battered to

pulp by defenders of a wicked conception of the Southern way of life. His mother, Mamie Bradley, insisted that he be sent back to Chicago so she could display 'what they did to my boy'. The thousands who walked past the open coffin would talk for a long time about the shock of seeing the victim whose offence, if it existed at all, had been to chat up a white woman storekeeper (Northern version) or 'put his hand on her and made a lewd remark' (Mississippi version). His two killers had only recently been acquitted, on the 166th anniversary of the signing of the Bill of Rights. Clearly, I told myself, I must find out more about the perverted values of this South.

I found it hard to decelerate from newspaper life. To a mind still subliminally on an edition timesheet, the cleverness in the academic studies on media seemed for the most part to consist of making the obvious obscure. Where's the headline point? Living off very little, I was housed in International House, with people of fifty nationalities. I had to save if I was to keep my Oliver Twist pledge not to ask for more support when my wife arrived. Like Rockefeller, I counted the dimes. In the cafeteria I was charged 35 cents for breakfast: 20 cents for cereal with milk and 15 cents for a banana; but I found a grubby supermarket where I could buy 10 tiny packets of Kellogg's cereals for 33 cents, enough milk for 10 cents, and a whole bunch of bananas for 15 cents. This meant breakfast for ten days on 58 cents, instead of $3.50.

The theory of International House was that by living together as individuals, the world would eventually live together more easily as nations. I wondered about this when my corridor neighbour, the engagingly rambunctious thirtyish Swedish novelist and broadcaster Par Radstrom, in Chicago to study 'contemporary American culture', made a habit of banging drunkenly on my door at 3 a.m. to discuss the ethics of his involvement with American women: he was a Harkness bachelor, his journalist wife remaining in Sweden. He had no enthusiasm for my suggestion that a diet of cereal and bananas would solve his hormonal problems.

He made up for his nocturnal intrusions by giving me a copy of a novel of his, in Swedish, embossed with a vamp's pouting red lips, and introducing me to a jazz hangout he'd found, Club de Lisa. It

Cartoonist Mark Boxer ('Marc') takes a rise out of my skiing obsession in the mid-seventies. Luckily, I left the extravagant Astrakhan overcoat in a cloakroom somewhere.

Wedding-day photograph of Frederick Evans and Mary Haselum, 1924. The next day Dad was back in the steamy grime, servicing locomotives at Patricroft railway yard, and Mum was in the cotton mill.

Vanished times . . . The sooty grittiness of my dad's daily life for nearly fifty years as a steam train driver is epitomized for me by Stephen Dowle's photograph of a Newton Heath loco heading into the winter darkness.

Above: Rhyl seaside front 1938. Dad and three of his four sons, Harold, Fred and Peter. Yet to arrive: John – and the Second World War.

Right: When steam trains were phased out, Dad drove diesel trains: 'It's a toff's job.'

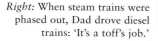

Summer, 1946. The family at Butlin's holiday camp at Skegness on my last day in 'civvies' before reporting to the RAF. We'd just emerged from the 'no this, no that, bugger-off' bleakness of the war, so we were impressed to be wooed by anyone, not least our hosts, Hollywood beauties (or so they seemed) in red coats and white skirts, and if that promise went unfulfilled there was always the knobbly-knee contest.

Weekends free of pursuing news were devoted to chasing the little white ball in table tennis tournaments. My doubles partner Ron Allcock waits for me to deliver what I hope will be an unreturnable backspin at the East of England championships. Ron won the singles; we'd have won the doubles if I'd been half as good as he was.

Dad and me after a swim in the sea. Dad's expression is truer: the North Sea was choppy and chilly.

Mum and Corporal Evans (answering to 2318611).

Empire Flying School Review: Diana Dors to the rescue.

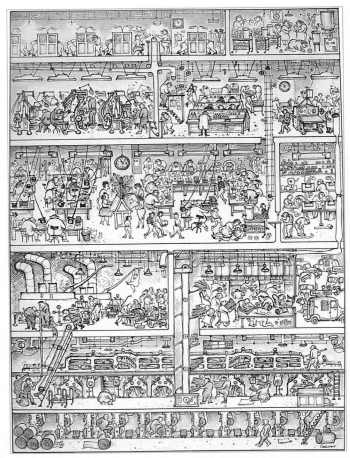

The newspaper office. If you had X-ray eyes and looked through the brick façade of any newspaper building from our vanished century, this is what you would have seen: the stacked floors of worker ants and machinery transmuting the typewritten word into newsprint. Basement: reel room and presses. A pressman (far left) yells about the shape of the plate cast by the foundry above; (right) newspaper bundles on their way to the world. Ground floor (left) the foundry casting plates for the rotary presses; and (right) newspaper bundles on their way to the world. First floor: reporters, subs, copy boys and indispensable tea lady and (right) wire-room collecting news and photos from afar Second floor: linotype operators. Top floor: proofreaders.

I've treasured the drawing for its antic wit ever since I commissioned it from an art student at Manchester University when I was editor of the spoof newspaper we put out during the university's annual rag week to raise money for charity. 'Caesar's drawing' prefigured Martin Handford's *Where's Wally?* – and yes, I'm in there somewhere, in prominent spectacles.

The battlefield: time and space were our enemies on the subs' desk at the *Manchester Evening News*; our weapons – black pencil, spike, glue and scissors, and caffeineated concentration, always fearful of a call from Big Tom. *(Manchester Evening News)*

Big Tom: Tom Henry, the editor in chief of the *Manchester Evening News*, pushing the last page to the foundry – a rare honour from the comps to mark the occasion of his last edition. *(Manchester Evening News)*

It had rained and nobody was about for the promenade photographer at Llandudno, North Wales, except a couple of newlyweds. One year after graduating from Durham University, Enid was teaching and I was trying to survive on the subs' table at the *Manchester Evening News*.

Right: Enid with Ruth, Kate and Mike in the doorway of our final home in Darlington, Elton House.

Below: Four brothers: Fred, Harold, John, Peter, on John's wedding to Margaret, 2 April 1960.

In the *Northern Echo*'s campaign for the wrongfully hanged Timothy Evans, we distributed thousands of pamphlets nationally. Our lead article by Sir Frank Soskice made a powerful case for an official inquiry – but on becoming Home Secretary he refused what he had advocated in opposition. We chose to believe him the first time. *(Northern Echo)*

was open 24/7, boasting like the Windmill Theatre in London: 'We never close.' There was nothing fancy about it, no cover charge, just bare, cheap tables jammed together in the darkness, a solitary spot on a small stage for a cabaret: the place was packed with black people fresh from the South enjoying themselves. Nobody bothered one way or the other that the only whites were me and Par and a saucy young French novelist, Babette Rollins, he'd brought along. A dozen Negro matrons suddenly appeared on the stage, in their best dresses and flowered hats, and the room went respectfully quiet for a little ceremony where they presented a gift cheque to a local charity. I'd thought I'd been living dangerously. I might have been in an English church. Club de Lisa had a double life as a community centre. It made me more determined to spend time in the South they'd fled.

A sterner test of the principles of international amity by contiguity came on 29 October, only days before Americans decided between Eisenhower and Stevenson. In the months before sailing to America, I'd written editorials in the *Evening News* on the cascade of events in Egypt: Colonel Abdel Nasser's military coup; his arms deals with the Soviet bloc; US Secretary of State John Foster Dulles's abrupt withdrawal of funds for Egypt's damming of the Nile at Aswan; Nasser's seizure of the Suez Canal owned by British and French stockholders, throwing down the gauntlet to Churchill's just-elected successor as prime minister, Sir Anthony Eden; the abortive efforts, never entirely sincere, to fashion a diplomatic solution. We did not trust Nasser having a grip on 'our lifeline', and we condemned Egypt's refusal to let Israeli ships through the Canal, but we were critical, too, of the 'whirling dervish' volatility of Dulles.

The news that Israel had invaded Egypt to destroy commando bases – and that Britain and France were intervening militarily, without consulting Eisenhower – plunged International House into a frenzy of excitement, bewilderment and dismay. A crowd of us at the dining tables – Israelis, Egyptians, Iranians, Aussies, Nigerians, Japanese, Brits and French – raced pell-mell downstairs to the television. We yelled abuse at the set when the programme abruptly

abandoned the United Nations Security Council arguments in full
flow, switching unconcerned to the regular schedule.

That first night I barely slept, International House becoming a
mini-UN. Two scientists from Tel Aviv asked whether they were supposed to do nothing when more than a thousand Israelis had been
shot or kidnapped by Egyptian raiders since 1950. 'And you've
killed a lot of Arabs,' a couple of Egyptians retorted, albeit calmly
enough. An American professor (in an argument prefiguring those
over the Anglo-American invasion of Iraq in 2003) suggested that
military action would inflame the Arab world without achieving its
objectives. The professor asked me to 'speak for Britain' on an Arab
student's charge that we had secretly put Israel up to the whole thing
so we could regain control of the Canal. Were we capable of this per-
fidy? I could hardly think so.

In the cafeteria the next day, I couldn't get to a table with my tray,
accosted by people rushing up with the news that the RAF had
begun bombing Egyptian airfields. Memory has long encouraged me
to think I heroically defended the British–French intervention, but a
letter Enid found expresses a depth of revulsion that memory muted:
'I am on fire with the Suez Crisis. I hope by the time you receive this
someone has put Eden in a lunatic asylum. I thoroughly despise
Eden, the gentleman turned bully. And he's wrecking the Anglo-
American alliance.'

International House, already smouldering, was incandescent when
the Soviets used the cover of the Suez Crisis to crush the Hungarian
revolution. Someone hissed: 'See. You've sacrificed the Hungarian
patriots!' Then Khrushchev threatened to rain rockets on Britain. It
was horrible being 4,000 miles from home imagining the worst.

Study impossible, I escaped the hothouse. Alastair Hetherington,
a former Harkness Fellow only a few days into the editor's chair at
the *Manchester Guardian*, telegrammed asking me to assess opinion
in the Midwest. I was flattered. As a *Guardian* correspondent, I was
untried. Hetherington was only thirty-six. Did he know what he
was doing?

Since Professor Waples had said the real America was in Gary,
Indiana, I went there first. Mammoth cauldrons exhaled flames,

lighting the dreary industrial wastes of the world's biggest steel plant. Most of the brawny and highly paid workers were Polish. They were not very welcoming to an English reporter. They'd just seen Władysław Gomułka win their country a measure of freedom from the Soviets, after the summer suppression of an insurrection in Poznan. Now they blamed Britain's Suez adventure for giving the Soviets a cover to do to Poland what they had done to Hungary. A local Polish newspaper suggested there should be new Nuremberg trials with Eden and Khrushchev in the dock. I was too close to their furnaces for debate on the subject. I made my notes and left.

Purely in the interests of research, I then spent time in Chicago's city centre bars. My timing was not great. Britain had just had to ask the US to waive interest on the 1948 loan. In one darkened bar where the patrons were watching the election results on television, my accent caught the attention of a belligerent barstooler. 'Look, son, America paid for the drinks in the first two world wars, and this time you've gotta pay for your own.'

The *Chicago Tribune*, renowned for fostering this friendly attitude, was having a field day. There was no escaping where duty lay. I had to venture into Tribune Tower, the imposing neo-Gothic redoubt of the *Tribune* on Chicago's truly 'magnificent mile' of Michigan Avenue, to ask if they would discuss Suez with a representative of perfidious Albion. It was snowing. In the forecourt, I genuflected to the American patriot Nathan Hale unflinching on his pedestal; the Revolutionary War hero had been hanged by the British for spying, declaring: 'I only regret that I have but one life to lose for my country.' My lesser regret was that I wouldn't meet the owner of the 'world's greatest newspaper', Colonel Robert McCormick, 6 feet 4 inches of megalomania.

He had been barely a year in his grave, but I hoped to find that his spirit still flourished. McCormick was more than a bombastic libertarian of the far right. It's inevitable that we pin epithets on public figures; newspapers do it all the time in marshalling the stage armies of the good and the bad, and the most egregious characteristic tends to stick. It may not be untrue, but it obscures complexity.

McCormick undoubtedly fulminated against the British Empire, against Woodrow Wilson and the League of Nations, Franklin Roosevelt and the United Nations, against the World Court and Nuremberg trials. He was convinced all Rhodes scholars came back to the United States to spy for Britain, and campaigned to have them fingerprinted. His worst excess, in his anxiety to keep America out of war, was to behave like Geoffrey Dawson of *The Times*, in the thirties suppressing his own correspondent's accurate reports of Hitler's evil ways.

Yet it required more than polemics for the *Tribune* to become the most widely read full-sized daily in the United States; at its zenith, it had a million readers each day and a third more on Sundays, and the influence of the paper was not confined to the Chicago region. McCormick was a bold and innovative newspaperman, versed in all its skills. He could take a printing press apart and put it together again. He saw the future of colour very early and the possibilities of facsimile transmission, and he backed the *Daily News* in New York, the first successful American tabloid. He campaigned and investigated with a vigour that makes many corporate American dailies today taste like cold custard. The diversity of his life, rich in paradox, defies caricature. He was an inventor, explorer, engineer, municipal reformer, civic booster, artilleryman and athlete. He was an apostle of free enterprise capitalism who despised Wall Street. He was ruthless in crushing newspaper rivals, but won epic battles for the freedom of the press. It was the cranky Colonel who beat the villainous Mayor Big Bill Thompson in a libel defence that established the principle that every citizen had a right to criticize the government without fear of prosecution; it was the cranky Colonel who valiantly bankrolled a Minnesota scandal sheet to win the famous Supreme Court case (Near v Minnesota) that gave the American press the vital freedom from prior restraint we did not enjoy in Britain. He was, as Fred Friendly wrote in his study of the case, 'the Daddy Warbucks of the First Amendment'.

The Colonel had standards. Duty came before profit. He loved private gossip but would not run a gossip column – keyhole peepers, he called them. He deplored Eleanor Roosevelt but would not print a story about an old affair of hers with another woman, nor a story about a homosexual advance said to have been made to a black railway porter by Undersecretary of State Sumner Wells.

The editorial writers I met in the Tribune Tower did not disappoint. They were glad to talk about the Colonel and what it was like to be summoned to his 24th-floor eyrie where armed guards and German Shepherd dogs protected him – 'Hizzoner' Big Bill Thompson had once sent goons to rough him up. The Colonel's men were pleased to be able to practise their swordplay on a real live Englishman who would bleed. 'Let's face it. Britain is finished,' said the chief by way of opening pleasantries. I retorted that Britain had just opened the world's first atomic power station; it was one of my last science features at the *Evening News*. 'That's nothing. You're desperate for atomic power. We don't need it. You've got corrupt unions, lazy bosses, soon you'll be kicked out of your last colonies.' And we had double-crossed America by going it alone on Suez. They were backing Eisenhower in the election, but in rebuking Britain, Ike had invoked the United Nations and the rule of international law, so I wondered if they would have second thoughts on condemning the UN. 'Nah,' the chief came back. 'We like Ike, but Ike's like Woodrow Wilson at Versailles; he's the preacher trapped in a bawdy house calling for a glass of lemonade.' McCormick would have enjoyed that.

I could have filed for the *Guardian* on the strength of the anti-British sentiments I'd heard in Gary and Tribune Tower alone, but I didn't. I called up congressmen, editors, churchmen, academics, local Democrats and Republicans; no one I bumped into was safe from interrogation. It was intoxicating to say: 'I am a correspondent for the *Manchester Guardian*' and find doors opened, phone calls to powerful people returned within the hour, even invitations to 'drop in for a coffee'. It was my first taste of the different attitude to the press. And while I didn't find anyone in the Midwest who was uncritical of the British–French intervention, the alligator of isolationism seemed largely confined to the banks of the Chicago River.

It was gratifying to see my report – airmailed in those days – appear as a page lead in the *Guardian*, bylined 'from a special correspondent', and even more satisfying to hear that the special correspondent was denounced by the Director of the British Information Services in New York as getting it 'entirely wrong'. He'd been telling London that Eden had the support of the whole country, including the Midwest, when I had reported the opposite.

Having broken the ice with the *Tribune*, I insinuated myself into a rival afternoon paper, the *Daily News*, which had just sent a public official to jail by proving he milked public funds of $1.5 million. Running the *Daily News* was a legendary newsman, shaped like a beer barrel, by the appealing name of Snuffy Walters (after a famous second baseman). Working for Walters, newsmen said, was like being pecked to death by a duck. He spoke in rat-a-tat machine-gun sentences. 'Tell it,' he told reporters. 'Don't write it. Tell it. Period.' Jabbing the air with a fat cigar, he gave me a staccato account of how they'd caught the official with his hand in the till. Snuffy was rolling up his sleeves for intensified news warfare with the *Tribune*, which had bought the rival afternoon daily *Chicago American*, so he swiftly took me to the newsroom where the crackle of the police radio was counterpoint to the usual hubbub. 'Tell Evans about the funerals!' he instructed a cardboard cutout of what a city editor should look like – crew-cut, bow-tied, under thirty, but grey-haired. A reporter had noticed, I learned, that a certain mortician seemed to get all the business when people died intestate. The reporter had spent weeks on the case and concluded that the official entrusted with intestate funds had been authorizing $4,000 funerals whereas the ones the reporter had seen carried out were cheap $100 affairs. The pair of grave robbers had been splitting the excess profit.

The city editor was constantly in the hot seat, but he said it was not as bad as working for the United Press Association (UP). In the competitive agency business where every second counted, a UP man he knew in Raleigh, North Carolina, had been so short-staffed he'd been forced to have one operator frenziedly punching copy on two teletypes at the same time. His boss at the receiving station in Atlanta telexed: 'Hurry. Why so slow?' Raleigh replied: 'He only has two hands.' Atlanta shot back: 'Fire the crippled bastard.'

Even the vigorous Chicago papers had their work cut out monitoring the Ike v Adlai 1956 presidential election. On voting day, I went with a reporter to various polling stations in the tough, largely black area to the north of the university. In one station, normally a barber's shop, we were not welcomed by the Democratic precinct captain, a nasty piece of work. We caught him bullying a middle-aged woman. 'See here,' he shouted, 'I know your crowd's goin' and blastin' about what Jack Wilcox did and did not do last time. I've changed my name – legally! – because of your mud-slinging, see!' The woman was one of three election judges charged, among much else, with watching the voting. It was not unknown for someone to nip into a voting booth and set the machine the way they wanted it so the next person voted Democrat/Republican like it or lump it. Apparently, the captain, a master of such arts, was lambasting her for her insistence that one of the booths be moved into the line of sight.

The voting machines were also too complicated for many. One perplexed woman was ten minutes in the booth. A judge went in and voted for her. The next day at the *Daily News*, Snuffy vented. The rival paper had a better story, a page of pictures showing a Democratic captain in the act of passing dollars to voters. Stories of fraud and intimidation by Democratic operatives ran for several days; and one can hardly say fifty years have purified the electoral system.

The smell of printers' ink had been seductive. After two months of thrashing around on my project I was depressed. In Theodore Roosevelt's phrase, I found relating the abstractions of mass media theory to my concern with stereotypes like trying to pin jelly to the wall. Fortunately, my truancy pointed a way out of the morass. Suez! It had been so obvious I hadn't seen it. Here was a concrete, finite event in foreign relations I could put under the microscope. Britain and America were at the centre of it, so any stereotype, any bias one way or another, would surely become clear. And from this empirical study maybe I could construct a model for assessing press perform-ance generally.

The truth about Suez, I recognized, might take decades to emerge. But we could expect the press at least to record the contemporary raw material of the crisis. I'd heard numerous disputes about who did what to whom and when. Did the press report the public statements fairly, fully and accurately? Did it publish rebuttals as well as allegations? Did it publish speculation as fact? Did a newspaper's opinion page colour its reporting? Just how much of an understanding did a reader get of what was going on?

Getting to work, I collected three weeks' worth of eleven publications covering the crisis, eight newspapers representing independent and chain newspapers in different environments, and three news magazines.

I drew up a checklist of verifiable and freely available facts. I also noted wherever unsourced, pejorative, non-factual colour was introduced ('he arrogantly refused'). It was a considerable task and awkward in my cramped room at International House.

I did not, in fact, finish the thesis elaborating a test for bias until I had steamed back across the Atlantic – which was perhaps just as well in view of the critical nature of the findings. Surprisingly few facts made it into print, but performance varied in unpredictable ways. The *Chicago Tribune* would have been expected to score poorly in the factual reporting of the British–French arguments. Not so. It performed better than any other newspaper or magazine in the study. It did have a great deal of colour words and unsourced material, but the *Tribune*'s animosity towards Britain did not affect the news coverage, since it gave its readers enough facts to help them arrive at their own judgements. (In the British press, on the other hand, patriotism made it risky even to raise a question about the Suez venture. Alastair Hetherington's *Guardian* and David Astor's *Observer* suffered heavy losses in readers and advertising for opposing 'Eden's war'.)

All American newspaper coverage, though inadequate, was fuller and straighter than *Time* and *Newsweek* magazines, and to a lesser extent *U.S. News & World Report*. All three magazines offered a confusing mixture of fact, supposition, distortions of chronology and continually angled writing. Fact and opinion were so mixed the casual reader would have no idea which was which. *Time* magazine was easily the most adulterated – twice the amount of non-factual material compared with *Newsweek* (344 entries to 154). Here is *Time*, for instance, on Eden's speech in the Commons: 'When he had finished the House was chill with silence.' But in *Newsweek*: 'His fellow Conservatives, including an enthusiastic Sir Winston Churchill, responded with a three minute ovation, probably the loudest of Eden's career.' *Newsweek* was accurate, *Time* was not.

For a reader who hadn't the time or inclination to read the newspapers during the crisis, *U.S. News & World Report* was the erratic best for gaining some unbiased appreciation of the crisis.

Whatever misgivings my younger self had about American journalism as manifest in the reporting of Suez and of Joe McCarthy's witch hunts, a seminal influence on me was the way newspapers consistently engaged in time-consuming investigations of a kind virtually unheard of then in Britain. Before satellite transmissions, the US was too vast for the distribution of remotely printed national newspapers, so the regionals and locals had a chance to star. While I was travelling in the West, I was mightily impressed by the dogged courage of two reporters in their thirties at the Portland *Oregonian*, Wallace Turner and William Lambert, who busted a conspiracy to control a vice empire in the city. Behind it were officials of the International Brotherhood of Teamsters and a compliant District Attorney. The two reporters had seventy hours of incriminating tape recordings of gangsters, obtained from an ex-con who broke with the mob and subsequently had been threatened. The suspect nature of the source meant Lambert and Turner had to double-check everything on the tapes – three months of risky work, since once Portland's underworld got wind of what they were doing, the reporters were marked men. They stayed in hotel rooms, but not in any one for long; they switched rental cars almost every day; and they stored the tapes in the vault of a bank.

The management of the *Oregonian*, too, showed courage; the Teamsters crooks were sure the paper wouldn't expose the rackets because their union had threatened to disrupt production (a tactic I was later to become all too familiar with).

The work of a number of other investigative reporters ended up central to the Senate McClellan Committee's investigations led by young Robert Kennedy – Clark Mollenhoff at the *Des Moines Register and Tribune* on the trail of Jimmy Hoffa; Harold Breslin at *The Scrantonian* in Pennsylvania; John Seigenthaler at the Nashville *Tennessean*. It's painful to recall now how I watched the two fated brothers, Bobby and his brother Senator John Kennedy, sit side by side in McClellan's committee, confronting day after day the dregs of American society.

We liked to think that British public life was less stained by corruption, and by and large that was no doubt true, but the big nationals at home were profoundly uninterested in grassroots journalism: the quality newspapers preferred the rarefied air of Whitehall and Westminster (where so many 'scoops' were partisan leaks); the interest of the popular press was more or less confined to sex scandals. It wasn't just that the British laws on libel, contempt and official information were more onerous. It was, I came to see, the difference between two cultures: a British population conditioned to limited access; the Americans demanding openness.

Pretty well everywhere the status of editors was high in their communities. No doubt this is partly because the role of the press is honoured in the very first Amendment to the Constitution; partly because local ownership tends to boosterism, much appreciated by all being boosted; and certainly because the better newspapers are vigilant in exposing abuse (except in nearly all of the South, another story altogether). Of course, in visiting forty states I passed through many a Gopher Prairie ill-served by a slovenly monopoly sheet, met many Babbitts as editors; discovered much of the work on the average Main Street paper would drive anyone to drink. I had modified raptures, too, about the use of freedom when people were accused of crimes. In San Francisco, where I lived for a few carefree months, I was shocked when both the *Chronicle* and the *Examiner* effectively convicted an innocent man of serial sex killings before his trial. Day after day they branded this poor fellow, name of Rexinger, announcing with glee, for example, that they'd come across love poems he wrote. Love poems! Must be guilty! But the police and the papers had the wrong man. It was a shameful episode. In Britain, editors faced jail for publicity about crimes that prejudiced a fair trial. The Rexinger case was no better than a Southern lynching.

Along with the high regard I developed for the dedication to good first-hand reporting on local and domestic issues, I questioned foreign coverage even before finishing the Suez study. The trauma of Senator Joe McCarthy's attacks on the press earlier in the 1950s seemed to have made editors neuralgic on anything to do with the East–West conflict. The coverage in most newspapers, wire services and radio stations of McCarthy had been inept and timid. I was also bothered that throughout the 1956 election the press let Eisenhower and Nixon brush aside Stevenson's proposals for making health care available to millions more, and his unanswerable case for stopping the poisoning of the air due to the continued testing of atomic bombs in the atmosphere. 'Catastrophic,' Nixon called it, falsely suggesting that ending tests would leave American defenceless. Eisenhower, too, had been allowed to distort Stevenson's proposal. We learned later he actually favoured the idea and he decreed a test ban only a year later.

The Suez turmoil had died down when I said goodbye to International House and freezing Chicago in February 1957 and headed for the softer climes of Raleigh, North Carolina, where my wife joined me. All my scrimping had enabled me to save for a car and camping gear. I would have to bear the humiliation of not driving one of the latest models of Detroit's creativity, but my 1953 cream and chocolate Plymouth without a prehensile fin was special, a gift of history. I had taken it to a dingy space below the elevated railway where a shaky man in his seventies, with four cats, a couple of dogs and a barefoot wife, had gone to work on it. In the 1920s, he had owned a big factory doing specialized body work until the Great Depression put him out of business. He'd survived all the years since by renovating baby carriages and bicycles, but he could still summon his old bodywork skills. With hinges and bolts and upholstery, he made it possible and easy for me to join the front bench and back seats to form a double bed (cost $62). 'What else?' I paid another $7 for two copper gauge screens to keep out mosquitoes on sleepovers in national parks. It was the best investment of the entire expedition.

Eisenhower's Interstate superhighways were as yet unbuilt, but with my wife as navigator we stayed off the main arteries, such as they were then ('Get your kicks on Route 66'), and explored the quiet blue highways. I won't forget the thrill – absurd as it sounds today – of my first motel stay one night when we couldn't find anywhere to camp. To a Brit reared in the war, the motel was the pinnacle of romantic luxury: a television, a telephone, free bedside tissues the colours of the rainbow, and a toilet seat sanctified by a strip of paper like a Good Housekeeping stamp of approval certifying it was unsullied by a stranger – what more could puritan American civilization offer?

I was keen to see something of the America of legend, so we spent time in the West. We joined the cowboys on a roundup of cattle on a Montana ranch. We spent an improbable tea time in Fort Sill, Oklahoma, with Mr and Mrs Betzinez – improbable because Jason was the last surviving member of Geronimo's Apache band, and his wife a former missionary teacher. He was ninety-three. As a prisoner of war, and later Army scout, he had been taught the blacksmith's trade, but on release was too proudly independent to accept the government's gift of the forge and the other assorted ironmongery he would need to set up business on his own.

In the eastern highlands of the Sierra Nevada, we trekked through blinding dust storms to the wild gold-mining camp of Bodie, now a ghost town of tumbledown saloons, storefronts and church, long empty of human life. We stayed among the Cherokee Indians in the Great Smokies of North Carolina, where mothers carried babies in papooses; we visited the Hopi in their clifftop dwellings in New Mexico, and the Navajo in their hogans at Bluff, Arizona.

Aware of why the blacks in Chicago had left the South, I was keen also to see how these other minorities were faring. The Navajo, herding their sheep and goats and gambling and trading, seemed happy enough, but they were undernourished, with a high incidence of tuberculosis, and only three in a hundred could read or write. Uranium and vanadium had just been found on the reservation, however, portending big royalty revenues for the Tribal Council, and an active Catholic mission ran two schools and a clinic. The Southern Cheyenne we visited in Hammon, Oklahoma, had nothing so promising on their horizons. The ten bands of the Cheyenne Nation were once among the fiercest tribes of the Great Plains, but all the families we saw depended on government handouts of food. They were living in leaky wooden sheds, with piles of rags to keep out the rain, no electricity, no gas, no running water, the women doing their cooking over open fires on the ground. A Cheyenne proverb had a prophetic ring: 'A nation is not conquered until the hearts of its women are on the ground. Then it is finished, no matter how brave its warriors or how strong their weapons.' A chiefly-looking man of eighty-three sat on an upturned bucket, staring into space, oblivious of drops of rainwater falling on his head.

Big Tom, always looking for feature articles, read somewhere that you could put all the people of the world in the Grand Canyon in Arizona and roof it off. It wasn't clear what he had in mind, but when we saw the huge hole a mile deep and 4 to 18 miles wide, the idea seemed feasible. It was a lovely fine day in June when we set out to walk from the North Rim to the Phantom Ranch guesthouse at the bottom. We were practised hill walkers in England, even having backpacked the entire 250-odd miles of the Pennine Way.

Fourteen miles downhill was a small thing to attempt for one of the world's most spectacular sights, each mile of the descent into the chasm revealing its geological history through millennia. Eight miles down and into the cacti desert we found Bright Angel Creek roaring across the trail, its footbridge a wreck of broken planks and wire. We were stuck. Eight miles was a long climb back. It was hot. Swimming was out of the question: Enid had never learned how. The swollen creek was about 20 feet wide. We tried a running jump to get as far across as possible. The onrushing water knocked us both down and wet the backpacks, but we got up again on the other side and triumphantly resumed the trail to the ranch.

We didn't know there were five more crossings, all destroyed by the melting of exceptionally high snows on the North Rim – and not even a hint of a bridge left on any of them. At the next crossing, the creek raced even faster between rock faces. Looking round for a wider, slower course, I interrupted the sunbathing of a rattlesnake. It hissed. I ran and stumbled on a long strand of telephone wire, which gave me an idea. My plan was to tie the wire to a tree, take both backpacks and somehow get across the water trailing the wire so that Enid could hold on to it for her crossing. I jumped from a ledge jutting out over the creek. Once I hit the water I was swept along but was able to scramble onto a rock, still holding the life-saving wire. I dumped the backpacks and yelled for Enid to come over. Her first few yards, waist-deep and holding the wire, were all right; then the current swept her up so she was stretched horizontally downstream and I was straining every sinew to hold her. I had made a mistake: I should have tied the cable to a tree on my side. Enid might have inched along if the wire had been firm. I just could not keep a grip. She vanished.

I went after Enid in the same instant, reached her and got her head out of the water quickly enough, more by panic strength than skill. We ended up far downstream, very wet and frightened – and on the wrong side of the torrent, with our backpacks of food, matches, maps and flashlight on the other side of the creek.

We couldn't go forward, couldn't go back. So we went sideways up and along the top of cliffs. In a few hours, we climbed a few hundred feet to traverse downstream for maybe a hundred yards, but it looked more and more foolhardy. Gaps opened. The rockface crumbled. We negotiated a retreat, to try again to ford. Without a wire, we were both tossed aside like twigs, once more dumped back on the wrong side. The spires and buttes of the canyon passed into shadows. Night fell too soon. We made a shelter of logs and leaves, aware of every stirring in the undergrowth.

At dawn, not having been devoured by mountain lions, we spent eight hours inching along the canyon walls, then came to a full stop where the cliff wall rose a sheer sharp vertical 1,000 feet from the torrents. I'd have to reach the ranch alone and get help. I found a high spot with an overhang, and took a running jump into the torrent. I went under, then surfaced and got tossed around trying to swim. I wasn't in charge, but I'd got far enough across to make it to the other side, albeit with a cracked shinbone. There were four miles to go in the heat and four more crossings to leap and swim.

The last two crossings were wider but easier and in late afternoon I reached the ranch. Within a few minutes ex-bronco buster Jay and a kitchen hand, Ray, just out of the US Marines, were off up the canyon. They took two sturdy mules. The mules lurched and lunged in the rapids but Jay – who'd made a living in rodeos from riding outlaw horses and Brahma bulls – drove those mules across. And at dusk Enid returned in the saddle of one of them. We recovered quickly enough at Phantom Ranch, but to go back up to the North Rim to retrieve our backpacks was considered impossible. We had to climb to the South Rim (much easier) and hitch a ride for the two hundred miles to the North Rim and our Plymouth.

The adventure in the Grand Canyon was scary, but what followed was the darkest experience of my time in America. I approached the states of the Deep South with foreboding. There were ghettoes in the North, as I'd seen in Chicago, and there was discrimination for sure; the white Northerner, if he had an opinion, could be indignant about the way the sharecropper in the Southern cotton fields was still treated as half slave, but hardly thought about the black American with a Ph.D. who could only get a job as a waiter and was excluded from buying a home in certain residential districts. But racism was of a different order in the South. Since the end of World War Two (as in World War One) scores of Americans had been murdered because they were black, hundreds maimed, thousands abused, and millions deprived of elementary rights.

The America that elected Barack Obama in 2008 is a very different place from the America of the 1950s and 60s – but only those who lived through the traumas of those years fully appreciate how dramatic the transformation has been. The full fury of what the blacks endured has faded in the popular imagination, and with it an appreciation of how extraordinary it was that the freedom they achieved was much of their own making: they had no new revolutionary doctrines, only the old ones enshrined in the Constitution and the Bible and the dedication to peaceful change. Most people I met on my travels who thought about it at the time expected that reform would have to be led and exacted by the white community. Almost no one anticipated that blacks would take the lead themselves.

On the way south I spent a few days in Kentucky at the *Louisville Courier Journal*, which by cool, positive reporting and quiet editorials had coached the city so well on school desegregation that all fifty-four schools opened to black children without incident only two years after the 1954 Supreme Court ruling ending segregated (and inferior) schooling. It was an inspiring example of what a newspaper could do by reporting and advocacy. It was cold water in the face to stop off further south in the sullen town of Clinton in the Cumberland Mountains of eastern Tennessee, where the influence of a decent enough paper, the weekly *Clinton Courier*, had not prevailed against baser passions. An outside agitator had gone about showing a picture of a black man kissing a white woman and a riot had ensued. Order had been restored by the National Guard, but I didn't like the look of the knots of young toughs hanging about in leather jackets and jeans and the thin-faced mountain people who sat unsmiling in a pinball diner; they stared hard at me when I stopped for a coffee.

Relieved to leave the ferment in Clinton (where the high school was blown up a year after my visit), I found an antidote to the poisons in the resolute manner in which the professors at Tuskegee University in Alabama faced the indignities inflicted on them. 'It's not conducive to confidence in the system,' said a doctor with the irony of the long-patient, 'that when I come back here from my home in Atlanta, there's not a single place where I am allowed to stop or eat or go to the restroom – that's 150 miles of willed restraint.' Whenever I could, I talked to black people of all kinds about their experiences. In the South they were uneasy talking to me at all in a public place; I might be compromising them if I instinctively put out my hand for a handshake.

Why should they trust a stranger? Anyway, how could I, a privileged white foreigner, possibly get the feeling of what it was like to be an ordinary black citizen relegated to the most menial work and degraded services not just in schools, but restrooms, parks, waiting rooms, elevators, bowling alleys, bars, cinemas, restaurants, beauty parlours, hospitals, professional organizations, railways, buses and streetcars? When I mentioned this to a white reporter in Mississippi, his response was: 'How'd you like to be one of 8,000 whites in Holmes County among 24,000 blacks?'

At Morehouse College in Atlanta I talked with the mentor of the newly emergent Martin Luther King – the scholar and humanitarian Benjamin Mays – about what newspapers might do. Editors, he told me, had an inescapable duty to be sensitive to the wrongs and injustices and to strive by faith and reason to close the gap between America's ideals and its practice. Only a handful of newspaper editors anywhere were doing that. The watchwords of liberalism were 'moderation' and 'patience', as if the denial of the fundamental right to vote could wait another century or two. In the North the interest was sporadic even among liberal organs such as the *New York Times*, *Newsweek*, *Time*, and the *Washington Post*. A sensational crime like the Till case or, earlier, the brutal blinding of the Pacific War vet Isaac Woodard, Jr. in South Carolina would make its way into headlines with strong editorials. Then the case would be allowed to fade, the reporting (not controlled by the editorial page editor) would diminish or vanish, as would the editorial pressure on local leaders, business and Washington's lawmakers and bureaucrats.

Mays' words were the origin of a conviction I was to carry with me into editorship: it may not be enough to print the truth once. Amnesia is a characteristic of all newspapers. It is natural. We have to move on to the next day's story and the next. It's an effort to keep connecting the dots, and worthwhile only when the dots look as if they're adding up to a significant picture.

In the South, editors like Ralph McGill at the big *Atlanta Constitution*, Hodding Carter II at the *Greenville Delta Democrat-Times*, Mississippi, and Harry Ashmore at the *Arkansas Gazette* in Little Rock were at least pinpricks of light in a dark scene, if not rallying points for reformers, but I was disappointed at the gradualist caution that considered it brave to give a black man the prefix 'Mister'. At the time I was there, McGill was regarded in the North as the conscience of the South, but he felt the Supreme Court school ruling must be obeyed not so much because it was social justice but because nine men had said it was now the law. In that view there was no passion to right a historical wrong. Those newspapers making a moderate, reasoned case for accepting the Supreme Court ruling for school desegregation were not speaking out against the Jim Crow laws, but rather the brutality that went into their enforcement. The ritual hypocrisy was made clear to me while I spent time at the liberally minded *News and Observer* in Raleigh, North Carolina, edited by the doughty Jonathan Daniels, a New Dealer and for a short time press secretary to President Truman. I took a drink at a water fountain marked 'White' next to one marked 'Colored', and looked up to see that the nearby statue was dedicated to Liberty and Equality.

In due course, McGill came around to despising the 'chloroforming myths' of white supremacy, but he was exceptional in his society: most Southern editors and their readers regarded anyone who advocated obeying the Court as a radical.

I travelled extensively through the plantation belt of the Deep South, sweltering in the humid 100-degree heat as big flying beetles hit the porches while I sagged listening to the same expositions on how well the races were getting on before outsiders started to interfere. The insistent theme was 'Leave the South alone; we'll solve our "problem" in our own good time; we understand our "nigras" and you don't. And, yes, the North can't talk about segregation and there have been race riots in Chicago.' At lovely dinners given by gracious Southern hosts, I knew it was my job to listen, but I got to the point where I had difficulty restraining myself from protesting as I heard again how kindly 'good Negroes' in their town were treated, how much happier they were than in the ghettoes of the North, or how any attempt to rush things would only stir up the ignorant mob terrified of miscegenation.

Worse almost than the violence against blacks as respectable white leadership averted its eyes was that the crimes escaped punishment. All too often they were committed with the assistance or acquiescence of law enforcement. What tormented me in the South was that the middle-class white people one met were ostensibly kindly folk of generous impulses. At home we thought of ourselves as a generous nation, but compared with American philanthropy ours was meagre. In every town on my American travels I had become aware of middle-class groups organized for benevolence. Alexis de Tocqueville wrote long ago of this American gift for association and it was just as true a hundred years later. Alas, in the Deep South in the 1950s the most active groups were organized for repression. I saw the dark side of the gift for association in community after community; the clergy-men, shopkeepers, politicians, auto dealers, lawyers, doctors and the like escaped scrutiny as they swelled the reactionary White Citizens Councils movement. Inspired by a Yale-educated Mississippi circuit judge, the Councils declared they forswore violence and would resist school desegregation by legitimate means.

It sounded like democracy in action, but it wasn't. They were determined to keep blacks down in every respect, and especially to stop them voting. The Councils' weapons were not billy clubs but denial of work, credit, supplies, housing, and a boycott of any white newspaper advocating compliance with the Supreme Court. By 1957 only 5 per cent of Mississippi blacks had been allowed on the voting register. The immediate past president of the American Chamber of Commerce took me around black schools in Jackson to show how happy they were, and I asked him about this denial of the vote. 'Only isolated cases,' he said. The Attorney General of the state was more blunt. 'Yes, we don't encourage them,' he told me in a disqui-sition on their inferiority. 'Maybe a wrong was done to the babbling natives of Africa brought here, but I am not willing to accept that the race of Negroes can get to the same position in 200 or 300 years that yours and mine attained in several thousand years. Would you know, I saw a Negro boy urinating in the street today?'

There were many acts of individual decency among editors. Eugene Patterson, who succeeded McGill as a bold editor at the *Atlanta Constitution*, rejected an FBI offer to let them catch Martin Luther King with a woman. That was not surprising for a progressive like Patterson, but even the most rabid segregationist editor in the state refused to touch the story. Rarely, though, was any white brave or

imprudent enough to express an outrage proportionate to the outrages. I spent time with such a man in the small town of Petal,
Mississippi, across the river from Hattiesburg. His name was P. D.
East, and his house had just been firebombed when I visited. East was
thirty-three then, 6-foot-2, and heavy; a rawboned product of the
lumber camps, a million miles from the colonnaded pretensions of
plantation homes set among their azaleas and Spanish moss. In the
Army and heaving sacks in a store and working on the railroads, he
had never thought twice about blacks and segregation until the
Supreme Court ruling in May 1954. He did not think much then
either. The year before, he had talked himself into starting a weekly
newspaper in Petal, having learned the ropes on a union paper. He
worked eighteen hours a day to build a six-page newspaper with 2,000
readers and was making money. He didn't entertain any thought of
coming out against the mores of the society in which he had been born
and raised. And then he found he could not live with himself.

The way he put it to me was that he just got sick of the daily
hypocrisies: a cunning law to stop blacks voting; the humiliation of
black leaders who turned up at a meeting called by whites to discuss
schools, then were told they couldn't stay when a politician present
said that by Mississippi law whites and blacks could not be in the
same room. 'One Sunday morning last month,' he told me, 'I was
in my office and I felt that if I didn't say something about what
was stuck in my craw I'd explode.' Who can imagine what a nightmare of the soul it was for a man like East to pull himself out of
the swamp of a deep-seated prejudice that seemed a natural way of
life, and do it in such a way as to hazard his own livelihood and even
his life? His epiphany took the form of a satirical column comparing
the progress in his native state to that of a crawfish. The progressive
Hodding Carter II wrote to him from Greenville: 'I hope you leave a
forwarding address.' He stayed, in pursuit, as he put it, of his hobby
of self-destruction. Week after week he poked fun at the beasts in
the Magnolia Jungle, reckoning it was a complete waste of time to
deliver sermons. He offered membership in a Better Bigots Bureau,
the privileges of which included 'Freedom to interpret the constitution of the United States to your own personal advantage! ...

Freedom to yell "nigger" as much as you please without your conscience bothering you!'

A typical send-up announced: 'Don't suffer the summer heat by using your regular uniform of muslin bed sheet. Be modern! Inquire about our complete stock of cotton eyelet embroidery; Klanettes may enlarge the holes for the arms but your heads will fit nicely through the eyelets as they are.'

His telephone calls would tell him he was a nigger-loving, Jew-loving, communist sonofabitch. He met everything with humour. Stopped at a light in Hattiesburg, a man on the kerb said: 'Aren't you P. D. East? If you'll get out of the car I'll mop up the street with you.' East replied: 'I am sorry, that's not sufficient inducement.' The *Petal Paper* was outrageous – silly if you like – and effective in killing his business in Mississippi. But to me it was a gold standard.

I'd had a taste of the feudal pathologies at work from reading the novels of William Faulkner – a quiet admirer of P. D. East's *Petal Paper* – and the 1941 classic *The Mind of the South* by Wilbur Cash, but by the end of my months in the Deep South I found myself simply unable to take it any longer.

I argued with the belligerent Robert Patterson, the organizing genius of the White Citizens Councils movement who'd been signing up thousands of members all over the South at Kiwanis, Rotary and Farm Bureaus lunches. Sitting in his office in Jackson, I told him in the middle of the strong exchanges that I'd shaken hands with a Negro, and yes, I'd have a Negro to dinner and no, we didn't discriminate in England (I was too sanguine on that score). He was a big, hulking man; I was intemperate, and he took offence.

It was probably just bad luck, but when we left town we had a nasty experience. On a lonely mountain road heading into Arkansas, I saw cars coming up fast behind me. The lead car had me in a dazzling spot. I pulled over to let the cars pass but they pulled over, too, and several men in rough farm clothes got out and approached. 'Didya notice that little bitty of a stop light at the crossing back there?' Well, I said, I'd seen a blinking amber light and I'd paused several seconds and both roads were clear. 'Yeah well round here we say that an amber is a stop light. Come with us.'

We were taken back to the little town, to a dimly lit bare room, while the gang kicked stones outside. My imagination had been inflamed by all the stories of police violence I'd been hearing. Were these men even police? 'Ya been in Mississippi, right?' said a man who claimed to be the sheriff. 'Not from these parts?' I said No, we're from England. It seemed an age before he absorbed this information, then asked me for $20 which I gave him. It was a lot of money in 1956 – in fact, $140 at today's values. But it was a relief we were allowed to go. I had a shameful feeling: I was glad I was white.

Which was the real America? The schizophrenic towns of the Deep South or the dour enlightened German city of Milwaukee, the Li'l Abner country in the wooded hillsides of Kentucky or hedonistic San Francisco? At the end of thousands of miles of travel through forty states, defeated by the immensity of space and the infinite complexities of the people, I decided there was no real America; but when pressed on my return home I settled for a small town in the corn-and-hog belt of the Middle West – the flyover country of today.

Smalltown USA! What is left of it? In one decade exposed as a small-minded hell by Sinclair Lewis's *Main Street*, in another pickled in nostalgia by Norman Rockwell's *Saturday Evening Post* covers, more recently satirized in the movies *American Beauty* and *The Truman Show*, and then claimed as the heartland of Karl Rove's 'red state' empire. But Smalltown USA was real enough for me in 1956 when I escaped from Chicago to Paris, Illinois. It was a township of 13,000 people, living in white clapboard houses overhung with maple and elm and fronted by unfenced lawns and pole-perched mailboxes. I passed through the little town square, with sandstone courthouse and tower, and the Farm Bureau where men in earmuffs stamped their feet in the cold. Five miles of gravelled, unpaved roads brought me in sight of a corn crib and the sturdy redbrick farmhouse where Ed Gumm and his family had offered to put me up.

It was what I came to see as an act of generosity typical of Smalltown USA where strangers were welcomed. The Gumms had no idea who I was: they had just extended an invitation to any foreign student to spend Thanksgiving with them: Ed, forty-one, a short,

sturdy man with sharp blue eyes of German–Scots–Irish–Swiss ances-
try; his schoolteacher wife Isabel and their six-year-old daughter. His
grandmother crossed the Atlantic alone at twelve; his grandfather built
the twelve-room farmhouse and planted a screen of trees.

Families were closely knit. All the races had become thoroughly
integrated as Americans. On Sunday everyone was at one or another
of the fifteen churches of fifteen different denominations; the Gumms
were Christian Scientists and told me that when Ed broke his col-
larbone in a fall from a corn crib, he let the fracture heal itself while
he read from his Bible texts.

The temperature was 14 degrees below freezing. Icicles hung from
the long white front porch. It was snug inside, warm with the smell
of a beef stew. I looked out on the desolate prairie. A heavy silence
pressed down from the sky. Ed predicted snow. It was not hard to
imagine the icy, howling wilderness it was a little more than 100
years before when the pioneers came with their oxen and their covered wagons and crude rafts. Then there were 7-foot prairie grasses,
swamps, mosquitoes, wolves, panthers and bears, and marauding
Sac Indians, led by the pro-British Black Hawk, finally defeated by
the settlers' militia in 1831 in a battle an arrow's flight from Ed's
farm. An old tomahawk turned up in the soil while I was there. I was
up at 5 a.m. with Ed on a round of his 480 acres of corn and soya
beans with his one hired hand. The federal government offered sub-
sidies to farmers like Ed. 'They can keep their dollars,' he told me.
'All those government dollars come out of the pockets of poorer
townsfolk paying taxes. And I don't like government officials on my
land.' That meant him turning away $2,000 a year (around $20,000
today). Money like that would quiet the conscience of most men, but
Ed, when I pressed him, insisted in his slow, cheerful voice: 'A man's
substance is what he believes in.'

In Paris, Illinois, I felt I was very close to the old Midwest and the
men and women who had turned the wilderness into America's
larder. They seemed to me, when I mingled with men like Ed, to have
inherited not just the land but the pioneer virtues that have been lost
or overlaid in the big cities. There the primitive vigour remained,
titanic and miraculous, but unaccompanied I thought by those other

original qualities such as devoutness, simplicity, patience, deep independence of thought and neighbourliness. And if Smalltown USA seems in retrospect like a product of my imagination, individuals like Ed Gumm – and Benjamin Mays in Atlanta and Jason Betzinez in Oklahoma and P. D. East in the South – were real enough. People like that were the real America.

I was going back to England conflicted by all I had experienced: exhilarated – outside the Deep South – by the restless optimism; warmed by the breezy unpretentious friendliness of a society that was more open than my own, with similar values but more vigour; moved by a common unabashed search for redemption in doing good; inspired by what a truly free independent press might achieve, and for the same reason inflamed by its passivity in securing equal protections for the most vulnerable. I admired how editors and reporters had achieved a fruitful status by demonstrating a commitment to their communities, as much as to their corporations, and the way they had done it through public-spirited investigation, professional pride and a sense of decency. Yes, their newspapers were duller than ours at home, and profligate, too. I envied the big city editors who had imaginative separate sections for books, science, business and society, yet the news pages everywhere were slackly edited and designed, with rivulets of news pages leased to supermarkets.

I now longed for a chance to marry the best of American and British journalism. Whether I would get to do so after such a long absence from the battlefront was another matter.

11

FROM DELHI TO DARLINGTON

One of the most versatile, courageous and creative editors in the history of newspapers perished on the *Titanic* on 15 April 1912. William Thomas Stead (1849–1912) was on his way to lecture in America. Men desperate to get into one of the last of the sixteen lifeboats were held back at gunpoint while Stead, a solitary bearded man in his sixties, sat in the first class smoking salon, apparently oblivious to the dramas around him or his own mortal peril. One survivor saw him reading his Bible as the ocean flooded in below. Another said Stead gave his lifejacket to someone escaping in the last lifeboat.

At the *Pall Mall Gazette*, Stead had investigated and exposed the evils of child prostitution, sanctioned by Victorian high society, and gone to jail for it. He'd made his name long before that in his very first editorship when he wrote passionate editorials that roused the whole of Europe against Ottoman Empire atrocities in Bulgaria – the Holocaust of the nineteenth century. Only in his twenties, he did this from the relative obscurity of the market town of Darlington in the north-east of England, where for nine years he edited the regional daily newspaper, the *Northern Echo*.

As I steamed safely back across the Atlantic at the end of the Harkness Fellowship, I could never have imagined that I would soon

assume my own first editorship in Darlington, sitting in Stead's
worn-leather editorial chair.

Curiously the route to Darlington was to be through Delhi. On my
return, I became an assistant editor of the *Manchester Evening
News*. Eleven months into my duties, which included editing the
paper on Saturdays (but only Saturdays), Big Tom suggested I might
like to step off the treadmill and spend a few weeks in India. He may
have indulged me because, as I learned many years later, he had
secretly vetoed the intention of Alastair Hetherington to invite me on
my return from the Harkness trip to be his assistant editor at the
Manchester Guardian. 'You can take time off to help out Mr Nehru,'
was the grandiloquent way Tom released me.

Ten years after independence, Prime Minister Jawaharlal Nehru
was exasperated that the Indian press was still stuck in the Victorian
mode bequeathed by British imperialism, in touch with officialdom
but out of touch with the millions of newly literate masses. The
country had 40 million literates in a population of 465 million, but
the total circulation of all the newspapers, vernacular and English,
was less than 3 million. 'I can't reach the people through the newspapers,' Nehru told Jim Rose, the visionary first director of the
International Press Institute. One of the founders of IPI, Rose was
passionately concerned with human dignity and freedom; as a high
British Intelligence officer in the war, he'd protested directly to
Winston Churchill that bombing Dresden would be a crime. After
the war he became literary editor of the *Observer*. He was a sensitive, graceful man, gifted with the ability to listen with such evident
appreciation that the speaker of the most mundane truisms felt elevated in his presence. He followed up on Nehru's remark at once by
getting the Rockefeller Foundation to fund a programme of technical training at the shirtsleeves level of newsroom and printing shop
and accounting practices.

Big Tom, a keen member of the IPI, had suggested I could teach
newspaper editing and design for two or three weeks. As soon as Big
Tom's recommendation was accepted in Zurich, bundles of newspapers rained down on me from all over the subcontinent: a score of

titles in English and another score in the scripts of Hindi, Punjabi, Tamil, Urdu, Malayalam, Marathi, Bengali, Kannada, Gujarati, Konkani, Oriya, Assamese. I could see what was wrong with the disorganized layouts and unimaginative photographs in these, and even wonder at the apparent rambling prolixity of multi-deck headlines I could only scan. The English-language papers that I could understand had news columns written in treacle topped by don't-read-this headlines ('Fissiparous Tendencies Remarked in State Government Report').

At the first workshop I conducted with thirty or so Indian editors in Delhi, I urged that news headlines should focus on people and be written in short, simple words with a verb in the active voice. On the blackboard I chalked as a basic example of a good headline the old definition of news: 'Man Bites Dog', shorter and superior, I suggested, to 'Canine Bitten by Human', whereupon I was denounced from the front row by a silver-haired man in a dhoti. What I had proposed, he flared, would corrupt the Hindi language. It was cheap, nasty sensationalism to have verbs in the active voice in the present tense; furthermore, he knew of no case in India where a man had bitten a dog.

Jim gravely explained that Mr Evans was attempting to make a point by parody, but then there was another eruption of protest – not at my insensitivity, but at the obduracy of the older man. 'We must change!' cried one of the younger editors. 'He resists it because he belongs to the old India of the Raj. Yes, "Man Bites Dog." Yes! Yes!' From round the room came a rapid-fire declension of 'Man Bites Dog' in Gujarati, Bengali, Urdu, Punjabi and Malayalam.

The discussions about the state of Indian journalism, afire with enthusiasm, spilled over from the hot seminar room to the hotel, and they were still going on when I went to bed very anxious. I learned later I worried too much about all the head-shaking I'd encountered; for an Indian a head-shake was a sign not of dissent but agreement.

It's fair to say that the IPI workshops, of which this was only the first of many over the years, encouraged a revolution in Indian newspapers, broadening their appeal, reinforcing their viability and their capacity to monitor government and business. But by no means was this renaissance all inspired by British and American missionaries, and certainly not carried out by them, but by editors like K. M. Mathew of the *Malayala Manorama* in Kerala, who put everything he learned into practice and doubled his circulation; his newspaper became the foundation of a media empire of twenty-five publications and television.

Lightning struck the subcontinent most effectively in the form of a chubby-cheeked ebony Asian, Tarzie Vittachi. He always appeared to be as urbane as the Western-educated elite of the post-colonial era he satirized in his book *The Brown Sahib*, but it was merely a convenient mask for passion. Editor of the *Ceylon Observer* at thirty-two, he'd had to flee the country after exposing the role of the government in the incitement of race riots. Jim Rose had persuaded him to be director of the IPI Asian programme, in charge of training missions in South-east Asia, and Tarzie and Jim had made prodigious journeys throughout the south-east, identifying the new generation's leaders in newspapers and the opportunities open to them for reaching a vast untapped readership without unaffordable expense. They found, for instance, that 10 per cent of the costly newsprint was wasted by bad pressroom practices. There was no concept of copy flow. Only six of India's 500 dailies used a make-up sheet to instruct the printer on the placement of headlines, stories and picture, so the printer just threw the paper together with much confusion and delay. Tarzie demonstrated the utility of the sketched page plan from which editor and printer could work. For decades afterward, until the arrival of computers, the layout sheet was referred to throughout the subcontinent as 'a Vittachi'.

Tarzie burst into our Delhi discussions with the fire of a revivalist preacher – he was a member of the spiritual brotherhood of Subud – but he was also a Rabelaisian, vastly entertained by life, and a champion deflator of pomp. He visited practical, informed vehemence on any journalist unable or unwilling to relate the columns of his newspaper to the hard daily life of the people: the children dying from dehydration during the yearly 'diarrhoea season', the families caught in the toils of debt to loan sharks, the street trader persecuted by petty officials. For twenty-five years he mocked the paraphernalia of

bureaucracy by travelling everywhere with the documents of a ficti-
tious Republic of Amnesia, bearing, for the health regulators, a
stamp of approval by 'Dr Portly Rumbel of the Quarantine
Department'.

Working with a variety of British, Asian and American advisers, I
sweated design and editing for several years on other periodic ventures into newsrooms in Malaysia, Korea, Japan and the Philippines;
in Manila we wrote headlines about an earthquake even as it arrived
to shake our desks. In Davao, in the Philippines, I joined in design-
ing a discretionary code for reporting racial and religious tensions.
Thousands had died in India because newspapers and broadcasters
had carelessly publicized rumour but community tensions had
exploded, too, in Northern Ireland and in the United States.

I learned much from what I saw and from the others in the travelling circus. Amitabha Chowdhury, from the Bengali paper
Jugantar, inspired us all in leading what was almost certainly the
first-ever professional discussion in India of the ethics and purposes
of investigative journalism. He described how he got into it when
two shy middle-aged clerks in the office of the Director of Statistics
of the West Bengal government came to see him because they were
uneasy about the way their boss manipulated statistical reports to
serve a political group – small beer you might think, but the fake figures that were used to justify a fare increase on the tramways
provoked a week's bloodbath in the streets of Calcutta. Chowdhury
spent months tracking nepotism and corruption in the department
and had no hesitation in fixing blame. 'For positive journalism,' he
said, 'there is no role for the neutralist, no scope for timidity in the
name of so-called objectivity.' Chowdhury made waves.

I remember most the young Serajuddin Hussein, news editor of
the Bengali-language daily *Ittefaq* in Dacca, then East Pakistan.
Serajuddin took to heart Chowdhury's mantra that if you stayed
with a story your paper would become a magnet for people with
information. A missing child was not a story in Dacca. Serajuddin
made it one. Every time he heard of a child vanishing in the busy
streets and bazaars, he noted it on his front page and reminded
everyone that this was the second, third, fourth, fifth, sixth child that

month and none of them had returned home. His persistence revealed that not a handful of children were missing, but scores. He asked the authorities to investigate the possibility a kidnapping gang was at work. They laughed at him.

A month or so later he went to the authorities with a tip from an informant. Police raided a remote village eighty miles from Dacca and found most of the children, deliberately maimed – some of them blinded – so that they would make pitiable beggars on the city streets. The gang leaders were hanged. Within six months, the *Ittefaq* nearly doubled its circulation: Serajuddin was so proud he wrote to me and others about his plans for investigating other abuses. When East Pakistan rebelled in 1971, he was among the 'intellectuals' sought out and murdered by the Pakistan army.

When I landed in London after a very long flight from Kuala Lumpur, I almost missed a small item in the *Guardian* telling its readers that Mr Harford Thomas, editor of the *Oxford Mail*, was joining Alastair Hetherington as deputy editor. No successor was named. Could it mean that an editor's chair was going begging in Oxford? But who would I have to beg? Nobody in Oxford. The *Mail* was the property of the Westminster Press group, owners of a number of provincial newspapers and the *Financial Times*, too. All the editorships, I discovered, were in the gift of the editorial director in London, one Charles Fenby, whose work I had admired without knowing it was his. *Picture Post* and *Leader* were two of the wartime and early postwar magazines, both dazzling in their different ways – *Leader* was more literary – and Fenby had been assistant editor on the *Picture Post* from 1940 to 1944, and editor of *Leader* in 1944–48. He had also helped to found the *Oxford Mail* – he was an Oxford graduate – and with his best friend at Oxford, the future Poet Laureate Cecil Day-Lewis, he compiled *Anatomy of Oxford* in 1938. He'd been editor-in-chief of the *Birmingham Gazette* before becoming editorial director of the Westminster Press.

A thin dry voice I could hardly hear came on the line when I telephoned Fenby. 'Ah, yes, the *Oxford Mail*. Applications have been falling on my desk like confetti. What makes you think you could

edit the *Oxford Mail*?' I told him. Silence. My pitch had been too
long. Clearly while I waffled he had gone off to read *War and Peace*.
I bit my tongue. A small movement of air I interpreted as a sigh eventually struggled along the cable from London to Manchester,
followed by words. 'I suppose you'd better come down for a little
chat if you don't mind what might be a wasted day. Good morning.'
Click.

Arriving in Newspaper House, Great New Street, for the 'little
chat' a few days later, I found Fenby to be a pale, dome-headed man
in his early forties who punctuated his glacial speech with light,
mocking laughs. He'd warmed up since I phoned. It transpired that
my IPI connections had come into play. Jim Rose's beautiful actress
wife, Pamela, was the sister of Pat Gibson, who was vice-chairman
of Westminster Press. Jim had mentioned our adventures in India to
Pam, she'd mentioned them to Pat, who'd mentioned them to
Charles, who also just happened to be chairman of the British committee of IPI.

'The *Oxford Mail* is not for you,' said Fenby at once, to my disappointment. But he went on: 'I've heard about the work you did in
India. Rather surprised you didn't tell me about *that*. You'll know
our *Northern Echo* in Darlington from your Durham days, read by
the coal miners' families, edited by the great W. T. Stead. You know
Stead I trust?' And he then drifted into a rumination as if I weren't
there. 'Now Mark Barrington-Ward is the editor of the *Echo*, Balliol
man, not too happy in County Durham. Perfect I'd think for
Oxford.' Pause. 'As indeed Evans may be for Darlington. Let me
think about it.'

So it was that in June 1961, Westminster chessmaster Fenby designated me as the bishop to move diagonally north from Manchester
to edit the *Northern Echo* and Barrington-Ward as the castle to
move directly south to Oxford. 'It comes as no surprise,' said Big
Tom in a generous note about my nine years with him.

It did to me. Finally given the challenge of editorship, I stood
astonished at my own pretension. I'd been inordinately ambitious to
succeed in all the stages of newspaper life. I was assiduous in learning the crafts. An editorship had always seemed the logical goal, so

I had applied, but now that it was about to be realized for something more substantial than the *Empire Flying School Review* I had a sudden loss of confidence.

I knew I could do all the nuts and bolts of newspapering. But there was more to editing than a sequence of crafts. It was all very well to carry out the instructions of Big Tom in reporting and editing or find fault with papers in Asia and America. I didn't really risk much beyond the shame of getting it wrong. As a critic, I was not hazarding a whole newspaper. Here I was about to have care of a venerable title, but one beset by competition, its circulation ebbing, headquartered in a small town, staffed by people whose skill I could not guess, whose attitude to a stranger might be unfriendly, and whose management I didn't know in the way I knew Big Tom and Laurence Scott. Hmm . . . I was thirty-two. This was it.

I arrived in Darlington, a pleasant market town, in August 1961, with Enid and our bright-eyed one-year-old daughter Ruth, who'd been born in Manchester. I touched for good luck a large granite boulder outside the redbrick offices of the *Northern Echo* in Priestgate. Stead used to tether his pony to the ring on the boulder at his home in Grainey Hill, a village two miles out. I saw the boulder, which had been moved to Darlington in the 1950s, every day when I walked to work, its bronze inscription identifying the granite as a fitting symbol of his indomitable courage and strength of character and proclaiming 'His Spirit Still Lives'.

Charles Fenby had something approaching reverence for Stead's professionalism – Stead had invented the big-time newspaper interview, and the cross-heading to break up slabs of text – but admired him most for his crusading journalism. Fenby had seen to it that I read *The Maiden Tribute of Modern Babylon*, Stead's exposé of the white slave traffic in London. To shock Victorian society into acknowledging what it furtively condoned, in 1885 Stead bought a girl of thirteen for £5 to expose how the trade and hypocrisy were locked in embrace. The sensation of what he called his 'infernal narrative' in the *Pall Mall Gazette* succeeded in shaming the House of Commons to raise the age of consent for sexual intercourse from

thirteen to sixteen, an overdue reform that had been blocked in the
Commons after its passage in the Lords. His enemies saw to it that
Stead was prosecuted for spoiling the fun. He was jailed for three
months for abduction on the trumped-up technicality that while he
had the permission of the mother for his symbolic transaction, he
hadn't secured that of the absent drunken father.

Enid and I renewed Barrington-Ward's rental agreement for a
spacious ground-floor flat in a solid Victorian house by a park. I was
so puffed up at finally being an editor and one in line from a legend
that the first morning I was due to start work I marched naked from
bedroom to bathroom declaiming: 'Here comes the editor!' forgetting
that along with the apartment we'd retained the services of Barrington-
Ward's spinster housekeeper, Miss Edith Mullis, who wished me
'Good morning, sir' and got on with folding towels. All her life
she had been 'in service' as she put it, meaning she had been one
of the aproned Downstairs ladies facilitating the Upstairs life of the
landed gentry in the heyday, long gone, of north Yorkshire's fashionable country-house parties.

The *Northern Echo*, in its antiquated appearance with a fake
Gothic titlepiece, small type and rambling headline style, resembled
one of those faded Edwardian establishments. It had a history and
character, but its carriageway was unweeded and the plumbing gur-
gled all night.

Reginald Gray, editor for the fourteen years before Mark, was a
Darlington grammar schoolboy who'd been at the paper all his life,
chief sub for twenty-two years before reaching the chair. He was a
big man, saddened by disappointment; he'd lost a leg in the fighting
at Arras in France in 1917 and didn't for a decade return to his field
of dreams, the cricket pitch. His left-arm spinners still eviscerated the
opposition but he was reclusive. He mixed little with the staff and
was very strict with those he did encounter. He did not encourage
visitors to his office, where he read a great deal and wrote book
reviews. Reporters dare not show up in Fair Isle pullovers or corduroy trousers. 'Few of you need to be told, I expect,' he told a
training conference, 'one does not wear a white tie with a dinner
jacket or a black tie with tails.'

The female secretaries and copy-takers invited censure if they wore make-up or earrings. He imposed a lot of unbreakable rules on the newspaper, too. One was that no regional news could appear on the front page. Another was that on the inside pages a place name had to feature in every headline. He was an excellent judge of sub-editors, and was content to hand over the paper to the chief sub when he left the office in the early evening.

The *Northern Echo* of his day, and Barrington-Ward's, too, was assiduous in covering an impressive range of local news, but it had not even the whisper of a voice. The editorials were written in London, exclusively on national and foreign affairs; so were the main editorial features (including a pre-formatted half-page for women). Only London writers were allowed bylines. When statistics were released or someone made a speech, the paper duly reported the adversities facing the basic industries of coal, chemicals, steel, heavy engineering and shipbuilding but it took them as a given, an act of nature.

Fenby told me the London editorials and features were not imposed. They were on offer as a service to all the newspapers in the Westminster Press group. I took him at his word. I intended relying less on London. How could I not, sitting every night in Stead's very own chair, confronted by a letter in his copperplate handwriting framed on the opposite wall?

'*What a glorious opportunity of attacking the devil, isn't it?*'

Stead had written the letter to a clergyman friend on being appointed editor in 1871 to ask whether a God-fearing man could edit the Monday morning edition when it meant being in the office later than 7 p.m. on Sunday evenings. His contract stipulated that he did not have to work after 9 p.m. any night, but evil being no respecter of the clock, Stead was often still at his desk after 9 every night, including Sunday, doing the Lord's work. In those days he conceived that as attacking Benjamin Disraeli and the Tory party. Stead was a committed member of Gladstone's Liberal party. I liked the maxim by Sir Linton Andrews, editor of the *Yorkshire Post*, that an editor of a great newspaper was the temporary cus-todian of a tradition, but much as I admired Stead I couldn't follow him undeviatingly down this anti-Tory road. I was tired of party political journalism; it wasn't the opinions I minded, but how they corrupted news pages.

Of course, I knew too well how pre-war Tory administrations had neglected the industrial regions, North-West and North-East, but five years of Labour government hadn't made an appreciable impact, and in 1961 we had in Harold Macmillan the best Tory prime minister we could have had.

'Supermac', as he was called for picking up the broken bits after Suez, had in 1929 been the MP for Stockton-on-Tees, a key town in my area, when every third man was out of a job. The old Etonian and classics scholar at Balliol affected to be a tweedy Edwardian patrician, but he'd seen the hardships first-hand and understood what it meant for a man to be out of work for years and without the dignity of owning a home. In the 1930s he'd broken ranks to press for social reform, just as he had to defy the policy of Chamberlain and the Tory machine, which he saw as asking Hitler what he wanted and gift-wrapping it for him. During my editorship, the conviction born of his Stockton experiences led Macmillan to give jobs and expansion a higher priority than preserving the exchange rate for the pound sterling, the cause of the walk-out of his entire Treasury team of monetarists. He neatly dismissed the exodus as 'a little local difficulty'.

So I regarded Supermac as a good bet; if we reported and argued effectively, we might win a better share of public sector investment to tackle our twentieth-century devils: a male unemployment rate twice the national average; little new industry; thousands of slum homes without a bath; air and water pollution; schools falling down; landscapes scarred by derelict spoil heaps from exhausted coal mines. My view was that the industrial areas had contributed so much to the nation's wealth – indeed, sacrificed so much – that reparations were due to them.

Of course, for all his virtues, Macmillan couldn't by himself regenerate the region. It was psychologically depressed by daily life amid the debris of the industrial revolution and the careless 1930s. It had to be roused from stoicism to strenuous endeavour, it had to

inspire more civic service, it had to nurture its own culture: two
cathedral cities, two universities, the Northern Sinfonia Orchestra
and the creative talents that had somehow flowered among the pri-
vations of the pit villages, most notably in the paintings of Norman
Cornish, thirty-three years underground, and the novels of Sid
Chaplin. I envisioned the *Echo* as forging the agenda here, yet the
paper itself hardly relieved gloom with a design in typography and
layout ideal for Dickensian times. The single-column editorial was
sometimes flanked by a black tombstone, an advertisement placed by
a local undertaker. Nor could I expect to find eagerness for change
among a staff long drilled in working to formulas.

Entering the *Evening News* office in 1952 had been like being
tossed into the rapids of Bright Angel Creek. Nine years later, entering the *Northern Echo* office the day Mark was to hand it over to me
was rather different. For a start, I saw no human life on the editorial
floor until I reached the editor's sanctum down a long, dark-green
corridor. Inside, Mark Barrington-Ward bore the cares of the world
on his shoulders (a genetic disposition: his father, Robert M.
Barrington Ward, DSO, MC, and Balliol, too, had been editor of *The
Times* from 1941 to 1949). Tall, waistcoated with a pocket watch on
a chain, droll when he wasn't melancholy, charmingly shy for a man
of intellect – he took a first at Balliol – Mark was very generous in
describing all the problems he'd encountered in his eighteen months
in the chair, getting sadder and sadder as gave me his note-to-self,
listing changes he thought imperative that he'd not yet been able to
carry out in that time.

I began to get one idea why after he strode off to catch the train
to Oxford and I sat alone in his book-lined office. Editors work by
command; there was nobody to command. The first day was emblem-
atic. Nobody came into my office except the secretary I'd inherited,
a young Darlington woman called Joan Thomas (she was to prove
a treasure; I knew she recognized my difficulties when she came
in one day wearing a Salvation Army bonnet). She asked brightly
if I'd like to dictate. I would have liked to rattle off something
along the lines of 'Editor's Note to Staff: Where the hell are you all?'
Nothing else was on my mind, but never having had the privilege

before of dictating to someone else, I wrote a redundant note to Fenby saying I had arrived and seen the granite boulder. I noticed that Miss Thomas's outlines were very good and said so. As a former teacher of Pitman's shorthand, I was referring to the clarity of her pencilled loops and dashes; these days I would no doubt have been reported and drummed out of office by a sexual harassment tribunal, but Joan Thomas had a sturdy common sense, coupled with knowing where the bodies were buried. She was to save me from many a misstep.

Of course, I'd not expected that a daily morning newspaper, going to press around 11 p.m., would be anywhere near as busy during the day as an afternoon newspaper like the *Manchester Evening News*, but my isolation was uncanny; no, it was unnerving.

I'd failed to realize quite what it meant to have the main reporting energies stationed outside the office. Darlington was the only town in the country producing a paper with a daily sale (then 100,000) bigger than its population (60,000). Its area of circulation was the largest of any provincial newspaper in England: 120 miles long and up to 60 miles wide, stretching from Berwick-upon-Tweed on the border of England and Scotland in the north, to York in the south, the east coast, and inland west to Penrith. This meant the paper was serving readers spread over 5,000 square miles of cities, towns, villages and hamlets, and nearly fifty reporters were not in Darlington, but scattered in fourteen branch offices, supplemented by 130 correspondents, twenty of them professionals, the rest part-amateurs – clergymen, teachers, clerks, owners of newspaper shops, retired policemen.

Even so, I was disconcerted by the absence of any executives. The *Echo* did not have a news editor. It had a chief reporter, a rather suave, dark-visaged Dick Tarelli, but only half of him: we shared him with the *Despatch*, the small-circulation Darlington evening newspaper published from the same building by the North of England Newspaper Company, the Westminster Press subsidiary that owned the *Echo* and two thriving weeklies (the *Durham Advertiser* and the *Darlington and Stockton Times*). The evanescent Tarelli was preoccupied with pleasing the *Despatch*'s editor, the immaculately tailored

Frank Staniforth, a senior figure of uncertain temper in the North of
England Newspaper Company whose responsibilities as group managing editor included administration for the *Despatch*, the *Echo* and
all the weeklies. Tarelli, like the chief photographer and the editor,
was accustomed to going home at 6 p.m.

The lassitude enveloping the floor was also partly a product of
head-office geography. There were separate quarters for reporters,
sub-editors and photographers and wire room. In all the daily newspapers I'd known, in Europe and even in India, there'd been a news
hub, a big central arena where people could be seen at work to the
same clock and you could feel news rippling across a floor, a place
for newspaper shop talk and gossip, a place where directions could
be defined, instructions shouted, enthusiasm raised, arguments concentrated, layouts examined, disputes resolved by crossing a few feet
to another desk. If Darlington was the cortex of the *Echo*, it
appeared to lack synapses.

Not until near dusk did some semblance of activity occur. A frail,
stooped figure in a cardigan knocked and very timidly advanced into
the room. 'Would you like to look at hear all sides?' I got it. This was
the letters feature 'Hear All Sides', destined for that night's editorial
page, for which Dick Yeomans was responsible. He wished he'd never
asked. He was unlucky that it was my first chance to edit anything.

My pent-up energies fastened obsessively on a letter from a
Shildon man who wrote that 'like all women', his wife loved a nice
cup of tea, but had been asked to pay ninepence in a small Lake
District café (as near as I can work out, that would be like paying £4
now). Our outraged correspondent had calculated all the costs of
making seventy cups from a quarter-pound packet, added the cost of
sugar, milk and overheads and concluded that the 100 per cent profit
was capitalism at its most rapacious. I asked Yeomans if we should
check it out with a tea-brewing experiment of our own. Could you
really get seventy good cups from the leaves of a quarter-pound of
tea or would it taste like dishwater? Should we challenge our readers to do it? Were a small café's overheads as high as the
correspondent suggested? Yeomans, with good reason, got paler and
paler. Was I joking? Miss Thomas came in to say the sub-editors had

started to arrive. I settled for a headline: 'How much profit on a cup of tea?' enthusing to Yeomans that his page would ignite a national controversy we could run for weeks. He gently suggested it wouldn't start unless we got that page to press on time. I released him.

While I was fooling around with tea-brewing, the world had moved to boiling point. Khrushchev, working through his East German stooge, Ulbricht, was threatening to close the East–West Berlin border, isolating West Berlin. President Kennedy, facing his first test since the ignominy of the Bay of Pigs cock-up, was dispatching Vice-President Johnson to Berlin; Britain was sending more fighter aircraft to West Germany. All this was chattering out of our four agency wires as I went down the corridor to the subs' shabby quarters opposite the composing room.

Here sat about eleven men, and one middle-aged woman, heads down over piles of dimly lit copy. In the absence of the deputy editor – on a perfectly timed holiday – a nice roly-poly balding man called Stanley Senior was in charge. He was the chief sub-editor, occupied in riffling through bundles of copy from the far-flung reporters phoning or sending packets by train. It was early in the evening, but already the printing room overseer was pressing a maddening buzzer to indicate he had men at the Linotype machines and no work to give them.

I was disinclined to breathe down the amiable Senior's neck when I hadn't yet met the deputy editor who ran the room. I wanted to see how the pulleys and levers worked before I tried to pull one, but a few days later, on a somnolent Sunday, I had to change my mind. At 5 p.m., the chief reporter in the Middlesbrough office phoned in to say his copy would be a little late because of the riots. What riots? Hadn't we heard? On Saturday several thousand people had taken to the streets. Coloured people had been attacked, a Pakistani café set on fire. There hadn't been anything like it before. Oh, yes, I felt like saying, thanks a lot, and while you were on the phone I forgot to mention that World War Three broke out this morning.

One of the characteristics in which I'm deficient as an authority figure is that I don't scare people. To say I'm even-tempered is not a boast but an admission. I should have thrown a fit in the subs' room that night. Tantrums are useful for making people sit up; they tiptoe around the volcano. Big Tom's incipient growl kept everyone on their toes. Rupert Murdoch has only to pick up the phone and men a continent away genuflect before he utters a word. Some geniuses have had very short tempers – Ben Jonson and Isaac Newton seem to have exploded with ease – and some well-regarded political leaders have had horrible tempers. Truman for one, Eisenhower for another. Senior decently made excuses for the reporter, a taciturn older man, he told me, who did things by the book. We would catch up somehow. Besides, the riots had happened too late on a Saturday for the Sunday newspapers, so we still had first bite at the story.

The lapse was actually quite useful. I told Senior I'd help out by handling the editing and layout on the story, and please to tell his good friend not simply to file the facts of the night but write 500 words on the history of relations with coloured people in Middlesbrough. I was sensitive on race, having smugly told the segregationists in the Deep South that British people were immune to any kind of racial prejudice.

On that Sunday night, immersed in subbing the story, I woke up with a start. I'd done nothing about Dick Yeomans and there he was on his way to the composing room to send his page to press. The editorial was another London offering on West Berlin. I told him we'd surely want to replace it with a local comment on the riot, and please to hold off for the moment. He came back into the subs' room paler than he had exited. 'It's too late.' The composing room overseer had refused to accept the request. 'I told him it was the editor's wish,' said Yeomans wanly.

I went into the composing room. The overseer had already sent the page to the foundry for plate-making. I cut him off at the pass by intervening with the stereo department. I told its bearded young chief (who belonged to a different union from the overseer) not to make the plate of the page he'd just received because a page with a new editorial was coming. He was both flummoxed and trapped. Who was boss – the new editor or the established composing room overseer? The standoff between overseer and editor got rather tense. I decided to proceed as if all we had was a little local difficulty, and rushed back to write a Middlesbrough editorial.

It was as imperative for the *Echo* to find a voice on issues like this as it was to excel in the reporting. The trouble with my impulse was that I was too busy to write myself, and the only writer around was a young man so shy he had difficulty getting to the end of a sentence. I had only just met David Spark and had no idea that his prematurely bald head contained a keen analytical intelligence, a rapid-fire writing ability when required, and a profound knowledge of everything about the North-East. I should have been reassured by Yeomans' reaction. He regained his colour; he knew that Spark would deliver insightful comment in double-quick time, and so he did. The overseer set the new editorial; the pages were a little bunched going to press on first edition, but we were not late. The very nimble, thirtyish stone hand, one Bill Treslove, made a lightning change on the editorial page, shuffling type slugs like a card sharp. I designed a simplified front page, half of it given over to the riot.

The facts from the reporters at the scene made it clear the violence in Middlesbrough was only superficially a repeat of the 1958 riot in London's Notting Hill (in which 76 whites, mostly youths, were charged with offences, as were 36 'coloured' people). Notting Hill was undoubtedly a 'race riot' in that both whites and blacks were charged with assaults. Middlesbrough's was more like hooliganism. Drunken youths coming out of the public houses had exploited a Friday night street fracas between an Arab and a white youth to attack anyone of colour: West Indians, Pakistanis, Africans, Chinese. The minorities, only 3,000–4,000 in the whole town, had not retaliated; they had run away. So I wrote the simple streamer MOBS OUT IN MIDDLESBRO' (instead of RACE RIOT IN MIDDLESBRO'). The editorial endorsed the point; and so later did the police chief and the magistrates.

No sooner had we sent the edition to press than the public houses closed and drunken mobs came out again. The chastened chief reporter was on the telephone within minutes of a baton charge by the police. Once more we rushed to press. The simplified layout made it easy to change and the next day we had a double gratification: all the nationals with earlier deadlines missed the baton charge, and they did not get around to an analysis of race relations in

Middlesbrough until a day later. We stayed way ahead of the competition, and, I thought, put the riot in the right perspective.

Or did we? A local teacher wrote to differ. He agreed the riots
were the work of louts, but he believed there existed a deep-seated
colour prejudice – about jobs, about lifestyles, about sex. It smouldered and it would burst into flames unless we could deal with it.
I published his views prominently on the editorial page on the
Wednesday – but with another feature on two big North-East soap
firms fighting it out for a monopoly of washing-up liquids. There
was the glimmering here of the kind of editorial page the *Echo* should
have. For the first time, I felt I was editing the paper instead of going
through the motions. Charles Fenby sent congratulations. The staff,
once roused, had done all I could have asked.

Still, news and photo editing didn't exist, sharing reporters in
Darlington didn't serve either the evening or the morning paper
very well, the feature pages had no sparkle, and the editorial page
had no authority. You would have had to try very hard to diminish
an editorial in the way the *Echo* routinely did, with small type in a
single column mixed in with the cinema and theatre ads and
random display advertising. But if we were to get anywhere, we'd
have to redesign not simply the editorial page but the entire paper,
as well as rethink the way it was created. We needed a news editor
of our own, reporters specifically allocated and a night production
editor.

I was eager to discuss all these matters with the deputy editor
when he returned from his break. Maurice Wedgewood was a small
dapper man in his forties with big glasses, a wispy moustache, a
words-per-minute rate of utterance almost beyond comprehension,
and a conviction that the world was going to hell and that it would
happen on his watch; no, it would happen that very night, in fact it
would happen right now while he was wasting time giving the new
editor a rundown on the night's news. (There was no written news
schedule. It was all in Wedgewood's head.)

The structure of his utterances was marvellously complex, with
subordinate clause upon subordinate clause; and then having erected
the structure he would take it apart bit by bit with qualifiers, so that

what began as an imposing edifice ended up as dust in your ear. To render it into prose is to do violence to a work of art, but here goes:

'Considering all the circumstances, and in the light of the fact that the story was in the *Despatch* last week and picked up also by the *Darlington and Stockton Times*, I've put the outbreak of foot-and-mouth disease on the front page because I think this thing is going to blow up. Though one never knows. One never knows since the last time we had an outbreak on a pig farm at Barnard Castle, it turned out not to be what it was feared to be. You weren't here at the time of course and can't be expected to remember what happened in Reg Gray's day – he was very keen on this kind of story, said the farmers were the heart of the region and Goddammit! we ended up looking very silly, in fact some of the farmers in the area said we had caused needless perturbation because the pig in question only had a cold and Gray got upset though he had no reason to be since he was the one who had told us to watch out for this kind of story, so perhaps you may not think Page One a good idea after all and we might be better off running a short paragraph on the front and cross-referring to a page inside, which I think would be prominent enough in the circumstances, don't you?'

All by himself, Wedgewood made up in kinetic energy for the inertia that marked the days. He had four editions to see to press every night except Saturday and immersed himself in editing the front page with frenzied concentration. When it neared time for the page to go to press, he got up a head of steam. If the phone rang, he didn't just replace it on its cradle – he slammed it with a force that rattled the tea mugs. Then the sound of the composing room buzzer would provoke him to flush, roar, break his pencil in half and fling it at the door. Nobody ever took any notice. It relieved the tension. One time, a damp inside-page proof held for his inspection was a mess in its layout because the stone sub had not followed the plan. Wedgewood raised himself to smash his fist through the page. Senior barely blinked at such outbursts. A day or two later, when Wedgewood was working pell-mell to close the edition, the messenger put proofs on the wrong nail. Senior, sensing Wedgewood's exasperation, wordlessly handed him a pencil so he could break it in triumph.

I was alarmed. Clearly, to get a moment for reflective discussion I'd have to wrestle Wedgewood to the ground. (It was doable; he was smaller.) A few days observing what he did to agency and staff copy won him a reprieve. He was a text editor and judge of news values in the class of Norman Thornton. His assistant, Frank Peters, was, so to speak, just a whisker behind his boss in editing and theatrics with dramatic Dundreary whiskers, a tartan waistcoat, a thesaurus of oaths from his service days on a Royal Navy cruiser, and a long cigarette holder tilted at the angle made famous by Franklin Roosevelt. He began the night with a quiver of sharpened pencils, all reduced to stubs by the end.

I came to regard the Wedgewood–Peters histrionics as a small price for the way these two hirsute Horatios stood on the bridge every night to intercept the verbiage that got through into so many newspapers; we regularly had fewer pages than our competitors and had to make every inch count. When they were hard-pressed I gave them a hand. I had an early wager with them both that for every unnecessary word I could save on any story they'd subbed, they would owe me a penny, and I would owe them a shilling for every challenge. I'd have made a fortune on American or Indian newspapers. Very little money changed hands in Darlington.

Years later Don Berry, who joined us as an Oxford graduate entry in Fenby's fruitful Westminster Press Training Scheme, offered me a theory for Wedgewood's curious marriage of conciseness on the page and volubility in speech. The torrent in the latter represented a release of the plethora of words he had absorbed in dutiful excision during the night's editing. When not besieged, Wedgewood was a patient teacher of lean writing, taking new reporters through the labyrinths of redundancies they'd created.

As I geared up to change almost everything in the time-honoured conduct of the paper, starting with the tortuously fussy design, I still didn't quite know how to deal with Wedgewood. It must have been cruel to have been passed over first for Barrington-Ward and then for me. I wanted my deputy to be a partner in the adventure, but in my first months he seemed to regard himself as the custodian of the archaic. I mentioned that I thought place names deadened the headlines and robbed them of universal appeal (Missing West Hartlepool Boy Found, instead of Gang of Kidnappers on the Run). Wedgewood repeated at length all the reasons place names had been the style for 'donkey's years'. I came to see he wasn't being obstructive. He could only guess whether I knew what I was doing or just making change for change's sake. And over my shoulder he could see the shadow of his former boss, Reg Gray. Wedgewood had a very quick mind, but like any batsman facing a spin bowler he could see all the horrible possibilities of any stroke. He felt obliged to do justice to the cons as well as the pros of every alteration in the *Echo*'s normal practice. This took time.

In the end, I simply promulgated my first edict as editor: place names are to be dropped from headlines! The editor's memo explained that the main effect of place names was to deter the circle of readers who didn't live there, i.e., the vast majority. Place names were henceforth to be included in new small-type bylines which had the virtue of advertising our on-the-spot presence. I waited for the ceiling to fall in. Senior plucked up the courage to whisper that the change would be much welcomed by the subs who had struggled for years to fit the 17 characters of Chester-le-Street into a headline of 12 characters per line. Wedgewood, without a word, faithfully executed the first Evans rule, and not a single reader complained.

If I was developing some hope for the night operation, I had none in the day. There was no morning conference to discuss news and photo assignments and establish priorities. I tried starting one with Tarelli and Charlie Westberg, the chief photographer. I had developed a toothache looking at the pictures in the paper. There were innumerable small 'grip and grin' photographs of retirement ceremonies, flower shows, well-equipped bulls, empty buildings, councillors on rostrums. These were fine for the group's weekly papers. They were the kind of pictures for which I'd written a lifetime of captions in my first year at Ashton-under-Lyne. I couldn't believe they represented the changing dramas and personalities of life in a region as vast and diverse as ours. Westberg's five photographers were run off their feet trying to cover all these repetitive functions, to the exclusion of less regular events. I laid it down that we had to be more selective, shunning routine images, seeking out scenes of promise, and always ready to cover breaking news. Westberg got the point, but Tarelli had half his mind on the *Despatch* and the news lists from the districts were thin and predictable. The conferences were a flop.

I was flying blind. We were assailed round the clock by competition. We had a few hours' grace over the national dailies printed in Manchester, but to the north, in Newcastle, we had the big morning daily, the *Journal*; to the south the *Yorkshire Post*, regarded as the leading provincial morning; and we had evening newspapers in Newcastle, Middlesbrough, West Hartlepool, and our own Darlington. In Darlington, moreover, I shared reporters with the *Despatch*. Day after day we'd nothing distinctive planned. In desperation, I suggested a sally in consumer journalism. Enid, who knew about these things, had found fruit and vegetables in Darlington expensive by comparison with similar provisions in Manchester. Perhaps the newsroom might check the prices and quality in the region's major towns? 'Can't do that,' said Mr Tarelli sweetly. 'Too busy with the Darlington Show for the *Despatch*.'

I was downcast when I walked home through the busy town at midday. I wasn't getting anywhere with the news operation. I vented my frustration on the cavalcade of truck drivers thundering through the centre, their exhausts belching black fumes. The Great North Road ran right alongside the elegant esplanade shops on High Row. I felt so impotent in the office that there and then in the street I began a little campaign pointing at the filthiest high-pipe exhausts and shouting at the drivers to look at how much they were poisoning us. They roared on. It was ridiculous, and a wonder I was not arrested as an eccentric, menacing the flow of British commerce. Well, Stead had gone to prison, hadn't he? So what if I got in trouble? Yes, but Stead had used his paper and that's what I should have been doing. The daily scenes of havoc created by the heavy trucks running through towns and villages reminded me of the campaign for St Ann's Square, how hard it had been to civilize it, and how very far I was from making the *Echo* anything like as effective an instrument as Big Tom's *Evening News* or for that matter Barry Bingham's *Louisville Courier Journal*.

At home for lunch I banged on a bit about what I called 'the lorry menace' to my waiting guest, the newspaper's industrial correspondent Don Evans, as if he was to blame. I knew he was a very sensible fellow when he agreed it was worth looking into why a long-planned bypass of Darlington hadn't come about and why railways weren't carrying the bulk loads for which they were most suited. After all, Darlington was the birthplace of the first railway in the world to run freight and passenger trains: George Stephenson's *Locomotion* did it from Darlington to Stockton in 1825. *Locomotion* then graced Darlington's Bank Top station, and I saluted it every time I rushed into the station for Westminster Press conferences in London.

I'd asked Don if he could introduce me to his friend Sid Chaplin, and my clouds lifted when the novelist arrived. He was so warm, so unpretentious, so full of zest for what the *Echo* might do. I felt a kinship with him. Sid had gone underground as a miner but got an education from the Workers' Educational Association through my University of Durham. His portrait of coal-mining life, *The Day of the Sardine*, spoke to me of my life as a working-class boy and he was intrigued by my own WEA experiences. Over a jolly lunch we identified the causes and the people who could make things happen. 'There's an ache for leadership,' said Chaplin. He thought the *Echo* was better placed to do it than the flashier Newcastle *Journal*. Lunch was exhilarating. By the time it was over I felt we had already retrained miners displaced by pit closures, grassed over the scores of hideous slag heaps, diverted the heavy lorries, cleaned up the beaches and rivers, purified the air, and capped it all off with a spectacular celebration concert in Durham Cathedral.

I felt emboldened to ask management to end the practice of shared staffing so we could have reporters of our own and a news editor and night editor reporting to me. I canvassed my thoughts with Frank Staniforth. Nobody had spelled out the degree of his authority over the *Echo*, if any. I half-imagined he might like having Tarelli all for himself and his own dedicated reporters, and I was sure, as an experienced newspaperman, he'd see the virtue of relieving the strain on Wedgewood.

He didn't. He arrived in my office on a thundercloud, which did not disperse when I asked him to contemplate how much we'd save on Wedgewood's pencils. The 1961 budget – drawn up before I arrived – made no provision for a news editor and a night editor, so that was that, wasn't it? I said I would wait and ask for the investment for the following year. This did not appeal to him. His second objection, probably his first really, was that the changes would hurt his *Despatch*. I didn't see why they should; he would have the same man-hours of reporters' time. He was flushed, and I was sick at heart. To me, he was a hidden minefield; to him I was a loose cannon. It was an uncomfortable confrontation and more wrenching than the one with the overseer.

Eventually the staff and budget argument went to the managing director of the Darlington group, Shannan Stevenson, a crisp former Royal Navy commander with newspapers in his blood; his family had funded the *Shields Gazette* in 1849. He heard us out and I waited. Perhaps Fenby intervened. A few weeks later I won my new positions and control of my own newly agreed budget for the following year.

This was intoxicating. It also made the days more fraught. I'd be sunk if our sales continued to slide after the approved reorganization. They'd fallen by 10,000 the previous year after a price increase. One of the hardest things for a newspaper to do is to halt a slide.

I began to see Stead's letter facing my desk as a nightly rebuke from the grave.

12

JUST CAUSES

The BBC's television crews, setting up their paraphernalia of cameras and cables and lights at the *Northern Echo*'s Priestgate office, created a stir in Darlington. Somebody famous must be coming.

Not so. The TV crews were there because I'd somehow convinced the Newcastle studios that they had the chance of a lifetime to create a documentary on the remaking of a newspaper. I cringe when I see the film today. There's nothing wrong with the production. It's the sight of the owlish, clench-jawed editor trying to give the impression he's in the middle of one of the greatest news stories of all time when all he has on his desk is a report of a Women's Institute dance.

The BBC broadcast helped us in the North-East – it certainly irritated our regional competitors – but frustratingly we were still obscure nationally. We were not quoted in roundups of national opinion; I was made to feel we didn't count. We had no money for promotion. How *could* we break out? Darlington was regarded as a dead end, and I was having difficulty even finding a news editor. We couldn't compete in salaries with the big nationals in Manchester, or for that matter with the pay scales of the *Journal* to the north, and the *Yorkshire Post* to the south. When I went to Newcastle and York,

I made a point of stopping in newsagents as an ordinary customer, asking for a copy of the *Northern Echo* and expressing amazement when they hadn't one.

In my search for a news editor I went south – far south. The editor of a weekly paper called the *Independent* in Ibadan, Nigeria, had read about my appointment and enquired if I'd have an opening for him sometime in 1962 when his contract ended. The name was familiar – Mike Morrissey. I remembered a terse, slim industrial correspondent on the *Manchester Evening News* moving mercurially through the newsroom before he took a chance and left for Ibadan to start a Catholic newspaper.

I tried him in Darlington for two weeks as a sub. He didn't shine. I sent him to cities and towns all over the circulation area to find stories. He dazzled. By insistent sleuthing, he discovered that unthinking magistrates were mistakenly sending children in need of care to remand homes. His story put a stop to that.

It was investigations and campaigning journalism that were to put us on the map. I didn't have a deliberate plan to do that; it was circumstantial, arising from frustrations and disquiet as we encountered instances of a vast carelessness in public life. I recoiled from the partisan political filters of the dailies and resolved never to start a campaign of any kind until we had first investigated thoroughly and had an achievable target. And if we began a campaign, which meant intensified reporting and opinion writing, we had always to give space to dissenters – and not give up after a few days. All this was as yet untested theory of mine.

I appointed Morrissey the *Northern Echo*'s first news editor. He made an astounding difference with no more full-time reporters than we had before. He wasn't everyone's favourite – he irritated the branch offices by his insistence on follow-ups. When they complained, I told them he was right. After the street riots in Middlesbrough, for instance, it was important for us to keep an eye on relations between the coloured and white populations. Six months after miners were thrown out of work by a pit closure, we had to find out what had happened to them, check where in the bureaucracy the Darlington bypass was stuck and when the ground would be broken for the factories promised for the new town of Newton Aycliffe.

Such efficient news editing was essential, but we'd not get very far with follow-ups and recycling all the events the dailies and weeklies were covering. We had to be different, but with an eye clearly on the community's needs. We had to monitor speeches and reports, from councils and courts, but I'd grown impatient with the notion, common then, that covering these scheduled events was about all a newspaper need do.

Fortunately, Morrissey ran on one of those batteries that never wear out. This became quite clear when I gave him an early endurance test in an investigation that led to a significant improvement in the well-being of hundreds of thousands of people.

It was a perfect spring day in the village of Hurworth-on-Tees, four miles south of Darlington. We'd moved to a house there, the family having grown with the arrival of our second daughter, Kate, and it was refreshing to escape town for an hour or so at lunchtime before returning for night work that tended to get later and later. Hundreds of daffodils bloomed on the village green; we thought it would be nice for Kate and Ruth to see the celebrated display. On the walk home, a mist swirled in, blotting out the bright sky. It was not a mist of mellow fruitfulness. It stank of rotten fish and it didn't go away. It made me gag and it followed us into the house. I mentioned it in the subs' room that night. 'Oh, yes,' said the chief sub-editor, Stan Senior, 'that's the "Teesside Smell". Everybody hates it, but not to worry. It comes and goes.'

I couldn't leave it at that. No doubt being a father again made me over-anxious about the Hurworth haze. I fretted it might be not only noxious but a health hazard for infants. I sent to the library for clippings, but drew a blank. I asked around, and got the same response from everyone: the smell wasn't news. It was a fact of life, get used to it.

Had I raised the questions in my first year of editing, I'd have had little hope of getting anywhere; I'd have felt like apologizing for the distraction from the routine news gathering. By the middle of 1962, however, my morning news conferences had begun as I hoped. When

I put the Teesside Smell on the daily agenda, I volunteered to carry a test-tube into the thick of the next noxious mist. We'd have it analysed and then send a sample for Prime Minister Harold Macmillan to sniff; as the former MP for nearby Stockton-on-Tees, he'd surely come to the rescue if he got a whiff of it.

I've had better ideas. Carrying a test tube in the hope of ambushing the smell was tedious; I broke a couple. Nor did the odour soon come back. Morrissey applied himself doggedly and duly reported that nobody in local industry would acknowledge responsibility for *any* smell. He asked the surveyor for Darlington Rural Council, a Mr J. D. Collins, if he'd investigate. He ran a mile. 'No comment. Least said, the better, I think.' A few regional patriots assailed Morrissey for asking around, contending that it was bad publicity for the region to admit it smelt of anything other than roses and new-mown hay. Some maintained that it was all in the editor's imagination: wasn't he from some effete metropolis to the south?

During a long spell of clear air, I began to doubt the authenticity of my olfactory senses; I almost longed for the nuisance to return to reassure the staff the editor was not an obsessive hypochondriac. Then one morning a haze thickened, and with it came the Teesside Smell. Our Stockton office reported coffee bars suddenly crowded with refugees. All who caught the merest whiff wanted to know the source and what 'they' were doing to suppress it. Clearly, 'they' were doing nothing, and we'd not been very effective ourselves, either, until David Spark, visiting Westminster Press in London, had the bright idea that we should check with industrial chemists whether there were pollutants that gave off a distinctively bad fish smell. The answer was methylamine, used in the production of pesticides, dyes and solvents. But where did it come from? And why did it linger?

Our chief suspect became the Imperial Chemical Industries plant at Billingham; they made amines there, did they not? A public relations manager we asked wanted to know why we were picking on ICI. They'd had no complaints locally, said the manager. Surely it was obvious that when there was a temperature inversion, low stratus clouds coming off the cold North Sea, known locally as the fret, would carry a whole cocktail of pollutants over a large area of

Teesside, not just downwind of Billingham. In short, fog wasn't a
local issue; it was an inescapable regional phenomenon, God's work.

At the end of the next morning conference, I suggested to my team
that when it returned, we should be ready to photograph the track of
the persistent noxious vapour. A giggle ran through the building.
'Guess what now, he's asked Charlie to photograph a bloody smell!'

Not long afterwards, Ossie Stamford, one of Charles Westberg's
photographers, was driving through Houghton village in Teesside on
a lovely day. No mist, no smell. But when he reached Stockton-on-
Tees downwind of Billingham, there it was: a pall enveloping the
High Street. He photographed that, then rushed back ten miles
inland to Houghton's clear skies. The images came out wonderfully –
the first photograph of a smell ever published! I splashed the two pictures across a whole news page. They proved that the Teesside Smell
was localized. Nor did the haze disperse quickly as did the sea fret
blowing inland. The haze, with its pollutant, lingered. So we had two
mysteries: the source of the smell and the persistence of the haze that
carried it.

We called ICI again and received a long letter from the process
investigation manager at Billingham. He strongly protested against
'bias in *The Northern Echo*'s implication that pollutants and smells
come only from the ICI factory at Billingham, ignoring the other
numerous sources of pollutants and smells among the busy industries
of Teesside'. Furthermore, he maintained, 'the smells observed and
described at various distances from the factory cannot be related by
"nose" with any smells inside the factory . . .' At this point he added:
'with one or two exceptions such as the amines or "fish smell".'

One or two exceptions? The game was up!

I was invited to lunch at Billingham with the division chairman,
Rowland Wright (who became chairman of ICI), and the factory's
top managers. I brought the incriminating photographs. ICI came
clean. Yes, they'd been plagued by leaks of amines and were working hard to stop them. It wasn't easy because the stuff was so potent
a thimbleful would smell across a county. As their process investigation manager put it, 'The quantities involved are very small indeed
and obtaining large enough samples and their subsequent analysis

calls for methods of very great precision.' So my test tube idea wouldn't have worked, but persistence did.

ICI now conceded that the mists carrying the fish smell weren't just naturally occurring sea frets. Instead, they were principally created by leaks from their own ammonia plants which rapidly combined with the amines to form malodorous mists. ICI committed urgently to plug leaks, install more gas scrubbers in the ammonia plant and replace worn-out plants at considerable cost. It refined its detection techniques for leaks. It fitted electrical precipitators to reduce emissions from the sulphuric acid plant. It sent out a mobile laboratory sucking in air and making analyses.

We'd done well following our nose. Only years later did I think we missed a trick: early in our inquiries, we should have called the relevant union officials. They knew all about the Teesside Smell, though perhaps they would have been too embarrassed to brief us. The men working in the amines tank wore protective clothing and breathing gear and changed and showered, but complained that the smell accompanied them home and put their wives off sex. A labour manager who went into the tank to assess whether they had a case for extra pay forgot to take off his wristwatch and smelt of stinking fish for weeks afterwards. He awarded the amines men an extra sixpence an hour. (I am not in a position to judge whether this was a valuation of intimacy in his own marriage or his estimate of the losses endured by the workers.)

ICI had performed a perverse service. Their reaction to the attention we gave the noxious lingering problem dramatized how feebly other firms controlled gases from other chemical factories, and the grit and fumes from the steelworks, power stations and brickworks. Black smoke also poured out of the thousands of household chimneys in the area. We applauded the housewife who took her laundry to a council meeting to show them the sheets she'd washed white and hung out to dry that morning only to have them ruined by black smoke.

Despite this, Darlington and Stockton local authorities had still not insisted that fuels should be smokeless (as Manchester had done years before). People smouldered with resentment, but as disparate individuals they hadn't formed into a well-organized pressure group. We had to speak for them.

Some of our critics saw our reporting as hostile to industry. On the contrary, as industrial editor Don Evans confirmed, the entrepreneurs invited to establish highly necessary new businesses in the region were not infrequently deterred by pollution. Perhaps it was as well we didn't stumble on the difficulties ICI had created for the sex lives of chemical workers; we'd have had to report it and the region would never have attracted anyone.

Out of the concern to attract new businesses we conceived a series of features highlighting the successful experiences of companies who'd located new plants in the North-East. The results justified the title, 'They Came North to Success'. But there were too few of these new companies. Government policy for the so-called depressed areas was to induce manufacturers to locate wherever unemployment was highest. It was good politics, lousy economics. Most of these areas lacked the communications, skilled labour and decent infrastructure to support fledgling enterprises. What the *Echo* was able to add to the relevant academic analysis were insights derived from grassroots reporting. David Spark had written 200 profiles and a series on the centres of Stockton, Darlington, Durham, Ripon and Newcastle; Don Evans had slogged round shipyard and steel mill and heard the grouses of management and union leaders. I asked Don and David to join me in defining the paper's policy. Trained as reporters, they were uneasy about opining. Soon enough, though, the three of us were sharing the writing of a double column of argument on a new editorial page uncluttered by advertising from undertakers.

With each passing week, the news got grimmer. The last shipbuilding yard on the Tees closed; so did Darlington's railway workshops. We hammered away at the piecemeal, short-term, and incoherent government policies for the region. We emphasized the crucial interaction between the economy and the environment. You couldn't walk in the shadow of the giant pit heaps without wondering why everyone had not fled long ago: skilled labour migrated south all the time. The vile winter of 1962–3, the worst in living memory, exposed the inadequacy of the road system. Giant snow-drifts cut off thousands of people for days. The effect on the local economy was devastating; nearly 90,000 were unemployed.

Amid the never-ending storms that winter, a tornado touched earth at Middleton St George airport (now Durham Tees Valley airport) one chill February morning in the person of a bleary-eyed man with flyaway hair, tie askew, boots untidily laced, and a cloth cap pulled down over his pugnacious face. This was Quintin McGarel Hogg QC, then the second Viscount Hailsham, a vigorous supporter of Churchill after the disaster in Norway, a platoon commander in the North Africa campaign, a barrister of charismatic brilliance, and our very own Merlin, charged by Prime Minister Harold Macmillan with conjuring up a long-term brief for the regeneration of our North-East region. The press cynics scoffed at his cloth cap as a gimmick to iden-tify with a mythic regional figure, Andy Capp, the earthy *Daily* and *Sunday Mirror* comic strip character supposedly located in Hartlepool, who was into pigeon racing, snooker, football, getting drunk and abusing his wife. No, Hailsham witheringly explained, as if talking to an idiot, he wore the cap to keep his head warm.

Hailsham was perhaps easy to underestimate. He'd been regarded as something of a clown for his stunts for the television cameras, rushing into the sea in baggy pants to celebrate an election victory, closing a Tory conference by ringing a big handbell to symbolize Labour's death knell. But Tom Little, our veteran chief reporter in Newcastle, had seen officials come and go and testified that not since Winston Churchill visited the region during the war had a minister of the Crown seemed so seriously possessed by the urgency of his mission. Hailsham defined it as 'lifting the quality of life at all levels'. He was shocked by the dereliction. He drove through South Durham and thought much of it should be pulled down. Lights blazed into the night in his Newcastle headquarters as he worked himself and his team from 8 a.m. into the small hours.

He didn't finish the Hailsham Plan until the autumn, but we were thrilled to read it when an embargoed copy arrived in the office in November. Our managing director even agreed to increase the size of the paper so we could publish four full pages. Her Majesty's

Stationery Office heard what we planned. They told us no, no, it was too much: 'It's our copyright.' Yes, I replied, but it's our lives. You'd think they would want the widest dissemination of such a key report, but they lacked the imagination Hailsham possessed. We went ahead hoping they wouldn't sue. (And indeed, they didn't.)

The Hailsham Plan – 'as long as a washing list' – projected a bright new future for the region. The conurbations of Tyneside, Teesside and the Darlington, Aycliffe area would become 'growth zones' for investment with new airports, motorways, revived seaports; a regional council would make decisions on the spot so that everything didn't have to await the nod from London. Hailsham envisaged making towns and villages more pleasant with decent housing, schools and hospitals, by removing the industrial scars, tackling pollution and fostering the arts.

I couldn't contain my glee, hopping about the editorial floor like a kid with candy. In my exultation, I felt emboldened to contact the region's leading industrialists – Swan Hunter, ICI, Vaux Breweries, Head Wrightson, as well as the heads of Durham and Newcastle Universities and others – and urged the formation and funding of an organization to sponsor schemes of improvement. They seized the moment with vigour and generosity, setting up an office for a Civic Trust for the North-East in 1965. The paper meanwhile attacked the Coal Board for dumping waste on a once lovely beach and highlighted shoddy development in villages of real architectural merit. But I wanted us to be creative as well as critical.

Geoffrey Broadbent, an architect friend from Manchester, toured the region for us with Bert Hackett, who'd drawn St Ann's Square for the *Manchester Evening News*. We couldn't pay this pair enough; they just liked the challenge. Their illustrated series, 'The Big Clean Up', showed how wretched and squalid landscapes could be made inviting. They produced plans for adding bathrooms on to the terraced houses in the colliery villages. Our attention to the derelict wilderness between Thornaby and Middlesbrough near a tatty racecourse was the genesis of the amusement park and modern shopping area funded in the 1980s.

*

There are no small stories (though some are bigger than others). And so to the Battle of the Broccoli. It was the fate of a clever bluestocking, by the name of Valerie Knox, to be assigned the investigation originally inspired by my wife, that of local produce. I'd abandoned the story in the face of the lassitude prevailing in the old shared newsroom, but Valerie was new blood, one of Fenby's graduate trainees. Doubtless wondering why she'd worked so hard for her Oxford degree, she took her shopping basket around Darlington, Newcastle, Middlesbrough, West Hartlepool and Manchester, buying fruits and vegetables. She found that the prices were indeed higher in the North-East than in Manchester, and highest of all in Darlington.

On the morning of publication, a posse of angry Darlington greengrocers arrived in the office of our managing director, demanding that the editor come down and eat his words – and their broccoli. Nervous that I could easily have been tripped up by an inability to distinguish between a mangel-wurzel and a yam, I offered up our investigative reporter Valerie instead and asked the beatific David Spark to go along as a pacifier. (I also calculated that his presence would calm management, still not sure whether London had imposed a madman on them.) As I fretted in my office, three floors above the battleground, a telex arrived from Fenby. He liked the story; in fact, his wife had also noticed how highly priced vegetables were in Darlington. I felt it should be put in a cleft stick and rushed by runner to the managing director.

Spark reported back that the confrontation with the greengrocers had been heated, but essentially came down to an argument about the comparative quality of broccoli and King Edward potatoes. I offered to repeat the exercise with an independent shopper and a Darlington greengrocer riding shotgun. The result was pretty much the same. We 'won', but it was another lesson on how sensitive local communities could be when 'their' paper seemed disloyal.

I read fifteen newspapers daily and ten on Sundays. One Sunday morning, scanning the heavyweight *Sunday Times*, I came across a three-line 'filler' paragraph at the foot of a column. It said that

Vancouver in British Columbia was expanding a programme to save
women from dying of cancer. That was all. A hundred questions
buzzed in my head, propelled by one of the most consistent emotions
of my life since the days I'd seen people in Lancashire coughing
blood from soot-blackened lungs. If preventable, why not prevented?
Why did it take so very long for medical knowledge to percolate and
have effect?

Ken Hooper was a 6-foot-2 history graduate and cricketer from
Wadham College, Oxford; rather enigmatic, certainly not prone to
my emotionalism, and likely, I thought, to wrestle every fact to the
ground. He was by now fairly experienced, having joined us in
January 1961 and survived the subs' room and reporting for both
the *Echo* and the *Despatch*. I could ill afford to lose him from the
reporting staff, but I gave him the clipping on the Monday morning
and asked him to go to Vancouver straight away. I knew I'd have to
worry about the impact on the budget, but I was eager to get started
before the *Sunday Times* or someone else followed up. Nobody did.

Hooper saved me the expense. He started his research in Britain
(much tougher to do before the Internet) and never went to Canada.
He spent endless hours in libraries, hospitals and ministries, heaping
his findings in a carrier bag to the amusement, if not derision, of
some of the big shots he visited. He was gone about seven weeks,
but four well-informed articles landed on my desk. They were disturbing. Thousands of women were dying from cancer of the womb
who might have been saved; thousands of others had died already
and thousands more were certain to die because of chronic inertia in
the National Health Service.

The technique that could save lives was exfoliative cytology, the
study of the characteristics of cells shed from body surfaces. The possibilities had been known to science on both sides of the Atlantic
since the 1920s, thanks to an American, George Papanicolaou, at
New York Hospital and Cornell Medical School, and Professor L. S.
Dudgeon and his colleagues at St Thomas' Hospital in London. It
was another twenty years before their work was put to practical life-
saving use by Dr Joe V. Meigs, a Boston gynaecologist, assisted by a
biologist, Ruth Graham. Graham took vaginal smears of three of

Meigs' patients. The patients appeared perfectly healthy, but she reported that the smears, read under a microscope, showed very early cancer cells. At the state of medical knowledge then it was risky/courageous of Meigs to remove the uterus from each of the three women, certain he would see a tumour not detectable in a routine examination. He didn't. He was horrified. He was roundly condemned – then vindicated. Three days after the visual inspection, the sections of each uterus, examined under a microscope, contained early curable cancer that would have been fatal if undetected.

What this all meant was that a simple smear test, requiring only a few minutes of a patient's time, could detect a threatened cancer in women and have the danger obviated by simple cone biopsy or removal of the uterus, depending on the condition. It was another five years, in 1949, before the potential was realized by two doctors in Vancouver and one on the other side of the world, Mr Stanley Way.

Hooper reported that all his findings kept bringing him back home, not with the finished articles, but to see Way – who was just up the road from us in Gateshead. Beginning in 1949, Way's gynaecological research unit at the Queen Elizabeth Hospital had screened upwards of 150,000 women and found 601 of them harbouring very early cancer. None of the women treated after that discovery had died; of those having the minor operation, 46 women had gone on to deliver 57 children.

Way's sample was smaller than the one in Vancouver. By 1963, researchers there had screened 214,900 women over thirty years of age, and compared the records of another 248,400 who hadn't been screened. The death rate was seven times greater in the unscreened group.

When Hooper called on Way, he heard how Way had tried for years to have screening adopted as a routine national test. There was interest in a few centres (London, Birmingham, Derby, Edinburgh), but none in the Ministry of Health. So every year something like 2,500 women died needlessly, about double the number dying in road accidents. It was so different in the United States. Early in the century, more women died from cervical cancer than from any other form, but the death rate began to fall remarkably after the American Cancer Society started to campaign for Pap smears in 1957.

I took up the Hooper articles with passionate urgency, running all four in June 1963, with editorials asking the Ministry of Health to start a national programme to save women. I sent everything the *Northern Echo* published to news organizations, and wrote personal letters to a group of MPs: three activist North-East MPs – Labour's Dr Jeremy Bray from Middlesbrough, Ted Fletcher from Darlington, Ernest Fernyhough (Jarrow) – the Tory supermarket magnate Wilf Proudfoot (Cleveland), Labour's Dr Kenneth Robinson (St Pancras) and Laurence Pavitt (Willesden).

They sprang to it, all of them submitting Parliamentary questions for the Minister of Health, Enoch Powell. They ran into a brick wall. 'I am advised,' Powell intoned, 'it would be premature to aim at a general application.'

How many more women had to die, we asked in the paper, before the minister acted on the evidence, already years old? He acknowledged that there had been 2,504 deaths in 1961, but every time the MPs came back – as they did month after month – the answer was always some variation of No.

'I cannot estimate how many deaths would have been prevented . . . I cannot suggest an average cost per smear . . . I would refer the hon. Member to my previous answer(s) . . .'

So it went on through the whole sickening year as we pounded away and the minister stonewalled. Regional hospitals, Powell said, would consider any proposals, but they'd have to find the money. We learned that the city of Stoke-on-Trent had done so, then had to wait three years for Ministry permission to establish a clinic. One of the MPs I'd recruited, Jeremy Bray, did not let it rest. At the end of the year, on 2 December 1963, he asked what further consideration the minister had given to setting up a comprehensive early diagnosis and treatment service for cervical cancer.

The gratifying answer was: 'I have asked regional hospital boards to expand cytology services. Before screening can be offered to all women in the age groups at risk, more trained staff are needed and I have asked five hospital boards to set up special training centres.'

It didn't represent a miraculous conversion. Powell had been replaced by Anthony Barber.

It was a victory, the road to a comprehensive national programme, but I couldn't help doing the arithmetic. A national programme could have been started ten years earlier (Stanley Way had been screening women for fourteen years). Since 2,504 women died in 1961, the unnecessary loss of life was ten times that number – 25,040. And in the developing world many still die needlessly.

Besides our campaigns for public health and revamped economic policies, we were now getting some recognition for our news reporting. We proved at least as good as the nationals in responding to the assassination of President Kennedy on 22 November 1963.

I heard of the Dallas shooting on the radio when I was in a dinner jacket driving to the Teesside press ball, and turned back to the office. Wedgewood was busy editing the diverse flow of copy – from the agencies and from the London office – with just over three hours to deadline. I added to the tension by saying we would publish a four-page special on Kennedy's life and discuss how often the presidency had been ended by murder. We sent for photographs from the library. None could be found. The day manager of the picture library, Shirley Freeman – known as Shirley Fileroom – had gone home, and the night manager, Bill Webster, had the night off. The indispensable Joan Thomas suggested we call Shirley's parents. 'Oh, she's out with her boyfriend.' Where? 'I think they went to the cinema?'

The Odeon was the most popular. Joan got the Odeon manager on the telephone for me. He hadn't heard of the Kennedy shooting. He was aghast when I asked him to stop the film and find our staffer. Then I had a better idea, with the result that Shirley and her boyfriend, canoodling in the back row, saw a flash on the screen – a handwritten message on a Perspex slide – 'Miss Shirley Freeman call the *Echo* urgently.' Her date was ruined, the paper was saved.

By 1963, circulation had risen by 10 per cent on the way to a rise of 14 per cent, and year on year our profit had tripled. Winston

Churchill had been a big help. I came across an old copy of his *My Early Life* (1930). I'd read his war histories, but not this, and I suspected few of my generation had. I was so enchanted by it that I wrote to him and asked permission to serialize it. He sent a warm note back saying go ahead. It proved popular.

1963 was a significant year, as the poet Philip Larkin made clear:

> *Sexual intercourse began*
> *In nineteen sixty-three*
> *(Which was rather late for me)—*
> *Between the end of the* Chatterley *ban*
> *And the Beatles' first LP.*

As a happily married man with three children (Michael had arrived that year), I, too, missed the sexual revolution – but I kept pace with the music. I could hardly miss the Beatles' first record, 'Love Me Do'. My wife was a Liverpudlian; our Granada TV broadcast the Beatles' first appearance in October 1962; we bought that first album, *Please Please Me*; and I could hardly forget how my acerbic producer friend Barrie Heads told me he'd thrown another new group out of the Granada studio because they weren't presentable like the Beatles – 'Mick Jagger and his group were so scruffy.'

The break into music for the *Northern Echo* came out of a snowstorm. George Carr, Westberg's deputy, took a sixteen-year-old printing assistant, Ian Wright, on a long slog to reach people trapped in a blizzard along the route that went over the Pennine hills. All Carr and Wright had was a broken-down Ford Popular car with no snow chains, no snow tyres and no heater. They loaded the boot with four bags of coal to weigh down the back axle, and a shovel and hessian coal sacks for when they got stuck. In this way, with Thermos flask and sandwiches, they got through the traffic jams and jackknifed trucks where all others, including the police, the rescue services and ambulances, had failed. Between taking photographs and conducting interviews, they helped people get their cars out of drifts.

As it happened the best photograph was taken by Wright, who was normally an unseen elf, filing the negatives, mixing the chemicals and cleaning up. I put his dramatic picture on the front page. Soon after the first edition had arrived there was a knock on my door, and there was Wright, asking very nervously if there was some reason why he'd not been given the credit. It was an oversight. I put his name under the photograph in the next edition and that began Wright's career as a photographer. He was the only photographer with any interest in pop groups. Westberg despised these long-haired rockers. It was a hard day's night getting him to concede that if Wright took the pictures in his own time, he wouldn't impede him.

Week after week Wright was out with the Beatles, the Rolling Stones, the Searchers, Lulu, the Dave Clark Five, Manfred Mann, Dusty Springfield, Cilla Black, Roy Orbison, Billy J. Kramer and Gene Pitney. I assigned junior reporters to write the stories. They knew more than I did about who was worth covering, though I was keen enough to drive them to and from Newcastle for the first North-East tour of the Beatles in March 1963.

Our youngsters struck up a rapport with the new pop stars, and with managers and roadies such as Brian Epstein and Neil Aspinall. Wright and Guy Simpson were the only pressmen who showed up when the Beatles gave a concert at the Globe Theatre in Stockton and had no problem going backstage. 'John Lennon,' Wright remembers, 'was always asking for complimentary prints. "Wrighty, don't forget to send those photos, the family love 'em."' I was so impressed by the initiative of these juniors, I started the paper's first weekly supplement, The Teenage Special, which attracted some 30,000 sales on Mondays – almost a 30 per cent increase. With the zestful Arthur Clifford, who was revitalizing Tyne Tees television, the *Northern Echo* organized very loud talent shows in Newcastle, the American Idol of Tyneside.

The music juniors all went on to make names for themselves. Philip Norman won a *Sunday Times* magazine essay contest, then became a best-selling author with *The Stones, Shout, Rave On*, and biographies of Elton John and John Lennon. David Sinclair wrote biographies of Lord Snowdon and the Queen Mother. David Watts became the South-East Asia correspondent for the London *Times*, John Cathcart editor of the *National Enquirer* and

Guy Simpson picture editor of the *Independent* newspaper in London. They must have taken their cue from Tyneside's own Eric Burdon and The Animals, whose great hit was 'We Gotta Get Out of This Place'.

Granada Television came calling on me at the *Echo*. Since returning from America, I'd written a couple of documentaries for them and a pamphlet on their fight to televise a Parliamentary election. It's an indication of how suspicious the authorities were of this dangerous new medium of television that Granada had to mount a full-scale legal and public relations assault before managing to bring television cameras to the Rochdale by-election.

The call was from Jeremy Isaacs, whom I'd met at a Granada function. He was to become renowned for producing a series on the Second World War and the Cold War, later becoming the founding chief executive of Channel Four, and Sir Jeremy, director general of the Royal Opera House. In 1961–2 he was winning his spurs commissioning a rotating group of commentators for a programme critically examining the week's newspapers, *What the Papers Say*, one of the world's longest-running television programmes which continues to this day, albeit now on the BBC. Would I care to audition for *What the Papers Say*?

Had he not heard of Lewenhak and the talkative gypsies? Five years had gone by, which for television people must have meant it was lost in the mists of time. I didn't bother to brief him on that history but wrote a script for the audition and did a dummy run in Manchester with Michael Frayn of the *Guardian*, Colin Welch of the *Daily Telegraph* and Tom Lambert of the *New York Herald Tribune*. The outcome was a letter from Isaacs: 'I hope I can persuade the boys here to let you have a bash on behalf of the provincials.'

The boys apparently weren't in any hurry to risk a hick from Darlington and it was a few months before Isaacs was back. He was, he explained, bringing cameras for the Parliamentary by-election at Harold Macmillan's old constituency, Stockton-on-Tees. He asked me to provide commentary on the press treatment of the election. The Labour candidate was an Oxford graduate named Bill Rodgers, who was to become Secretary of State for Transport, then one of the gang of four Social Democrats who broke with Labour, and later the SDP leader in the House of Lords. Young and dashing, with a fiercely pretty wife, Rodgers was running rings round his Tory opponent. His theme tune 'My Darling Billy Boy' caught on. The sound that permeated my own broadcast was a howling wind. I stood in the town square, orating into a gale and feeling foolish, as I squinted at the teleprompter, watched by a group of giggling urchins.

Soon afterwards, Isaacs was succeeded in control of *What the Papers Say* by Barrie Heads, who'd produced my interview with the painter L. S. Lowry. He invited me to join what was now a regular panel. This was hard. Brian Inglis, the anchor for the series, was dry, ironic and authoritative; Michael Frayn and Peter Eckersley were very witty. Barrie's main problem with me was my North Country pronunciation. The Queen's English was still the standard on television. Any regional accent was judged déclassé, unless in a slice-of-life show like Granada's own *Coronation Street*. In one run-through of my script for 'The Papers', Barrie rushed out of the control room shouting: 'Butcher, Butcher!' He meant that my Lancashire accent was overly stressing the 'u': 'Don't say boo-ocher! Say butcher! Try it again.' I did. It satisfied him. But on the show I was so concerned to pronounce it right it came out 'betcher'. Thereafter, I continually rehearsed to myself, reciting 'butcher, baker, candlestick maker,' but the flat a's and deep u's kept coming back all the same.

For the next two years, I was on about once a month. It was a slog in Darlington scouring scores of newspapers scattered amid the children's toys, as well as writing and rewriting, counting and recounting the words to fit the allotted fifteen minutes – all in between hours at the office, followed on the Wednesday night by a long drive over the Pennines for a recording session in the Manchester studio the next day. The newspaper extracts were read by actors, and the tone of their voices, pace and timing had to be rehearsed.

How I sweated over the early scripts! I had not merely to read all the papers, but compare them for news-getting, accuracy and fairness. I'd known from childhood, for instance, that the *Daily Express* (circulation 4 million) believed in putting an optimistic gloss on all news (unless it was about the Labour party). Its most famous editor, Arthur Christiansen, laid it down that the *Express* 'should make everyone feel it is a sunny day'. Nice sentiment, but it was remarkable how far they were prepared to go to make everyone believe all was for the best in the best of all possible worlds. Milk in Britain was being contaminated by radioactive iodine from a Soviet 57-megaton bomb test in the atmosphere, reported the Agricultural Research Council; the government made a statement in Parliament that it was keeping a day-to-day watch in case the contamination got to a danger point. These two items were in every paper except the *Express*. Instead, it wrote: 'there is little danger milk will become contaminated.' When all the other papers reported that Britain could expect additional strontium-90 to arrive next spring, the *Express* reported that 'many experts' believed the Soviets could produce 'clean' bombs with little fallout. But they hadn't produced them; theirs was a singularly dirty bomb. 'All this talk' about fallout, said the *Express*, was 'unpatriotic, because it made the Russians think they could scare us.' Next, I said on air in my commentary, we'd be told by the *Express* that strontium-90 was good for us.

Though that sort of absurdist journalism was meat and drink to *What the Papers Say*, I also tried to highlight any great reporting I'd read in the national papers. I contrasted the *People*'s robust pursuit of the crooks running football pools for bogus charities with the malicious invasions of privacy by the *Daily Sketch* gossip writers simply to make someone miserable. I praised the *Sunday Times*' exposé of the slum landlord Peter Rachman. I chastised the *Daily Mirror* for rejecting a Conservative advertisement without saying why, and teased the *Sunday Express* for not disclosing that the lively letters it ran were all written by staffers posing as readers.

Some took this better than others. The editor of the *Sunday Express*, John Junor, invited me to lunch. The editor of the *Daily Mirror* slammed me, thundering prominently in the paper: 'Evans dedicates his spare time to denigrating the rest of the press. Loftily he lectures the national newspapers as if Darlington exudes a special degree of insight and wisdom denied to newspapers in London and Manchester.' I did the most detective work tracking how the newspapers had failed to find out what lay behind the resignation of Lord Mancroft from the Norwich Union Insurance Society. It transpired that the Jewish Mancroft had been forced out by Arab business interests that had dealings with the Norwich, but the *Financial Times*, which had first reported the resignation, was slow to find out why and even slower to comment.

My commentary did not win friends on Fleet Street. I heard that Lord Drogheda, the fastidious chairman of the *Financial Times*, was upset with me; and I was well aware that Pearson Industries, which owned the *Financial Times*, also, through the Westminster Press, owned the *Northern Echo*. Drogheda was far from alone. Big Tom wrote a friendly warning letter from the *Manchester Evening News*: 'It so happens that at a large gathering in London last night I saw a number of our Top Boys, one of whom went into a long diatribe that your Granada programme was intended to try and kill newspapers and that you were determined to single out *The Sun* for often quite unjustified criticism which, if persisted in, could put the newspaper and 2,000 employees out of business.'

I'd actually commented very little on the struggling *Sun* (then owned by the Mirror group, which got tired of trying to make it succeed and sold it to Rupert Murdoch, who made it a building block of his empire). Tom wrote: 'I tried to reason with one editor but the conviction appeared to be that instead of one of their own kind trying to help newspapers at a critical time, "a newspaperman is selling us down the river to the commercial television companies who are delighted at the spectacle".' Tom concluded: 'I can also tell you that one of the top boys let it drop that they're watching your paper like hawks every day and they even quoted headings and certain things to me. Keep your powder dry!'

I told Big Tom I had the curious notion that if 'helping newspapers' survive was the criterion, surely improving their performance would help. And no Granada producer ever once tried to influence me one way or another in the commentaries. Big Tom understood; I thought that storm clouds had lifted. I was stunned when Charles

Fenby told me I had to stop appearing on *What the Papers Say*. The icicle I'd first encountered had become a warm and perceptive booster, but now he noted that my contract required me to seek the permission of the Westminster Press board for doing anything other than edit the newspaper, and he was not giving it.

I would not lightly accept the ban, I told Fenby, because the publicity had drawn attention to the *Echo*. It was now being noted and quoted much more often. Fenby was adamant, so I requested permission to appeal to the Westminster Press Board. It so happened it was meeting on the Thursday I was due to do the show that Fenby insisted should be my last.

As soon as I'd finished the recording that afternoon in Manchester, I drove straight back to Darlington. Fenby and the board had just finished viewing the actual programme going out at 10.30 p.m. I entered the boardroom in trepidation. They all applauded. It was a tremendous relief, a ruling in character with the open way the Westminster Press ran their newspapers. Fenby took his defeat with grace, and I continued the programme until the end of my editorship of the *Northern Echo*.

When I'd met Sid Chaplin at the start of my editorship, the region was sunk in gloom, and we'd wondered if we could persuade someone to stage a spectacular celebration of its heritage, its art, architecture and scenic beauty. In 1964 Tom Little, our chief reporter (and music critic) in Newcastle, watched a son et lumière concert in the radiant white basilica at Vézelay in France, and in his review for the paper wondered why we could not do the same in the much grander and more glorious setting of Durham Cathedral. Well, why not? I called in David Spark. 'We're going to have a son et lumière concert in Durham,' I told him, 'and you're going to organize it.'

Of course, it meant borrowing the cathedral, and having the city of Durham amenable, and finding a writer and composer, and raising money for script and music, and finding a brilliant lighting engineer, and selling tickets and praying that people would come. We started by seeking the blessing of Durham's Dean, the Very Reverend John

Wild. He and his wife gave us lunch in the cathedral Close, which David remembers was trout with a delicious sauce. I can never remember anything I eat; on this occasion, too, I was concentrating on not talking like an irreverent show business impresario.

The Dean warmed to the proposal. So did Mayor Norman Richardson, who throbbed with energy. We made him chairman. We engaged Christopher Ede as director and Charles Passmore at Atlas Lighting. I asked Sid Chaplin to write the script; Flora Robson, born in South Shields, agreed to narrate. We dragooned the cathedral choir, the Horden Colliery Band, the Cornforth Men's Choir and the cathedral's bell ringers.

To guard against financial failure, I asked Tyne Tees Television to give us a £1,000 guarantee. Arthur Clifford said yes instantly, and so did every organization we went to. As manager, we hired the fiancée of the effervescent director of the North-East Arts Association, Sandy Dunbar. She set up to sell tickets from a caravan in Durham City's Market Place and was besieged. We circulated the Women's Institutes with leaflets, and issued invitations through the paper.

It was the single most exciting and uplifting experience of my time in Darlington, a magical marriage of North-East enterprise and artistry to reflect the splendours of human faith and endeavour. You could hear the intake of breath among the crowds as the lighting revealed the hidden beauties of the interior and the pageant of 900 years unfolded: the translation of the body of St Cuthbert from Holy Island, the start of building on the rock, the battle at Neville's Cross, Charles I praying alone on his way to London, a murderer seeking sanctuary hammering on the great doors, the entry of miners' bands to dramatize the role of the common folk as well as the ambitious princes and clerics.

When it was over, we were able to give the cathedral the profit of around £70,000 at today's values. It was more than a concert. It was agreed most of the money should go to pay for the installation of permanent floodlighting. In the years since, I've never been able to look on that glorious heritage of the cathedral shining in the night without a rush of exaltation and gratitude.

*

I'd edited the *Northern Echo* for four years when I had a letter that would provoke the biggest of the campaigns.

It was March 1965, and I was on an express train from Darlington rattling down to London for a Westminster Press conference. I'd caught the train with seconds to spare, which was normal in those madcap days. I made it to my reserved seat only because Joan Thomas pushed me out of the office and – as always – phoned ahead to the station staff, so when I ran onto the platform with the train about to leave they had the right carriage door open. She never told me this at the time. I just knew there were sixty-one minutes to the hour and assumed everyone else did.

In my haste, I grabbed sheaves of articles and correspondence reproachfully piling up in the pending tray. Among them was an article submitted for publication from a Darlington man I didn't know. Herbert Wolfe had escaped the Nazi persecution of the Jews in 1933. He'd brought with him one shilling – from which he built a thriving chemical business – and a passion for justice. The story he told in his letter and article accelerated my racing heart, carrying me back to a cold night fifteen years before in March 1950, when a young man called Timothy Evans – no relation – sat in the condemned cell in Pentonville Prison waiting to be hanged. He was twenty-five, a bakery van driver and not very bright. He'd had no normal schooling and he couldn't read. He whiled away the time playing Chinese patience and chatting about football and boxing. His companions said later he didn't seem to realize his position.

'The one thing that sticks in my mind,' Evans would say to the warders in the cell with him, 'is that I'm in for something I haven't done.' He'd been found guilty at the Old Bailey of the murder of his baby daughter Geraldine; he was charged with, but not tried for, the murder of his wife Beryl, whose strangled body was found with the baby's, bundled up and hidden in the washhouse at 10 Rillington Place, a small, squalid house in a seedy area of Notting Hill, London, where the Evanses had a poky flat. The trial excited little attention. The chief prosecution witness was a bespectacled clerk called John Reginald Halliday Christie, who lived in the ground floor flat at 10 Rillington Place.

All that Evans could say in his defence was that 'Christie done it.' He couldn't suggest a motive. The jury was out only forty minutes. The appeal was dismissed. Our neighbour in Failsworth, one Albert Pierrepoint, the official executioner, was summoned from the pub he ran called Help the Poor Struggler. It was just another of the several hundred hangings he'd carried out with great efficiency at £15 apiece. There was no crowd at Pentonville at 9 a.m. on 9 March 1950, when the uncomprehending Timothy Evans was executed for a murder he did not do.

The cold facts Wolfe summarized gave me an urgent feeling that I should pull the emergency cord that would stop the swaying high-speed train so I could shout to the world that here was a monstrous injustice we must lose no time in correcting. It pained me that I'd put off reading through the pending tray, for the sequel to Evans's execution was as horrifying in its way as the terrible crime.

What the judge and jury didn't know, what counsel didn't know, what Evans never knew, was that the star witness for the Crown was already a psychopathic strangler. Even as Mr Justice Lewis donned the black cap and pronounced sentence on Evans, the bodies of two of John Christie's victims, Ruth Fuerst and Muriel Eady, were lying buried, undetected, in the little back garden in Rillington Place.

Three years after the execution of Timothy, there was a new tenant in Christie's old ground-floor flat. He started to put up a wall bracket, pulled off a piece of wallpaper to reveal a papered-over cupboard, and found himself looking at the bare back of a human body. There were two more corpses in the cupboard, another under the floor in the front room (Mrs Christie), plus the two female skeletons in the garden, six in all. Three years after the trial of Timothy, Christie stood in the same dock at the Old Bailey and confessed that he was a necrophiliac and that it was he, not Timothy Evans, who had strangled Beryl Evans for sexual gratification at the moment of death.

The Christie confession confronted the public and the legal system with an appalling probability: that British justice had hanged an innocent man – and had done so on the evidence of the man who framed him, a man of such sangfroid that when his garden fence slipped he propped it up with a human femur.

How could it have happened? It wasn't surprising that judge and jury at the time chose to believe Christie. He was fluent, he was ingratiating, he'd been in France in the First World War and been gassed in his country's service, and from 1939 to 1943 he'd been a War Reserve policeman with two special commendations. What a nerve this illiterate wretch Timothy Evans had, trying to blame an upstanding ex-policeman! And hadn't he admitted the crime? But it was a bogus confession. Christie had offered to perform an abortion on Beryl Evans – one of his tricks to indulge his vice – and Evans felt guilty when Christie told him it 'didn't work' and Beryl had died in the procedure.

We can still get a very good idea of the diabolical nature of Christie from the movie *10 Rillington Place*, where the wily whispering serial killer (played by Richard Attenborough), believed by the Crown, is the cobra, and the pathetic Timothy Evans (John Hurt) the mouse. 'Playing Christie,' Attenborough told me at the film's world premiere, 'was the most disturbing, distressing role I've ever played.'

In Parliament and the press, following Christie's conviction and confession in 1953, there was an insistent demand to re-examine the case. The Home Secretary Sir David Maxwell Fyfe announced that he'd asked for an inquiry by a Queen's Counsel. The QC he chose was John Scott Henderson, a selection that proved to be a landmark in hypocrisy. The Home Secretary gave Henderson only nine days to review the complexities on the grounds that Christie's execution shouldn't be delayed. It was an absurd request and Henderson complied by rushing out an absurd report in only seven days. He did not merely say that Timothy Evans was guilty after all. 'There is,' he concluded, '*no ground for thinking* that there may have been a miscarriage of justice.' Nobody else got a chance to interrogate Christie. On 15 July he was hanged on the same gallows where the man he'd framed had died.

The Home Secretary, a devout believer in the infallibility of trials for murder, declared it 'a fantasy' to think there could have been a miscarriage of justice, but there were a number of people in Parliament and the press who remained disturbed, for good reason.

Michael Eddowes, a London solicitor, published an investigation revealing pressure had been brought to suppress the testimony of witnesses to Christie's lying and violent nature. Christie, 'this perfectly innocent man', in the words of Mr Christmas Humphreys, the QC prosecuting Evans, had in fact six entries on his police record, including six months in jail for maliciously wounding a woman he nearly killed. The authorities ignored Eddowes. The *Daily Mirror*'s Peter Baker interviewed the Roman Catholic chaplain at Pentonville and concluded that Evans didn't confess to either murder before he died saying the rosary. The authorities were unmoved.

The next Home Secretary, Major Lloyd George, maintained the intransigence. A private delegation of Sir Linton Andrews, the retired editor of the *Yorkshire Post*, Ian Gilmour MP, John Grigg (*National and English Review*) and David Astor (*Observer*) demonstrated the inherent falsity of the implausibly perfect confession the illiterate Timothy Evans was supposed to have written. I asked Sir Linton what happened: 'It was a waste of time. Lloyd George's mind was clearly made up before we began.'

In her work for Notable British Trials, Ms F. Tennyson Jesse, a crime reporter and editor (and a grandniece of the poet Lord Tennyson), again underlined the fallacies in the prosecution case. The authorities dug in. Ludovic Kennedy, the celebrated writer, TV performer and Liberal candidate for Parliament, was moved to spend five years writing a masterly demolition of the case. It produced a Parliamentary debate in June 1961 where the Conservative Home Secretary, Rab Butler, conceded that no jury of the day would convict, but he made no attempt to explain the crime committed in the public's name or exonerate the victim. There was nothing he could do, he murmured, it was all too long ago.

The debate produced something that made me still more agitated in 1965. Among a number of speeches from the Labour opposition there was one by Sir Frank Soskice QC, which passionately demanded a new inquiry, a free pardon, and that the body be handed over to Timothy's Catholic family (a mother and two sisters) for burial in consecrated ground: 'I believe,' he said, 'that if ever there was a debt due to justice, and to the reputation of our own judicial system and to the public conscience of many millions of people in this country, that debt is one the Home Secretary should pay now.' Three and a half years after that, Sir Frank himself became the Home Secretary. He then had the power to do what he'd urged the government to do in 1961. He didn't, proclaiming: 'I really do not think that an inquiry would serve any useful purpose.'

Sir Frank was the fourth Home Secretary in eleven years to reject a reopening of the case, and MPs and editors had other things on their mind then. Given the calibre of the people who'd already protested, the fate of Timothy Evans was a lost cause.

To Herbert Wolfe this was intolerable. The integrity of British justice was precious, and it had been polluted. He'd convinced the Liberal party to pass a resolution; it made no impact. He'd written letters to the press; they were discarded. He'd chosen the fifteenth anniversary of Timothy's Evans's death, 9 March 1965, to send me a short article. As soon as I returned to Darlington, I read all I could on the case and was overwhelmed by the magnitude of what we'd been led to believe.

If Timothy Evans and Christie were both killers, we were not merely being asked to accept that there were two stranglers of women in the same two-up two-down house, operating independently and in ignorance of one another. Both men had used the same method of strangulation, and both made confessions to the police using the same language. Both confessed to 'using a piece of rope'; and a piece of rope 'off a chair'. Both disposed of the strangling ligature, both concealed their victims' bodies; both temporarily used the same place of concealment; both wrapped their victims' bodies in blankets; both left them without shoes, and without underclothing.

Not only were these men independently strangling in the same way at the same time in the same house, but it was pure chance that Timothy Evans accused the one other man who, unknown to him, shared his own supposed murdering characteristics. Evidence to overwhelm this series of coincidences would need to be formidable. The likelihood of finding two people with the same fingerprints is 4 billion to one (twice the number of people in the world then). The

Evans–Christie 'coincidence' was like finding two people with the same fingerprints in the same house.

I edited Wolfe's article and published it along with a full editorial setting out the reasons justifying a new inquiry.

I knew it would take much more than this to break officialdom's wall of certitude. What could a provincial newspaper and one of its readers possibly accomplish after all these years when all the distinguished testimony had been to no avail?

Soon after my trauma on the train – and it was that insistent – I was back in London, sitting on a cold stone seat in the lobby of the House of Commons. The man I'd come to see had written the fatal words 'let the law take its course' on the death warrant for Timothy Evans. This was Lord Chuter Ede, who'd been Labour's Home Secretary at the time. He was the man with the least to gain from reopening the case, yet he had the humility and courage to say he now believed he'd sent an innocent man to the gallows and society should make amends. I asked him if he would visit the Home Secretary with a group of MPs and he agreed – a unique event for a former Home Secretary to appeal to his successor for a pardon for a convicted person.

I put that news on the front page with a little white-on-black box (a logotype) I intended to use to flag every story about Timothy Evans: 'Man on Our Conscience'. I wrote personal letters to all our regional MPs. In an editorial, we asked: Why has Sir Frank changed his mind? If he'd discovered some new element in the case, he should tell us; if not how could he explain his volte-face? But Sir Frank would not be drawn. Chuter Ede had warned me how hard it would be to make any impact. 'We are up against the full weight of official Whitehall.'

I sent Wolfe's article and my editorials to every regional and national editor and broadcaster. Nobody picked up on the case or the Soskice contradiction. The silence was broken only by the chief whip of the Liberal party, Eric Lubbock. He put down a House of Commons motion for a new inquiry and invited signatures from members of all parties. A month later, he had only nine signatories.

An editor asked me: 'Why are you flogging a dead horse? Why

give a dead man any space?' I sent him a quotation from Michael Stewart MP (later Foreign Secretary): 'The moment we say we cannot be bothered, we have other important things to do, we turn from our progress and start walking along the road that leads to Belsen.' A radio interview I secured after a few weeks brought a stinging rebuke from Douglas Nicholson, the chairman of Vaux breweries in Sunderland. He wasn't clear, he said, whether my call for an inquiry was 'a newspaper stunt', but it did seem to him and others he had spoken to that an inquiry would 'waste the time of important people'.

It was a strange period for me. I don't have a thick skin: emotional, rather than phlegmatic, is the adjective that follows me around. But as the discouragements multiplied I grew preternaturally calmer. It was a weird out-of-body experience, like the time in New York when I was mugged and regarded the mugger with a gun to my head with ridiculous detachment. I just went on publishing everything I could. Every time an MP signed Lubbock's motion, I put it on the front page with the Man on Our Conscience logo. Every day I selected one question after another about the conviction and put it under the logo. This got to be a bit much for Maurice Wedgewood and Frank Peters, who saw their precious front-page space taken up by Man on Our Conscience paragraphs. Said Peters: 'Isn't it time to call it a day?'

I fell back on the famous editor Horace Greeley, who'd observed that the point when a newspaper begins to tire of a campaign is the point when readers are just beginning to notice it. But how to keep up the momentum and not bore everyone to tears? I assigned a bright reporter, Jim Walker, to examine how the authorities had reacted when confronted with other miscarriages of justice. Arthur Conan Doyle, the creator of Sherlock Holmes, had exposed the wrongful conviction of Oscar Slater, who nonetheless had to spend nineteen years in jail before the Home Office admitted error. Then Doyle, after a Sherlockian investigation, campaigned for a pardon for the former solicitor George Edalji, erroneously convicted of mutilating animals, where the authorities held out against a pardon but had to concede the establishment of the Court of Criminal Appeal.

Letters did begin to trickle into the paper. Ludovic Kennedy came back from abroad and we formed a Timothy Evans Committee of all those who over the years had campaigned on Evans's behalf. On 19 May 1965 I collated all the editorials and news reports and features and letters in a four-page *Northern Echo* pamphlet and mailed it to every MP, every editor, every television station and BBC radio. Gradually Lubbock gathered allies, and four months into the campaign, 108 MPs had joined the call for an inquiry. I was now regularly interviewed about the case on radio and television. Supportive comment began to appear left and right – in the *Catholic Herald* and in the left-wing *Tribune* and by the scorching columnist Bernard Levin in the *Daily Mail*, but nowhere else in the national press. The going was made easier by the provincial newspapers. I urged all the editors to collaborate on a joint letter to the Prime Minister. They took up the *Northern Echo* campaign without a trace of jealousy.

Eddowes, so unrelenting in his concern over all the years, had bought the house in Rillington Place with the intent of preserving evidence of the physical impossibility of Evans doing what the prosecution said he did, when he did, especially hiding two bodies in the washhouse at the very time workmen were there doing repairs. We decided to summon the press to the house – and created a flurry of activity we didn't seek. Eddowes had arranged access with his tenant, a West Indian lady who suddenly decided that she didn't want a posse of newspaper and television people in the house. Kennedy had led in four of us when she opened an upstairs window and shouted abuse at our arriving reporters. Then she came downstairs and put her large presence between us and the front door. The newsmen couldn't get in, and short of forcing her aside, from which we flinched, we couldn't get out. We were reduced to pushing notes through the letterbox imploring the press to wait. After ten minutes of this nonsense, landlord Eddowes persuaded his tenant to open the door, but as Kennedy showed everyone the washhouse she thumped downstairs and again furiously barred the exit. Twenty or thirty of us were hostage for half an hour in the murder house and rescued only by the arrival of the police, drawn by the commotion. 'It would have served you right,' Bernard Levin wrote to me, 'if Christie had come down the chimney and necrophilised the lot of you.'

We survived the ridicule. On 22 July, Lubbock's motion had 113 signatures. With Chuter Ede, he led an all-party group to see Sir Frank Soskice, who agreed to think again. A month later he gave in. He overruled the advice of his Civil Service officials, and returned to his original position, appointing Mr Justice Brabin to conduct an inquiry in public in the Royal Courts of Justice.

I was there in the Queen's Bench Court No. 6 in the Strand Law Courts on Tuesday, 23 November 1965, with Herbert Wolfe and Ludo Kennedy, when Brabin opened the inquiry. The court was packed with QCs, government officials, press, witnesses, police, and Evans relatives. Day by day the inquiry revealed the missteps in the dreadful labyrinth to the execution; we reported them all and Wolfe wrote a commentary for the *Northern Echo*.

The judge took a million words or so of evidence and examined seventy-nine witnesses – and then on 12 October 1966 he presented the oddest judgement of all: Timothy Evans had probably not murdered his baby, for which he was hanged, but he probably had murdered his wife, for which he was not even tried. 'This was certainly an arresting theory,' remarked Ludo, 'especially as there is virtually no evidence to support it.'

I wrote an examination of the flaws in the Brabin manoeuvre based on all the evidence that had been taken over a year, and all the Timothy Evans committee joined in urging the new Home Secretary, Roy Jenkins, at last to do the decent thing. The testimonies at the inquiry, the judge's findings on the murder of the baby and the years of advocacy were enough for Jenkins, a man who made all the Whitehall stonewallers look like straw men. Wolfe and I were in the House of Commons on the 18th of October when Jenkins rose to make a unique announcement. On his recommendation, the Queen had granted Timothy John Evans a free pardon, and the state returned his remains to his family for burial in consecrated ground.

Many people had worked for years to end the death penalty on religious and ethical grounds. The execution of Evans and the long refusal to face the shame of that brought the cause to a climax. Two weeks after the Brabin inquiry was announced, our ally and the stalwart long-time abolition campaigner MP Sydney Silverman won a motion for the suspension of the death penalty, which had sent 799 men and 16 women to the gallows that century. On 9 November 1965 the House of Commons voted to suspend executions for murder for five years.

Four years later, on 18 December 1969, on a free vote, the death penalty was abolished altogether.

BOOK TWO

Scoop, Scandal and Strife

13

THE ROLLS-ROYCE OF
FLEET STREET

Twenty-five years almost to the day since I waited while my father sat on the sands at Rhyl with the burned-out soldiers rescued from Dunkirk, I encountered a survivor who was to change my life.

Denis Hamilton, editor of the *Sunday Times*, was one of the most powerful people in British journalism. In 1940, this debonair, soft-spoken man had been a 22-year-old junior officer shoulder-deep in the Atlantic waters of the English Channel desperately trying to save the remnants of his battalion. He got to Dunkirk with only 160 men, the survivors of the 1,000 in his 11th Battalion of the Durham Light Infantry.

Now he was not only the prodigiously successful editor of the *Sunday Times*, the flagship of Thomson Newspapers, but editorial director of five Sundays, five morning and eleven evening newspapers. He'd ended the war as the British Army's youngest brigadier, decorated with a Distinguished Service Order for holding back a German thrust near Arnhem. He moved in exalted circles. He was close to Field Marshal Montgomery, Prime Minister Harold Macmillan and South Africa's Prime Minister, Field Marshal Jan Smuts. He was photographed with members of the royal family, the Shah of Iran, President Kennedy and President Nasser. He was a friend of the Grahams at the *Washington Post*, the Sulzbergers at the *New York Times*.

The three-hour-plus train ride from Darlington deposited me in King's Cross station, a good walk from the copper-faced Thomson House at 200 Gray's Inn Road. Passing through the imposing double glass doors at the entrance embossed with the coat of arms of the owner, Lord Thomson of Fleet – motto: *Nemo me impune lacessit* (No one provokes me with impunity) – I was intercepted by a very martial commissionaire in a white peaked cap, his uniform ablaze with battle ribbons. I had the impression he checked the shine on my shoes as he telephoned someone to confirm the authenticity of my letter of introduction to Hamilton. Once confirmation arrived, he showed me into the lift to the fifth floor, where I was escorted to an outer office and then to the inner sanctum that the secretary breathlessly told me had been designed by Lord Snowdon, then husband of Princess Margaret. It was more like an elegant drawing room, with sofas and silk cushions. Hamilton seated me in a stylish Eames chair while he took a corner of a sofa beneath a Matisse print. No sign of a typewriter anywhere.

He was unhurried with me (the former corporal), and not at all intimidating. We established a bridgehead in our shared attachment to the North-East of England – he'd been born in South Shields and worked in Newcastle – then he veered away to Asia and the training assignments I'd carried out for the International Press Institute. 'I heard what you did for all those newspapers in India,' he said. 'Very important.' He said nothing more for what seemed like an eternity, his mind, I imagined, roaming the subcontinent during the absences that I later learned were unnervingly characteristic of him. I didn't interrupt his reverie. Then his soft voice resumed. 'The Timothy Evans affair in the *Northern Echo* and the campaigns on pollution and for a big clean-up of pit heaps ... well done. A really good provincial newspaper can make a difference to a community.'

I presumed he must be sounding me out on switching sides to join his Thomson regional newspaper group; at the *Northern Echo* I was competing against three of their papers every day. After the geography discussion, however, it seemed it was the *Sunday Times* that was at the top of his agenda. The *Sunday Times*! I hadn't allowed that possibility to enter my mind when he'd asked me down to London; I'd guessed it was either about the regional papers or the role of the provincial editors on the National Council for the Training of Journalists, where I'd joined discussions in which Hamilton occasionally took part. I tried to look calm. It was harder when I caught up with his ruminations. 'I'm looking for a practised newsman who might be groomed to be managing editor here.'

Managing editor? Now that was a heady thought. The job was impressive enough in itself, and a managing editor was also clearly in the line of succession to the editor's chair. But 'might be groomed' was tentative, the list of potential assignments he enumerated was long – features, news, campaigns, sport, long-term planning for the colour magazine – but without specifying who would have final say over any of them. How many jostling managing editors were there at the *Sunday Times* already? Then he murmured something, too, about looking for a successor to Pat Murphy, a seasoned professional who reported to Hamilton on the performance of Thomson's twenty regional editors. Murphy's current job held no interest for me, nor did I think I'd be much good at it. Twenty editors! I'd found it distracting enough to be looking over the shoulders of just three editors of an evening newspaper and two weeklies after I was promoted to editor in chief of the North of England newspaper group while still editing the *Northern Echo*.

The opportunity of the *Sunday Times*, though, did make my head spin. How could it not? This was the biggest of what we called the quality Sundays, bigger in circulation at more than a million, bigger in number of pages; it broke news more often and its staff was legendary. It is not every newspaper that could boast Ian Fleming, the creator of James Bond, as its foreign manager and upscale gossip columnist. Or where else in a lift you could meet such literary luminaries as Cyril Connolly, George Steiner and Raymond Mortimer and ask if they'd read any good books lately? The newspaper's critics and foreign correspondents trailed clouds of glory. The magnetic Fleming, coming out of the war as assistant to the Director of Naval Intelligence, recruited eighty-one men and seven women as

correspondents for Lord Kemsley's Mercury foreign service, their
locations indicated by coloured lights on a map behind Fleming's
desk in Gray's Inn Road. He liked to say, with a wave of his long
ebonite cigarette holder, that their average age was thirty-eight and
they spoke 3.1 languages apiece. Godfrey Smith, then the young personal assistant to Lord Kemsley – K as he was known – endeared
himself to the irreverent Fleming by letting him have the key to K's
very private loo. He remembers Fleming instructing the awed young
men and women in his circle never to use a subordinate clause and
to call only God and the King 'Sir'. And Fleming's Atticus column,
like the man himself, was sophisticated entertainment.

Admittedly, the glow of the paper's political history was less
impressive. In the 1930s owner and editor-in-chief Kemsley was an
errand boy for Chamberlain in appeasing Hitler, and in 1956 he'd
been a cheerleader for the invasion of Suez (and gained circulation at
the expense of rival owner-editor David Astor's anti-Suez stand in
the *Observer*). Under the ownership of the Canadian-born Roy
Thomson and Hamilton's editorship from 1961, however, the
Sunday Times had become less of a mouthpiece for Conservative
Central Office. It was a far richer, more influential newspaper than
my provincial daily, with 56 pages then to our 16, and at 1,300,000
it had more than ten times our circulation, nationally and interna-
tionally.

I was flattered, but I didn't dive in, as I sometimes did without
checking whether there was any water in the pool. Editing the
Northern Echo, I was 'with child'. The paper was thriving as part of
the community. We'd moved the family from Hurworth to a listed
period house in town where we gave strawberry tea parties on the
lawn while my two-year-old son Michael ate the daffodils. I'd identified so much with the North-East and Darlington that a year before
I'd written to the *Sunday Times* to protest against a book reviewer's
slighting reference to the town, typical of the South's snotty disdain,
I felt, for anything north of Potters Bar. Hamilton himself had telephoned to apologize; the values he prized most were civility and
loyalty.

London itself – the alien metropolis – was a splendid mystery. On my fleeting visits I remembered the bewildered excitement of the pair of Newton Heath cubs just before the war when Dad used a free railway pass to take Fred and me in our best suits by night train from Manchester. We arrived at Euston as the streets were being cleaned early in the morning and then he proudly showed us Big Ben and the Houses of Parliament and Madame Tussaud's waxworks and Regent's Park Zoo and the Tube. We had tea at Joe Lyons corner café, where the nippies, as the waitresses were called, wore white aprons and white lace caps, and then, and then . . . the magical day ended and we were on the night train back to Manchester.

I was thirty-six. I'd watched all my young friends and colleagues in the provinces head for Fleet Street as soon as they could. I'd had the occasional envious pang seeing their bylines from foreign capitals, or hearing of this or that ascent in the hierarchy, but I hadn't looked to London as my future, and looked still less when I became editor of the *Northern Echo*. One of Lord Beaverbrook's top men had recently invited me to go for lunch, but I had never got round to it. In any case, there were just too many big guns firmly in editor's chairs of the papers that interested me – not just Denis Hamilton, the ceaseless innovator at the *Sunday Times*, but Sir William Haley, castigator of the immoral from his pulpit at *The Times*; Alastair Hetherington, keeper of the liberal conscience at the *Guardian*; Michael Berry, the zealot for news at the *Telegraph*; David Astor, the gentle curator of all the cultures at the *Observer*; John Junor at the *Sunday Express*, both acerbic columnist and editor; and the popularizing genius Hugh Cudlipp at the *Daily Mirror*, the voice of the people.

Of course, Fleet Street had its magic then. It's become a dull London thoroughfare since the electronic diaspora to south of the river, powerfully assisted by the gratifying defeat of the Luddite print unions by Rupert Murdoch. But it wasn't like that in 1965. Nearly all the national newspapers had their headquarters in the street or nearby, with their presses roaring in the basements, the press barons barking in the penthouses, news vans and reporters racing out, and enough watering holes for a thirsty newsman, gossip diarist or cameraman to run from one to another in a rainstorm without getting wet. The spoof character Lunchtime O'Booze was an iconic expense account fabricator in *Private Eye*'s 'Street of Shame', but who among us with ink in his veins wouldn't be entranced by the tales of daring scoops and backstairs scandal, much improved in the telling by the bibulous hacks in the Printer's Devil, El Vino's, the Cheshire Cheese, the White Swan, the Punch Tavern, the Old Bell, the Stab in the Back? Or by the sight of Megalopolitan House in its sheath of black glass, where Evelyn Waugh's bewildered anti-hero in *Scoop*, country diarist William Boot, arrived for his unforgettable interview with the foreign editor of the *Daily Beast* and its owner, the autocratic Lord Copper, doppelganger for Lord Beaverbrook.

About Denis Hamilton's question of whether I'd like to join him, I felt like borrowing the response of Copper's underlings who, asked to confirm that black was white, tempered honesty with prudence: 'Up to a point, Lord Copper.' The *Sunday Times* was regarded as the most exciting paper in Fleet Street, albeit located in Gray's Inn Road, where its solitary watering hole was the Blue Lion – but I'd heard quite a few stories of newcomers to national papers being squeezed out of a role. The *Sunday Times*, glittering with competitive talent, had as many people with grand titles as old Mesopotamia. At least on the *Echo* I could get some things done, ungroomed.

Sensitive to my reservations about moving south, Hamilton suggested I had coffee with his deputy, William Rees-Mogg, the donnish epigrammatist (who in 1981 became the celebrated editor of *The Times*). I did so two weeks later, an encounter eased by the discovery that while Rees-Mogg was a country squire from Charterhouse and Balliol, we were both graduates of RAF Padgate. 'Joining the paper would be like joining a freeway,' explained Rees-Mogg, equably ensconced in his Georgian home near Smith Square, in the political heartland of Westminster, within division-bell distance of the Houses of Parliament. 'If you come, I'm sure you'll soon gather speed and get in the right lane.' With the caution I came to see as characteristic of Rees-Mogg, he added: 'Of course we can't see round corners.'

The columns of his I'd read in the *Sunday Times* resounded with such authority, it was a relief to find a shy bibliophile with an appealing little sibilance in his speech. His solemn ecclesiastical manner, hands fingertip to fingertip as if in prayer, dissolved into a self-effacing giggle when confessing a cheerful unfamiliarity with questions of typography and production. Rees-Mogg asked if I was inclined to accept 'Denis's' invitation, then persuasively sketched why I'd enjoy the weekly operations and the personalities I'd be working with if I joined. 'Perhaps you'll care to write some editorials, too,' he said expansively, as he saw me out into the sunshine of Lord North Street looking towards the baroque church of St John's. I visited the church before catching the train back to Darlington, and happened on a lunchtime concert of Beethoven sonatas. It seemed a happy augury.

Back in Darlington, I did some homework on my prospective new boss – Charles Denis Hamilton, known to his associates as 'CD' – as well as on the chairman, Lord Thomson of Fleet. Who were these controllers of the destiny of the *Sunday Times*? Would I be able to pursue the journalism that had most engaged me at the *Northern Echo* as freely as I had with the Westminster Press? Would Hamilton's position as an establishment figure be in any way inhibiting? If an investigation had to be defended legally, would Thomson balk at the costs? The self-made tycoon had amassed most of his fortune, in Canada and Britain, after he was sixty. He was flagrantly frugal. The gossip diarists were agog in 1964 that standing in a queue at Burberry's for a cashmere coat reduced from £70 to £40 was the newly ennobled Baron Thomson of Fleet.

I soon discovered that Hamilton was not the upper-class officer I'd assumed. He'd been brought up in a terraced house in Middlesbrough, his father an engineer, who'd been forced to retire early from Dorman Long's heavily polluted iron and steel works at Acklam with lung cancer and a miserable pension of only 10 shillings a week. Hamilton's scholarship to Middlesbrough High School put him among the handful of youths from the industrial slums, separate from the paying sons of professional people. He'd started in journalism as a junior reporter, as I had, but he had never sought to go to university.

So how had he risen in the ranks so quickly to become an Army officer? He'd learned leadership in the Boy Scouts, achieving the highest level of King's Scout. After Munich, he'd volunteered for the Territorial Army when the Durham Light Infantry needed thirty officers by the end of the month. He wasn't qualified by the standards of the time, meaning he wasn't a public schoolboy, he hadn't played rugby for Durham and his father didn't know the Colonel's family. What he did have was an eye for the relevant social signals. Mixing with officer candidates who'd been solicitors, bank managers, accountants and men from minor public schools, Hamilton assumed an upper-middle-class disguise like a second skin.

Hamilton had a good war, but of wider significance than that oxymoron is that he was a skirmisher in the shifting fault lines of the culture. His establishment aura – his commission, his decoration, his accent, his Savile Row clothes, his whole demeanour – enabled him to advance towards the redoubts of privilege. Absent the illusion that he was a member of the ruling class, his very real native abilities might well not have carried him into a position of power with the deeply snobbish Lord (and Lady) Kemsley, even though he was a war hero. Control of the so-called quality or serious national broadsheet newspapers in Britain, circulating among the more educated, tended to be the preserve of the traditional elites, with the graduates of public schools and Oxbridge predominant. In 1965 when Hamilton was talking about my joining the *Sunday Times*, the top four positions below him were all held by Oxbridge men. Hunter Davies, who'd followed me as a Castleman at Durham (senior man, no less) and editor of *Palatinate*, was the only provincial university man to have come via reporting in Manchester. (His breezy talents had taken him to an envied position as the successor to Fleming, Godfrey Smith and Nick Tomalin writing the Atticus column.) It was similar elsewhere. The *Guardian* was edited by an Oxford man, and the *Telegraph* and *Observer* were owned and edited by Oxford men. But the Canadian Roy Thomson, the son of a barber from a more open, non-deferential society, who'd appointed Hamilton on buying out Kemsley, didn't care where anybody came from so long as he knew where he was going. And William Haley, who oversaw *The Times*, had advanced himself by omnivorous reading. So perhaps there was some hope.

The press was just one strand of British life touched by the social changes accelerated by the war. In his 1940 essay 'The Lion and the Unicorn' George Orwell predicted: 'This war, unless we are defeated, will wipe out most of the existing class privileges.' The victory of the Labour party five years later seemed to fulfil his dream that England would assume its 'real shape' through a conscious open revolt by ordinary people 'against the notion that a half-witted public-school-boy is better fitted for command than an intelligent mechanic'. The two most powerful and able members of Attlee's 1945 Cabinet, Ernest Bevin and Herbert Morrison, were uneducated working-class lads. The Butler Education Act of 1944 opened the door for secondary education for all, as I have described earlier, but by the 1960s higher education was still very much a privilege: seven years after I graduated from Durham, only 4.2 per cent of the 18–21 age group had become full-time university students, hardly a lightning advance on the 3.2 per cent admitted in 1954, and nothing compared with the United States. Orwell had been right to protest that the working class ought not to be 'branded on the tongue' – a phrase borrowed from Wyndham Lewis – their status determined more by accent than by ability. He could not have foreseen how liberation from that perception would be more powerfully assisted by satire than by polemics or politics. The surreal mockeries of class in the phenomenally popular *Goon Show*, on BBC radio, inspired the satirists of *Beyond the Fringe*, leading to *Monty Python* and *Fawlty Towers*. My generation did not feel any need to affect the standard English accent of the BBC news readers and the hotel receptionists posing as Lady Bracknell. It was not that we were brave; it would just have exposed us to ridicule.

I would not be alone as a beneficiary of the late-breaking waves of political, cultural and social changes that gathered force in the mid-1960s. By 1965 the Conservative party had fallen apart in the aftermath of the Profumo sex-and-spy scandal. The Prime Minister was no longer Harold Macmillan, who had appointed thirty-seven Etonians to office, seven in the Cabinet, and played to perfection the role of the grand English gentleman. Now the Prime Minister was Harold Wilson, a scholarship boy at grammar school and university with a nondescript accent who liked to be photographed in his ordinary Gannex raincoat, taking every opportunity to be seen as a middle-class, middlebrow, non-conformist Little Englander. Labour's 'New Vision', epitomized by Wilson's bending the nation's ear about the white heat of technological revolution, narrowly won the 1964 general election over a Conservative party now seen as too much under the influence of the 'fuddy-duddy right'. It was led by Sir Alec Douglas Home, who'd had to demote himself from being the 14th Earl of Home so as to be eligible to sit in the Commons as Sir Alec and succeed Macmillan. He'd been cruelly caricatured as the Prime Minister who did his sums with matchsticks, and had been given only tepid election support in the *Sunday Times*. Afterwards, Rees-Mogg wrote that the party deserved to lose because it had lost the progressive middle class, while Labour had identified itself as the party of the young scientist and university teacher; the 'meritocrats', as identified in Michael Young's influential 1958 book *The Rise of the Meritocracy* – though Young wrote it as a warning against creating a narrow new elite. Rees-Mogg's scalding criticisms brought down Home, and his column predicting that without aligning itself with 'the new society' the Tories would lose the following election was prescient. Labour got back in 1966 with a thumping majority. The stars were thus not badly aligned for me, a young working-class non-Oxbridge graduate with a northern accent, whose political genes were suspect.

Lord Thomson said of Hamilton: 'He's a fellow that doesn't display himself.' He was indeed very private about his origins and his war, but I believe I was lucky that Hamilton's own rise from obscurity, his well-hidden resentment of the way his father had been treated, and his command of men in battle from all walks of life, combined to make him exceptionally open-minded for his time and his position.

My sense of Denis Hamilton's civic virtue, as much as his achievements with the *Sunday Times*, was a powerful attraction. He'd delivered on his promises to the International Press Institute and

Commonwealth Press Union, too, helping scores of editors in developing nations, so I trusted he was in earnest about a plan for one British provincial editor from an undeveloped region.

His boss was more of a puzzle. Roy Thomson was plainly tight-fisted, but he'd risked millions launching the first colour magazine in British newspapers in 1962 and installing machinery for a bigger newspaper. Visiting Thomson House I got no sense of hair-shirt austerities. But what of his attitude to editorial? I'd watched a number of television interviews of Thomson on his purchase of the *Sunday Times* in 1959; he was a tubby, cheerfully Pickwickian figure who blinked at the questioner from behind thick bottle glasses, occasionally twitching his neck as if his collar was too tight, as I had seen my dad do. The impression I had, reinforced later, was that he was psychologically incapable of lying or dissembling. He just blurted things out. The television franchise he'd won in Scotland in 1957, he said with a chuckle, was 'just like having a licence to print money'. Once, in negotiations in Egypt to buy a failing Cairo newspaper from President Nasser, I'd heard he told Nasser: 'You certainly are a cunning old Jew.'

His political philosophy amounted to a few homespun pioneer principles about honesty, humility and thrift, drawn from the life of a self-made man. He'd left school at fourteen but absorbed into his bloodstream the romances of Horatio Alger, poor boy made good. He had the conventional political opinions of the business class. The death penalty was good, socialism a sickness, government regulation bad. But enfiladed from right and left by tough interlocutors like Randolph Churchill and Keith Waterhouse, he wouldn't be shaken from insisting that he would never impose editorial policy.

Thomson didn't disguise that he was a cultural philistine indifferent to all the arts, or that his views were not those of the chattering classes, but he didn't expect anyone to take any notice, least of all copy him. After all, he once remarked, 'part of the social mission of every great newspaper is to provide a home for a large number of salaried eccentrics'.

His attachment to editorial independence had deep roots, practical, rather than philosophical. Failing early on – in trying to grow wheat, sell motor supplies, sell radios, sell anything – he'd learned the hard way how much expertise he needed to realize his ideas. When he acquired Kemsley's empire, he patiently explained that his commitment to editorial freedom was not a 'sales gimmick' by telling the story of how early on in Canada he'd learned to deal with this or that complaint about an item put out by one of his radio stations or small newspapers. He had his policy printed on a card he carried around for twenty-five years like an oath:

> I can state with the utmost emphasis that no person or group can buy or influence editorial support from any newspaper in the Thomson group. Each paper may perceive this interest in its own way, and will do this without advice, counsel or guidance from the Thomson Organisation. I do not believe that a newspaper can be run properly unless its editorial columns are run freely and independently by a highly skilled and dedicated professional journalist. This is and will continue to be my policy.

He'd fish it out from his pocket when accosted by critic, favour-seeker, advertiser or politician wanting him to pressure an editor.

'You wouldn't expect me to go back on my word, would ya?' he'd say, showing them his card.

The word of Thomson and Hamilton was good enough for me. In June 1965 I accepted an invitation to become chief assistant to C. D. Hamilton. I passed through the crested glass doors to start work in January 1966. Hamilton's formal letter of invitation spelled out a clearer prospect of being 'indisputably the key managing editor within a reasonable time', while still floating the idea of succeeding Pat Murphy as the regional newspapers' editorial director if that didn't work out.

I left Enid and our three infant children, Ruth, Kate and Mike, in Darlington while I tested the ice, travelling back home at weekends aboard the midnight sleeper, with an inky third edition of the *Sunday Times* for company.

Longtime foreign manager Ian Fleming bequeathed his successors a warning of the hazards of being deceived by the editor's Tuesday conferences of department heads: 'Beneath the surface friendliness, lurk all the deadly sins with the exception of gluttony and lust. Each one of us has pride in our department of the paper; many of us are covetous of the editorial chair; most are envious of the bright ideas put forward by others; anger comes to the surface at what we regard as unmerited criticism, and sloth, certainly in my case, lurks in the wings.'

The 'sloth' was the giveaway, an obvious exaggeration for effect, since this was the time – between 1945 and 1959 – he was turning out a succession of his James Bond bestsellers (*Casino Royale*, *Live and Let Die*, *Moonraker*, *Diamonds are Forever*, *From Russia with Love*, *Dr. No* and *Goldfinger*). Well, so I told myself, hoping the rivalries were not so intense. It seemed to me on arrival that Hamilton and Rees-Mogg set an agreeable, gentlemanly tone to the weekly proceedings, more reminiscent of a senior common room than the frantic ways of Fleet Street dailies. There were no women in the conference and hardly any on the newspaper. Still, the men who assembled in Hamilton's office each week were an impressive bunch, and it would have been surprising if there wasn't hot competition between them for the managing editorship, or even the editorial chair in the unlikely event of Hamilton leaving it. I'd only been in the office for a day or two when my old friend from Manchester and Durham, Hunter Davies, the only person I knew on the paper, took me aside. 'What are you doing here? You'll get eaten alive. You haven't even got a proper job (as he had as Atticus). You've been a big fish in Darlington, but you'll just be carved up by these *Sunday Times* slickers.'

The leading players were exceedingly clever Oxbridge men who'd vaulted over the traditional route to Fleet Street from the provinces. Presidents of the Oxford Union were in two of the top four positions: Rees-Mogg, the political editor and columnist, and Godfrey Smith, the irrepressibly creative editor of the colour magazine. The foreign editor who controlled Fleming's old domain was Frank Giles, whom Hamilton had filched from the *The Times* where he'd been chief correspondent successively in Rome and Paris. The fourth Oxonian, editing the business news, was Anthony Vice, who'd started out at the *Financial Times*, like Rees-Mogg, and was for five years City editor of the *Daily Telegraph*.

Among the older stalwarts were Leonard Russell, who'd been literary editor for thirty years, and was married to Dilys Powell, doyenne of film critics. Russell was now in charge of the Review Front, then the most cherished showplace in the paper for the best original feature writing, and first serializations from as yet unpublished books of literary quality or sheer excitement ('Three men in a boat on a boiling ocean' was Russell's characterization).

In contention for managing editor, I could see, were a number of 'young Turks': Insight editor Ron Hall, news editor Michael Cudlipp, star writer Nicholas Tomalin, and Mark Boxer, the wild card.

The scintillating founding editor of the colour magazine, Boxer had first made headlines at Cambridge where, editing *Granta*, he'd published sacrilegious doggerel that carried the lines: 'You drunken, gluttonous seedy God/You son of a bitch, you snotty old sod.' But though leaving Cambridge without a degree, Boxer subsequently proved the sharpness of his eye as art director of *Queen* magazine. He was known, too, for a felicity for making enemies via the sharpness of his tongue as well as the wit in his pen-and-ink caricatures. He'd resigned the editorship of the colour magazine, and when I arrived was features editor without controlling any space, so he wandered round in a vaguely insurrectionary role. In conference he was often deftly offensive, which gave an edge of excitement to the proceedings. People resented his disdainful manner and Byronic good looks as much as the substance of his remarks, since he was usually right about what was 'dreadfully dull'. Of all the competing executives, he had for some reason been the most welcoming to me, apart from Hunter Davies. Cudlipp and Hall, some ten years younger than me and both with rare provincial experience, were probably the most put out by my arrival; when I'd ventured a mild criticism of Insight on *What the Papers Say* Hall had sent me a rude postcard. I probably deserved it.

Hamilton's style in the editorial board – a grand name for his Tuesday morning conference – was like none I'd seen before. There were no news schedules, no clipboards, no set agenda, no inquest on things that went wrong the week before. It was more of a conversation about what people had seen, or read, or were puzzled or entertained by. Hamilton let it drift. Having no agenda meant people just talked about what interested them, and this often led to happy sequels for the paper. A remark about the prevalence of short skirts on the streets elicited the information that a revered Parisian film critic had referred to the phenomenon as the 'English Revolution', and then someone else said the revolution was in the moral standards the English young were developing, so different from their boring parents.

Hamilton took hold of that balloon. Who might understand what was happening, someone with authority but wit? Names were batted around. He didn't reject any, so a kind of cultural bidding war developed, everyone trying to come up with a still more appropriate, still more distinguished, still more surprising name.

My diary of 1966 reflects the shifting nature of English culture and the haphazard way I tried to keep up. Memos to myself survive in a tiny diary of 1966 and reflect the eclectic collisions as I struggled to come up with ideas and writers for all sections of the paper. I'd caught the tail-end of a dismissive remark, 'He's just a newsman.' Was it about me? Not wanting to be typecast, I tried to cover all the bases:

- Rebecca West on Feminism
- Court magistrate who thinks 70 miles an hour speed too slow. Eccentric magistrates? Justice as comedy? Tomalin.
- Who Lord Goodman? Lewis Chester to write.
- Jean Shrimpton's knees.
- Find husband/wife writing team, perceptions each other.
- Hector Berlioz letters. Other composer letters?
- Malcolm Muggeridge and Jesus. Fix lunch.

With Leonard Russell's approval, I got to know the London publishers and agents, in the hope we might have early warning of literary coups; I was unused to long, lavish lunches where pound notes were discreetly palmed for the wine waiter. I took bags of books to skim in my cheap room in the loft of the National Liberal Club that I shared with the pigeons and the cleaning ladies outside my door rattling their buckets. I made good use of the ideas and contacts gained as the host of a new weekly BBC radio discussion programme, *Word in Edgeways*.

I can no longer remember why I thought we might bring fresh light to the question of Jean Shrimpton's knees. But I do remember that a breakfast with my old friend Tarzie Vittachi of the International Press Institute led to him writing a stunning two-part Review Front for us revealing what had gone on in Sukarno's Indonesia during a news blackout. First the communists murdered generals in an attempt at a coup, then Suharto's generals murdered the communists, and then fanatical Muslims started killing 'infidels', so that 300,000 died before Indonesia returned to normality.

In the third month I'd been with the paper, Prime Minister Wilson called an election, giving me an opportunity to observe how far the paper's Conservative sympathies affected news coverage. I was in charge of the election pages, writing up the polls and monitoring the press. The *Sunday Times* reporters, I found, were wholly free to report what they saw, hardly commonplace in the fiercely partisan press.

These were difficult months, because in the third week Hamilton told conference I'd be revamping the sports pages. Boxer whispered: 'That's the kiss of death.' Apparently none of the executives cared to tangle with Ken Compston, the very professional but belligerently independent sports editor of seventeen years. He blew smoke in my face, making it clear he didn't want any bloody fancy new ideas mucking up his pages: I'd asked David Hillman to redesign them. I signed Michael Parkinson as a sports columnist (Parky was not yet a TV celebrity), and cut a deal with the renowned yachtsman Francis Chichester. He'd announced he was going to attempt sailing single-handed the 28,000 miles to Australia and back, following the romantic and dangerous path of the famous clippers. We gave him a marvellous send-off on the Review Front with a profile written by Philip Norman, last seen earlier in these pages reporting pop concerts for the *Northern*

Echo. He'd become a staff man on the magazine, having won a writing contest set by Godfrey Smith. The Chichester signing turned out to provide a year-long exciting series, the whole world absorbed with his regular dispatches, climaxing when experts predicted on his setting sail from Australia that he would never survive the dangerous straits round Cape Horn. It was the start of the *Sunday Times* in adventure journalism.

I was tense at Hamilton's first Tuesday conference after the launch of the new sports pages. There was bound to be criticism. I just hoped it was specific so I could try to grapple with it. Leonard Russell knocked his pipe on an ash stand and spoke before anyone else. 'Damned good sports pages this week.' Whatever anyone was about to say, Russell's endorsement was enough; a quiet murmur of assent and we were off on other topics. All that was required was for England to win the World Cup, which they did in July against Germany; and they hadn't needed to adopt the strategy advocated by Parkinson of having ten goalkeepers and one forward. The following week Hamilton announced I was to be managing editor.

The corner William Rees-Mogg had said we couldn't see around opened on unexpected vistas in September 1966, when Hamilton made a dramatic announcement. The separate companies of Lord Thomson's profitable *Sunday Times* and Lord Astor's loss-making daily *Times* had agreed to merge into a new Times Newspapers Company, 85 per cent of whose stock would be owned by the Thomson Organisation. 'The main obstacle to the merger,' said Lord Thomson, 'had undoubtedly been me. I don't think Lord Astor could stomach the idea of giving control of his paper to a roughneck Canadian.' Thomson volunteered to give up the chairmanship, though he remained the principal risk-taker. He said he calculated that the ample profits of the *Sunday Times* would cover losses by *The Times* – £285,000 that year – but if the company moved into loss he and his son pledged their private fortune. And, he reiterated his pledge that neither the organization nor any individual Thomson would ever interfere in editorial policy.

Both newspapers were judged so important to the national life that the merger was referred to the Monopolies Commission. There was no other ground for a referral, since it would increase the Thomson stake in the circulation of the national and provincial press to only 6.5 per cent – compared with 26 per cent for the Mirror group, 21 per cent for the Mail group and 18 per cent for Beaverbrook. (An even more striking comparison is that in 1981 Prime Minister Margaret Thatcher stopped a referral to the Monopolies Commission of Rupert Murdoch's acquisition of Times Newspapers, though it gave him control of 36 per cent of the national circulation.)

The merger was approved by the Monopolies Commission in December 1966. Both William Haley at *The Times* and Denis Hamilton at the *Sunday Times* relinquished their editorships, Haley to become the first-year chairman of Times Newspapers, Hamilton to become in editor in chief of both papers. He promised the Monopolies Commission he would not attempt to impose identical policies on the new editors of the *The Times* and *Sunday Times*.

Rees-Mogg was clearly destined for *The Times*. I had no great expectations I would be high on the list to succeed Hamilton at the *Sunday Times*, and I was surprised when Mark Boxer remarked casually: 'You'd have been a candidate for editor, you know, but you're considered too left-wing.' I'd originated several big features, led an Insight investigation of the crooked car insurance company headed by Dr Emil Savundra, revamped sports and overseen news, but I'd been on the paper for only a year, managing editor for only three months, and there were several senior contenders. The clear favourite was the foreign editor Frank Giles, an unruffled administrator who was an accomplished linguist and writer. He'd been Ernest Bevin's private secretary at the Foreign Office and knew many world leaders.

After Giles, it turned out the rivals for the *Sunday Times* chair were fewer than I'd expected. Godfrey Smith made it clear he had no ambitions to edit the paper. Michael Cudlipp and Anthony Vice were privately earmarked for *The Times*; Ron Hall, Mark Boxer and Nicholas Tomalin were, it seems, judged not to have sufficient experience setting political and economic policy. This left two older and formidable frontrunners inside the building – Giles, and Pat Murphy, the Thomson group's editorial director – and one powerful outsider, Charles Wintour. The volcanic Randolph Churchill was hoarse in his incessant and often drunken private lobbying of Hamilton and Thomson for the appointment of Wintour, the acerbically clever editor of the excellent *Evening Standard* (and the father of American *Vogue*'s future editor Anna Wintour).

In the week the decisions were made, Hamilton took Giles to dinner at Prime Minister Harold Wilson's official weekend residence at Chequers, along with Lord Thomson, William Rees-Mogg and the *Sunday Times* political correspondent, James Margach. They didn't get to bed until 3 a.m. because Wilson reminisced for hours. Only later, when it was announced that Rees-Mogg had been appointed editor of *The Times*, did it occur to Giles that he and Rees-Mogg had both been eyed as top prospects and that, for some reason, Hamilton changed his mind about giving him the editorship of the *Sunday Times*. Perhaps Frank's eye drooped mid-Wilson. Or it could have been that Roy Thomson had told Hamilton he preferred Evans's 'North-Country cheek' to Frank's more polished style. (An assessment I was to learn about only years later.)

All I knew was that on a Friday Hamilton summoned me to his office and asked for a brief, to be delivered on Monday, on how I would develop the paper. I was so nervous typing it at home I filled a whole wastebasket with crumpled false starts: in those days every second thought meant retyping the whole thing. Hamilton said nothing about the report I gave him on the Monday, but the following day he sent me over to the *Times* offices to see Sir William Haley. Though we both had got serious ink on our hands at the *Manchester Evening News*, this was my first meeting with the legend of whom his subordinates at Reuters and the BBC had said he was the only man in London with two glass eyes. Haley was warm enough, but not in the mood to reminisce about his days in Manchester. His rectitude during the interview was focused on how, if I were made editor, I would resist any pressures or temptations in the conduct of the paper to promote other Thomson commercial interests in magazines, holiday travel, book companies and directories.

Two days later, I was wheeled into the grand boardroom of *The Times* at Printing House Square for scrutiny by the full board of the new Times Newspapers. I sat isolated in a chair facing twelve solemn directors around a long walnut table with intimidating oil portraits on the walls. In addition to the chairman, editor in chief and general manager, there were three Thomson nominees (one of them Kenneth Thomson, Roy's son), two Astor nominees, and the fulcrum was four independent 'national directors'.

'*How independent will you be as editor?*'

'I'm certain that the judgement of the Monopolies Commission was correct. I shall be completely independent. Unless I was certain of this I would not be prepared to accept the job.'

'*What is your attitude to the Thomson commercial interests?*'

'The same as my attitude to any other commercial interests.'

'*Even if it is news adverse to the Thomson interests, say in travel?*'

'If there is any news in we will print it.'

The directors spent a full hour examining my halo as someone who would embrace and defend the freedoms defined in the Monopolies Commission report, not to sell out to Mammon or twist the news for a political agenda. Looking back at the commitments they demanded, I can't help but wonder at how much journalism has changed.

I was confirmed as Hamilton's successor.

Frank Giles, for his part, accepted the deputy editorship. He was forty-eight, I was ten years younger. Often, talking to colleagues when I was out of earshot, he got into the habit of referring to me as 'the young master'. I didn't mind. It was good-humoured; he was incapable of malice. For all fourteen years we were together he was an engaging and steadfast deputy.

On the last Saturday of his editorship in January 1967, Hamilton, in his immaculately tailored suit, looked down from the steps leading to the composing room floor where shirtsleeved subs scurried about with galley proofs and page plans. 'I'm handing you a Rolls-

Royce,' he said. It was true. His *Sunday Times* purred. I was determined to match his dedication to quality, though constitutionally incapable of achieving it in his inimitable style. He was a master delegator. I was a meddler. He was reticent. I wasn't. But we shared the same high hopes of what journalism might achieve. In the years to come I could always hear the Boy Scout in Denis Hamilton asking, as he frequently had done when I was managing editor, 'Have you done your good deed for today, Harold?'

14

THE THIRD MAN

A gale is blowing in from the Atlantic. It rattles the windows of the cottage behind a beach dune in Quogue, Long Island, where I'm writing this. If I take my eyes off the pines bending in the gusts and glance to the right of the windows, there's a framed photograph on the wall that carries me back to the heart of a great newspaper which had more than its share of storms – and created a few of its own.

The black and white photograph is of a news conference at the *Sunday Times* in London. It's unremarkable enough in itself – a dozen people sitting on sofas below a spotlighted world map. It would mean little or nothing to anyone else, yet for me it has the exalted resonance of a Nocturne painting. I'd admired James McNeil Whistler's work in the Tate Gallery near my last home in Pimlico, but John Ruskin didn't. The celebrated critic said Whistler's *Nocturne in Black and Gold* was no more than a pot of paint flung in the face of the public. Whistler sued him. Asked in cross-examination by Ruskin's attorney how long it had taken him to paint it, Whistler famously replied: 'All my life.'

That's what the photograph on my wall represents, the culmination of my life in journalism, thirty-five years in newspapers from weekly reporting in Lancashire, to subbing and editorial writing for the *Manchester Evening News*, to foreign reporting in Europe and South-east Asia and the United States for the *Evening News* and the *Manchester Guardian*, to five years of daily newspaper editing in Darlington, and then fourteen more years editing the *Sunday Times* of London.

I'd started this national editorship in January 1967, feeling very much an imposter as I was driven by a chauffeur to Gray's Inn Road and the grand office where Hamilton in the summer of 1965 had first broached my joining him. I'd barely got used to being managing editor of the paper. Now I'd taken his place at the helm and he'd moved across a bridge to the *Times* offices. In the perpetual remodellings of the editorial floor ordained by management, I ended up in the photograph's large white and chrome office planned by Terence Conran – benefactions a million miles from all my previous newspaper habitats – after moving from a smaller one decorated in rather startling red and black tones decreed by Snowdon. He explained it was to match my character (I'm still working that out). He'd designed it very practically for transactions with galleys and page proofs, but he was always darting in to remove any object that offended his taste – one day an ashtray, another a cushion, another a clipboard, another a small potted plant. My secretary predicted: 'You'll be next.'

One day two Scotland Yard detectives did come in looking for me, but what they wanted to take away was a Civil Service report we'd published which revealed the Ministry of Transport officials were privately pressing to shut down one-third of the nation's railway system. It proposed leaving large areas of Scotland, Cumberland, Lincolnshire, East Anglia, Central and the West of England without any trains at all. I truthfully told my visitors they wouldn't find the incriminating documents in my office; I'd taken home the background paperwork after seeing the story to press on Saturday night.

I don't think their heart was in the detection, but I was duly cautioned that by publishing the information I could be charged with a criminal offence under Section 2 of the Official Secrets Act (Section 1, dating back to 1911, being concerned with espionage). In the outcry after our report, the minister rejected the scheme. And the detectives didn't come back.

Other stories we ran or wanted to run, however, provoked so many subpoenas and writs summoning me to the Law Courts in the Strand I could have found my way there blindfolded. I didn't seek confrontations with the law. They arose only because government, corporations and individuals sought to suppress information of public concern discovered by diligent, painstaking efforts by the *Sunday Times* staff and its contributors.

Collectively, the conflicts provoked by our attempts to answer numerous questions dramatized a chronic but unsuspected malaise in the functioning of British democracy. The resulting confrontations with authority also proved the severest of tests for the *Sunday Times* itself. Closer to home, would the solemn promises of editorial independence made by Denis Hamilton and Lord Thomson be maintained under unprecedented pressures and at grave financial risk?

I would soon find out.

In my audition memorandum for Hamilton I'd suggested the paper needed a full-time investigative unit. I wanted to reflect W. T. Stead's governing function of the press – 'its argus-eyed power of inspection'. My appetite had been whetted by the *Northern Echo*'s unifocal investigative ventures (cervical cancer and Teesside pollution); by the big car insurance fraud I'd worked on as managing editor; and by the earlier three exposés by the *Sunday Times*: the investigation of the crooked landlord Peter Rachman; the piquant case of the Chippendale Commode by which the newspaper was able to prove the existence of an antique-dealers' ring swindling sellers; and the 'bogus Burgundy' story in which we found a bottling factory sticking prestigious but false labels on cheap blended wine. These three stories had been published under the rubric 'Insight', but the title was otherwise used to identify a weekly page of short undifferentiated background features contributed by several writers. I devolved the feature writing to three staffers with a more focused mission, charging them to keep watch on all the scientific 'ologies' on a page we would call 'Spectrum'. Then I created a new investigative Insight team of four reporters and a researcher. Their exposures of unsuspected scandals of significance and compelling narrative reconstructions of major events (the Yom Kippur War for instance) soon powerfully reinforced the identity of the *Sunday Times*.

Team journalism is difficult to manage but I'd no doubt then and none since that it facilitates the best investigative journalism. No single reporter then – or instant blogger today – could be expected in timely fashion to follow a multiplicity of trails, false and real, and grapple along the way with unpredictable technicalities in civil engineering, company law, accounting, aeronautics, physics, molecular biology, or whatever the relevant area of expertise. At various times over the next few years when I visited the cramped Insight offices there'd be the engineering blueprints on the wall of the fatal DC-10 airliner and a scale model of its defective cargo door that sent 346 people to their deaths; another time there'd be diagrams of the organic chemical structure of thalidomide that robbed children of an arm or leg or left them limbless trunks; and for another investigation – the killings on Bloody Sunday – there'd be annotated maps of the maze of streets in Londonderry plotting the moves of paratroopers and civil rights demonstrations.

But it is no easy matter to create and monitor a team. The chemistry and direction of the group is crucial. This is a subtle business and there were periods when I got the mix wrong. You don't want four clones side by side; you want distinct but complementary skills. Each member has to like and respect the others' professionalism; all must be prepared to subordinate their egos, the thirst for a byline, and accept direction from a team leader. Then they have to be willing to yield control of the final writing to a leader they trust to respect their words and judgements – without being pushovers when he doesn't. The most persuasive criticism of team journalism touches on this point. As an anonymous Conservative party critic of Insight's reporting of Northern Ireland wrote: 'While the subjectivity of one writer can clearly be seen in a newspaper under his byline, that of a team is blurred and made more difficult to spot by the common, but unfounded, assumption that anything written by a team must be more dispassionate than that of a single writer.'

In the early years the pace and style were set by Ron Hall and his deputy, at that time Bruce Page, two men in their late twenties–early thirties of very different temperaments who shared a taste for exuberant hair styles – Hall a curly black mop, Page long angry sideburns. Hall was a scholar in scepticism, honed by his study of statistical method at Pembroke College, Cambridge. It was Hall who made the breakthrough in investigative journalism for the *Sunday Times* with a three-part series on the slum landlord Peter Rachman, giving birth to tighter regulations and the new noun for tenant exploitation, 'Rachmanism'. But Hall didn't regard himself as a dragon-slayer. In fact, he distrusted crusaders in journalism. He felt they'd make the facts fit the thesis. He affected boredom, yawning ostentatiously when someone canvassed a story that seemed freighted with virtue. For me as editor, though, it was comforting to see Hall, a pipe clamped in his mouth, slowly taking a reporter through the back-up for his assertions and analysis. He was a lucid writer, a rigorous editor of text, and he had a flair for headlines and display introductions beaten into him during his apprenticeship at the *Daily Mirror*. The worst thing Hall could tell you was that he was 'combing a dog', which meant the story scheduled for the feature page he controlled had come in with a full consignment of fleas.

Page was not at all interested in the arts of presentation, but as scrupulous as Hall in what was fit to print. He was a member of his local Labour party but never once in all the years I was to work with him did a hint of partisanship infiltrate his work. There came to be a certain creative tension between the two men because Page was zealous to set the world right. Whereas Hall, a dogged Yorkshireman, concealed his analytical sharpness in lethargy, Page, a drop-out from Melbourne University, displayed his in breathtaking pole vaults over shelves of the collected works of Hume, Burke, Popper, Coleridge, Marx, Keynes. His long auto-didactic digressions were relieved by an ironical style and his energy was contagious.

He and Hall developed strong opposing views on team journalism. Page believed all those involved, from the reporters to the designated collating writer, had to trust the judgement of competent colleagues or team journalism could not flourish. He was very careful, though, about who qualified as technically and morally honest enough for membership of a team. Hall thought Page's concept imposed too great a sacrifice on individual integrity. He was not prepared to have an article articulate a view until he was personally intellectually satisfied to the last comma. His statistical training inclined him to calculate the odds against a story having the level of accuracy he required, i.e., 100 per cent. He was the kind of editor who'd not publish a chess annotation until he'd played the game through himself. As Insight developed, Hall became the chief 'space baron' for the whole first section of the paper, selecting and editing pages he controlled; no second-rate work would survive Hall's scowling scrutiny.

Page had particular gifts for investigation and he had an eclectic mind. He was an ingenious originator of theories to connect apparently unrelated dots, but had the remorseless intellectual integrity to discard them when the dots didn't connect and the imagination then to construct another working hypothesis. Some people found him hard to take; he could be summarily dismissive of individuals he suspected of deviation from his standards; he could be tempted into fascinating but unnecessary digressions in the writing; and edition times were vulnerable to his search for the definitive. But he was also able to inspire a group with a common animating curiosity. Much of the renown Insight was to win was due to Ron Hall and Bruce Page and the path they set for the very varied editors who followed: Lewis Chester, Godfrey Hodgson, John Barry, Simon Jenkins and Paul Eddy.

Insight had a baptism of fire.

Does the Flap of a Butterfly's Wings in Brazil Set Off a Tornado in Texas? Edward Lorenz didn't present his Chaos Theory paper until 1972 – and the mathematics would have been beyond me – but I've often thought of the principle in relation to a major investigation we began in 1967 in my second month as editor. The dynamic of the whole saga is of initial small changes producing unpredictably large effects. For my own part, I had no idea that an idle remark I picked up at lunch would nearly a year later lead to my being denounced by Foreign Secretary George Brown.

The lunch was with Jeremy Isaacs, my Granada producer on the first *What the Papers Say*. Isaacs had now become head of current affairs at rival Thames Television. He remarked in passing that the *Observer* had bought the serial rights to a memoir by Eleanor Philby – 'you know, the wife of that other man Philby in the affair of the missing diplomats.' Sixteen years before, in 1951, two British diplomats, Guy Burgess based in Washington and Donald Maclean based in London, had disappeared together and officially surfaced in Moscow in 1956. They were presumed to have been Soviet spies. Philby – 'that other man' – had been in Washington with Burgess, vanished from Beirut in 1963, and six months later Russia announced he, too, was in Moscow.

Back at the office I remarked to Bruce Page how interesting it was that all three defectors had been undergraduates at Cambridge in the 1930s. Maybe we could identify the subversive don who recruited them to the communist cause. It didn't prove difficult to identify the don (Cambridge economics professor Maurice Dobb), but the unpredictable trajectory of Project X led us to a far bigger story about Harold Adrian Russell 'Kim' Philby.

The Philby investigation was the most taxing we ever undertook – a frustratingly tedious process of assembling and assessing tiny scraps of information from hundreds of interviews with denizens of a closed world whose stock in trade is deceit. Central Casting couldn't have selected a more suitably varied bunch of independent minds for penetrating Philby's secret world. Australian Phillip Knightley's quiet unassuming manner exuded an empathy that attracted confidences despite his distinct resemblance to Lenin – bald dome, black goatee. He'd knocked about the globe as a seaman, vacuum-cleaner salesman, South Sea Island trader and reporter. David Leitch, like Guy Burgess, was a golden boy at Cambridge, though twenty years younger: both good-looking, charming, bohemian romantics, and brilliant; Leitch was already showing the writing gifts that would win him acclaim describing his days among the Marines at the siege of Khe Sanh in Vietnam. John Barry, a dropout from Balliol, was a contrarian with a quicksilver mind.

The austere, cerebral Hugo Young was not on the regular Insight team – he was chief editorial writer and an impeccable political reporter – but he contributed because he knew the ways of Whitehall and of Washington, as a Harkness Fellow and also a Congressional Fellow.

Most of the ink over the years had been spent on Burgess and Maclean and the mysteries of their last-minute getaway, rushing together on the ferry from Southampton to St Malo at 11.45 p.m. on Friday, 25 May 1951, one of them drunkenly shouting 'Back on Monday!' to a sailor concerned about the big white Austin they abandoned on the quayside.

There had been articles about Philby but nobody had even begun to peel the onion. Nothing had been said on what he did, when he started spying for the Soviets, how he escaped detection, and, importantly, no assessment of the damage he did, if any. He was assumed to have been a low- to mid-level agent in Britain – and in Moscow he'd become the invisible man. His address was a secret; his telephone was ex-directory; there was nothing about him in the Soviet press; and in the city if glimpsed one minute he was gone the next. For our part, we knew next to nothing about him. David Leitch had tried to use an interview with Khrushchev in Moscow in 1964 as an avenue to the mysterious exiled Scarlet Pimpernel, but nothing came of it. Right at the start of our inquiry we tried again, writing to Kim Philby, Moscow. (It seemed necessary to do that, but in retrospect I'm glad he maintained his silence. If he had talked to us, we would have been accused of being his mouthpiece.)

In the biographical sketch with which we started, Philby surfaced only as a series of snapshots: the blazered head boy at the elite Aldro prep school; the handsome youth who'd won a King's scholarship at Westminster posing with his proud bearded father, Arabist explorer, scholar and convert to Islam, St John Philby, who'd had to struggle financially to send him there; pipe-puffing Kim in flannel bags and tweeds at Trinity College, Cambridge, working hard to get a good degree in economics and history; and Kim at twenty-five, an adventurous journalist reporting the Spanish Civil War for *The Times*, his head bandaged from a shell burst. He appeared to be the quintessential upper-middle-class Englishman, a member of the Athenaeum, the premier gentleman's club in London, decorated as a CBE, addicted to the *Times* crossword and cricket and premier cru claret, and repelled by displays of emotion. Even under stress in 1955 when he'd just been accused by a Labour MP of tipping off Burgess and Maclean to flee in 1951, we see him unruffled by the uproar, debonair in grey pinstriped suit as he smiles into the press cameras admitted to the living room of his mother's Drayton Gardens home. In the tape we watched, he was calm and assured, speaking with amused condescension, controlling his charming little stutter; he had a get-out-of-jail card in his pocket, a statement to Parliament by the Foreign Secretary Harold Macmillan: 'I have no reason to conclude that Mr Philby has at any time betrayed the interests of this country, or to identify him with the so-called "third man", if, indeed, there was one.'

The press, too, exonerated Philby. Poor fellow, they concluded; he'd lost his job as a diplomat just because he'd been unwise enough to let the wild drunken Burgess, an old friend, have a basement flat in his large house in Washington. This was the period when there was revulsion in Britain for the witch hunts of Senator Joe McCarthy. The MP who'd made the charge against Philby had to withdraw, shouted down by his fellow Labour MPs.

After his official clearance, we next see Philby in shirtsleeves at a picnic in the hills outside Beirut, squatting on the ground all smiles and sunglasses, the Middle East correspondent of the *Observer* and *The Economist* at work on a bottle of wine; an American diplomat at another lunch described him as 'an arrogant, condescending jerk'.

And then we don't see him at all.

On 23 January 1963, on the way to a party with Eleanor, he got out of a taxi in Beirut 'to send a cable' and didn't show up again. Six months later, Edward Heath, the Lord Privy Seal, told a questioner in Parliament that Philby had confessed to having 'warned Maclean through Burgess', but this was all that emerged. The government had maintained total silence since. It had never even been officially acknowledged that Philby had been a spy working for Britain's Secret Intelligence Service. (The SIS is authorized to operate abroad and is popularly known as MI6, as distinct from MI5, the domestic counter-espionage agency.)

We made some progress putting together the jigsaw of Philby's
life. Leitch snooped round Cambridge, his old university, looking for
leads. Burgess and Maclean were members of a communist cell
started by Maurice Dobb. Philby did not join, but did become a
Marxist, spending his £14 prize money at Trinity on the complete
works. He was moved by the sight of hunger marchers who'd
walked all the way from the North-East and organized meals for
them. At Dobb's suggestion he visited the Paris Comintern and on
graduation in 1933 he rode his motorcycle to the bloody ideological
battleground of Vienna. Page called Eric Gedye, the *Telegraph* correspondent who'd been in Vienna then. The news from him was that
Philby had married a vivacious communist – we tracked down her
first husband in Israel – and worked with the underground to smug-
gle communists out of Austria to safety.

How could such a dedicated Marxist win entry to the Foreign
Service a few years later at a time when fear of 'Bolshevism' was
acute? The answer is that by then it was not the same Philby. The
Philby smuggling clothes to communists hiding in the sewers in
Vienna was next lending his energies to the hated fascists. Back in
London, he was nominated editor of a planned Anglo-German
Fellowship magazine. 'Look,' said Page, coming excitedly into my
office with a framed photograph and a shrewd deduction. 'Here's
Philby building a new identity.' The picture was a swastika-bedecked
black-tie dinner given by the Anglo-German Fellowship
Organisation in July 1936, and there clearly was young Philby.
Maclean and Burgess, too, had both conspicuously and abruptly
retreated from their Marxism.

When the Spanish Civil War broke out, Philby took himself off to
the battlefront as a freelance reporter – not, like most of his generation, allied with the uneasy coalition of the left on the Republican
side supported by the Soviet Union, but on the side of General
Franco's monarchists, fascists and the Roman Catholic Church. In
1937, when he was only twenty-five, he became the special correspondent of *The Times* with Franco. We looked at his dispatches in
the *Times* library. They were slanted in favour of Franco's
Nationalists, even after the bombing of Guernica by the German

Condor Legion, the first mass air attack on civilians. One thing stuck in the minds of journalists we spoke to who'd observed him in Spain. He wanted to know details of the movement of Nationalist troops – numbers, directions and regiments – way beyond what readers of *The Times* needed.

'Maybe,' said Page, 'he'd already been engaged by Soviet intelligence.'

It was a prophetic insight. He had. But he had also been talent-spotted by MI6, the reason we deduced for his abrupt departure from *The Times* in July 1940. What did he do in the service? We went through all the reference books to find the names of the staff in our embassies where Philby had worked. There were some clues about who had been intelligence officers: an entry in *Who's Who* naming someone as a member of the Diplomatic Service but whose name did not appear in the Foreign Office list seemed a likely target. Few of the people we approached at first in MI6 or MI5, the counter-intelligence service, would divulge anything. 'Sorry, Official Secrets.' And click.

Things improved when we knew enough to appear knowledgeable in the hope that the conversation would inch us forward, but I got used to the expression of apology that my depressed reporters brought back from a fruitless day. Knightley had a typically tantalizing talk with an MI5 retired officer who told him: 'Of course it was the defector in 1945 who put us on to Kim. After that you had only to look in the files to see it all.' Yes? And what did you learn? 'Better leave it at that, old boy. Don't want to get into trouble with the OSA [Official Secrets Act].'

I had known it would be a difficult assignment. We were asking questions about a non-person, a disgraced member of a Secret Intelligence Service that did not officially exist, whose head man was a letter of the alphabet ('C'), and whose headquarters address was a state secret (so different from the American practice where the Central Intelligence Agency, its director and its location are publicized). I could not keep Insight knocking on closed doors if there was nothing behind them. Perhaps I had given them a bum steer and there wasn't much more to Philby.

What happened next was like a fluke in a crowded pool hall where, as you make a shot, someone jogs your elbow and the cue ball caroms wildly round the table and ends up potting the black. Two high officials, striving to be unhelpful, jogged our elbow at the right moment.

The first was the former head of MI6, who'd retired to Wiltshire and was no longer the anonymous 'C' but the aristocratic Major-General Sir Stewart Menzies. He'd been in charge of the agency during the war and through the defections, a decent, canny man, much sounder than the upper-class clown portrayed as the head of the service in *Our Man in Havana* by Graham Greene (who served under Menzies in the war). We wrote to him for an interview. No, he said politely, he wouldn't talk to us. He was known in the service as the man with sealed lips who wouldn't agree it was a nice day for fear of giving something away. But he could not resist adding a sentence in his letter: 'What a blackguard Philby was.' Oh, really? A man of such notorious discretion as Menzies must have been driven by deep feelings to resort to the vocabulary of Victorian melodrama.

The second elbow-jogger was Lord Chalfont, a new minister at the Foreign Office. Leitch, who'd previously been on the staff of *The Times*, had known Chalfont before his elevation on joining government, when he was Alun Gywnne Jones, the newspaper's defence correspondent. When Leitch and Page met Chalfont at the Foreign Office and mentioned Philby, the Minister began by saying Philby was a man of no importance, not worth a reporter's time and effort: *Let me save you the trouble. Anyway you couldn't possibly uncover anything about Philby. And if you did you'd not be able to publish it.* Then, like Menzies, he felt compelled to say more. 'You must stop your inquiries. There is the most monstrous danger here. You will be helping the enemy.' He was more charmingly restrained with me when I had a drink with him at the Garrick Club. Would the Foreign Office at least answer some questions I had? 'Afraid not, but we'll not stand in your way.'

I told Denis Hamilton that we were going to go flat out to find out what Philby did that caused so much alarm. He was troubled.

'How can you be sure you won't help the Russians?' he asked.

'Well, we can't tell them more than Philby must have already told them. Denis, we're the ones in the dark.'

'And what about the Official Secrets Act?'

'Can't we judge the risks of that when we know more?'

'Let me think about it.'

He didn't tell me the results of his deep think until a few days later. I was surprised. He called me to his office to say that 'in great secrecy' he'd been to see Prime Minister Harold Wilson and the current 'C'. 'The Foreign Office is alarmed. I told them you're not a man who would want to damage his country. But I've seen too much slaughter in my life, Harold. Will you let them see a draft to make sure you don't put anyone at risk? All I've said is that you will consider representations.'

I said I would. None of us wanted to risk the life of an agent by some unwitting reference. The trouble is we had nothing about which anyone could make representations. The trail was not just cold by 1967. It was frozen. I took up Hamilton's suggestion that I see Sir Denis Greenhill, deputy undersecretary at the Foreign Office; I discovered later he was the main link between the Foreign Office and MI6. After a first mutually wary meeting in the Travellers' Club in Pall Mall, I saw him once in a Bloomsbury hotel, once in his unpretentious house in West London where his vivacious wife Angela served tea and biscuits, and once we met grandly, in the Foreign Office. He was then fifty-four, silver-haired but well-muscled in a double-breasted chalk-stripe suit, curt and brisk in manner. The son of a top manager in the Westminster Bank, he'd reached Christ Church, Oxford, by way of the lesser public school Bishop's Stortford and then got a job as a traffic apprentice on the London and North Eastern Railway, the ladder by which middle-class young men became the bosses of railwaymen like my father. He'd been a staff colonel in the Royal Engineers in the Second World War before entering the Foreign Service in 1946. Not a typical Foreign Office man, but he exhibited the same hostility to our probing Philby as did Minister Lord Chalfont.

About Burgess he was droll in his detestation. Burgess had been foisted on Greenhill when he ran our Washington Embassy's Middle

East department during the time Burgess and Philby were there. He recalled Burgess as an idle shambling drunk who dropped cigarette ash on other people's papers, drank other people's whisky, paraded his homosexual promiscuity and told entertaining tales to discredit the famous. 'I've never met a name-dropper in the same class.' Burgess had a gift for caricature, and once drew a Christmas card for Greenhill's small son with Stalin as Father Christmas. 'I should have paid more attention to it at the time,' Sir Denis noted, somewhat wistfully. But Greenhill's agreeable facility for recall eluded him over Philby. Not a word would he say about the man who'd fooled them all.

'You'll do more damage with the Americans if you write about Philby. Who's this fellow Page. What's *his* game?'

Why did this minor figure, Philby, continue to excite such anxiety? Any number of people we'd reached were willing to reminisce about Philby as a Special Operations Executive trainer of men and women dropped into occupied France. We were regaled with the prowess of Philby as 007 – a master of unarmed combat, night sabotage, pistol shooting and seduction of women. He shone, too, we learned, as an executive within MI6, which he entered in the summer of 1941, though his style was not to everyone's taste. Sir Robert Menzies, a Foreign Office security officer, was dazzled by Philby's 'sense of dedicated idealism', his mastery of the English language in his reports, submitted in neat, tiny handwriting; Miss Kennard Davis, on the other hand, from the vantage point of the typing pool, told Insight that Philby was harsh in his rebukes for mistakes. 'I used to shrivel up like a worm. He used it on the men, too, just as effectively. I can remember walking into Graham Greene's office and his eyes were glinting with anger. I asked him what was the matter, and he said, "I've just had a caning from the headmaster."'

All of this was very helpful for sketching the outlines of Philby's personality, but none of it told us where the 'most monstrous danger' lay.

Around this time, I had a call from Michael Frayn. I'd seen him socially from time to time in the years since we shared a canteen table in my days in Manchester at the *Evening News* and *Guardian* long before he was acclaimed for his farce *Noises Off*, the intellectually brilliant dramas *Copenhagen* and *Democracy*, and the rollicking Fleet Street novel *Towards the End of the Morning*. He'd told me then he'd turned down an invitation to join MI6. He called me to say he had a bright acquaintance who wanted to start a new career in journalism. I'd have seen him on Michael's recommendation but I did with alacrity when he added: 'By the way he's in the Foreign Office at the moment.'

John Sackur was a mystery. A pale, earnest man in his late thirties, he presented himself as a crusader for black Africans. He was upset that Britain had not quashed the coup in 1965 by which Ian Smith imposed white minority rule on what was then British Rhodesia (now the benighted Zimbabwe). But was that really his motive in seeing me? I'd expected to draw the usual blank when I mentioned our interest in Philby.

Sackur appeared incredulous.

'Philby? You'll never be able to print it.'

'Why not?'

'It'll get stopped, D notices, the Queen. It goes to the highest in the land.' And then he bit out with real emotion: 'Philby was a copper-bottomed bastard.'

It emerged that he had written a report on the damage Philby had done, but more he would not say. He'd already met Frank Giles, my deputy and foreign editor, who asked him if he was 'a friend', the Foreign Office term for someone in MI6. He said he was. When later I accused Michael Frayn of foisting a spy on me – he recalls I was 'very angry' – he said he had no idea Sackur was in MI6 and I believe him. 'John was a natural deceiver. He deceived me on several occasions at Cambridge.'

I introduced Sackur to Bruce Page, who took him off to Manzi's seafood restaurant in Soho. The one clue Page prised out was that if we ever got to the bottom of Philby's betrayal we'd realize that what mattered was less what Philby did in the Cold War than what he did in the Second World War. Eventually we discovered this was a reference to Philby's role in blocking evidence in 1944, before the German officers' plot to kill Hitler, that the German army was putting out feelers for a separate peace with the US and Britain. He may have also had a hand in the fate of a number of Catholic activists in Germany who'd been identified as possible leaders in an anti-communist government after the war. They did not survive.

Knightley, who has become a specialist in writing on espionage, believes today that Sackur tipped us off because he represented a small group of young rebels in MI6 who thought the service had not had enough of a purge after Philby. It is also just possible, on the other hand, that M16 encouraged Sackur to seek a foreign corre-spondent's job with us as cover for working for the agency in the Middle East, just as they infiltrated the *Observer* and *The Economist* with Philby. On this supposition, Sackur's hints about Philby might not have been indiscretions, but cunning bait to suggest he was disaffected enough to be a genuine defector whose integrity could be trusted. Recalling the intensity of expression on his chalk-white face as he expounded on foreign policy at our first meeting, a lunch at the Ivy, I am inclined to conclude he was not a plant, but a young man whose conscience would give him no rest. I intended to talk to Sackur again, when I conceived of writing this memoir, but he died before we could meet.

Only later did I realize the significance of Sackur's glancing refer-ence to the Queen. Leitch had given Page the names of a number of leftist undergraduates in *Trinity Review*. One name was Anthony Blunt. At the time, in 1967, he was Surveyor of the Queen's Pictures, a part-time job in which he oversaw the care of the Queen's publicly owned collection. He was a pale, chilly, fastidiously mannered aesthete, a compulsively promiscuous homosexual, a favourite of a small group of the more arty courtiers – he dined often at Marlborough House with the Queen Mother and her set – but an enigma even to his friends. Twelve years later in November 1979 Margaret Thatcher named him as a Soviet spy after Andrew Boyle, the founding editor of the BBC Radio 4 programme *The World at One*, had featured Blunt in his book about the Philby scandal, *Climate of Treason*, disguised as 'Maurice', the figure in E. M. Forster's story of homosexual love. Blunt then became an object of universal execration. He was stripped of his knighthood, but what must have disturbed Sackur (as it did me, among many others, when the facts became known) was the immunity Blunt had been given in 1964 and the retention of his job at Buckingham Palace in return for a confession, whereas three years earlier the less well-connected gang in the Portland Spy Ring stealing naval secrets had been sent to prison for between fifteen and twenty-five years.

Page wrote to Blunt in 1967, asking for an interview. Knightley took the letter round to his grace and favour apartment at the Courtauld Institute. Blunt read it and slammed the door in his face. The next morning Page got a letter from Blunt's solicitor warning he would sue for harassment if we ever tried to contact him again. We would not have been deterred by that if we'd had anything on Blunt – but we didn't. He'd been investigated by MI5 fifteen times and proved to be small fry by comparison with Philby, but we didn't know that at the time. Not to pursue Blunt was a mistake I regret – one that got away – but we were by then excitedly preoccupied by leads developing on Philby.

Our collection of espionage books had netted one titled *British Agent* published the year before by someone named John Whitwell. Knightley winkled out his real identity, A. L. (Leslie) Nicholson, who'd been an MI6 man in Prague and later in Riga. Knightley found him to be a drunken burnout living on a miserable pension over a seedy café in east London. It was hard to believe he had ever been an MI6 officer; another wasted expense thought Knightley as he treated Nicholson to a good Italian lunch and several brandies. But as Knightley gently pressed questions – inevitably revealing we knew Philby was important and by inference that we didn't quite know why – Nicholson's enjoyment increased. He was aware of the seriousness of his illness (he died two years later) and over coffee and another brandy, he told Knightley what Philby had really done.

'The reason for the flap, old man,' he said, 'is that Kim was head of our anti-Soviet section.'

As Knightley put it, 'I can remember trying to clear my head of brandy fumes.' He pressed Nicholson. 'Let me get this straight. The man running our secret operations against the Russians after 1944 was a Russian agent himself?'

'Precisely.'

This meant not only that any intelligence operations against the Soviets were doomed from the start but that the days were numbered of all the MI6 agents already in place in the Soviet Union and Eastern Europe.

In the *Sunday Times* office, we puzzled why Philby's crimes remained undetected for so long. Two luminaries who talked to us about their wartime experiences with MI6 – the Oxford historian Hugh Trevor-Roper and the journalistic provocateur Malcolm Muggeridge – spoke freely of their contempt for the quality of MI6's staff apart from the clever code-breakers. Trevor-Roper said the permanent officers were drawn from two classes of men – 'ex-Indian policemen and metropolitan young gentlemen whose education had been expensive rather than profound and who were recruited at the exclusive bars of White's and Boodles'. But even if Philby's colleagues were as dim as alleged by these critics, both of whom took a poor view of the human race anyway, wouldn't one of any number of the KGB defectors from the Soviet Union surely have given the game away?

The Sheriff of Shropshire gave us an answer. He was then Mr John Reed, living in a great house in a forest, but before retiring to Shropshire he'd been First Secretary in our Embassy in Turkey in the last year of the war. He was worried how our series might portray his role in a great blunder.

I sent Knightley to see him. He would only talk anonymously for the moment, concerned that the Foreign Office would not approve. Thus masked, he told a fascinating tale. On a hot August day in 1945, the area head of the Russian Secret Service (the NKVD, later KGB), one Konstantin Volkov, had walked into the consulate in Istanbul seeking asylum. For a safe passage to Cyprus and living money, he would identify Soviet spy networks. 'In return he told me he would offer the real names of three Soviet agents working in Britain, two of them in the Foreign Office, one the head of a counter-espionage organization in London.'

The ambassador, Sir Maurice Peterson, wanted nothing to do with the nasty business of spies. He told Reed to let London handle it. Reed sent the information to London in a secure diplomatic bag, and waited.

It took two whole weeks for an agent to arrive to debrief Volkov. It was none other than the head of the anti-Soviet section, Kim Philby.

Volkov was never seen again. Philby, who must have had a fright that he was so nearly outed, had taken time with his Soviet masters organizing a safe passage for Volkov – but not to Cyprus. A Soviet military aircraft made an irregular landing at Istanbul airport and within minutes had taken off again with a heavily bandaged figure on a stretcher carried to the plane. 'The incident convinced me,' said Reed, 'that Philby was either a Soviet agent or unbelievably incompetent. I took what seemed to me at the time the appropriate action.' Nothing happened.

Knightley reported: 'The memory of the betrayal made Reed's voice shake.'

If Philby was that important in 1945, what was he doing in Washington from 1949 under the cover of being First Secretary in the Embassy? All the public attention had been on his possible role in tipping off Burgess and Maclean. There'd been nothing about what he did day to day. Nobody had asked and nobody had talked. In view of the run-around we were getting in London, Knightley was entranced to be in Washington. He called the CIA and was directed to several retired officers who'd known Philby.

Lyman B. Kirkpatrick had been with the CIA since it was set up in 1947. This was a few years before Ian Fleming created the Bond fantasies – which Kirkpatrick regretted for misleading the public about the painstaking nature of intelligence work – but the Americans had been in awe of MI6 for its legendary history and the dazzling code-breaking achievements that won the battle of the Atlantic. The doors were wide open for Philby, whose experience was so much richer than anyone's in the fledgling CIA.

When Knightley found Kirkpatrick he had just retired as executive director of the agency. He had contracted polio in Asia on CIA business and was teaching politics from a wheelchair at Brown University. He combined secret knowledge with an intellectual zest for freedom. He wouldn't go into detail, but on the main point he didn't equivocate: 'Philby was your liaison officer with the CIA and

FBI.' This was as astounding as Nicholson's revelation. It meant that for three years of the Cold War, Philby had been at the heart of Western intelligence operations. Put it another way: having penetrated SIS he was then able to penetrate the CIA. The director, General Bedell Smith, gave him clearance at all levels, which meant that in a secret service's typically compartmentalized operations Philby would know as much as anyone except the director himself and perhaps one or two assistant directors like Kirkpatrick. Kirkpatrick would not say much more than 'Have a look at Albania,' but that chimed with vague hints we'd picked up. Tom Driberg MP had told us the Foreign Office expunged from his book on Guy Burgess a scornful reference by Burgess to Western meddling in Albania and a former MI6 man in Rome had told Leitch: 'Philby lost us a lot of lives in Eastern Europe.'

Back in London, Page asked a researcher to see if among the émigré groups in London there might be some Albanians who could give us a clue as to what lay behind Kirkpatrick's cryptic remark. They could do better than that. When the researcher found a bunch of them working as woodsmen for the Forestry Commission, he was directed to one of the few survivors of an ill-fated joint MI6–CIA operation. The two secret agencies had armed, trained and funded a small army of guerrillas and put them into Albania by boat and parachute in the spring of 1950. The communist rebels in Greece were faltering, Yugoslavia's Tito had broken with Stalin, and it was hoped a communist collapse in Albania would ripple throughout the Balkans. Hundreds of Albanian exiles, including the exiled King Zog's royal guard, were trained in a fort in Malta. They were doomed from the start. One of the few who escaped alive told us: 'They always knew we were coming.' At least 300 died.

The disaster, reminiscent of President Kennedy's Bay of Pigs blunder infiltrating anti-Castro guerrillas eleven years later, was put down to leaks from the infiltrators and the extraordinary efficiency of the Albanian frontier guards and police. Super-clever those Albanian cops, you know; they must have worked out the radio code by which the first infiltrators could signal back that it was safe to send in more men – when it wasn't safe at all.

The operation was jointly commanded by a CIA man and the British liaison officer, Kim Philby.

Hugo Young, meanwhile, was making good use of his inside knowledge of Washington: he found that the significance of Maclean, too, had been missed by everyone. The urbanely supercilious diplomat didn't go home after the Washington cocktail parties. Several times a week, unknown to Admiral Lewis Strauss, chairman of the Atomic Energy Commission, Maclean was unescorted in Strauss's headquarters.

It was a crucial time in the transition from hot to cold war. The Russians were already making good use of the bomb-making secrets from Klaus Fuchs and Co. but were desperate to find out all they could about the allied policy for the atomic bomb. Britain, Canada and the US had all cooperated on the Manhattan Project, but in 1947, through the McMahon Act, the US abruptly ended the exchange of information on atomic weapons. Nevertheless, an Anglophile manager, feeling it was unfair to exclude their British ally, had given Maclean a pass not authorized by the Atomic Energy Commission. Young found that despite McMahon, Maclean had been given access so rare it was denied even to General Leslie Groves, who supervised the building of the bomb, and J. Edgar Hoover, head of the FBI. Between 6 August 1947 and 11 June 1948, Maclean had been in the AEC headquarters twenty times, sometimes at night.

One of the strengths of the leaders of Insight was a readiness to admit a weakness and a resolve to remedy it by identifying people who did know. At the *Sunday Times*, we didn't have the expertise to determine the significance of the information Maclean had likely gathered, so we asked the atomic energy historian Margaret Gowing to assess how important it might have been to Maclean's Moscow masters. Answer: very. Especially useful were the quantities of uranium being bought, from which Stalin's scientists could calculate the projected size of the US nuclear arsenal. In the geopolitical poker game, this was a valuable face card.

We'd compiled many hundreds of thousands of words in notes and drafts with multiple cross-references. Page, ringed in cheroot smoke, had been at his typewriter early in the morning and late at night collating and sifting what we knew, and what needed more checking, into a longer and longer 'state of knowledge memorandum'. If he was not doing that he was testing hypotheses on the inner circle: we kept Project X as tight as we could. I wanted to publish before the *Observer* began its serialization of Eleanor Philby's memoir, scheduled for October.

By the first week in September Ron Hall had the text ready for the first of a four-part series. Greenhill was still protesting. 'Drop Philby, he's a bore.'

On 1 September I received a letter from the Services, Press and Broadcasting D Notice Committee. The key injunction (my italics) read: 'You are requested not to publish anything about identities, whereabouts, and tasks of persons of whatever status or rank who are *or have been employed* by either Service [MI5 or MI6].'

This was a direct attempt to wipe our entire investigation.

The D Notice (now a DA – or Defence Advisory – Notice) was a request approved by a joint committee of government and media representatives. The system was set up to warn the press against inadvertently publishing or broadcasting information that would 'compromise UK military and intelligence operations and methods, or put at risk the safety of those involved . . .' The D Notice did not have the force of law, but it could be cited against us if the Attorney General chose to bring an Official Secrets case. Our lawyers were anxious. I told Denis Hamilton I was ignoring it. He didn't argue.

The team wanted another two weeks and I agreed to hold off publication then for two reasons: we were following a lead about 'another defector' (who turned out to be Volkov) and we had our own Philby in Moscow – not Kim, but John, his son by his second marriage to Aileen. Leitch had the inspiration to check the London telephone directory and rang Philby, J. He was living in a basement flat in Hampstead with two pet Alsatians and an ambition to be a war photographer. Leitch, who had an engagingly jolly manner, casually asked him if he'd like an assignment to photograph his father in Moscow. He would.

The secretive Kim Philby broke his cover to greet his son and came out to stand in Red Square in an open-necked shirt, looking into the distance, his left hand nonchalantly in the pocket of his jacket. 'My father told me,' said John, 'the Russians had given him the task of penetrating British intelligence in 1933 and that it did not matter how long it took.'

We'd already worked that out. What we hadn't calculated was that John would have dinner on his return with the journalist Patrick Seale, who was at the rival *Observer* and directly responsible for the Eleanor Philby serialization. The first extract had been scheduled to begin late in October, but they rushed it into print. A copy of the *Observer* landed on my desk at 6 p.m. on Saturday 31 September. Not so fast! By 6.30 our 'Spy Who Betrayed a Generation' was on the presses with the scoop picture of Philby on the front page and the lead headline 'Philby: I spied for Russia from 1933'.

As photojournalism, it was dramatic, but a short-term tactical error on my part. The combination of photograph and quote could give the impression that our investigative series had sprung from Philby, or from the Soviet ministry of disinformation. We had enough disinformation agents on our side. When Philby let us know he had written a memoir we all recoiled: I couldn't stomach the monstrous egotism – what else? – that allowed him to stay loyal to his masters after the Soviet–Nazi pact and the years of Stalinist terror. (He offered to suppress his manuscript in return for a deal in which the Soviets would release a British prisoner, Gerald Brooke, and Britain would release the Krogers of the Portland Spy Ring. His sardonic memoir eventually appeared in the *Sunday Express*.)

Disturbing as our findings of Philby's betrayals were, to me the most sobering revelation was how long Philby was able to exploit the class-conscious and social attitudes of the club and old school tie echelons of MI6. They could not believe one of their privileged own would betray his service, his class and his country. Here was a Soviet agent within a breath of the final triumph, his appointment as head of MI6, yet still his friends in the service continued to resent the vulgarly suspicious security men of MI5. Even after he was dismissed from the service, 'cleared' by Harold Macmillan on the understanding that MI6 would reorganize and institute a 'general clean up', MI6 continued to employ him as a field agent in the Middle East and assured the *Observer* and

The Economist, who hired him, that he was no longer active. It was simply impossible for these gentlemen to accept that one of their own could have been a traitor to his class, let alone his country.

When we published our revelations in September–October 1967, I naively expected a demand for reform. Instead there was outrage, directed not at Philby or those who protected him but at us. Sir Stewart Menzies, the former head of MI6, who at the outset revealed his anger with the 'blackguard' Philby, now somersaulted to vouchsafe that Philby had never been important in MI6. In the eyes of Donald McLachlan, a former intelligence executive and editor of the *Sunday Telegraph*, we had even undermined the concept of the English gentleman. Several newspapers ran stories – not discouraged by official sources – that our life story of Philby was a Soviet plant. The accusations that we were handmaidens of the KGB seemed to me the product of minds incapable of confronting a real spy story without constructing an ersatz conspiracy around its origins. Only a political paranoid could have imagined, as the Foreign Office put about, that the iconoclastic Bruce Page was a communist. I reassured them that he was safely locked up in a slave labour camp in Gray's Inn Road.

Next, the rumbustious Foreign Secretary and Deputy Leader of the Labour party George Brown got into the act. The first I knew of it was a late-night phone call to my home from a very upset Denis Hamilton. 'The Foreign Secretary has just denounced you as a traitor at a business dinner and in front of Roy. You'd better be in the House of Commons tomorrow when the Foreign Secretary will speak.' I opened the next morning's *Times* with some trepidation. 'Ebullient Mr Brown Hits Out' was the euphemistic headline, ebullient being a press parlance adjective to get round the libel risk of saying he was drunk.

The next afternoon I sat in the House of Commons gallery waiting to be dragged out by the serjeant-at-arms. The victim turned out to be the Foreign Secretary himself, carpeted that morning by the Prime Minister for once again showing undue ebullience in a public place; the *Daily Mirror*'s front page the next day headlined 'THE BOWED HEAD' featured a penitent Foreign Secretary in morning suit facing a stern Wilson on the platform at Waterloo Station as they awaited the arrival of a dignitary.

When Roy Thomson was asked about the protests at our Philby series, he had an economical answer: 'Bunk!'

My experiences as a provincial editor had given me some inkling of the ramparts behind which the bureaucracies conducted the nation's affairs then. The Philby story was my first prolonged experience as a national editor of dealing with central government and what, for want of a better name, I have to call the political establishment: those over-lapping 'charmed circles' of influence and power whose strands of DNA were the elite public schools, Oxbridge, the aristocracy, the City and the blue-chip boardrooms, the Civil Service, the legal profession and the conservative press. British society had become more solvent, more meritocratic, less deferential than it was in the 1930s when the Soviets saw very well how it was run in their recruitment of Burgess, Philby, Maclean and Blunt. I don't for a minute believe there was in the sixties or now a homogeneous conspiratorial establishment – a 'tightly knit group of politically motivated men', to misappropriate Prime Minister Harold Wilson's phrase against striking seamen. Obviously, people in the establishment and the various professions differ on issues today: the privately educated Labour men contend with the privately educated Tories. But a penchant for secrecy, social privilege and the nurturing of an educational elite remained pervasive in the culture and has not been quite expunged to this day.

A secret service is a secret service, I accepted that, but the well-tried administrative precept that efficiency improves with accountability is not irrelevant even to the secret service. It was shocking to me that Blunt, having condescended to betray his country, was still in place at Buckingham Palace, a socially sought-after figure. It was a revelation that the closing of the ranks that had allowed Philby to survive was manifest again in the rebukes we earned for exposing him and the cover-up.

The consolation at the end of the Philby affair was in the awareness of my good fortune: that Thomson and Hamilton had been steadfast in their support, and that in the staff of the paper, if I could manage it well enough, I had a resource of extraordinary intelligence, vitality and inde-pendence of mind. We could tackle anything!

15

CHILDREN ON OUR CONSCIENCE

I'd never heard of the word 'teratogen' until 1963. After that I could never forget it. Between 1958 and 1961 pregnant women who reported morning sickness, anxiety and lack of sleep to their doctors were prescribed a 'wonder drug' – a pill with supposedly none of the side effects of barbiturates. It was thalidomide, a teratogen, meaning it interfered with the normal development of the embryo. Taken between the fourth and twelfth weeks of pregnancy, it caused babies to be born with foreshortened limbs or no limbs at all; numbers of them were born blind and deaf and with damage to internal organs. More than four hundred children were affected in Britain, and at least another 10,000 around the world. The director of the Thalidomide Trust, Dr Martin Johnson, who has made an extensive study of thalidomide, writes that apart from war and genocide, thalidomide was the cause of the largest man-made disaster in European history.

I first became aware of the thalidomide children, as they came to be called, in 1962. We published some early pictures in the *Northern Echo* of thalidomide infants at Chailey Heritage in Sussex, a hospital, home and school for disabled children. I expected an outpouring of sympathy. I was wrong. Most of the readers who wrote did so to protest that it was not right for 'a family newspaper' to do this: 'We don't want to know.'

I should have known better than to expect anything else. I had already experienced the awkward emotions in encountering people who are severely disabled. One of the patrons of St Cuthbert's, a Catholic hospice in the trees by the river in Hurworth village where I lived, had promised a few of the patients there that she would find someone who 'knew about print'. She nominated me, so I called at the hospice one morning and met John Tinsley. He could not control his limbs. His head bobbed and his mouth twisted when he spoke. The vowels were prolonged and the consonants were lost so that what came out was part howl, part speech. It took me some minutes to work out what he was saying – a plea not to laugh at his idea. He wanted to print a magazine created by patients like him in St Cuthbert's.

John had been born with athetoid cerebral palsy; he was highly intelligent and could get around in a cycle-chair (an electric cycle of sorts). Peter Jackson, the sports editor of the magazine he conceived, was a severely spastic young man who had to be strapped into his wheelchair – 'Thaaaat's J-J-Jaaaco,' John said, jerking an elbow into him. And the magazine's cartoonist was a boy with spina bifida.

I naturally said I'd be glad to help, but to be honest my heart had sunk at the thought of spending time with John and Peter and their group. Of course, I felt sorry for them, but what was it Graham Greene said about 'pity' being a way of distancing ourselves from the other? It was a form of reassurance, an acknowledgement of our own wholeness. That was an uncomfortable thought.

It took me a couple of visits to St Cuthbert's to stop regarding the patients as victims and treat them as people, real personalities with their own individual identities rather than a 'case' of spina bifida, a 'case' of muscular dystrophy, a 'case' of spastic diplegia. When I said what I really thought about an article, a poem, a cartoon, we all started having a good time. John would then tell me with a huge convulsive laugh why I was wrong.

The thalidomide scandal was the most emotionally draining of all the stories I became involved with at the *Sunday Times*. I came to think of the letters to the *Northern Echo* as a metaphor for how the

British legal and political institutions had responded over and over again to the tragedy. They made the thalidomide children invisible.

The children were between the ages of four and eight when I became editor of the *Sunday Times*. Having published those early pictures in the *Northern Echo* in 1963 I wanted to find out what had happened to them. By 1967, I learned that not one of them had received a penny in compensation.

This was a consequence of a heartless decision taken by my old political adversary in the *Northern Echo*'s cervical cancer campaign, Enoch Powell, who was Minister of Health between 1960 and 1963 and thereby responsible for the National Health Service, which had told doctors it was safe to prescribe thalidomide – 'a remedy of proven value' in the words of the government-appointed drug-safety advisers, the Cohen Committee. In all the attention paid to the thalidomide story, Powell's crucial role in the long nightmare has been neglected.

Powell was a baffling figure. There was no doubting his academic brilliance – a double starred first at Trinity College, Cambridge, a professor of Greek at the University of Sydney when he was only twenty-five. Nor his bravery: he was the only man in the war to rise from private to brigadier. He had high velocity, too, as a political thinker. He ricocheted from the impeccably lucid to the paranoid crazy: it was one thing in the 1940s to accuse the United States of wishing to see an end to the British Empire, and something else again to blame the CIA for the bomb that blew up Lord Mountbatten in Ireland in 1979, a crime clearly committed by the IRA.

Millions paid attention when, in a carefully prepared speech in Birmingham in 1968, he said the threat posed by West Indian and Asian immigrants to Britain was comparable to the threat posed by Hitler in the 1930s. Britain, he said, was madly building its own funeral pyre by allowing in 50,000 immigrants a year and the anti-discrimination bills before Parliament would be match to gunpowder: 'Like the Roman, I seem to see the River Tiber foaming with much blood.' As policy, Powell's speech was defensible. But the tone and language was something else – an incitement. The speech blamed immigrants for all the social problems of the cities, indicting every person of colour on the basis of a number of unverifiable ugly anecdotes, and in emotive language about 'wide-grinning piccaninnies'. Then he refused to disavow the personal and mob violence that followed.

William Rees-Mogg in *The Times* had called the speech evil, but it was the *Sunday Times* criticism that roused Powell to sue for libel. Shortly afterwards, when I bumped into him at a reception in the House of Commons, he turned his pale, moustached face towards me and said: 'I will bury you.' In fact, when ordered by the courts to produce letters he'd quoted to justify his extravagant rhetoric, he refused to obey and then did not proceed with the libel action.

Like many people, I was puzzled by the loose screw that turned Powell's brilliance corrosively inward. That he refused to help the dispirited and powerless thalidomide families is hard to understand or forgive. He received a delegation of affected parents in January 1963 and rejected their every request: No to a public inquiry on the origins of the disaster. No to immediately setting up a 'drug-testing centre' – 'anyone who takes an aspirin puts himself at risk'. No to a public warning against using any of the pills that might still be in medicine cabinets – 'a scare-monger publicity stunt'. No to giving a statement afterwards – 'no need to bring the press into this'. And No to his setting eyes on a thalidomide child. No to Frederick Astbury without legs, arms and right hip; Louise Mason, no legs; David Bickers, no legs, no arms and just three fingers from his shoulder; Gary Skyner, a short left arm and no thumbs; Eddie Freeman, no legs and foreshortened arms.

It was an extraordinary lapse of public duty to deny society the knowledge essential to understanding the origins of the tragedy and preventing anything similar happening again. Powell's intransigence left the families with only one remedy, to sue the manufacturers for negligence. It was bad enough thus to condemn the parents and their children to live in *Bleak House* legal torment. The courts, in any case, could not be relied on to find the facts. The primary objective of the judicial system is to settle conflicts. It is not to find the truth come what may. A civil action for damages is an indirect, laborious, very slow and costly way of unravelling the facts. The families were not well endowed for that exhausting exercise.

They were up against a formidable defendant. The thalidomide pill was marketed by Distillers Biochemicals, a subsidiary of Distillers, the giant liquor company retailing famous brands of whisky such as Johnnie Walker. It had assets then worth more than £400 million – £4 billion at today's values – and pretax profits of more than £500 million at today's values. Its chairman, Sir Alexander McDonald, was a Glasgow University graduate of accountancy and law who'd been with the company since 1946. He'd gathered a reputation as a man of granite, which suited the Distillers' image, and he'd engaged the rapier mind of John Wilmers QC, much feared for his capacity to eviscerate witnesses (as Malcolm McLaren, manager of the Sex Pistols, was to discover in a conflict with band members).

While the families' counsel changed four times, Wilmers stayed on the case throughout. The families had to rely on public funding through the Legal Aid fund administered by the Law Society. It begrudged spending on what it regarded as a weak case. Three and half years passed before it authorized paying expert witnesses.

Distillers wasn't a long-established pharmaceutical company. It had no research scientists and didn't hire a pharmacologist until it had decided to manufacture thalidomide under licence from a German company called Chemie Grünenthal that was also relatively new to the business. By one of those mocking twists of history, the *Sunday Times* had a part in the company's decision. Aldous Huxley, the author of the prophetic 1932 novel *Brave New World*, contributed an article to the paper in June 1956 in which he speculated that modern science might be able to produce a happiness drug (called Soma 6 in his novel). 'Will the pharmacologists be able to do better than the brewers and distillers?' he asked. Provoked by the question, a Distillers director read Huxley. Might a pill be found that would eventually become an alternative to whisky? This new non-toxic sedative from Chemie Grünenthal seemed to fit the bill. Distillers sold it as a safe sleeping pill and tranquillizer called Distaval from April 1958. Another company, Richardson-Merrell, sold it as Kevadon in the United States. Millions of American mothers escaped the catastrophe because Dr Frances Kelsey, at the Federal Food and Drug Administration, while not predicting the dramatic phocomelia deformities, became suspicious of Richardson-Merrell's sloppy procedures. Even so, some seventeen American mothers and their babies were affected by premature releases of the pill. What a savage irony that a 'happiness' drug was to cause so much human misery.

So upset were hospital midwives and doctors at the births of the first thalidomide babies that they often concealed the children from the mother – making excuses until it came time for her discharge. The mothers, isolated from one another, struggling with the same emotional and physical difficulties, the stares of others, did not know where to turn. They had paroxysms of guilt; something must be deeply wrong with them or their families or their husbands' families. Some believed God had punished them for a lapse in their lives. Some felt ashamed they'd complained of the symptoms that prompted their doctors to prescribe the dangerous pill. Scores didn't know for several years that they were victims of thalidomide. They didn't connect the news stories about the drug to their own predicament. The psychological traumas were intense. Mothers hid at home rather than encounter people who recoiled from the sight of an afflicted child. Marriages were wrecked. 'If you bring that monster home,' said one husband, 'I leave.' And so he did.

The impulse to put the tragedy swiftly out of mind was understandable. It was too painful. Somebody, surely, would look after those unfortunate children and their families so we could get on with our lives. Somebody didn't and wouldn't.

Here again Health Minister Powell was no help. He'd left the families no choice but to seek redress through the courts, then put the whole weight of the ministry behind discountenancing the very grounds of negligence they'd have to prove to win damages. Thalidomide, he said in Parliament and in a television interview, was properly tested by Distillers according to the standards of the time, when nobody thought a drug could reach the foetus. And unanimity prevailed on this key question. *The Economist*, *The Times*, the *Manchester Guardian*, the *Sunday Telegraph*, all said the same thing.

As we were to discover, none of those apparently authoritative statements was true.

In fact, reproductive studies had been routinely done by pharmaceutical companies a decade before Distillers made thalidomide. The tranquillizers in direct competition with thalidomide were tested for teratogenic effects and the results published by Hoffman La Roche, Lederle, Pfizer, Smith, Kline and French, among others; while in Britain studies were done at Burroughs Wellcome and at ICI under Dr Edward Paget. If reproductive tests had been done with thalidomide they would not necessarily have produced the precise deformities, but they would have shown that it could pass through the placenta and might endanger unborn children.

How could it be that everyone got it wrong? We learned later that all the assertions about the inviolability of the placental barrier originated with Distillers. The senior civil servant signing the letters to parents and advising Powell had taken his cue from a Distillers medical executive who'd been with the Ministry and called to brief him. And the newspapers found the company most helpful. Like some primitive medicine man's incantation, the unceasing repetition – the standards of the time, the standards of the time – hypnotized everyone who heard it.

When I first arrived at the *Sunday Times*, I longed to take up the cause of the children. Editorial action, however, was forbidden on pain of a jail sentence or heavy fine. Some sixty-two of the abandoned families had begun civil actions in August 1962, while I was still with the *Northern Echo*, and British law on contempt of court meant their writs sealed the whole affair in a legal cocoon. Once the writs had been issued, it became illegal to bring out facts or comment on a pending trial, whether civil or criminal. With thalidomide, this meant that nothing could be published that might influence a judge until every case – every single case – had been settled by the courts. This is a plain denial of free speech, but common law had long held that this right of free speech had to be balanced by the right to a fair trial uncontaminated by outside

pressure on any party or information and comment that might sway
a judge or jury.

In my first months as editor I had a narrow squeak when, thanks
to a slip by a writer, compounded by a duty lawyer's misjudgement,
we'd accidentally published the previous convictions of a man about
to stand trial. I was personally exonerated but the newspaper was
fined £5,000. The thalidomide actions were in civil court, to be tried
by a judge alone, but the law was no different. And to the courts it
didn't matter either that there had been no movement on the cases in
all the five years to 1967. Indeed, in 1973, a Law Lord referred to
eleven-year-old pending thalidomide cases as being 'in the early
stages of litigation'.

The families had been told by their lawyers on no account to talk
to 'mass media', but what we most wanted to know at this stage
was how the disaster had occurred. Nobody in Distillers or Chemie
Grünenthal would help, but we suddenly had the chance to look
into the files of both companies. John Fielding, a reporter, brought a
Dr Montagu Phillips to see me. Phillips had been engaged by the
families' solicitors, Kimber Bull, as a consulting pharmacologist
and chemical engineer. He was a small, rumpled man who fidgeted
a lot – not, I thought, likely to be impressive in a witness box under
Wilmers' brand of interrogation, but he possessed 10,000 Distillers
internal memoranda and reports that he said documented a scandal.
They'd been made available through the legal process known as
'disclosure' by which both sides are obliged to supply all files in
their possession relevant to the issues in contention. In short, he
was a whistle-blower, or what we called a FINK – Fair Insider
with Necessary Knowledge. But was he 'fair'? He had a grievance.
His wife had taken thalidomide as a sleeping pill and he believed
that was the cause of her irreversible nerve damage, known as
polyneuritis. How far was that influencing his judgement? Moreover, he was breaking a legal honour code and he was asking me
to risk a breach of journalistic ethics: he wanted £8,000 to help
care for his wife, he said.

Was this the chequebook journalism I'd inveighed against on
What the Papers Say and in speeches criticizing newspapers that paid

for the memoirs of a criminal? I'd never done that. In the office and at home, I debated the ethics of paying him. It was a consideration that he offered us his technical advice and, more important, promised to keep us informed on what went on behind the closed doors of the legal negotiations. Every last doubt fell before my intense curiosity about what the documents revealed on the origins of the disaster. Was I to put my precious journalistic conscience before gaining access to crucial information that might never see the light of day if, as seemed likely, an out-of-court settlement was reached? No. We collected the documents and I assigned the unflappable Phillip Knightley to evaluate them and prepare a narrative for publication sometime when we were free of legal restraint.

More urgent was a second set of documents from Chemie Grünenthal. Henning Sjöström, a Stockholm lawyer representing 105 Swedish victims, was concerned that since it had taken the Germans seven years to mount a criminal trial of nine company executives, it might take another seven years of court testimony to resolve the case: the prosecution alone said it had 352 witnesses. Other than wanting his expenses covered, Sjöström was simply looking for international publicity to shame the company that had caused so much havoc. The German newspapers dare not publish anything for fear of punishment under their own laws on contempt.

Collected in three suitcases, the German papers, when translated and indexed, were to reveal a get-rich-quick mentality in the Chemie Grünenthal company. The safety in pregnancy of Contergan (as they called the drug) was a main selling point, but the company had not tested to see if it could pass through the placenta to affect an unborn child. Chemie Grünenthal sales leaflets for doctors stressed safety, quoting a March 1960 article in the *American Journal of Obstetrics and Gynecology* by Dr Ray O. Nulsen, practising in Cincinnati, Ohio, the hometown of Richardson-Merrell. In his deposition for the German trial, however, Nulsen admitted he had not tested it on pregnant women at all and was not even the author of the article. It had been written for him by an employee of Richardson-Merrell – who'd relied on Chemie Grünenthal!

In the light of what I knew was in the German documents and

emerging in the Distillers documents, I was very surprised when Mr Desmond Ackner QC (later Lord Ackner) appeared in court for the families in February 1968 to say they were withdrawing charges of negligence. Distillers had agreed to pay 40 per cent of what they might have had to pay should the actions have been wholly successful. Both parties still had to agree what sum of money would represent an award of 100 per cent, but the 40 per cent, said Ackner, would amount to 'very substantial' damages, whereas if the actions had continued, 'the plaintiffs could have failed to recover a penny apiece'.

Mr Justice Hinchcliffe endorsed Ackner: 'I have given anxious consideration to the issues and to the prospects of success in law and fact, having regard to what the reasonably careful manufacturer would have done before marketing the drug in the then state of knowledge. In my judgment the plaintiffs are well advised to accept.'

This sounded absurd to us. By this time Godfrey Hodgson, the new editor of Insight, had constructed a shocking four-page narrative of the history of the German company's invention and marketing of thalidomide. James Evans, the elegant and indispensable full-time staff lawyer at the *Sunday Times*, advised me that the law on contempt almost certainly made it too dangerous to publish. Not only would revelation of Chemie Grünenthal's reckless conduct cast Distillers in a bad light, but the announcement of Ackner's interim settlement had stimulated more families to sue Distillers, so the rule of sub judice extended into the unknowable future.

James Evans had to be heeded. He was not one of the legal fraternity schooled in the scholarship of suppression; he was a facilitator. If publication was in the public interest, he regarded it as his duty to justify it in law. Now, unusually unsure, he suggested we seek yet another opinion by consulting a specialist in one of London's grand Inns of Court, a new experience for me.

We'd hardly taken a chair in the Brick Court rooms of David Hirst QC before he pronounced: 'Contempt! Flagrant contempt!' I tried suggesting that on this logic when the German trial started every British newspaper reporting it would be in contempt. Mr Hirst – later Judge Hirst – was disturbed by my belligerence (so was I). All these years later I see his eyes, unblinking behind his glasses, evoking the sensation of being in *The Great Gatsby* looking up at the gigantic blue irises of the oculist Dr T. J. Eckleburg brooding on his billboard over the Valley of Ashes. There is no escape! Flagrant contempt!

Sulking on the way back to the office, I pressed James Evans, who went back to Hirst and got the same answer in writing. His own doubts, as much as my persistence, led him to seek yet another opinion. Mr Peter Bristow – another QC on the way to the bench – spelled out the risks, too, but ended on a somewhat less alarming note than the steely David 'Eckleburg' Hirst.

I decided to ignore them all and publish. This was not only my heart speaking, but my head. I realized that in the long run, without any challenge, the oppressive British press laws were not just a threat to the thalidomide victims and their families, but a real threat to democracy itself. These laws were a teratogen in themselves, stunting and deforming our freedom and liberty. I was so appalled by the way Chemie Grünenthal had disregarded early warnings that I emotively juxtaposed photographs on the Review Front of a deformed German child and one of the architects of his misfortune, a white-coated head of research at Chemie Grünenthal.

I waited in a defensive crouch for action by the law officers of the Crown or Distillers, but they stayed behind their battlements. Distillers had clearly blundered in relying on Chemie Grünenthal. Their own documents revealed how little independent testing they'd done, how similar to Grünenthal they were in unjustified marketing and the inexcusable delays in sounding an alarm: the Australian obstetrician William McBride notified at least two, and possibly six Distillers Sydney employees of his suspicions by the first week of July 1961, but the company continued to promote the drug as safe for another four months (in which time about a quarter of the British children known to have been affected were damaged in the womb).

Our publication of the German story would, I assumed, stiffen the sinews of the families' lawyers about what constituted 'substantial' in the damages Ackner had said were in train. But we had to wait a whole year to find what that meant. Unable to agree on what 100 per cent of damages would be, the parties came back in July 1969 to ask Judge Hinchcliffe to resolve the deadlock by making monetary awards in two test cases. One was in the top bracket – David Jones, then nearly nine, who had neither legs nor arms and would need help for the rest of his life, never being able to toilet himself, dress or undress. The other, Richard Satherly, was in the middle bracket. He had legs but only a single digit protruded from his shoulder; he brushed his teeth by holding the toothbrush in his feet.

The press hailed Judge Hinchcliffe's resultant awards with the usual 'fortune' headlines associated with lottery winners. We didn't. Nicholas Harman had joined us from *The Economist* and I made space on the editorial page for a critical article. He noted the judge's conclusion that his award to Richard of £32,000 'would be sufficient to keep him free from financial worry and would go some way to ameliorating the discomfort and deprivations that he is bound to suffer'. All very well, said Harman, but if £32,000 was 'sufficient' to these ends then the 40 per cent he would actually receive – £12,800 – would be 60 per cent insufficient.

It was a temperate article, but I wrote the aggressive headline 'What Price a Pound of Flesh?', and soon had one of James Evans's duty lawyers in my office. 'Afraid this is risky. Not happy about your headline. Contempt.' He pointed out that since even more families were now suing, the contempt restrictions continued. 'You could be accused of interfering with the course of justice.'

I let the article and headline run.

Partly as a result of these stories, families kept coming forward to press their claims. By 1971, some 266 had won waivers from the three-year statute of limitations and another 123 victims had identified themselves, making 389 not provided for by the first settlement. Even if all but one case remained, nothing could be written. Every year pressed harder on the families, whereas the legal entity of Distillers enjoyed immortality, immune from criticism.

In the meantime, outrage followed outrage. The lawyers representing the 266 new claimants as a group went back to Distillers, but ice had formed on the Scottish granite. The company declared that it would set up a trust fund but it was worth only £3.25 million, averaging some £7,500 for each victim – half the 1969 settlements.

Moreover, the offer was conditional on every single family accepting.

The lawyers commended the offer to the group of families. Six families objected, led by David Mason, a sophisticated Mayfair art dealer who was the father of a legless daughter. The six dissenters regarded the offer as miserable charity, whereupon their own legal advisers – yes, the parents' legal team! – took them to court on behalf of those ready to settle, and Judge Hinchcliffe removed parental rights from the dissident six. Henceforth a Treasury solicitor would decide what was best for their children, i.e., accept the Distillers offer.

Mason had a friend who knew David English, the editor of the *Daily Mail*, so Mason took his personal story there. English published three articles: 'My Fight for Justice by the Father of Heartbreak Girl Louise'. When the Attorney General warned the *Daily Mail* that these articles constituted contempt of court, English backed off. The Court of Appeals resoundingly restored Mason's rights, but the *Mail* did no more, BBC television's *Twenty-Four Hours* cancelled a related programme and Mason stopped giving interviews that never appeared. Once again, the cloak of invisibility enveloped the thalidomide children.

As we entered 1972, I had plenty of other issues to deal with, but I just couldn't get the thalidomide negotiations out of my mind. I was convinced something was badly wrong. If the Knightley article presented, as a judge later said, 'a powerful case of negligence', why had the lawyers been eager to accept only 40 per cent of the less than adequate 100 per cent? And why were they now ready to settle for something like half of that?

What made me even more determined was a new perspective in a long memorandum from Bruce Page. His successes as head of Insight had led me to create a Special Projects unit around him with Elaine Potter to assist. Elaine was a South African whose tenacity matched her scholarship. She'd not had a great deal of experience in journalism, but she'd acquired an Oxford Ph.D. and, as important, squatter's rights to a freelancer's chair in the features department. Some of our most successful recruits were squatters; they were tested by the exigencies of sudden demands for labour and the best, like

Elaine, survived with the complicity of editors until I could find a place on staff.

I'd asked Page to revisit the whole thalidomide project with Elaine. His first initiative was to compare the money awards with a more precise assessment of the children's needs; his second was to send Elaine to pharmaceutical laboratories in the United States and Britain to check the routine story that Distillers did all the tests that were standard at the time – exposing the myth I've mentioned. His memorandum on the compensation money was as startling as the medical blunders. In the *Modern Law Review* of May 1972, he read a two-part article on the absence of any coherent method by which judges assessed personal injury damages. It was written by John Prevett, a Fellow of the Institute of Actuaries with the London firm of Bacon and Woodrow. Prevett, it turned out, had given expert evidence to Judge Hinchcliffe that the lead test case, David Jones, required £135,000, whereas the judge had awarded less than half that amount with that sum in turn subject to the 60 per cent reduction agreed upon by the lawyers. This meant his actual cash for the rest of his life was only £20,800.

When recently I spoke to John Prevett, now in his retirement, he remembered wondering if he was making any impression at all on the judge. 'He seemed to be asleep during the long time I was cross-examined on the numbers by the Distillers lawyer [John Wilmers].' The judge said he had to be fair to Distillers as well as to the children, but he must have been hypnotized by the mesmerizing Wilmers to swallow the QC's contention that inflation should be disregarded because the government had promised to control inflation. Ah yes, said the learned judge, all 'speculation' and 'hearsay'.

As for the inflation that judge and Distillers counsel regarded with such amused disdain, the 1969 award was by 1972 worth 20 per cent less, and in 1975 alone the inflation rate was 24 per cent. Prevett told me: 'Altogether the awards were 16 per cent of what I reckoned was justified. I worked out that the money the judge awarded David would run out by the time he was twenty-nine.'

Why did nobody, including us, fully report Prevett when he was in court in 1969? It was hardly rocket science. And here's a terrible thought: if the *Modern Law Review* had not, three years later, asked Prevett to write on actuarial advice, and if he had not chosen thalidomide as his example, and if Page had not read the journal, it's possible we might have underestimated just how rotten the personal injury system had become.

The priority now had to be to make the case for decent compensation and to do it before more families were sold down the river. It was hard to find out what was going on in the negotiations. Distillers' solicitors refused our every request for information with heavy breathing about contempt, and our contact, their adviser Dr Phillips, was not privy to the secret negotiations. But Knightley had formed such good relations with the families that a number of them confided in him, including the fearless Mason. The shock of the Page–Prevett assessment was searingly with me when Knightley strode into my office, his phlegmatic personality unusually agitated. 'Can't we do something? They're being told they'll lose their legal aid certificates if they don't sign. Most of the parents are ready to give up and yet they'll still get only half of what the 1969 families got. Half 1969!'

The new pressure on the families was the last straw for me. The much-feared law on contempt was going to sanctify a gross injustice. It was urgent to shout it must not be allowed to happen. Was I emotional about the thalidomide families? Yes, I was, but my decision that Tuesday to launch a campaign in the next issue of the paper, five days hence, was not a sudden impulse. My experience of campaign journalism at the *Northern Echo* had convinced me that certain conditions had to be fulfilled before a newspaper undertook a campaign. The paper had to have investigated the subject thoroughly enough to be sure that there was a genuine grievance; it had to have defined a practical remedy; it had to be ready to commit the resources for a sustained effort and it must open its columns to counter-arguments and corrections of fact. No campaign should be ended until it had succeeded – or was proved wrong.

I called James Evans: 'I'm going to campaign on thalidomide starting this Sunday come what may, contempt or not.' He preserved his celebrated equanimity. 'I have the picture perfectly,' he responded. 'Alpine tourist asks guide to take him to the top of the Eiger by the safe route. Let me think about it, mm?' I told Denis Hamilton we were going to denounce the proposed settlements, and was phoned by the advertising manager, Donald Barrett. 'You know, Harry, Distillers is our biggest client, £60,000 a year.' Then he added: 'I know that won't stop you and it shouldn't.'

Page came in from holiday to convert his Prevett memorandum into a three-page analytical narrative for the upcoming issue of 24 September 1972. It was a bitingly cool piece, but the display by Ron Hall and our new design chief Edwin Taylor incorporated an editorial across the top of the page with a picture of a pretty young girl who had no arms. James Evans drafted the editorial. We would, he proposed, acknowledge Distillers' duty to their shareholders and their denial of negligence, but demand the company fulfil its moral obligation: 'The law is not always the same as justice.'

I did very little to James's draft. I headlined it 'Children on our Conscience' and devised the emotional slogan for the coverage I hoped we could continue: 'Our Thalidomide Children, a Cause for National Shame'. At the end of the three pages demolishing the levels of compensation, there was one paragraph where I'd intended to announce our upcoming article on Distillers' documents. 'May I say that it would be wise,' murmured James, 'to give yourself and the courts a little more time to sort that out?'

Wise indeed it was. I simply wrote that 'in a future article' we'd trace how the tragedy occurred.

It proved to be the matador's cape.

We were engaged on a high-risk enterprise, but after all the delays, all the anxieties, all the legal frustrations, this was an exhilarating time. We all felt as if we'd been let out of prison.

I invited David Mason and his wife Vicki to watch the presses start up. Over the din, he yelled: 'Until now I never believed it would happen!' It was quite a contrast with the media silence that followed, but that first Sunday morning a most important telephone call came to my home from a man who lived in a permanent silence. Jack

The Tuesday conference in the editor's office at the *Sunday Times*. Prince Charles happened to be there the week the 'Uganda Sensation' was on the contents bill. This was the detailed revelation of the atrocities of Uganda's dictator Idi Amin, written by a fugitive hiding in my Essex cottage.
(Sunday Times)

Roy Thomson

Lord Thomson of Fleet by David Low.

Twelve years into my editorship of the *Sunday Times* and William Rees-Mogg's of *The Times* we were asked to pose with the 'indispensable, elegant' Denis Hamilton, as Cyril Connolly called the chairman of Times Newspapers. The photographer was one who had to be obeyed, Arnold Newman, in Britain to prepare a show for the National Portrait Gallery and the *Sunday Times* magazine.

The Insight trio who led the Philby investigation: David Leitch, Bruce Page and the Lenin look-alike Phillip Knightley. The intrepid photographer Bryan Wharton managed to get them to stand still for a minute.

Bryan Wharton travelling in style on the West Bank of Luxor with the Valley of the Kings in the background. He was there to photograph the tombs and temples in readiness for the Tutankhamun exhibition that *The Times* was bringing to the British Museum. He had also packed equipment in readiness for yet another threatened war – a good enough excuse for hiring a bearer and a noble steed.

(Shirley Freeman)

David Blundy interviews Israeli leader Ariel Sharon on the Golan Heights during the Yom Kippur war of 1973. He survived his hazardous years as an irrepressible reporter only to be killed by a random bullet on 17 November 1989, during El Salvador's civil war. (Sally Soames)

Press Association

Neil Libbert

Mark Ellidge

Saturday moments in an editor's life. Everything begins with the reporter. Jon Swain (top right) vanished in Ethiopia in July 1976. Only later did we learn he'd been kidnapped by Eritrean insurgents and held in the desert for nearly three months, accused of being an 'imperialist spy'. It was huge relief when he was released and I was able to welcome him home. Translating the reporters' words into a page display (middle) has Ron Hall, with pipe at left, in a huddle over a page proof with Colin Chapman (foreign news editor), Richard Vickers (then chief sub-editor) and the new editor. Hot news finally in hot metal. A last-minute look at all the type in the completed front page with editorial and comps clustered around.

Tatler magazine in London was about to expire when Tina assumed the editorship. I didn't notice at the time that the window display behind spells FUTURE. She'd only recently returned from New York where she made friends with an author I'd signed for the *Sunday Times*: S. J. Perelman, the celebrated *New Yorker* humorist, and scriptwriter for some Marx Brothers films and Mike Todd's *Around the World in Eighty Days*. (Ken Sharp)

At the age of seventy-four, Sid Perelman declared he was going to drive his 1949 MG YT tourer in a rerun of the epic Paris to Peking motor race (9,317 miles). He told me he had a blonde from Pine Bluff Arkansas as travelling companion: 'She knows zilch about engines, but she's six foot two inches of dimpled beauty.' In the end he settled for travelling with MG expert Sid Beer, and London art gallery dealer Eric Lister. Perelman and I are explaining all this to a London meter maid when Sid parked the MG for a farewell lunch. (Bryan Wharton)

Our Nick Tomalin and David Blundy died reporting war. David Holden was murdered, mysteriously, in reporting peace. (*Sunday Times*)

The man in the Muscovite fur hat and sunglasses was our more or less permanent nightmare: union leader Reg Brady, linking hands with his mates who are carrying a coffin – representing the *Sunday Times*.
(Sally Soames)

The deserted composing room at some miserable moment in the year the paper was shut down. (Sally Soames)

Saying goodbye on the composing room floor, on my last day as editor of the *Sunday Times* after fourteen years.
(Mark Ellidge, *Sunday Times*)

As a former corporal, I was outranked by the retiring chairman of the joint chiefs, Colin Powell, and his associates, but we all got the joke about 'the one that got away'.
(Random House)

At the end of the devastating year of non-publication of the *Sunday Times*, we came back with a bang with the White House memoir of Henry Kissinger, which I'd edited for serialization. (UPI)

And then there were four . . . The birth of Isabel Harriet in October 1990, recorded by photographic royalty Annie Leibovitz.

Our refuge, the 1928 cottage by the sea in Quogue, Long Island, seen from the top of the dune. (Mike Evans)

The best birthday gift – my five children all together from both sides of the Atlantic. Top row: Ruth, Kate, Mike; bottom row: George, Isabel. (George Brown)

In the courtyard of Buckingham Palace in 2004, having bent the knee to be dubbed a Knight Bachelor of the British Empire. They've been awarding KBE's since the reign of King Henry III (1216–72) so I was a Johnny-come-lately.

Ashley, the Labour MP for the Midlands potteries town of Stoke on Trent, was stone-deaf. I was amazed to conduct a telephone conversation with him: his wife Pauline, listening in, enunciated my words to Jack, he read her lips, and responded.

Ashley was one of my heroes. He'd left school at fourteen, become a labourer and crane driver in Widnes, a sprawling industrial area, and a shop steward for the Chemical Workers Union. Then he'd won scholarships to Ruskin College, Oxford, and Caius College, Cambridge, produced radio and TV documentaries for the BBC, and got elected to Parliament the same year, 1966, that I joined the *Sunday Times*. He wasn't deaf then, but one ear was less good than the other, and since he was in line for a ministerial appointment he decided he had to have an operation to equip him for the rapid interchanges in the Commons. It went wrong. His first instinct was to give up his seat, but there was an uprush of support for him so spontaneous and moving that it encouraged him to stay – and to do what he could in Parliament for all handicapped people.

Ashley came to the office with Pauline to meet Page and Knightley, asked questions and said: 'Well, that's decided it. I'll give up writing my autobiography until we've won.' It's a little commentary on the postwar social changes that Ashley was swiftly joined as an ally by another Northern working-class boy who'd left school at fourteen and got to Oxford on an adult scholarship, my old schoolmate Alf Morris (who later became the first Minister for the Disabled). So we had a partnership of Widnes elementary school and Brookdale Park embellished by Oxford and Durham. The cause soon became bipartisan when two Tory physician MPs, Gerard Vaughan, a paediatrician at Guy's Hospital, and Dr Thomas Stuttaford, joined with Ashley and Morris.

Yet we might as well have been publishing on the moon for all the attention we got. One BBC radio programme gave us a few minutes of air time – with a jumpy BBC lawyer hovering in the control room – and that was it. To the media we were Typhoid Mary. Twenty-three days were to go by without another mention on radio or a single story in print or television. Even David English, the enterprising editor of the *Daily Mail*, was unwilling to follow up his newspaper's original Mason series; not until the eighth week of the campaign did the *Mail* comment. 'Saving our space to cover your trial,' was the joking response I got to the press and television phone calls I made.

There was silence in Parliament, too. The efforts of the four MPs to get the issue raised were squashed. A letter from Ashley to Prime Minister Edward Heath brought only a rebuke: 'Legal matters are not for this or for a Labour government.' This was a fair statement of the long Parliamentary tradition that the House of Commons never intervened in any subject being decided by court of law, but it meant Ashley couldn't get a resolution before the House or even raise a question. I went to see the melancholy Minister of Health, Sir Keith Joseph, in his gloomy office at the Elephant and Castle south of the river. I came back empty-handed, as depressed as him and the area – another very clever man like Powell with the same aversion to getting involved. The law must take its course, etc.

The first intimation there might be legal trouble came three days after our 24 September blast. I was handed a letter in an embossed envelope. It was from the Solicitor General warning that our editorial and article could be considered contempt of court. The Attorney General was in Strasbourg and would deal with me upon his return. Meanwhile, said the letter, 'you will no doubt wish to consider your position'. I replied that we were canvassing moral obligations, not legal, and were not to be deterred from continuing. James Evans then applied his emollient forensic skill in several phone conversations with the Attorney General's office.

In the third week of the campaign, we got another embossed envelope. 'The Attorney General instructs me to say he has now considered the material in *The Sunday Times* of 24th September and 1st October and does not propose to take any action over the matter already published.' By not accusing us of contempt of court on the first article, he legitimized the moral campaign. I put in an immediate call to give Ashley the news, but didn't get through all morning. I had to leave the office for a lunch appointment, not knowing that Ashley had that very afternoon arranged to see the Speaker of the House to make one last plea for Parliament to discuss thalidomide.

I'd just arrived at the Ivy restaurant when a call came through to me on the cloakroom attendant's phone in the vestibule. It was Ashley speaking with Pauline listening on an extension so as to enunciate my words for Jack to lip-read. What I heard from Jack above the bustle of the lunchtime crowd being greeted by the maître d' was that he could not speak for long because he was due any minute in the Speaker's room in a last-ditch effort to have the Parliamentary restrictions removed. I had a rush of blood to the head. In my excitement to tell him that the Attorney General was not taking us to court over the first article, and hence was recognizing the distinction between moral and legal justice, I forgot that everything I said had to be mouthed by Pauline so that Jack could read her lips and respond. Jack's patient voice came on the line: 'Sorry, Harry, didn't get that. Say again slowly please.' When I'd calmed down, I was able to say that if the Attorney General accepted the distinction between moral and legal justice, surely the Speaker would have to follow suit.

It was not that easy. It meant the Speaker would have to overrule the Prime Minister and shake, if not sever, the precedents of barring any Parliamentary discussion when an issue was before a court of law.

Jack argued his case that afternoon, and the Speaker said he would rule the next day. It was then Jack's turn to rush a call to me. The Speaker had just authorized Jack to put down an Early Day motion and they'd agreed on the language Jack might use. This was a vital breakthrough that opened the way for Parliamentary activity. Within days, 265 MPs had signed in support of the Early Day motion.

Two days later I got another letter from the Attorney General. He was going to court to ban publication of our promised future article on the manufacture of thalidomide.

The campaign I began on 24 September was to run more than three months into January 1973, and the reverberations continued for years after that. Just as in the Timothy Evans case, there were misgivings from within the newspaper regarding the editor's obsession; we'd offend some readers, bore others. Elaine Potter still remembers

the theatrical yawns she encountered from some staffers as she produced 'yet another thalidomide story'. I understood the concern.
There was clearly the risk, too, that I'd get distracted, that I'd not
organize enough talent, time and space for other stories. The world
was not standing still. On 5 September, Palestinian terrorists murdered Israeli athletes at the Olympic Games, and in October three of
the killers were released in Germany following a hijacking. In
November Richard Nixon was re-elected, but there was this shadow
called Watergate. Stephen Aris in New York was agitating to investigate and Kissinger said 'peace was at hand' in the Vietnam war;
Ulster was reeling from the killings of civil rights protesters on
Bloody Sunday; Prime Minister Edward Heath was leading Britain
into Europe while the Labour party wrangled with itself about
whether to stay in or pull out; Idi Amin was terrorizing Uganda. And
the Yom Kippur war started.

I was in the thick of all these events as an editor, but determined
to keep faith with the thalidomide children by campaigning week
after week, month after month. The challenge was to keep readers
interested.

The editorial template was human interest stories, argument on
personal injury law, news of the Ashley–Morris activities, and powerful photography that would engage readers' compassion and dare
them to look away. I wouldn't have done this without my experience
in Darlington with the programme to save women from cervical
cancer and in vindicating Timothy Evans. I'm as eager as the next
editor to find something new and exciting, but living close to the
readers, as I did then, I'd noted how we in the trade, absorbed by
every page, every story, became bored before the readers did. Our
challenge was to keep dramatizing the pain. We achieved it with such
photographs as one of a figure, wearing laced black shoes and white
ankle socks, hung up on a steel stand. The legs were artificial limbs
fitted to an otherwise empty full body harness, ready for the limbless thalidomide child to be hoisted into the frame like a jousting
medieval knight lifted into his armour. The hands were metal
talons. I remember thinking there was no way a thalidomide victim
could put on the socks, tie the shoelaces.

I identified everything we published with the 'Our Thalidomide Children' logo. From readers I had a quite different reaction in 1972 than I'd had ten years earlier in Darlington. Now they didn't turn away, perhaps habituated to the shock; instead, I had hundreds of letters and telephone calls of support, asking what they could do. Many of the letters came with cheques, scores came from thalidomide families. In the legal profession and the press, however, we had severe critics. The *Law Society Gazette* (representing solicitors) denounced the campaign as having 'all the subtlety and legal justification of Robin Hood's activities in Sherwood Forest'; the columnist Peregrine Worsthorne in the *Sunday Telegraph* condemned it as nauseating to focus on a company that had only done what the country willed. The Oxford historian A. J. P. Taylor described it as 'a witch hunt, an exploitation of popular feeling such as Dr Goebbels would have rejoiced in'.

That the *Sunday Times* had been attempting to print true facts was a nicety Taylor and others chose to ignore. But I was buoyed by these ordinary readers. The letters from thalidomide families were affecting. David Jones's father, a former male nurse, had taken on the full-time task of looking after his legless son while his mother, a teacher, went out to work. 'When the compensation awards made headlines,' he told us, 'people withdrew their sympathy. They treated us as if we'd had a lucky win on the pools. After the years of struggle it took time to register what a piffling sum we had. Had I fully appreciated the problems we are facing now – David is growing too heavy for me to lift – I'd have stood up in that courtroom and shouted.'

I said we'd run a family story every week until we succeeded. 'And what will you do when you've run out of 450 families?' someone asked. 'Start again,' I said on the spur of the moment. 'They'll all be older!' To do that we recruited Marjorie Wallace, who was directing television programmes for the BBC. She had a gentle nature and a degree in psychology, and managed to depict the struggles without being mawkish. It was she who found nine-year-old Terry Wiles, a highly intelligent two-foot limbless trunk with one eye, abandoned by his mother, adopted by an inventive sixty-year-old van driver,

Leonard, and his young wife Hazel, living in a dilapidated cottage near Huntingdon. The National Health Service equipment was no use to him. From scrap metal and old army surplus, Leonard had invented a 'supercar' chair for Terry on the principle of the fork-lift truck, so the boy could press a button with his shoulders and raise himself to talk to people. These tragedies could not be ignored – but the authorities were about to try again to switch off the light.

We lost 3–0 in the High Court on 17 November. We were forbidden to publish the Knightley article based on the Distillers documents revealing the company's unjustified reliance on Chemie Grünenthal's own questionable marketing activities. The ban itself probably earned as much ink as the article would have if we'd been allowed to publish it.

Sir Alexander at Distillers counter-attacked. Tony Lynes, who'd inherited sixty Distillers shares, took up the cause in a letter to the company, and got a stiff lecture from Sir Alexander on the chairman's legal responsibilities. It was easy for a single shareholder, he declared, to take a moral stand – 'even easier for a newspaper editor' – but the chairman would be sued by shareholders if he gave money away without the unanimous approval of the 250,000 share-holders holding 300 million shares. Legally, said Sir Alexander, the parents were probably entitled to nothing. And if the *Sunday Times* campaign led to the breakdown of negotiations, well, that's what they'd get, nothing. The company would go to trial – a danger to the families because their lawyers had already unwisely conceded they had no case on negligence.

It sounded like blackmail. 'For three hundred and seventy children,' said Ashley, 'the sword of Damocles has been replaced by the jagged edge of a broken whisky bottle.' Alf Morris, too, had been working away in the background. He invited me to come to the Commons to meet the Leader of the Opposition and soon-to-be Prime Minister, Harold Wilson, and Sir Elwyn Jones, a former Attorney General who was soon to become Lord Chancellor. Morris was the front-bench spokesman for social policy and in the meeting, with me cast in the role of Greek chorus, he begged Wilson and Jones to give up precious opposition time for a debate.

The Labour opposition had only four days in the whole year when they could decide the agenda, but they agreed, and on 29 November Morris and Ashley spoke to a packed House, calling on Distillers to recognize its moral debt and for the government to set up a trust fund for the children.

On the way to see the Labour leaders, I'd been stopped in the lobby of the Commons by Prime Minister Heath's parliamentary private secretary, Timothy Kitson, to ask whether we'd end the campaign upon hearing the information they'd just received: Distillers was willing to increase its offer of a trust fund from £3.25 million to £5 million. I said no; I'd been advised that any realistic assessment of need had to be closer to £20 million.

The Distillers' £5 million, announced by the government, was brushed aside in a debate in which massive emotional indignation and vivid personal testimony swept both sides of the House. 'How can an eleven-year-old girl look forward to laughing and loving,' said Ashley, 'when she has no hand to hold or legs to dance on?'

Heath relented with the announcement of a £3 million fund for the congenitally disabled, with a further £3 million for the thalidomide children. Moreover, he set up a Royal Commission to examine the whole question of personal injury damages.

Two months into the *Sunday Times* campaign, it was now self-sustaining. It gathered momentum from an unexpected quarter – Distillers' shareholders. Tony Lynes joined with Sarah and Roger Broad to take up Sir Alexander's challenge. They circulated a letter to thousands of shareholders. Sir Alexander had blithely assumed that the shareholders were interested only in maximizing their dividends, but that proved a misjudgement. Ron Peet, chief executive of the Legal and General Assurance Society, the second-largest life assurance company in Britain with 3.5 million Distillers shares, concluded not only that corporations had moral as well as legal responsibilities, but that the obduracy of Distillers was provoking such consumer hostility it would damage its own commercial interests.

And a trade union pension fund chairman declared: 'Distillers is blundering around like a Glaswegian drunk.'

Peet's snowball started an avalanche. More big companies, insurance brokers, merchant bankers and local authorities joined in. Stores and customers boycotted whisky made by Distillers. The duty-free stores at London and European airports reported customers saying: 'Anything but not from Distillers.' In the US, Ralph Nader planned an international boycott, briefed by the indefatigable David Mason who lobbied passengers on his transatlantic flight. Over nine days Distillers shares lost $35 million in value. This was arithmetic Edinburgh understood.

On 23 January the company gave in with an immediate commitment of £20 million, about ten times the original offer. Jack Ashley rang me on the Saturday to say he'd discovered the Treasury intended to tax the money. I wrote an editorial for the next day. With intervention by Ashley and Morris, the Prime Minister – now Harold Wilson – made the trust good with £5 million from government funds. The families and the campaigners were overjoyed by the victory and a settlement by which Distillers, in the end, accepted a liability of £28.4 million, embracing all the cases started in 1969.

I was delighted but strangely numb. I'd never doubted we'd win more money once we were able to let people know what was happening; my faith in free journalism and in the common decency of ordinary citizens had been reinvigorated, but I'd lived with the story for so many years I kept imagining the daily lives: getting into that harness, opening a bottle with one's teeth, holding a toothbrush between's one's toes, wondering if ever they'd know the joys of marriage and family life.

And then there remained the fact that we had not yet laid bare how the whole appalling mess had been created. A few weeks after Distillers had made their new acceptable offer, I sat in the Appeal Court to contest the ban on our draft article – and won 3–0. The Attorney General would not accept that. He took the case to the House of Lords who restored the ban by a 5–0 vote. Eleven judges had now pronounced, and only by one vote was the original moral campaign regarded as legitimate.

I kept Page and Potter on the investigation and a few months after the monetary settlement – not years – they were able to conclude there had been an excellent case waiting to be developed, only the parents' legal teams had failed to assemble it. Because the contempt rule still applied, it was not until 27 June 1976 that we were able to publish the Page–Potter findings documenting the powerful and scientifically sound case that the parents might have had all along. Solicitors and counsel had not secured decisive testimony available in Britain and the United States. No doubt the legal aid system had restricted them, but we spent relatively little energy establishing the falsity of the position taken by Powell and the 'quality' press that Distillers were blameless. In this regard, Dr Phillips turned out to be a poor choice of expert adviser. The documents he gave us were significant, but his advice on why the tragedy was foreseeable was not, and, in so far as we mentioned him, our draft article would have been seriously flawed.

The occasion for publication was our triumph – no other word for it – in a declaration by the European Court of Human Rights. By the vote of 13 international judges to 11, the Court ruled that by banning our report on the origins of the tragedy, Britain's law on contempt had breached the free speech Article 10 of the European Convention for the Protection of Human Rights. This meant the British government had to enact a statutory reform so that the years of silence on thalidomide could never be repeated: report and comment could henceforth be allowed in civil litigation until a case was actually set down for trial.

So in the end, it was all worthwhile. We exposed the real reasons for the disaster, and achieved reasonable compensation for the families, a Royal Commission on personal injuries, and somewhat more freedom of the half-free British press.

An extraordinary coincidence provides a coda to this chapter. I was writing this account when a stranger came on the phone from Yorkshire. It was Guy Tweedy, a property investor in Harrogate, wanting to come and talk about a campaign. Not the *Sunday Times* campaign of the 1970s, which he knew very well, but one he'd started with Nick Dobrik, who had a jewellery business. They are both thalidomide victims, relatively able-bodied, but joined now with other more typically damaged thalidomiders. They've already, with the help of Jonathan Stone, a former assistant of Lord Goodman, succeeded in getting Gordon Brown to rescind his decision as Chancellor to tax benefits payable through the Thalidomide Trust. (Does the Treasury have a tin heart?) Furthermore, they've briefed the successor company to Distillers, the Guinness group (now Diageo, the world's largest beer and spirits company), to such effect that it is repairing the damages of that 'hearsay' inflation with another £160 million over thirty years. Still, the payments from the trust, very fairly distributed, cannot meet the needs of the most affected of the 457 surviving thalidomiders. Money that seemed adequate three decades ago is no longer able to assure a decent life for someone like Lorraine Mercer or Vivien Barrett. Lorraine has no legs or arms, and only one hand emanating from her shoulder; she longs for the independence of being able to get about in a car with wheelchair access, now possible thanks to advances in technology, but such a car would cost £50,000. Vivien Barrett, no arms, legs or feet and only one hand, teaches music theory part time but fears how advancing age may affect her. Those thalidomiders who were able to work are finding they cannot continue.

The indomitable Jack Ashley has been moved to action again, calling for the state to recognize its responsibility for the disaster. Unfortunately, the then Labour Minister of Health, Alan Johnson (promoted to Home Secretary in 2009), is in the Powell mode. He has said he is 'not persuaded' there is a case for financial aid.

The thalidomiders feel a bond with their 'brothers and sisters' in other countries. In Italy, Spain and Austria, the victims have had no financial compensation at all. In Germany, where there are more than five times as many thalidomiders as there are in Britain, the maximum annual payment is meagre. And Chemie Grünenthal had insisted in the stingy private settlement made in 1969 that none of the victims there could ever complain or campaign.

I called the *Sunday Times* editor John Witherow, who immediately took up their cause.

I find it inspiring that the thalidomider activists, whose early years were such an ordeal, are now extending a helping hand to others, and then I realize with a stab of pain that many of them have no hands at all.

16

SPACE BARONS

Did I mention how invigorating it was to have a big-time national newspaper with the best staff in town? I still get a high from the fumes of those Saturdays when a vague idea from the beginning of the week – or an investigation started months back – crystallized into a thriller package of story, headline, photograph and graphic; and then the glorious moment when we got our hands on the first copies of the newspaper, expunging all the raw urgent untidiness of the passion and fine-tuning in the making of it. How authoritative everything looked! How delicious the smell of the still warm newsprint! How envious the rivals would be! Truth requires the admission that the rivals, the *Observer* and the *Sunday Telegraph*, sometimes arrived with a story that eclipsed ours or had escaped us altogether. Once we'd reduced the shock by declaring to each other 'Nothing new in that,' we scrambled like mad to catch up.

The week began at the editor's conference on Tuesday. Early on I had felt it necessary to issue my first edict. The head printer knocked up a sign I pinned to my office door: 'Smokers are welcome but not their cigarettes.' My peace offering to ease the pain was a souvenir I'd brought back from a Moscow trip, a samovar that was supposed to keep going a flow of hot tea.

Most of the talking was done by 'collectors', heads of departments who said what they hoped to bring in from reporters and columnists, photographers, graphic artists, critics and reviewers. These executives were responsible for people, not space on the pages. As the week accelerated, they bid their best efforts to the space barons, the handful who decided what should go in the premium spots in the paper: Ron Hall had the main feature space, Don Berry the news pages, Peter Wilsher the business pages, Leonard Russell the Review Front. One thing distinguished all the space barons: a vigilance about standards, expressed by Berry with a gentle headshake and big question marks on the copy, but with scorching scepticism by Wilsher. Business writers would do a lot to avoid Wilsher's high-pitched bray: 'That's all very well, chum, but what does it mean?'

It's endlessly fascinating to me how the tumult of the world can be made comprehensible by the orderly calibration of values within the discipline of the printed page. In newspapers that we are familiar with, the coded signals of headlines, space and placement tell us at once the gradations of content from the amusing to the awesome. I found it impossible to stay away from the 'back bench' where managing editor and chief sub-editor assessed stories, chose photographs and planned pages. The Saturday news pages were designed by Robert Harling, who'd worked in the war with his chum Ian Fleming on black propaganda operations run by the navy's Unit 17Z. Ingenious ways had to be devised to keep me from making observations that might impede the haste to go to press. I heard later that space baron Berry deputed Harling to distract me in the last minutes of closing page one. 'Tell me, Harry,' I can hear the saboteur now, 'which do you prefer, sex or skiing?'

I had my own source of relief from the week's tensions: squash. It required careful calculation and downright furtiveness to get away with it. At some stage during an afternoon in the week, at a time decided at the very last minute, I went down in Lord Thomson's private lift in our offices at Gray's Inn Road, jumped into a waiting car and sped off to the Royal Automobile Club in Pall Mall for a match. 'Sped' is the wrong verb for the times when I got snarled in the

Trafalgar Square nightmare and I ran the last 220 yards to make my game. I think it was then I decided that I must return to motorcycling as a superior form of transport. Every minute counted. I could not be out of the office for more than an hour (and since there were no cell phones then I had elaborate arrangements with my secretary, Joan Thomas, how to get word through if the Russians landed in my absence).

I came to share the half-hour with different discreet staff players at the paper, notably Peter Roberts, Magnus Linklater, James Evans and Lewis Chester. The urgency of chasing news carried over into the precious half-hour we had rushing like maniacs about the court. Sometimes the small black ball metamorphosed into the wily barrister from Lincoln's Inn who had convinced the judge that there was no possible public interest defence for our newspaper's desire to report on, say, the bribing of a British MP by a foreign government; sometimes it was the lupine grin of the communist union leader in the pressroom who had once again sabotaged our production (calls to him from Moscow came collect, which was a bit much). In any event, just hammering the ball, even though it was too often returned with nonchalance, was therapy for several days.

Not one of my staff members, curiously, was willing to give the editor the benefit of any doubt about questionable line calls. I will say in defence that we often continued *Sunday Times* business in the locker room. I didn't join the regulars who repaired to the Blue Lion pub opposite the office to discuss what had happened that week to their paper – everyone regarded it as their paper.

Over the years, various allegations have been made about my treatment of staff and guests – that I sent a 98-pound young woman reporter into a field with a bull to illustrate a story on the risks ramblers face; that I had to be cornered in the gents to sign 'pink slips' for cash advances for indigent reporters; and most commonly that I'd invite visitors arriving for lunch at the paper to decamp for a brisk cheese salad at the RAC club, then keep them waiting at its poolside while I swam my customary twenty laps. These stories and worse are all, regrettably, true. Very few appreciated the offer to jump in the pool with me. One interviewee preferred to stay fully clothed, obliging me to conduct our discourse standing at the shallow end between laps.

The *Sunday Times* staff was small by American standards, never more than 160 men and women on newspaper and magazine, but one of the paper's strengths, as it grew to 64 and then 72 pages, was that it was informed by a pool of unconventional talents. Today, when journalists tend to come into newspapers and television by the same conventional route – college, journalism course – my staff at the *Sunday Times* would seem eclectic to the point of parody, but they knew how the real world works. Time and again the richness of their backgrounds enhanced the paper. Among those who'd come to newspapers in mid-career, we had a molecular biologist, a professional pilot, a clinical psychologist, a civil servant, a university lecturer, an antiques dealer, a television producer, a research chemist, a bond salesman, and an accountant going straight – very helpful when we were looking into the financial records of some crook or other.

Most of the staff were graduates – two of them Harkness Fellows, so there were three of us – but a number had not completed high school. Insight's Paul Eddy was one, a relentless investigator who is now a bestselling thriller writer but who left school at fifteen without an education certificate to his name; the newsroom's pertinacious Anne Robinson had been expelled from school and worked as a chicken gutter and sales lady before trying journalism; later she became a transatlantic television celebrity as taskmistress for *The Weakest Link* quiz show. On the other hand, Oxford classics graduate Anthony Holden, who was only twenty-five when he joined the *Sunday Times*, had already written two books on Greek poetry, and another on Graham Young, the Neasden teenager who tried out poisons on his family, and continued his mad murdering ways when prematurely released from Broadmoor. And while reporting for a local evening newspaper, Holden had come top of the national training scheme proficiency examinations. These days he maintains his humiliating versatility by writing literary biographies and competing in the world poker championships.

A number of staffers had reached the *Sunday Times* via the cauldron of the Fleet Street populars; many had pounded pavements in
the provinces; a few had experience of American newspapers and
one, John Lovesy came from Time Inc's *Sports Illustrated* to take the
sports pages way beyond what I'd been able to do. We had regular
infusions of renegade 'colonials' from Australia, Canada and South
Africa, never inclined to take anyone's No for a final answer. And we
fostered active relationships with a corps of freelances, paying the
ones we'd learned to trust for their effort even when the story didn't
pan out to our standards: next time it might.

Our coverage of wars was powerfully assisted by people with
experience of both front lines and deadlines. Among those who'd
seen military service of some kind we had a company of other ranks
infantry, an instructor in tank desert warfare, a tail gunner, a trio of
army colonels and naval commanders, a sprinkling of wartime intelligence officers and at least one corporal that I know of. When Tom
Stoppard became intrigued about pressmen coping with concepts of
freedom in the context of reporting the murderous idiosyncrasies
of an African dictator, the theme of his play *Night and Day*, he
explored the experiences of our roving foreign correspondent Jon
Swain and photographer Bryan Wharton, who'd dodged a lot of
bullets.

The staff photographers such as Wharton struck me as rather like
Battle of Britain pilots, lounging around with their cameras round
their neck ready to take off on hazardous missions at a moment's
notice. Wharton, in fact, looked the part, down to handlebar moustache and fur-collared leather jacket, sauntering into the newsroom
with a pretty girl on his arm. The entire news photographic team –
Steve Brodie, Frank Herrmann, Don McCullin, Sally Soames,
Romano Cagnoni and Wharton – were on the battlefields almost as
soon as a shooting war started. Photographers with their equipment
were more conspicuous in danger zones and they'd all absorbed
Robert Capa's injunction: 'If your pictures aren't good enough
you're not close enough.'

It's no exaggeration to say our cameramen had more experience of
combat than many of the young soldiers. McCullin always went

with the front-line troops. He advanced with the Marines foxhole by foxhole in the battle for the Citadel at Hue, carried a sniper victim to first aid; in Cambodia he was wounded in a Khmer Rouge ambush; in Uganda he was held in the mad Idi Amin's Makyinde Jail with prisoners led out to execution; when the Israelis fought yard by yard for the old city of Jerusalem in the Six Day War, he (and our Colin Simpson) were with them. McCullin's reputation of coming through gun and mortar fire alive preceded him wherever he went. Israeli soldiers were seen to touch his jacket for good luck. The paras regarded Jon Swain as a talisman.

I had loved selecting and editing photographs at the *Northern Echo*, enchanted by the way the photographers, bored with flower shows and factory openings, took advantage of their freedom. But none of this had the acrid taste of danger that came with the prints the *Sunday Times* men brought back from conflict and disaster.

In the Paris anti-Gaullist street battles in 1968, for instance, Wharton and Frank Herrmann were in the thick of it ducking tear gas, then found themselves overwhelmed by CS gas of military strength wildly unleashed by the back-up riot police, the CRS (Compagnies Républicaines de Sécurité).

The difference from tear gas was profound. Wharton got more of it since he was with the students. It dropped him to his knees and blinded him for about twenty minutes. Yet he went back into that gas twelve times to photograph the CRS beating everyone in sight with their rifle butts. 'I saw them corner a sixteen-year-old girl, pummelling her in the face with rifles, dragging out defenceless old men and women from cafés and beating them without mercy. I slipped on the blood on the floor when they charged and went down with camera straps entwined round my neck.'

Team journalism was vindicated by the way it all worked with Herrmann and Wharton feeding their experiences into the group of reporters coming in from the tumult to write in the old Gestapo haunt, Hôtel Meurice; they telephoned copy in fragments, and John Barry in London, working through Friday night, pulled the strands together in a single arresting narrative we ran over eight pages. Wharton, after a mad drive from blockaded and blazing Paris, had to catch the ferry from Ostend to bring back his and Herrmann's film in time.

I say 'bring back' because in those pre-digital days getting images to London required ingenuity – and stamina. One Friday afternoon, with little more than twenty-four hours to Saturday's deadline, we dispatched Wharton to an earthquake in Osoppo, Italy. The local airport was fogbound. He drove 350 miles through the night to arrive at dawn, took his pictures, drove 350 miles back, flew from Milan and raced into the London dark room just in time for the first edition. His narrative sequence was moving: a father waiting for the removal of rubble above an imploring outstretched hand, cleared only to find the boy was dead. Today nobody would have missed a heartbeat in the rush to press. A digital Wharton would have had time to improve his tan before making a leisurely return, picking up a paper with his pictures on the front page.

Photojournalism had centre stage in the colour magazine, though the magazine irritated fastidious media critics by the dexterity with which it could move from serious reportage to glamour and celebrity chic. But the *Sunday Times* was responsive to the vibrant popular culture and the fast-moving social currents – the Beatles and Stones; the Pill; liberal new laws on hanging and homosexuality; race and abortion; theatre censorship formally abolished; the satire boom sparked by Peter Cook and Dudley Moore and *Private Eye* and *That Was the Week That Was*; London's eclipse of Paris as the centre of fashion . . .

We weren't aware of it at the time but the magazine was itself a tiny chip in the mosaic of the swinging 1960s, its long-serving editor Godfrey Smith and art director Michael Rand matching the counter-culture with innovations of their own. They employed gifted young artists like David Hockney and Peter Blake to go abroad and paint the story for us; they gave rein to the turbulent talents of Roger Law, whose plasticine maquettes transmuted into the subversive and hip TV show *Spitting Image*; and they deployed such big-name photographers as Robert Freson, Arnold Newman, Norman Parkinson, Bruce Davidson, who were happy to work for the magazine at a fraction of the pay they could get from advertising because it gave them worldwide prestige (and they kept their copyrights). Snowdon was on the staff, liberating himself from the confines of fashion and theatre by serious photojournalism of a high order. One of his images of a nurse gently tending a mentally handicapped woman was so moving I stole it for insertion in an editorial I was writing on the state of mental hospitals. The flow of photographers was totally classless, with the East End boys Terry Donovan, Brian Duffy and David Bailey, and Patrick (Lord) Lichfield trooping in; even more pleasing to all the males, drawn like moths to the light box, was when Julie Christie dropped by to see our new pictures of her.

We felt affinity, too, with a group of young men in the advertising industry. Until the very early 1960s, it was stuck in the time warp of social class and condescension: don't even think of being an ad man if you're bereft of a military background, a public school–Oxbridge education, or a Southern counties accent, preferably all of the above. Then John Pearce, padding the corridors of the small bright new ad agency Collett, Dickenson and Pearce (CDP) in his stockinged feet, attracted an electric group of talents in their very early twenties – David Puttnam, Alan Parker, Ridley Scott, Frank Lowe, Charles Saatchi. We'd borrowed Puttnam for six months to help with the nerve-racking launch of the colour magazine.

These CDP youngsters, with Frank Lowe and Colin Milward, transformed advertising very much as the colour magazine transformed Sunday newspapers. The ad industry in the 1960s was like the TV series *Mad Men*: lose an account and you're fired. But when Ford Motors rejected a daring piece of creativity from CDP, the agency turned the tables. It fired the client. Creativity, they wanted to suggest, was king. Puttnam, Parker and Scott became celebrated filmmakers, Saatchi formed with his brother Maurice what became the world's largest ad agency, Saatchi and Saatchi.

I can claim a small part in their launch in 1970. Having seen how uncontrolled display advertising plays havoc with good design in American newspapers, I'd laid down the maximum size display advertisements could take on a page of the *Sunday Times*. The advertising director asked me if I'd see the young ad executive Maurice Saatchi to hear his pitch for our making a single exception.

Saatchi was preceded into the room by the largest pair of horn-rimmed glasses I'd ever seen, a fitting ad itself for the 24-year-old with a first class honours degree, parchment-fresh from the London School of Economics. He devised a cunning appeal to my vanity, patriotism and compassion. As an innovative editor, he wheedled, I should support an innovative business; as a citizen I should support a new business for Britain's sake so that the advertising trade would not be dominated by American companies; and as a compassionate person, I should bear in mind that without the prestige launch in the wonderful *Sunday Times* they'd never make it.

I relented, just this once, and its launch in 1970 put the new agency on the map. I'm not forgiven for this by some of my friends, since the Saatchi agency went on to devise devastating attacks on the Labour government which sadly were entirely justified. (A billboard of a long trail of men lining up for unemployment was headlined 'Labour Isn't Working'.) Their agency was a powerful promoter of Margaret Thatcher's ascension to Prime Minister and Maurice became Lord Saatchi, chairman of the Conservative party.

I must admit I afflicted the staff with every half-cocked rumour and vague hint I picked up. I can't recall anyone blinking; whatever they might say out of earshot, if there was anything in it, they invariably delivered. I came to expect them to spin gold out of flax. There were times when I half-regretted transmitting news whispers. To have any sympathy with that confession, you'd have to have dealt with Robert Maxwell, the bellicose and flamboyant Labour Member of Parliament, academic publisher, wannabe international newspaper baron and consummate charlatan. Maxwell was quite brilliant in finding new ways to punish the publication of grim truths about his business philosophy – first you see the profit, now you don't. Godfrey Hodgson, the reporter I put on Maxwell's trail, wrote: 'The impressive precision of Maxwell's sales claims bears about the same relation to reality as Falstaff's eleven rogues in buckram.' Maxwell showed appreciation of the literary effort by storming into our offices to demand my head first from Roy Thomson and then Denis Hamilton, only to be deflected to me.

Then he made the mistake in our meeting of shouting that Hodgson had been motivated by anti-Semitism. Hodgson had two Jewish children whose mother lost seven close relatives in the camps. He was incensed, but his response was one I stored up for noisy confrontations in the future:

'You remind me of the lobster,' said Hodgson coolly.

'A lobster! How dare you!' shouted Maxwell.

'No,' said Hodgson, 'I said "*the* lobster". You just reminded me of an incident in a restaurant where I ordered lobster. When it came it was smeared with Heinz Russian salad instead of the genuine sauce. So I sent it back, and the chef came roaring out of the kitchen shouting: "Where is the bastard who called me a cheat and a liar?"' Said Hodgson: 'That was the point at which I knew it was definitely a load of Heinz Russian salad.'

Throughout my editorship, hardly a year went by when Maxwell was not pitting his volcanic energy, dialectical skill and moody charm against us in endless legal actions.

Having sent a number of reporters to chase wild geese, it was good that I got a taste of my own medicine from Lord Thomson himself. He called me up on a Saturday night to ask whether I'd like to meet Howard Hughes and if I would – 'entirely up to you, Harold' – I was to join him at London airport the next morning. Thomson knew Mormons in the entourage of the famously reclusive Hughes and they'd told him that Hughes was ready to discuss how we might interview him for a book and newspaper serial.

We did indeed meet with Chester Davis (Hughes' lawyer) and Hughes' Mormon aides who shuttled between our waterfront room in Miami and wherever they were keeping their nutty boss. Hughes remained elusive, but it was satisfying in its own way to see how Roy negotiated money matters. He sat on his bed in his underpants, and calculated the sum he intended to offer.

For me, there were two tricky moments with the proprietor on this abortive mission to see Hughes. The first morning, coming into the dining room for a very early breakfast with Roy, I was carrying both the *Miami Herald* and the *Wall Street Journal*. 'Why'd ya buy

two newspapers?' he growled. When we came to the front desk to
pay our departure bills he had another spasm. He reckoned that
since we were leaving at noon he hadn't incurred a charge for a full
day and then he began myopically going through the charges item by
item. The duty manager was summoned and an unseemly argument
loomed between frugal peer and frosty manager. I suggested to Roy
that he leave me to sort it out while he accompanied the porter to his
room. I volunteered for this because when I ran my own eye down
his charges I was horrified to find the hotel had charged him for
some of my expenses, a massage, a suit pressing and two calls to
London. I suggested to the manager in the privacy of his office that
merely transferring the charges to the right room was not sufficient
recompense for inflicting all this embarrassment on a peer of the
realm. Roy's satisfaction, when I told him that the hotel had made an
error and his bill was being reduced, made him beam for the whole
trip home.

Can embarrassment be retrospective? In one of the photographs of
those days, I see I'm caught seated, gesturing in front of a news
poster on display behind my chair at the editor's weekly conference.
In big black type, the poster announces: UGANDA SENSATION.

The poster, sent to my office for approval for distribution across
the country, promoted a scoop we'd secured documenting the crimes
of General Idi Amin, otherwise known as the Butcher of Uganda, Big
Daddy, Emperor of all the Beasts and Fishes on Earth – the blood-
thirsty madman so vividly portrayed in 2007 by Forest Whitaker in
the movie *The Last King of Scotland*.

We didn't allow visitors to our editorial meeting, but this week
there was a guest by royal command: Prince Charles, the Prince of
Wales. He'd expressed an interest in how the paper was put together
to Denis Hamilton and our managing director Marmaduke Hussey,
whose wife, Susan, was lady in waiting to the Queen. I could hardly
demur, but I could wish a better day had been chosen: as head of
the Commonwealth, Queen Elizabeth was about to receive a bevy
of African leaders among the thirty-five prime ministers attending a
Commonwealth conference in her Silver Jubilee year. We intended

to rebuke them all for continually failing as a group to unite in condemnation of Amin (a situation similar to the failure of African states to unite against the outrages of Mugabe in Zimbabwe in 2008). Prince Charles would now have to hear how we planned to attack guests of his mother.

Enough was known of Amin's reign of terror to feel repelled by the way a sense of racial fraternity had given him immunity from censure. It was bad enough that the Organization of African Unity, predecessor of the African Union, had not only looked the other way but in 1975 unanimously elected him their chairman. It would be contemptible, I thought, if the Commonwealth and the UN too remained supine in light of the horrible story we were preparing for the coming Sunday.

The source for the sensation was a 37-year-old defector from Amin's government by the name of Henry Kyemba, who'd known him for twenty years and for the last five had been his minister of health. Kyemba had walked into my office a few days before in fear of his life. 'I want to ensure,' he told me, 'that what I know does not die with me.' That same morning I'd bundled Kyemba and his wife Teresa into an office car with a driver I knew I could trust and sent them to my weekend cottage in Alphamstone in Essex with the writer Russell Miller. It was melodramatic but necessary. Amin had dispatched agents to kill Kyemba and one had already been detained at Heathrow Airport by an immigration officer alerted by the Home Office, which had granted asylum to Kyemba.

His arrival in London had been daring. Sickened by what he'd seen, knowing that five of his Cabinet colleagues had been murdered, Kyemba had made elaborate plans to defect while in Geneva heading Uganda's delegation to a World Health Organization conference. So as not to arouse suspicion, he'd left his two infant children in Kampala in the care of relatives. Only when he received word they'd safely avoided Amin's goons and border guards by trekking through the bush to Kenya did he evade the other Ugandans and make his way from Geneva to my office.

It was a stroke of good fortune to have Miller ready to begin debriefing him immediately. Miller was well informed on Uganda because he'd prepared for an interview with Amin, fixed by a retired army officer who had something to do with the 'whisky run', the twice-weekly flights of spirits, cigarettes and luxury goods from Stansted airport to Entebbe by which Amin secured the loyalty of his thugs. It was good fortune for Miller, too, since he'd been due the next day to catch a plane to Kampala. Had he been there representing the *Sunday Times* when we published Kyemba's story he would not have survived. Amin had not hesitated to murder journalists: Nicholas Stroh, freelancing for the *Philadelphia Evening Bulletin*, and his associate Robert Siedele were killed just for asking too many questions about a massacre at Mbarare barracks.

Kyemba was the first senior member of Amin's government able and willing to speak with authority on the reign of terror because his position gave him access to all hospitals and mortuaries. By the next morning, when I rode my BMW motorbike to Suffolk, Miller had already solved the mystery of the 75-year-old British-Israeli grandmother Mrs Dora Bloch who'd vanished after Palestinian hijackers held 106 hostages at Entebbe airport, courtesy of Amin. She was unlucky to miss the electrifying rescue of the hostages by Israeli commandos on the night of 3 July 1976. The night before she'd choked on a piece of meat and been taken to Mulago Hospital. Kyemba visited her there and found her recovered. The morning after the Israeli raid she was nowhere to be found. To inquiries from the British High Commission, Amin said she'd been returned safely to the airport an hour before the raid and had presumably been taken by the Israelis; hospital records proved it. But in truth he'd ordered Kyemba to falsify them.

In the peace of the Essex countryside it was chilling to listen to Kyemba's description of how Dora Bloch had become a victim of Amin's rage after the Israeli raid. 'He went berserk. If he's provoked he reacts like a wild animal and goes into a kind of fit. No one around him is safe.' The morning after everyone else had been rescued, said Kyemba, four of Amin's 'State Research' officers arrived at the hospital, two of them carrying pistols. They shouted for staff to stand aside, grabbed Mrs Bloch from her bed and frogmarched her screaming down three flights of stairs and out of the main hospital door without shoes and dress in full view of patients, staff and visitors. Later they dumped her body by the road twenty miles from the city. A photographer who took a picture of her partially burned corpse was murdered.

Kyemba knew, too, what had happened to the Anglican Archbishop Janani Luwum and two Cabinet ministers who'd all been reported killed in a car accident. He'd seen their bodies in the mortuary. 'They were riddled with bullets, the Archbishop shot in the mouth. The country is littered with bodies. They're fed to crocodiles in the river.'

I left Miller at his typewriter and raced back to the office with a sketch of the hospital layout Kyemba drew for us; we had very little time before deadline.

Our Kyemba story had an instant effect. The Commonwealth conference condemned Amin for 'massive violations' of human rights. For the first time, African leaders allowed open discussion of the internal affairs of another African country. Britain broke off diplomatic relations. America's Ambassador to the UN, Andrew Young, denounced Amin in vivid language. Amin was ousted in 1979. He should have been tried as a war criminal for hundreds of thousands of murders, but Saudi Arabia gave him sanctuary as a convert to Islam. He lived with his four wives, fancy cars and chef until his death in 2003.

Only later did I realize that the Uganda Sensation headline might have been troubling for personal reasons to our guest that day, Prince Charles. Sitting to the right of Prince Charles in our editorial meeting was Ron Hall. He'd given a party at his house in Hampstead and, lacking a downstairs cloakroom, had asked guests to leave their overcoats and umbrellas on the upstairs bed. When the first departing guests came to collect their coats, they interrupted the wife of a political correspondent. She was thrashing about under the coats with an African diplomat.

'Don't mind us,' she said blithely, 'we're discussing Uganda.'

Private Eye at once seized on this unlikely explanation as a neat way of conveying libellous gossip about the sexual mores of people in public life. She or he was an expert on Ugandan affairs . . . they met often to discuss Uganda . . .

At this time Prince Charles, unknown to his public, was deep in an affair with Camilla Parker Bowles that was to continue through his marriage to Princess Diana. The Palace must not have been happy to see the future King of England in front of a poster blaring UGANDA SENSATION.

*

It was not by chance that Kyemba came to our office to start the chain of events that led the African nations to disown Amin. He might have chosen any one of four or five newspapers with bigger circulation, but he regarded appearance in print in the *Sunday Times* as the watermark of authenticity. Actually, the same credence would have been lent to his story by appearance in the *Observer* or *Sunday Telegraph* or BBC Television, but this was not an occasion to discuss the nuances of a newspaper's authority. Of course, others came to us with stories and pictures, and to our competitors, simply because they mistook a newspaper office for a bank.

The difficult part for me when there was a knock on the door from the bearer of apparently big news was the judgement call: Can we believe a word this person tells us? (And nowadays with pictures one must wonder if the photograph has been manipulated.) What if Kyemba had been a fabricator, what if he wasn't who he said he was, what if one half of what he said was true and one half wasn't . . . what if? That would have been gravely damaging to our reputation. We couldn't very well put in a call to Idi Amin; what we could do was check Kyemba's identity and assess his character and the consistency of his story with known facts. But almost always in these circumstances you have then to take some things on trust. The excitement of a scoop can overwhelm elementary prudence. You want to believe.

Redoubtable journalists fall for confidence tricks and hoaxes. Before I became editor of the *Sunday Times*, Denis Hamilton and the Thomson Organisation bought eighteen volumes of Mussolini's handwritten wartime diaries for book publication by a Thomson company and newspaper serialization. I knew nothing of the transaction. It was conducted during his editorship by Denis Hamilton and a skilled investigator, the former Insight supremo Clive Irving, who'd left the paper in 1965. Everyone was sworn to secrecy. Three years later, in February 1968, the Italian newspaper *Corriere della*

Sera reported it had discovered a mother and daughter from Vercelli forging Mussolini papers. Only then did Hamilton rather shame-facedly let me in on his acquisition. He called me to his office to say he'd kept quiet about it on my assuming the editorship because secrecy was a condition of the sale (i.e. con) and in due course he'd hoped to make either me or *The Times* the present of a world scoop. Hamilton and the Thomson group had already parted with a down payment of £150,000 in advance of the diaries being translated and edited. I was led to understand that the Thomson group would rather the deal was forgotten, but to me it was clearly a story we had to do – and it was irresistible to send an Insight reporter to grill Clive Irving, his former boss.

Famous publications have been burned time and again. A *Washington Post* reporter, Janet Cooke, fooled her editors and the judges of the Pulitzer Prize with her invention of an eight-year-old heroin addict; Jayson Blair long deceived the editors of the *New York Times*, plagiarizing other publications and pretending to go to places and conduct interviews he never had; Stephen Glass fabricated more than twenty stories for *The New Republic* and other publica-tions for several years before being caught out in 1988 when a drama of a teenage hacker and a computer company proved to be a figment of his vivid imagination; and in 1983, a year after I'd left the company, the forgers of Hitler's Diaries totally took in *Newsweek* magazine in New York and Times Newspapers in London. I felt for my former *Sunday Times* colleagues. Caught up in the excitement of a shattering scoop, their own doubts suppressed, they'd been let down by the vetting historian Lord Dacre (previously Hugh Trevor-Roper) and my gullible successor as editor of *The Times*, Charles Douglas-Home, who initially had charge of the project. They'd been rushed and pushed into the folly by the commercial imperatives of Rupert Murdoch and his macho management who would rather be caught dead than having second thoughts.

It could be said I was lucky in my editing years never to be caught in one of these disasters, and I suppose I was. Not a little of that, however, was because my door was always open. This was not a custom applauded by apostles of good line management, but at least anyone on the staff could barge in waving a galley proof to ask: 'Harry, why are you publishing this crap?' Transactions presented 'for your eyes only' flatter the ego, at the risk of having egg on one's face later. Had the paper's foreign staff been in on the Mussolini deal, it's very likely someone would have had a vague memory of the trial and conviction some years back of two women of Vercelli forging Mussolini papers, or at least thought to make a few discreet inquiries in Italy. Had Trevor-Roper as a Hitler scholar not contentedly accepted the idea that he was so experienced he could make the judgement all by himself, the falsification of the Hitler Diaries would very likely have been detected by a reputable German historian.

Retailers of trash invariably impose haste – 'We'll have to go to the *Observer* if you can't decide here and now' – and invariably insist on secrecy. Dealing with strangers, I came to regard both these conditions as red flags.

Who was Anthony Mascarenhas? The well-dressed man in his early forties who came into my office on 18 May 1971 had the bearing of a military man, square-set and moustached, but appealing, almost soulful eyes and an air of profound melancholy. I'd never met Mr Mascarenhas before, nor had the foreign editor, Frank Giles. We'd encouraged him to file freelance for us from Pakistan on the strength of his reports in the *Morning News*, Karachi. He was assistant editor there and had lived most of his life in Pakistan and held a Pakistani passport, but he was by descent a Goan Christian.

Two months before, in March, the Bengalis of East Pakistan, fired by Bengali nationalism, had rebelled against what they saw as their ill treatment by the non-Bengali military rulers of the geographically divided nation; President Yahya Khan and his administration were based in Islamabad, in the western wing of the country. In an untimely and ill-starred bid to hasten independence promised to East Pakistan, 176,000 troops in East Pakistan had mutinied. They joined thousands of Bengalis in a pogrom against non-Bengalis. Thousands of men, women and children had been butchered. I'd

kept a close eye on it because my youngest brother John was working for the Foreign Office in Islamabad; 'our man in Dacca,' he
wrote to me, 'says the East Paks have been meat-hooking people,
hanging them up and then slitting their throats like pigs.' Reports of
these atrocities had been filed by Mascarenhas and our own Nick
Tomalin in Jessore.

At the end of March, the government in Islamabad had sent in
two Army divisions to restore order. It expelled all international
reporters and imposed a news blackout. Thereafter the news from
East Pakistan was that the Army had made the province peaceful
again. Such was the story in Pakistan's press and television. Pictures
were broadcast of villages and towns coming out in parades with
Pakistani flags to celebrate the return of peace. A British Parliamentary
delegation went to West and East Pakistan and satisfied itself all
was well.

Mascarenhas, talking quietly for a long time with shafts of
afternoon sunlight coming into my office, told a different and very
harrowing story. In late April he'd been one of eight senior pressmen taken to East Pakistan by the Ministry of Information. The
government wanted to discountenance sporadic reports of Army
killings in East Pakistan, retailed mainly by a fast-growing stream of
Bengali refugees. 'The way Islamabad put it,' said Mascarenhas
'was to show in a patriotic way the great job the Army was doing.
'But what I saw,' he told us, 'was genocide.' He'd been shocked by
the Bengali outrages in March, but he maintained that what the
Army was doing was altogether worse and on a grander scale. It
had not been content to do the necessary job of restoring order, nor
was it confining its violence to rebels. Instead, Mascarenhas said, it
had gone on a huge killing spree across the entire country, soldiers
systematically moving from village to village, town to town, killing
any of the mutineers and other rebellious non-Bengali Muslims
they could catch. One of the victims, his body thrown in a brick-
field, was my Dacca journalist friend Serajuddin Hussein, who had
uncovered the child kidnapping gang.

'The top officers,' said Mascarenhas, 'told me they were seeking a
"final solution". I wrote down quotes all saying the same thing:

"We're determined to cleanse East Pakistan once and for all of the threat of secession even if it means killing two million and ruling the colony as a province for thirty years."'

Was this man to be believed? Seven of the eight pressmen invited on the trip had already written what they saw and it was nothing like the story Mascarenhas was telling me. I asked him why he had not filed a contrary story for his own newspaper. 'They wouldn't publish it – and they're under military censorship anyway.' He said he'd had a crisis of conscience. 'Either I had to write the full story of what I'd seen or I would have to stop writing. I would never be able to write again with any integrity.' But writing the full story, he said, was impossible anywhere in Pakistan; he'd been allowed to send us only a description of the Bengali atrocities. Even references to the danger of famine had been deleted by the censor. 'That's why I've come to London. I want the truth to come out but I cannot tell it and stay in Pakistan.'

Instinctively, I believed Mascarenhas. I could see a man propelled only by a decent Christian passion and immanent shame. Frank Giles, my deputy and the foreign editor, made the same judgement while passing on the foreign department's caution that we had known Mascarenhas for only a short time. He did not ask for money. I was impressed and moved that the sufferings he'd seen made him ready to sacrifice his life in Pakistan, abandoning all his possessions and his career, and uprooting his wife and their five children. His main anxiety was that he would first have to get his family out of Pakistan. Nothing could be published before he did, nor could we make other inquiries that would point to him as the source.

I took the risk. I told him that subject to vetting and his own determination to see it through, we were ready to pay for the evacuation of his family, but I could not give him a job. He'd not felt it safe to write his story in Pakistan, so he'd memorized notes, then discarded them. His 5,000-word report of ten days in hell was a detailed eyewitness account of unique precision and authority. It supplied the missing centrepiece of the East Pakistan tragedy: why people were fleeing in the millions. He named names. Here was a pitifully skinny tailor Abdul Bari, scared by the arrival of the Army in his village, running away and brought back for execution; here was Mascarenhas forsaking his neutrality and exclaiming to Major Rathore: 'For God's sake don't shoot.' Bari was found to bear the marks of circumcision obligatory for a Muslim, hence not a Hindu to be shot out of hand. He got away with a clubbing, but in the Circuit Headquarters at Camilla, Mascarenhas saw the truckloads of Hindus brought into the compound and heard the screams as they were bludgeoned to death.

Everything Mascarenhas described from his travels through the whole province made sense of fragmented, unconfirmed accounts from refugees and missionaries, like finding the missing piece of a jigsaw. He'd arranged with his wife Yvonne that if I accepted his report he would send a telegram to her saying 'Ann's operation successful' as a signal for her to fly out to relatives in Rome, leaving everything behind. She received the telegram, but after his return to Karachi, Mascarenhas was forbidden to follow her; only one foreign trip a year was allowed. To escape, he took a flight to Peshawar and walked across the border into Afghanistan and then sent the agreed message to a staffer's private address: 'Export formalities completed. Shipment begins Monday.'

I took the exceptional step of clearing the entire centre spread of the 13 June edition, one page headed in big black letters by the single word 'Genocide' and an editorial 'Stop the Killing'.

Our breach in the curtain of silence was an international sensation. President Nixon, concerned to protect Pakistan as an ally against the Soviets, ignored the genocide: 'To all hands,' he wrote on a memo, 'don't squeeze Yahya at this time.' But by the end of July more than 5 million refugees were in India's camps, and still they came. Years later, in Delhi, India's Prime Minister Indira Gandhi told me that the Mascarenhas report had shocked her deeply, setting her on a campaign of personal diplomacy in the European capitals and Moscow to prepare the ground for India's armed intervention.

The India–Pakistan war of 1971 ended with the creation of the state of Bangladesh. Mascarenhas had no political agenda; he was just a very good reporter doing an honest job. For that he earned the enmity of the Pakistan military and a telegram from the Black

September group (who the following year murdered Israeli athletes at the Olympic Games): 'You bastard, we'll get you, you went against your country.' I put Mascarenhas on a retainer. He amply justified that, and seven years later became a permanent member of the foreign staff with consequences I will relate.

The *Sunday Times* I inherited could fairly be described as a Conservative newspaper. Its editorials no longer slavishly echoed the party line as they had done in Lord Kemsley's time, but my conviction was that it should not have any party line at all.

I was well aware that even an independent, unpredictable leader column might have fewer readers than the race card, but the leader page was where we could speak to the opinion formers and indeed firmly establish the whole tone of the paper. The aspiration I brought to the page was that we should try to judge every issue on its merits, questioning the use of power by government, the courts and corporations, but fairly, and always balancing respect for individual human dignity and freedom with the imperatives of order. Easier said than done.

In 1983, two years after I had moved to edit *The Times*, Hugo Young, the political editor, contributed to *Political Quarterly* an assessment of the *Sunday Times* stance over fourteen years. His aim was to discuss the change of attitude he perceived in the paper following its acquisition by Rupert Murdoch in 1981 but his essay bore on this question of independence. He illustrated his argument with an incident I'd quite forgotten. In my first year on the *Sunday Times*, before becoming editor, I apparently got into an argument with deputy editor William Rees-Mogg about power and responsibility as applied to some burning issue of the day:

William Rees-Mogg took the position that a government which had responsibility without sufficient power was decisively worse for society than its opposite. He took the view that the paper should reflect this view in its leader; in other words should be ready to offer government its support in the never ending struggle to prevent events sliding out of control.

Harold Evans took exactly the opposite view. He saw power without responsibility as by far the greater evil. It was a fierce argument over a classic issue between two brilliant journalists who could barely comprehend each other's position. Each then went off to edit the paper suited to his political outlook. Rees-Mogg's *Times* continued the paper's ancestral supportive duties . . . Evans' *Sunday Times*, completing the break with its establishment past, developed a role as the most effective scourge of power in the whole of the British press.

Editorials under Denis Hamilton's editorship had been written by Rees-Mogg and Hugo Young with some contributions by me. I straight away replaced this troika with an editorial board of eight that I chaired for up to two hours every Friday morning. It included the foreign editor, the business editor, the religious affairs editor, who was also an expert on Northern Ireland, the labour editor, the political editor, a political columnist and a former editor of the paper who had retired to academic life.

The group brought special knowledge to the arguments – and at times they were strenuous. The most contentious issues, apart from the selectors' choice of fast bowlers for the Test series, were Britain and Europe (go in and stay in); Pershing missiles from President Reagan (yes, please); what to do about overweening trade unions; the propriety of our disclosing Cabinet discussions in extracts from the diaries of the late Richard Crossman; Enoch Powell's 'rivers of blood' speech on immigration; internment and ill-treatment of IRA suspects in Northern Ireland; and skirmishes between our editorial board's interventionists and the laissez-faire insurgents, all trying to find the way to the British economic miracle in the dark mazes of economic policy.

I'd nominate the writer who had to synthesize the group's opinions without producing a fudge. The unassuming Young – pedigree Ampleforth head boy, Balliol law graduate and *Yorkshire Post* – was a master of this. His editorials had such authority even the dissidents felt they'd written them. I hardly ever changed a word in editing him (and I always edited with the writer present, poised to leap for my jugular).

The inner strength of the editorials was that they were not spun off the top of the head. They drew on solid reporting, investigations we commissioned, seminars we organized on the economy and Northern Ireland and reconstructions of major political events. Instead of the staple editorial bemoaning Britain's low levels of productivity, for instance, we asked the feature writer Stephen Fay to go into the factories and solve a mystery: why does a British welder in the Ford Dagenham plant produce 110 Cortina doors an hour when a worker in Germany, Belgium or Spain, using the same machinery to the same management plan, produces 240 an hour? (Answer: labour–management trench wars.)

The tricky part of not having a party line was general elections, when all newspapers conventionally endorse a party and the red-tops ramp up the propaganda war. Denis Hamilton had told me on appointment as editor: 'You'll have total freedom from Roy [Thomson],' then he added: 'So long as you don't attack the Queen.' That idea had never impinged on the fringe of consciousness, but I tested the freedom of opinion in the October 1974 election.

Tory Prime Minister Edward Heath had called and narrowly lost an election in March based on the theme: 'Who governs Britain?' (The coal miners, going slow in a wage dispute, had forced him to ration power supply, restricting commercial enterprises to use electricity only three days a week.) We were certainly on his side in principle but persuaded that Labour's 'social contract' might end the warfare – it did only for a time – and Labour ministers were a more impressive bunch: Roy Jenkins, James Callaghan, Anthony Crosland, Denis Healey and Harold Lever.

Hamilton, reading my mind, gently suggested that Lord Thomson would be displeased if the *Sunday Times* endorsed Labour, then seeking to increase its tenuous working majority of three MPs. Thomson usually called me on a Saturday night to ask whether we'd yet overtaken the combined circulations of both opposition qualities (we were close). This Saturday I took the chance to mention I was inclined to endorse Harold Wilson and Labour against Edward Heath and the Tories. Thomson made some shrewd comments on the two leaders and concluded: 'Well, it's up to you, Harold. How's the run going?'

I wrote that editorial, after discussing it with my colleagues, as I wrote all the election editorials, and thought the Labour endorsement clear enough. I was rather proud of it. Innate yearnings to steer clear of party must have seeped through, since Hugo Young later wrote that it was a bit of mess, its principal virtue being that it was vague enough to preserve the paper's status as a non-combatant in the direct party struggle, a sceptical onlooker not a committed outrider on the march. 'Preserving *The Sunday Times* as a genuinely non-party paper was an essential prop to the credibility of all its journalism whether of fact or opinion.'

By 1979 the Labour party was a shadow of its purposeful self in the great days of Clement Attlee. It was frustrated by its ties to the trade unions, and the public sector unions in particular, who demanded more and more for less and less, their attitude to the nobler ideals of socialism climaxing in the 1979 'winter of discontent' strikes when they stopped cancer patients going into hospitals for treatment.

Michael Jones, who'd become political editor, realized sooner than most that the Conservative leader Margaret Thatcher, waiting in the wings, could not be dismissed as a right-wing harridan whose middle-class accent and suburban outlook would doom the Tories to the wilderness. I agreed. When she was a back-bencher I happened to be seated at the same table at some stuffy City of London dinner, with a group of financiers. These were regarded as pillars of the Tory party. She was not in the least in awe of their millions. I relished the way she assailed them for being more greedily interested in money manipulations than investing in the business of manufacturing and managing the unions more effectively.

The decay of the Labour party in the late 1970s was painful to report. It was infiltrated by Trotskyites creating cells in around 100 moribund constituency parties, working by stealth to undermine any Labour man lacking a taste for a Soviet state. Jones tape-recorded one of the Trots in full flow promising 'a civil war and the terrible death and destruction and bloodshed that would mean'. It didn't seem much of a vote-catcher to me. More serious were the strenuous efforts by left-wingers in the National Union of Journalists to impose a closed shop. Michael Foot, the Minister of Labour, was a cultivated and decent man, but he drew up a Bill to make the closed shop law. It would mean that nobody could write for the paper unless they had a union card. A few union militants, thankfully no more than a handful on the paper itself, were outraged that I gave columns to the polemicist Germaine Greer and 'Jolly Jilly' – Jilly Cooper, who became immensely popular for her comedies of domestic life.

Since a closed shop would hamper us in so many ways I resisted the move, with support from Margaret Thatcher – I was for a short time 'one of us' – while the Labour ministers I most respected sat on their hands. Alastair Hetherington, the editor of the *Guardian*, and I went to the Ministry of Labour offices to register our alarm with Foot. It was a waste of time; we were fobbed off with a junior minister. But as editors rallied, some moderates in the Labour party dared put their heads over the parapet and the proposed legislation died.

We all of us in the opinion group remained dismayed by two aspects of British life in the 1970s: the grip some recalcitrant unions had on the Labour party, and the stultifying secrecy in government. The great showdown was the diaries of Richard Crossman, a former Oxford don who was a member of the Labour Cabinet from 1964 to 1970. The rule was that ministers had to wait thirty years to publish a documented account of their experiences, and if they or anyone else wanted to publish sooner they had to accept official censorship on pain of a criminal prosecution under the Official Secrets Act.

Crossman's ambition was to illuminate how Britain was governed: he wanted to show that civil servants called the shots more often than the public realized, that Cabinet meetings were not the decisive forum of popular imagination and MPs had little real power. He'd learned in September 1973, when I first invited him to lunch at the paper, that he had only six months to live. The priorities in his mind were such that his first action, even before he finalized his will, was to finish his two years of editing and give clear instructions to his executors completely to reject any censorship. He predicted there'd be pressure for suppression and truncation of his work, both from Whitehall (the Civil Service) and from Westminster (the politicians) – and he was right. After his death, his executors were made to give an undertaking they would not publish without official approval, and the same was asked of us as serializers.

Denis Hamilton was in favour of giving it; I wasn't. He was against naming defenceless civil servants (I was, too) but also against allowing Crossman's accounts of Cabinet debates. Hamilton acquiesced when I assured him we'd studied the law and prepared our case. The stratagem I devised, with only two or three on the staff in the know, was to begin publishing uncensored extracts in the window of one weekend before we were bound by any undertakings. I sent the first of nine edited extracts I intended to publish to press on the night of Saturday, 25 January 1975, when Roy Thomson and his son Kenneth were paying a rare visit to my office. I told them that as soon as the Prime Minister's office got its hands on a copy we expected a court order to stop the presses. Kenneth was worried; his father simply said: 'You happy in your own mind, Harold?' I told him I was. There was no breach of national security. People should know how they were governed. 'A good read, eh?' said the owner as he went happily off with his paper.

No court order reached us that night, but the noises from Whitehall were menacing. Every day we expected an injunction and had a bevy of lawyers on standby; I was advised we'd surely lose. Then the Cabinet Secretary, Sir John Hunt, proposed we should discuss what we might and might not publish in future extracts. I declined to meet the Cabinet Secretary. I preferred Hugo Young and John Barry to do that because I couldn't trust myself to behave with the appropriate courtesy. Bernard Donoughue, who assisted the Prime Minister, recorded a conversation he had with Attorney General Sam Silkin in a diary entry on 14 January 1976 (his *Downing Street Diary: with Harold Wilson in No. 10* was published in 2005; I wasn't aware of this episode at the time):

He had met Harold Evans for the first time the other evening at the American Ambassador's residence and thought he was a 'fanatic' for open government . . . Sam said, 'He's very tough. He said to me "It's granite against granite." He may be granite. I certainly am not.'

It didn't sound like me, but then if I didn't recognize myself in this scene I didn't recognize the sheep Mr Silkin affected to be. For nine weeks I played cat and mouse with the Cabinet Office, accepting some requests for deletions, but at the end we'd published 100,000 words and broken every restriction. Then Mr Silkin shed his wool and bared his teeth. He sought a court order to force the book publishers to accept the censorship we'd defeated. I couldn't tolerate seeing the executors and publishers singled out in this way. Within days of the writ being served on them, we ran unpublished Crossman material and were duly joined in the action.

We lost in the High Court, but won in the Appeal Court. Soon afterwards, a committee of inquiry, to which I gave evidence, recommended that ministerial memoirs should no longer be regulated by statute. Ministers were asked to sign undertakings. A number refused. The logjam had been broken – but an even fiercer contest with government was pending.

17

DEATH IN CAIRO

The only qualities essential for real success in journalism are rat-like cunning, a plausible manner and a little literary ability.

I am quoting. My colleague and friend Nick Tomalin, who made the observation, protected himself – and entertained us – with irony and epigram. He concealed his real passion for a trade he described in a rare moment of self-revelation as 'a noble, dignified and useful calling'. In June 1973, before he took leave to write a history of the National Theatre, he cared enough to send me a critical appraisal of how far the *Sunday Times* and Britain's 'so-called quality press' were meeting the highest aspirations. Four months later, at the age of forty-one, he was dead on a battlefield.

Nick Tomalin was immersed in reading the notations of Mozart and Beethoven, playing the oboe in one of the regular musical gatherings at home, when we interrupted him on the early evening of Saturday, 6 October 1973. The Arab nations had chosen the holiest day in the Jewish calendar, Yom Kippur, to launch a war against Israel from Egypt and Syria.

Tomalin was a star writer, dazzling in his versatility but most renowned for his classic 'The General Goes Zapping Charlie Cong', describing an afternoon in the gunship of a Texas general who was proud to have killed more Vietcong than any of the troops he was commanding. We hesitated to break Nick's sabbatical, but his closest friend and editor, Ron Hall, thought he would like a change. Typically of Tomalin – and indeed every reporter I ever asked to go in harm's way – he said 'Yes' right away. 'Don't worry, it's safe enough,' he told his wife, the literary biographer Claire, 'the Israelis take good care of the press.'

In the first week, he filed a briefing for a long Insight narrative on the war, without expecting a byline. On the Sunday, he finagled his way into a closely guarded Tel Aviv hospital to take a gift for his taxi driver, who'd broken a leg taking him to the Syrian front. He was visibly affected by the long lines of stretchers waiting for the wounded. The following week he headed back to the Golan Heights as the Israeli Army fought to retake sections they'd lost in last-ditch stands against massed Syrian armour. 'I am only beta plus when it comes to courage,' he remarked at dinner on Tuesday, 16 October, to his colleague Philip Jacobson, a self-deprecating acknowledgement of the apprehensions correspondents felt about the shifting, ill-defined front lines on the Golan.

Early Wednesday morning found him sharing a car with a photographer, Fred Ihrt of the German magazine *Stern*, and the conducting officer, Major Hannan Levy, necessary to get them through roadblocks and not accidentally run into fighting. They passed an Israeli artillery battery, whose soldiers gave Tomalin mail to post, then descended into a bleak treeless valley to take pictures of clusters of wrecked tanks near a crossroads. Two hundred yards further on they could see what looked like an abandoned bunker and Tomalin drove them there. It was very quiet, no sign of life anywhere. In fact, without Major Levy realizing, they'd come right up to the Israeli front line. Concealed from view inside the battered bunker were Israeli soldiers who'd endured accurate Syrian artillery fire for several days; by some fluke they failed to see the correspondents' car arriving and departing again.

Major Levy judged the risk of running over a landmine too great for Tomalin to make a three-point turn against the bunker so as to drive them back the way they'd come, so the Major and Ihrt got out to direct Tomalin while he carefully reversed to the crossroads. He was turning there, with Ihrt and Levy some yards behind his car, when they heard a swooshing sound. Tomalin would have been unable to hear it above the car's engine. The noise was from an anti-tank missile trailing an electrical wire by which a Syrian hidden in the hills was guiding it onto the target. It flashed past Ihrt and Levy and blew up Tomalin's car with a direct hit, killing him instantly.

Moments later Syrian artillery shells were exploding around the crossroads, Ihrt and Levy were hiding in a rocky trench, a trans-porter arriving at the crossroads was hit by shellfire, five survivors were scrambling out and Israeli commandos in the bunker were yelling for everyone to crawl back to shelter with them.

And then there was other movement, a man running down the hill into the valley floor and towards the killing ground at the cross-roads. It was our Don McCullin, who'd arrived above the valley with his colleague photographer Frank Herrmann. At the top of a slope, they'd been stopped from going further into danger by an Israeli tank commander. McCullin, one of the most celebrated of war photographers – surviving under fire in Vietnam, Cambodia, Cyprus, Biafra, Beirut – was impelled by a surge of emotion to argue the warning and hazard his life yet again, not for a picture but for a friend. He took off down the hill, running half a mile to the smoul-dering car in the valley, identified Nick, retrieved his broken glasses, saw there was nothing more he could do and ran the half-mile back, choked, unable to speak.

In all my years in journalism, assigning men to take risks I did not have to take myself was more wearing than all the anxieties of legal threats and trials – except trying (and failing) to restrain people like McCullin, Murray Sayle, Philip Jacobson, Colin Simpson, Lewis Chester, David Leitch, Jon Swain, David Blundy, and others, from insisting they just had to do what they did, editor or not: Swain and McCullin, defying instructions to make for safety, stayed in the killing fields of Cambodia as the murderous Khmer Rouge reached the doomed city of Phnom Penh.

The death of one journalist is only another digit in the statistics of war, but I often wonder how much readers and viewers understand that the world-weary cynicism or vainglorious postures affected by the men and women who place themselves at risk conceal a deeply felt compulsion to 'bear witness when others can't or won't'. The phrase comes from the third of our reporters who lost his life, the adventurous and droll David Blundy, killed by a sniper's bullet in El Salvador in 1989 attempting to file a last paragraph for the *Sunday Correspondent*.

The second, after Tomalin, did not die in war, but in attempting to report peace. This was David Holden. We were plunged into many mysteries in my fourteen years as editor of the *Sunday Times*. The most profound was right there in our own office. It turned on how we could answer two related questions: who assassinated Holden, our chief foreign correspondent, in Cairo in December 1977 – and why?

I've brooded on this question for many years. I've not written about it before because what I now believe happened has only slowly and painfully been discernible through the shadows.

The beginning in 1977 was the momentous news that to make peace with Israel the Egyptian President, Anwar Sadat, would himself make an unprecedented journey to Jerusalem on 19 November to meet Israeli Prime Minister Menachem Begin and present his olive branch in person to Israel's Parliament, the Knesset. He had ambitions to make peace on behalf of all the Arab nations he'd led to war in 1973 on Yom Kippur, but also to finally resettle the Palestinians who'd lost their land. He was nonetheless denounced as a traitor by the 'rejectionist' states of Syria, Libya, Iraq and South Yemen, and by all factions of the Palestine Liberation Organization (PLO). They arranged to meet in a 'sorehead summit' in Tripoli at the time in December when Israeli negotiators, and the world's press, would be arriving in Cairo.

David Holden, the foreign department's star on the Middle East, did not jump at our invitation to go to Cairo. He was writing a book on Saudi Arabia during the six months a year leave of absence agreed upon in his contract. We still hoped he might do it, but in the meantime Cal McCrystal, the foreign features editor, flew out on Friday, 18 November.

At fifty-three, Holden was a vastly experienced correspondent and broadcaster, one of the chroniclers of the end of Arabia as romance, 'the immortal image of mystery', as he once put it. He shared the sense of style of his friend and *Times* colleague James (later Jan) Morris, who was to receive a last enigmatic message from him. Holden was a small, neat man, not a hair out of place, who somehow, in his bush jacket and debonair manner, still managed to bring a touch of Beau Geste to our newsroom hubbub. It was an echo of the dashing young foreign correspondent of *The Times* of twenty years before, flourishing his British passport at the Yemeni border guard with great curved dagger, seeking out the wicked old Imam Ahmed in his rocky fort, standing on a hilltop in Qataba to observe rebel tribesmen around him opening furious fire on British soldiers across the valley. Nobody on either side hit anything, he reported back, except a goat.

His career spanned the end of an Empire and the entrenchment of secular nationalism, not yet threatened by Islamic fundamentalism. He became intellectually absorbed by the politics of the transition as the former colonial states, through sacrifice and treachery, struggled to find their identity amid the eddies of big power politics and the ascendancy of Israel. He moved easily through the Arab capitals; too easily, the Israelis thought: they regarded him as unduly sympathetic to the Arab cause. In 1967 he had reported how the Israelis punished Palestinians for terror attacks by demolishing Arab houses on the West Bank. He disliked what he saw, but he reported accurately and without histrionics; he did not hate Israel, the emotion was alien to his character. He also wrote, with amused tolerance, of 'Arab venality, prejudice, opportunism and incompetence'. If he hated anything, it was the categorization of countries as good or bad and the manipulation of people's minds.

He was a cultured man, but unaffected; widely read in literature and history, he thought it impossible to write about the present without studying the past. Analysis rather than adventure became his strength. More information, he suggested, did not mean better information. The result of too much reporting was 'to turn up the decibels on the Tower of Babel'. He would not shun the ramparts but he sought his realism elsewhere in the nuances of his quiet meetings with diplomats and intelligence services, academics and Arab editors.

Holden was not all that popular among a few of our harder reporters who'd covered the Six Day and Yom Kippur wars. On his infrequent stays in the office, they thought him rather detached, even condescending, remote from the craft of reporting. This was unfair. He was generous in providing contacts – and very well aware of the dangers of practising journalism in tense exotic places. He'd been interned by the Egyptians during the Suez crisis. Reviewing a book by fellow foreign correspondent Noel Barber of the *Daily Mail*, he wrote, only a few months before his death: 'Thank God I have never suffered either bullets or the steel tearing into my flesh, but I have felt the boots going in and I have heard the prison door close behind me, and I know how sickening the fear of such moments can be.'

Holden stayed at home in London that weekend, 19 and 20 November, but the following week he suddenly told us he would go to Egypt after all. We learned later that Anthony Austin, the articles editor of the *New York Times* magazine, had reached him on 'about the 18th' with the request to write an essay from Egypt. Holden was, Austin recalls, 'very enthusiastic', rather different from our impression. The *New York Times* asked the Egyptian embassy in Washington to telex Cairo to arrange an interview with President Sadat. The upshot of all this was that Holden arranged to go to Cairo, but to first swing through Syria, Lebanon, Jordan and the Israeli-occupied West Bank for us, to test the strength of rejectionist feelings. He landed in Damascus on Sunday, 27 November.

The plans for his murder had already been made.

Holden's first optimistic article, which we headed 'Peace may break out after all', was filed from Amman on Saturday, 3 December 1977. The fire and fury of the rejectionist front, he said, had a 'disintegrating quality', adding laconically, 'very Middle Eastern'. His telex said that the following morning, Sunday, he would go to the simmering cauldron of the West Bank, where the Israelis were building settlements on conquered land. He wanted also to revisit Jerusalem, stay in the American Colony Hotel he loved in the Arab quarter, and then get back to Amman, crossing via the Allenby Bridge in good time

to catch the evening Royal Jordanian Airlines flight RJ 503 to Cairo
on Tuesday, 6 December.

Reviewing the news schedule on the Wednesday, I asked what
David proposed to write. Nobody had an answer. 'We've not heard
from him. Give him time to find his bearings.' The foreign desk put
in calls to Cairo's Meridien and Hilton hotels, where he had been
tentatively booked. He'd not checked in, nor been in touch with the
Reuters bureau where he would normally establish communications.
Nobody was alarmed. 'He'll pop up like a jack in a box, you just
see.' Communications in the Middle East were notoriously difficult;
it was commonplace to have to wait up to eight hours to send a telex
or get through on the telephone.

By Thursday, confidence had evaporated. We set off a full-scale
search operation, staff calling British diplomats and fellow journalists he'd travelled with. Progressively through Friday we confirmed
his departure from Jerusalem; his crossing of the Allenby Bridge and
his boarding the plane to Cairo as planned. The foreign desk suggested an explanation for his silence. The Middle East was racked
with cholera, his inoculations were out of date, and Egypt might
have unceremoniously quarantined him for three or four hours in the
isolation hut at the far end of the airport.

I saw the paper to press on Saturday, 10 December, then around
10 p.m. went to spend the night at an office short-stay apartment
near our building in Gray's Inn Road. I was back in the newsroom
five minutes after the dreaded call came. The British Embassy, chasing the police, had heard that on Wednesday, 7 December, the body
of 'an unknown European male' had been deposited in Cairo's Kasr
el Ainy mortuary, the Dantean repository of all the city's accident
victims. Bob Jobbins, the Cairo correspondent of the BBC, and
Reuters' Fuad al Gawhary went to the mortuary and at once identified Holden. Jobbins was struck by the lack of any obvious injury,
save a small exit wound in his chest. 'An apparent execution,' he pre-
sciently observed.

Holden's body had been found at 8 a.m. some eight hours after his
presumed departure from the airport late on Tuesday night. He lay on
a sandy patch littered with old newspapers by the highway which

runs beside the walls of the Al-Azhar University campus. The area was unfrequented at night, but he was certain to be found as soon as day broke either by students, a passing motorist, or soldiers from a camp on the other side of the highway. He was on his back, his feet neatly together and parallel to the road, his arms folded across his chest in a mocking parody of repose. His expression was calm, his hair as sleek as ever, the only discordant note being the way the dark-rimmed spectacles he wore for driving were lodged crookedly over his eyebrows. His shoes were clean, without a trace of the fine white dune dust to be expected if he'd walked or been walked to this spot.

There was nothing on his person or at the scene to indicate who he was. All marks that might suggest his identity or nationality had been removed, down to the maker's label inside his green and brown check sports jacket. Someone had emptied all the pockets. Only a few Jordanian coins remained untouched in one trouser pocket.

The manner of death was equally methodical. He had been shot once from behind by a short-cartridge nine-millimetre automatic, the classic shoulder-holster weapon. The range was so close, as little perhaps as two inches, that his jacket was scorched just below the left shoulder blade where the bullet entered. But the killer aimed his gun downwards as he fired the single shot so that the bullet pierced the heart. It left the chest with such little force that it was found in the folds of the polo-necked sweater he wore underneath his jacket.

The time of death was established as no earlier than 3 a.m., not later than 5 a.m. This meant Holden had been alive for at least three hours after leaving the airport, possibly a captive all that time.

The shock at the *Sunday Times* was profound. David had not been as closely knitted into the competitive jousting and gossip of our office life as the convivially mischievous Nick Tomalin. But that was the death of a war correspondent, bravely but knowingly exposed to risk in a battle zone; here we faced the death of a colleague reporting peace, and a death for which there seemed no explanation. We all felt a passionate urgency to do everything we could to find one, to nail the killers.

I called the Home Office and the Commissioner of Police at Scotland Yard. The Commissioner assigned two of the most experienced homicide detectives, Chief Superintendent Ray Small and Detective Inspector Tony Comben, but they had first to get permission to work on Egyptian soil and in Syria and Israel, too. We wanted to move quicker while the trail was warm – though not exactly hot given the time of the murder and identification of the body. Within a few hours a team of six reporters was on its way to the Middle East. Hamilton discouraged this initiative; he was as distressed as any of us, but believed we should leave inquiries to the police. Of course I was well aware that newspapermen can only ask questions; despite a common exaggeration of the 'powers of the press', we don't have means of coercion of the kind certainly available to the Egyptian security services, nor did we have knowledge of Cairo's criminal networks. But we had our own contacts, we knew the way David worked, and our team was especially resourceful: Insight editor John Barry and Cal McCrystal in Cairo, Paul Eddy and Peter Gillman in Amman, Tony Terry (a former British intelligence agent) in Jerusalem, and Helena Cobban in Beirut.

Barry and McCrystal visited the morgue, but their mission, apart from answering any questions the Egyptian police might have about Holden, was to track his movements in the last week. They were to look for clues to some of the questions the murder posed: Who knew Holden was arriving on Flight RJ 503? Who else was on the plane with him? Could he have spotted a terrorist on board? Was he seen leaving the airport with anyone? And by anyone he knew? Was the motive for his killing something from his private life playing out as public drama? Or was the trigger his work? Nothing of his we had published could be regarded as offensive, though some Israeli commentators had condemned him for a *Sunday Times* Insight report on the ill-treatment of Palestinian prisoners. The report, which angered the Israeli government, was later confirmed by the US State Department, but Holden had nothing at all to do with it as we made clear (and those who did compile it were never molested in any way).

Or was there something to suggest Holden had been chosen as a high-profile target by Palestinian rejectionists or terrorists? Would they have calculated that the death on Egyptian soil of a famous British correspondent would embarrass Sadat and demonstrate to the VIPs attending the peace talks that peacemakers were as vulnerable? Was Egyptian security all that tight?

Who did Holden see in his swing through the Middle East? Could one of the people he met have learned the time of his flight to Cairo? Had he alarmed somebody, seeing them in a politically compromising situation? Or had he perhaps been asked to courier to Cairo a message or document too sensitive to relay over telex and telephone?

Most of Holden's last week alive, we found, was spent interviewing Arab leaders, including those of the PLO, the West Bank mayors of Bethlehem, Nablus, Hebron and Ramallah, Arab journalists and academics, Syrian and Jordanian officials, and American, British and Australian diplomats. We pressed them for recollections of what transpired; none of these people had knowledge of his travel plans, but we learned that on the West Bank he'd been given a petition to take to Cairo appealing to Sadat not to negotiate with Israel.

Three other curiosities emerged. We were intrigued by Kenize Mourad, a thirty-year-old Frenchwoman reporter for *Nouvel Observateur*. She'd invited Holden for a drink on meeting at the US embassy in Damascus on 30 November. In Amman on 2 December they spent time together, ending with dinner in the hotel coffee shop. The next day they went to a restaurant; at 11 p.m. she'd gone to his room for drinks and stayed until 1 a.m. She told us she angled to join him on his West Bank trip and he declined. On 5 December, she said she'd gone back to Damascus, a curious move, we thought, for a journalist, since the Syrian leadership had flown to Libya for the sorehead summit. At first, we wondered if she might have followed David for some reason but she herself sought out Peter Gillman, and was very open about David being 'a wonderful man'. I came to the view she was an eager younger journalist admiring of an old Middle East hand.

Other than that, we came across two unexplained gaps in Holden's schedule and discrepancies in two testimonies.

In Jerusalem, on the afternoon of 5 December, Holden told Edward Mortimer of *The Times*, with whom he'd been working, that he was

going alone for a walk in the Old City. The taxi driver described to
us how he'd dropped Holden at its main entrance, the Damascus
Gate. Later that day, Holden described to Mortimer his long walk in
detail, remarking how much the city had changed in the ten years
since his previous time there shortly after the Six Day War. But did
he spend two-and-a-half hours in the Old City as he suggested?
It certainly did not square with the testimony of an academic at
Birzeit University who told us the two of them had spent the afternoon in a village twenty miles away where the Israelis, he said, had
harassed the population. And what was the meaning of the postcard
Holden sent from Jerusalem to his friend Jan Morris? He wrote only
nine words: 'In the Old City, citadels still have their uses.'

The next day, his last, produced a conflict about his time in
Amman. The manager of the Bisharat Travel Agency in the lobby of
the Intercontinental Hotel said he'd seen Holden around lunchtime,
about the time he'd have arrived in Amman. He saw him go into the
coffee bar of the hotel with two Americans, writers and archaeolo-
gists John Fistere and his wife Isobel.

Holden and the Fisteres had overlapped before in Beirut for the
first two and a half of the years Kim Philby had been there. (The
gossip then was that the Fisteres were keeping an eye on Philby for
the CIA.) Ruth Holden told us of a dinner she and David had given
with him as a guest. In the files of *The Times* we found that on
8 January 1957 Holden had recommended Philby 'the *Observer* man'
to the paper's foreign desk as someone who could fill the gap left by
a departing *Times* stringer. The mere fact of knowing Philby at this
time in Beirut is hardly significant, but what surprised me, and others
on the original Philby investigation in 1967, was that Holden himself
had not come forward either during our inquiries or after publication.

The Fisteres gave a very different account of David's last hours.
Only in the *evening*, they said, had they seen Holden, not lunchtime,
and then only for about five minutes when they exchanged a few
words by the hotel press centre. According to them, he was 'trying
desperately to telex to the Cairo Hilton to confirm his reservation
there'. He looked 'tired and dirty and worn out from his travels, in
a desperate hurry to catch his flight'. The travel agent's account

checked out better. No one in the press centre or wire room could recall Holden trying to send any last-minute telexes – and if he had he would have been given a telex from the Hilton that had been waiting for him since 4 December. He caught his plane with time to spare.

.

I felt justified in sending the team when John Barry reported from Cairo that he was disturbed by the Egyptians' initial response to the murder. The death by shooting of an unknown European was a rare event. In thirty years only two foreigners had been murdered in Cairo, both victims of domestic disputes, and December 1977 was a period when Egypt was on the alert for the arrival of a thousand of the world's press and the Israeli negotiators. But Barry said the Egyptians had made zero effort to identify the body from 7 December and performed no proper autopsy. Had Holden not been identified when he was, he would have been buried in a common grave. The initial line of the Egyptians was that the murder was the work of foreign agents (Israelis strongly hinted), though the Egyptians were worried enough about the rejectionists to deport two hundred Palestinian militants.

The Scotland Yard detectives were still stuck in London, awaiting travel documents from the Egyptians, but the questions the *Sunday Times* team started asking galvanized the authorities. We were assured that President Sadat himself had ordered a massive investigation. Hundreds of police were deployed. They grilled the airport staff and every one of the 128 passengers on the flight was traced and questioned. None was suspected of terrorist links. They were mostly American tourists. Mrs Willivene Bonnette from Clyde, Ohio, told us that Holden had the aisle seat and would not get up to let her in so she had to squeeze past. He was 'sarcastic and kind of surly', telling her it was 'absurd' she did not know what she was going to do and see in Cairo. He rebuffed conversation, saying only that he had been in Jerusalem 'on business'. His mood might be explained by a personal anxiety: the grumpy, experienced traveller wasn't sure he himself had a bed for the night. He had once held a booking at both the Hilton and the Meridien, but had changed his itinerary so often he had lost the Hilton booking and did not know that we had a room waiting for him at the Meridien. To arrive in Cairo late at night with no hotel booking was not an amusing prospect.

We tracked the way on landing he'd joined others in the wearisome scramble Egypt inflicted on its visitors. He changed travellers' cheques for $200 at the National Bank of Europe, completed a form to obtain an entry visa, then went through passport control and picked up his red Samsonite suitcase; he was alone then. That was the last fact about his life of which we could be certain. Presumably he walked through the 'nothing to declare' channel in customs and through a pair of swinging doors into the open. A double line of crash barriers formed a channel into the foyer of the arrivals building. A police guard of a couple of armed men stood at the end to control the throngs. From that point to the kerbside where the taxis waited was at most forty paces. In that distance Holden disappeared.

There was one curious feature of his arrival, probably innocuous, possibly sinister. Everywhere on his journey he had entered his occupation as 'journalist'; here he wrote 'writer'. This meant he avoided being drawn into the bureaucratic net the Egyptians had set up for the media arriving for the Egypt–Israel negotiations. 'Journalists' and 'press' were ushered into a press room next to the visa office and escorted directly to their hotels. It may have been a whim on his part, or someone might have advised him to do that so that he remained a free agent.

It was routine for the police at Cairo airport to log every taxi picking up a fare. Hundreds of drivers were interviewed. The police concluded Holden was not picked up by one of the authorized, registered taxis. If there had been a queue of people waiting, he might have veered right at the exit and gone to the car park to pick up one of the 'pirate' taxis, but there were plenty of regular taxis at the kerb and the cheaper gypsy cabs were uninvitingly small and uncomfortable. So perhaps someone else had picked him up.

Near midnight on Thursday, 15 December, four days after the identification of Holden's body, John Barry was summoned to the police station at Dukki, a pleasant quarter of Central Cairo on the west bank of the Nile. General Nabawi Ismail, soon to be Minister of the Interior, was there with a dozen beaming generals from security and criminal investigation – and a battered white Fiat 128 without licence plates a Dukki resident had found abandoned; it had a tangle of wires below the dashboard, indicating it had been started without an ignition key.

In the boot they'd found Holden's red suitcase. In it were two Christmas gifts for his wife and jumbled clothes. His Olivetti portable typewriter was in the car, too, along with unexposed rolls of film, a blue folder stuffed with a letter and notes for his book on Saudi Arabia; and the scattered pages of his loose-leaf contacts book built over three decades; the Egyptian section alone ran to eleven pages. Missing were his passport, travellers' cheques, his Olympus camera and lenses and exposed rolls of film, and material he must have accumulated on this trip.

General Ismail and his team doubted the motive was robbery. Holden had been alive for at least three hours, possibly five, after leaving the airport; and robbers would surely have taken what they could and fled. Nobody had attempted to cash the travellers' cheques, and no one ever did. Detectives combed through the known outlets for stolen goods and found nothing of Holden's. Surveying the found and the lost, the General remarked: 'It looks as if the killers knew what they were looking for.'

Our immediate thought was that they had been looking for material for Holden's book on Saudi Arabia. We could not tell whether the pages of notes that remained were the total of his work. Kenize Mourad said he told her he'd uncovered corruption in high places, but he did not intend to include that in his book. There was a reason for this. The book was being written in cooperation with the Saudis, its viability resting in part on the hope that the government would buy 10,000 copies. And we found that the part of the manuscript that had been completed was a thorough historical survey – nothing more.

The police at first assumed that the Fiat was a gypsy cab which Holden had voluntarily taken from the airport. The team told me they were not convinced. It struck us all as highly unlikely that as experienced a traveller as Holden, tired from a day in the West Bank and Jordan, would consider the saving of a few Egyptian pounds worth the discomfort and risk of a ride in a gypsy cab, especially if the driver had used the tangle of exposed wires to start the car.

Could he have been forced into the cab in one of those scenes that films like to portray when the victim is told to keep quiet and keep moving with the prod of the abductor's concealed pistol in his back? It seemed implausible. The airport was teeming with people and security men. None of the travellers or officials noticed the slightest thing untoward in the exit area, nor inside the terminal before customs. To penetrate inside the terminal to identify Holden during the exchange of money, the collection of the visa, or the acquisition of his suitcase, would have required a pass to get through security doors. Conceivably he could have been met by an Egyptian security person or someone posing as one, and invited to a waiting car, but by far the most likely scenario is that he was met outside the street barrier by one or more people who knew him and whom he knew he could trust.

If he'd been abducted in the white Fiat, it was not the car he died in. Just a little later the police found another Fiat, abandoned at Tanta in the heart of the rich delta farmlands eighty miles north of Cairo. In the rear passenger compartment there was a cartridge case matching the fatal 9mm bullet, and bloodstains between the front seats. The headrests on the passenger seat had been removed, making it easier for the gunman leaning forward from the rear seat to put a bullet through the heart. The headrest subsequently turned up in the first car used to capture Holden, the white Fiat dumped with the luggage at Dukki.

There were more provocative facts when we had the body flown home to London, and a thorough autopsy indicated that he had put up a fight, possibly that his wrists had been tied. The examination at the London Hospital by Professor David (Taffy) Cameron noted: 'Bruise on the principal knuckle of the left middle finger, to a lesser extent on the left little and ring fingers, and a bruise noted to front of the left wrist, approximately three inches above the wrist. There was also fingertip type bruising to the outside of the left arm above the elbow; and bruising was noted on the main knuckle of the right thumb.' If David had indeed been in a struggle, we reasoned it was unlikely to have been at the airport, since this would have caused a commotion that someone would have been sure to notice. Our best

guess was that he'd struggled on being transferred to the murder car.
There, thinking they might have done with him, he might have taken
his front seat quietly enough.

Nearly a month later a third Fiat was found with documents from
the murder car. All three cars had been entered in identical fashion
by breaking open the quarter light, all driven by hot-wiring the ignition, two resprayed, one green, one red. The security police thought
the logistics of the break-in, respraying, murder, transfer of the luggage, dumping the body and getaway would have required a team of
eight people. Robbery having already been discounted, the police
moved vaguely back to foreign agents, rejectionists now in the
starring role. The theory gained momentum when they established
that the owner of the first car found at Dukki was an activist, a
twenty-two-year-old engineering student with a Jordanian passport
(whose father had fled Jordan on terrorist charges). He was brought
in for questioning as were the owners of the other two cars. All
were cleared, we were told, but they did yield tantalizing information. The owner of the first car said he'd reported it stolen in the
third week of November – around the time Holden's trip to Cairo
had been decided in New York and London. The other two cars
were stolen when Holden was set to move from Jerusalem to Cairo
on 6 December.

But who had carried out what was clearly a well-planned abduction?
Over the Christmas holiday, I had a conversation about the murder
with a highly placed Egyptian visiting London. He told me the operation was carried out by Fatah hard-core rejectionists who would
stop at nothing to sabotage Sadat's initiative. More he would not
say. We followed up. Helena Cobban, our correspondent in Beirut,
had a good working relationship with Fatah's chairman, Yasser
Arafat. He promised he would investigate.

Barry and fellow reporter Gillman were summoned to Beirut to
hear the findings. 'Finally, after much fussing about changing cars,'
said Barry, they were ushered into a heavily curtained room in a
derelict building that had been wrecked in the Lebanese civil war. In

the gloom, a middle-aged man sat at a Victorian desk; they were given to understand he was head of Fatah intelligence. Nobody was identified, but Gillman had a tremor of recognition that one of the three men was Ali Hassan Salameh, believed by the Israelis to have organized the Munich Olympic kidnappings in 1972 (and subsequently blown up by the Israelis). Barry reported: 'He said on the chairman's orders he'd made inquiries and could assure us that "no arm of the resistance" had a hand in the murder. I asked if he could be so certain of other "organs of resistance" apart from Fatah and he said no Palestinians would have wanted Holden dead. They had a policy, he said, of not killing journalists, and the *Sunday Times* had been regarded as "a friend to our cause" because it had published that report on the ill-treatment of Palestinian prisoners.

I could not regard the interview as conclusive, but a strange development made Fatah's involvement seem less probable.

Even more alarming than the news from Cairo and the pathologist's report in London was the information Paul Eddy brought into my office late in January 1978. He'd asked for a closed-door meeting strictly between the two of us, and then in his cool, cryptic style proceeded to astonish me. 'The killers knew exactly when Holden would arrive in Cairo because they got the information from the horse's mouth – us.' Eddy had discovered that copies of telexes between Holden and the foreign desk were missing. Hundreds of telexes were filed in an unmarked cupboard on the fifth floor, not far from my office. Nothing had been taken or disturbed except eight telexes relating solely to Holden's changing travel plans from the day he decided to go. With the messages stolen from the cupboard, the plotters would have been able to track him as he travelled from Damascus to Amman to Jerusalem, back to Amman, and finally to Cairo.

The foreign department was very well run. Could it not be, I suggested, that this was just a mix-up, an unusual act of carelessness? Eddy had another shock for me. The thefts were continuing in January. He had discovered the December thefts only in the course of looking for more recent messages and was stunned to find that some of these, too, had gone. Among them were travel plans and reports on the progress of the investigation from Barry and Gillman who had returned to the Middle East in early January. One dispatch reported speculation that there might be a connection with the terrorist Abu Nidal's campaign to kill moderate Palestinians who favoured a deal with Israel. (The key moderate PLO leader, Said Hammani, had been shot dead in London in January.)

Someone had gained access to the editorial floor, not too difficult in those days pre-9/11. There were at least six entrances to the deep, rambling building on Gray's Inn Road. A thief could easily mingle with the hundreds of casual workers who were employed on Saturdays in the basement presses and in the huge distribution warehouse where copies came up from the basement for bundling and loading onto trucks. Those floors were removed from editorial on the fourth and fifth floors at the front of the building, but we were used to seeing new faces, assuming them to belong to casual messengers ferrying copy and coffee. Still, an interloper must have had intimate knowledge of the layouts and procedures to find the foreign department cupboards and find them when nobody was in the room. 'Horrible thought,' said Eddy, 'we may have a spy on the staff.'

On 24 January Eddy removed all material related to Holden from the foreign department and locked it in the Insight office with a single key to the filing cabinet. We did this very quietly, not wanting to alert a predator. The stealth was prudent but it meant the wire room that transmitted and received messages did not know of the thefts from the foreign department – and we were not aware the wire room operators had developed a practice of keeping a second copy of messages sent to the foreign department. They impaled them on a spike in a corner of their office hidden away in a back corner of the building. It took the thief thirty-six hours to realize that fact and gain access to the wire room when it was unattended during the night of 26–27 January. Every message had gone, including twenty-five related to the investigation. More surprising still, sometime between 8 a.m. and midday on 27 January Eddy asked the wire room for its copy of a telex from Gillman to Eddy announcing his plans to return to London on 30 January. It had vanished.

Again, we sounded no alarm but I spoke with Scotland Yard and we informed the Foreign Office. Very soon after my call, our windows began to receive a thorough cleaning inside and out. The cleaners were from the Yard's C-10, known as 'the watchers'. Without detection they hid infrared cameras that would capture any intruder on tape. Eddy and the managing editor were the only staff people who knew.

Discussing the schedule in conference, the foreign editor said that Gillman and Eddy were reporting a breakthrough and that Eddy would travel to Cairo. 'Tell them no heroics in any circumstances,' I told the foreign editor. I wasn't really worried. Eddy, making sure he wasn't followed, did not go to the airport but headed for North Wales (only later did he tell me, by the oddest of coincidence, that he went to my very own Rhyl). The Eddy–Gillman plan was that from there he would contrive to send messages purportedly from Cairo, Beirut and Jerusalem while the Yard's concealed cameras kept watch on the foreign department and wire room.

Over ten days no interloper appeared on the recordings. Either the thefts had been by someone on the staff pretending to go about their normal work, or the trap had been rumbled, or the thief had concluded that we were not on a dangerously hot trail. I had got so jumpy, especially after the Philby cover-up, I even began to think I'd made a mistake letting the Foreign Office know that we'd detected the thefts. What if our own secret intelligence service (M16) had played some role in the abduction of Holden? What if we were caught in a convoluted winding down of the Philby betrayal? Hadn't I read in Dorothy Sayers or Agatha Christie that the least probable suspect should never be ruled out? I invoked Occam's Razor to banish the mad thoughts.

Certainly one piece of solid ground was that the Yard was unstinting in its cooperation; the Egyptians were not. Chief Superintendent Small and Detective Inspector Comben were still in London. Assurances that they would be welcomed were endlessly forthcoming. What were not were the necessary papers. In the end, Small and Comben were never allowed to go to Cairo. This was baffling and infuriating because they were appalled by the Egyptian police work. An inquiry about whether fingerprints on the cars led anywhere produced a negative – because too many policemen had handled the vehicles. Instead of admitting the two Scotland Yard men, the Egyptians sent a senior officer to London. He seemed to us to be as baffled as we were by the purpose of his visit. He thought he might perhaps go to Paris to interrogate Kenize Mourad. However, since he was in London, he told the Insight team that he had settled for shopping at Marks and Spencer instead.

It was all very frustrating, but the timing of the thefts of the cars and the raids on our office did put a different perspective on an early theory, first advanced in a Lebanese newspaper. Holden, it reported, had been mistaken for David Hirst, a *Guardian* correspondent. In Arabic, the surnames Holden and Hirst have some differences – two dots over Hirst, only one for Holden – but they could have been mistaken for each other. Our access to the flight manifest found that European names were hopelessly garbled. A motive was apparent, too: revenge. Hirst had maddened Sadat and infuriated Mrs Sadat by writing about corruption and high living. 'True enough,' Hirst affirmed. 'Nine months before, four security men came to the Cosmopolitan Hotel, I was escorted out with a gun pointed literally at my head. On top of that I came back to Cairo deliberately when David Owen [Foreign Secretary] was visiting for two days, and Sadat was incensed that I'd been able to get a visa in Rome. They tried to stop me leaving on Owen's plane but Robert Fisk [veteran Middle East correspondent] said he wouldn't leave without me.'

Mistaken identity seemed the most plausible explanation to us for a time. Sadat was certainly very angry about David Hirst. One well-placed but very frightened informant confided that he knew Sadat had sent an assassination team to the airport and swore us to secrecy. The crucial difficulty was that David Holden was clearly the intended target. The thefts of the cars, and the thefts of telexes relating to Holden, could not be just a coincidence. And whoever held Holden for three hours would have known pretty soon that he was not David Hirst. Nor had Hirst signalled any intention to revisit Egypt.

We were forced back to the conclusion that the chess-like precision of the abduction, and the capacity to operate in both Cairo and London, must have been the work of an international organization with considerable facilities. Terrorists, we know to our cost now after

9/11 and the abduction of Daniel Pearl of the *Wall Street Journal*, can work in deadly stealth, and the Egyptian police pressed this explanation on us. But we did not find it convincing for a number of reasons. To accept it, one has to believe that an unknown group, undetected in the clampdown, arrests and deportations in Cairo, using methods without the slightest resemblance to those of other terrorist killings in the world, went to all this trouble to murder at random one of a thousand correspondents, for indiscernible motives, remove his clothing labels for no apparent reason, and then disappear without a trace, leaving their achievement unclaimed.

There are other suspects who had the means, and had been known to carry out assassinations. Not excluding the Egyptians themselves, there were the foreign intelligence agencies of Israel, the US, Russia, and possibly even Britain; and the Saudis, we were told, handled this kind of work by contract with professionals. But what on earth could be the motive? Was there an important clue in the killers so carefully leaving Holden where he could be found – a warning perhaps?

While the rest of the team resumed normal duties, I authorized Eddy and Gillman to continue the inquiry, as they much wished to do. To consider motives, it was agreed we had to ask not just who killed David Holden, but who *was* David Holden? It's not an easily answered question about any of us; all identities are evanescent. His career was well documented – the son of an editor of the *Sunderland Echo*, educated at Quaker schools and Emmanuel College, Cambridge, a teacher of geography for three years (a job he said he 'loathed'), a postgraduate student at Northwestern University, Illinois, a foreign correspondent for *The Times* and *Guardian*.

To go beyond these facts into the nuances and ambiguities of a personal life was a sensitive decision. I was troubled by the way newspapers and television in pursuit of the mass audience were intruding into private lives when there was not the slightest justification. People are entitled to personal privacy; it's integral to our sense of worth. Certainly there are grey areas where the private elides with the public; but photographers and reporters – and their editors – who regard private lives as fair game are for the most part taking the easy option. It is harder to expose the complications in a real public wrong than to make someone's life a misery (on the grounds of exposing hypocrisy, which is itself hypocrisy on stilts). Indeed, gratuitous breaches of privacy invite restrictive laws that protect the unscrupulous, all too ready to invoke the sanctity of private life while plundering the public purse. So I hesitated about authorizing our own inquiries into Holden's personal life; he was not around to defend himself.

Yet the thought persisted that the motivation for his murder might lie in some conjunction of the personal and public. I felt we owed it to him at least to explore the possibility of finding something relevant, without necessarily committing to publication of what we found. That is how we ran into contention with the CIA and FBI.

The most important relationship Holden formed before his marriage was a passionate ten-year friendship with an older man he looked up to. He was a chameleon named Leo Silberman, who'd been an ardent communist, first anti-America then pro, a supporter of Israel on its founding and then vehemently anti-Zionist. The CIA came to suspect he was a British intelligence agent in Africa. Silberman had been born into a Jewish family in Germany in 1915. As Hitler rose to power, the family escaped to Britain, where Leo joined the Communist party and, according to his brother Freddy, lost jobs because of his radical activities. He married a Communist party secretary in Vienna in the 1930s – as Philby had done – and thus came to the attention of the FBI when he later applied for a visa to visit the United States and denied any communist connections.

During the war, Silberman studied and taught sociology at South African universities – brilliantly, according to his professors, though he gave himself the title 'Doctor' to which he was not entitled. The British Colonial Office was impressed enough to provide him with a letter saying he was working on their behalf in East Africa 'in connection with social problems'.

Silberman was loud and flamboyant, the opposite of Holden, but they were lovers, according to Silberman's brother Freddy. Holden and Silberman stayed close until Silberman's death in 1960, whereupon Holden married the photojournalist Ruth Lynam, who worked for *Life* magazine.

We were surprised that Holden was bisexual. In letters to his brother Geoffrey, to former teachers, and in conversation, Holden made constant references to girlfriends and sex. He wrote to Geoffrey about the lack of sexual opportunity in Arab countries, saying: 'What is a fellow to do except turn queer?'

Holden's closeness to Silberman led us to ask the FBI first and then the CIA what they knew about him and Holden. An FBI official told us he had Holden's file in front of him and 'it looks to me as if some of this stuff is classified' and he'd have to ask if it could be released.

The agency dragged its feet so much we retained the Washington law firm of Williams and Connolly to press the FBI to meet its obligations under the Freedom of Information Act. In the meantime, we checked through unofficial sources and learned that within weeks of Holden being posted to Washington by *The Times* in 1954, he'd been observed meeting 'a known Soviet bloc agent'. None of us regarded this as conclusive, the FBI having an ability to put two and two together to make five. Many were the cases in the paranoid 1950s where individuals were put under surveillance for a chance meeting or an expression of social concern. A journalist might meet a Soviet agent, knowingly or not, in the course of his work. Indeed, I suppose I must have been observed meeting a number of Soviet bloc agents at diplomatic parties in London, and I'd been shown around Moscow by an Intourist guide so well indoctrinated I quickly realized the truth was the exact opposite of what she told me. The circumstances were the key, but the FBI declined to release any further details on grounds of national security.

The CIA was also less than forthcoming. Sixteen months after our requests under the Freedom of Information Act for documents concerning Holden and Silberman had produced no response, we filed a court action. John Barry met two CIA officials in Washington's Mayflower Hotel who said the agency had nothing on its files about Holden and no knowledge of his murder. 'I just don't believe you,' said Barry. 'You must at least have taken an interest in the murder of a British newsman at that critical time.' They acknowledged the point, but all they had collected, they said, were rumours, no more, that he had been killed by terrorists looking to use his press credentials in one way or another. They invited Barry to withdraw our suit; he didn't have to read my mind to decline their invitation.

In fact, the CIA did have a file on Holden. The court action led to the agency providing us with an index, but not the contents, of thirty-three documents it had assembled, four of them about Holden and the rest about Silberman. We learned much later that this file on Silberman was started when a CIA agent in East Africa met him at a dinner party where Silberman, on the basis of the Colonial Office letter, gave the impression he was a British agent working under cover of an American foundation grant. This annoyed the CIA man on two grounds: that British intelligence had an 'undeclared' operative in his area, and that he was using an American foundation as cover, something American operatives were forbidden to do.

In addition to the thirty-three documents from its own files, the CIA said it had turned over nineteen to other agencies, one to the FBI, thirteen to the Department of State, four to the National Security Agency (NSA) and one to the International Communication Agency to decide whether these could be disclosed to us. All of the agencies said no.

We appealed these decisions; all of them were denied. The CIA Assistant General Counsel John F. Peyton contended the Freedom of Information Act exempted matters that might be kept secret 'in the interest of defense and foreign policy'. Williams and Connolly advised that rather than go to trial, a slow and expensive business, we should propose that the documents be shown in camera to a judge who would rule whether the CIA was justified in maintaining secrecy. A judge supported the proposal; the CIA rejected it. Only when an appeals court ordered the agency to comply did it allow a judge to see its file in confidence.

He was swift. Disclosure would constitute a national security risk. The documents should not and would not be released.

What were we to make of this? A source told us that the CIA file simply recorded Holden as 'an informal contact', meaning that he would have met 'second trade secretaries at U.S. Embassies' on a fairly regular basis, presumably to exchange information. Holden was not, we were assured by this source, in the pay or under the control of the CIA, but it would have been possible for 'adverse parties' to mistakenly come to a more sinister conclusion.

But none of that could have persuaded a judge to seal the documents, certainly not the judge who'd forced the CIA to make them available for judicial inspection in the first place and was regarded as open-minded. We were compelled regretfully to consider whether David had in some way been involved in espionage for somebody and been killed for that reason, perhaps because he had been thought to be serving two masters, the commonest reason for what's referred to as the 'liquidation of an asset'. That would at least do something to explain why his body had been left as an obvious example of an intelligence killing: it was a warning – this is the price of betrayal.

But to go further into these shadows meant trying to identify which intelligence agency might have employed him in the first place as a straight agent, rather than a double, then which agency might have regarded this as treachery. Three agencies had surface plausibility: the CIA, Mossad and the KGB.

The CIA was the obvious first candidate, given its resistance to revealing its documents. There were incidents in David's life that lent some credence to the idea of a double identity on behalf of the CIA. Nobody could explain why he'd been arrested twice in Cuba and then deported. His flat repudiation of any CIA involvement in the bloody coup that deposed Chile's President Allende in 1973 was also an uncharacteristic misjudgement, and worded in uncharacteristically vehement language. And then there was the afternoon in Jerusalem when he was in two places at once and sent that cryptic postcard to Jan Morris: 'In the Old City, citadels still have their uses.' The notion did occur to us that the uses of the 'citadel' might not have been political but sexual. When I spoke to Jan Morris she discounted this, while saying she had never had such a strange postcard among many she received from Holden on his travels. Then we learned that the US Consulate in East Jerusalem did maintain a clandestine meeting place in a small rented room in the Old City walls. We'd previously been assured that by agreement with Israel there was no CIA post in Jerusalem, only in Tel Aviv. Moreover, the academic at Birzeit University who'd said he'd been with Holden that afternoon we discovered to be a paid agent of the CIA.

The theoretical case for Holden being a KGB agent was based on the one FBI sighting of him with a KGB operative and his association with Kim Philby. Holden might have been useful to the Soviets in gathering information and assessing trends: Moscow had been taken quite by surprise by Sadat's expulsion of the Soviet military in 1971.

And then there was Mossad, every paranoid's favourite mastermind. Rather than Holden being an agent for Mossad, however, the first hint the Egyptian police gave was that he'd been a Mossad victim. They said the bullet had been manufactured in Israel. Then they thought better of it and emphasized terrorists. But would Mossad have left such an obvious clue to a clandestine killing? Furthermore, unless one was totally cynical about the Sadat–Begin peace moves, would Israel have risked killing a reputable journalist who was writing favourably of the initiative they valued? I thought not. It was put to us more than once, however, that if Holden was an intelligence agent, then Israel was the country he could best serve. It was the one nation denied access and travel throughout the Middle East. His journeys, though infrequent, gave him valuable insights into the options and intentions of Israel's immediate neighbours, including their military preparedness. Perhaps there was a wider audience for his observations than the regular readers of the *Sunday Times*.

Eddy and Gillman were still sporadically on the trail when I left to edit *The Times* in 1981. They kept in touch with people they were sure knew more than they'd admitted. In 1988, after we lost the Freedom of Information case, Gillman confided what we'd found to a senior US contact in the Middle East and let the contact read the Eddy–Gillman unpublished Insight notes. It was suggested that we had to think about the case in the context of the CIA's changing role in the Middle East.

In 1973, at the outbreak of the Yom Kippur war, American intelligence capability in Egypt had reached zero with the expulsion of the last active CIA agent, a woman who for cover worked for an Alexandrian company, the splendidly named Société d'Alexandrie pour les Boissons Distillées et Vignobles de Gianaclis. After Egypt's defeat, the agency worked hard to re-establish itself and establish links with Egyptian intelligence. It was central to persuading Sadat to make his historic gesture. The peace negotiations leading to the 1978 Camp David Accords between Sadat and Begin had gathered great impetus, with Egypt and Israel offered comparable aid packages from the Americans. Nothing was to be allowed to jeopardize the rapprochement.

The contact did not admit any direct knowledge of the murder but suggested that Holden would have been vulnerable if he had been suspected of playing a double game in any way that clouded the prospect of a peace agreement. The contact in effect suggested we should not rule out a joint operation, instigated and encouraged by the CIA but carried out by the Egyptians. Why Holden should have been thought to be a hazard could have been because he was believed to be a hostile intelligence agent or carrying messages from the rejectionist front. I've mentioned that he did have a petition for Sadat, given to him on the West Bank. The team had not regarded this as really significant because it was in mimeographed form (that is, typed on a stencil and run off on a cyclostyle machine) and by the time Holden reached Cairo it had already been published by Edward Mortimer in *The Times*. But the stakes were high in 1977.

It proved impossible to verify or even follow up this lead; Eddy and Gillman had gone back to the source, but he'd left his position and over many months all efforts to find him in the Middle East and the US failed. In the mists of circumstance and conjecture, we are left the certainty only that Holden was foully murdered, and with the aching suspicion that he died not for journalism but for some secret cause he betrayed. We should give him the benefit of the doubt, but of one thing I am certain: no journalist should ever, ever agree to act for an intelligence agency, whatever the invocation, whatever the desire to be patriotic. And we should relentlessly expose the agencies and journalists who ever make that kind of arrangement. Vivid in my mind still is not only Philby passing himself off as a correspondent in Beirut but our own Jon Swain, held captive by rebels in Eritrea, and in mortal danger because of false suspicions that he might be a British spy. The credibility of journalism, and the lives of individual correspondents, are too valuable ever to compromise.

18

DIVIDED LOYALTIES

A newspaper is an argument on the way to a deadline. If there isn't any argument there's not much of a newspaper. And the editor's decision is final. That sounds straightforward, doesn't it?

The questions, in fact, are endless. Is this report credible and clear? Is it a rehash of the familiar or does it advance public understanding? Does it justify its space and position in the paper? Is its readability derived from malice? Is it legally risky? Does it betray a source? Is it faithful to the paper's espoused values of seeking truth fairly and without fear or favour?

As editor of the *Sunday Times*, nothing impeded my ability to make the final decisions except my own ignorance or cowardice. But I did have to decide under the pressure of time, and palaeontology kept me on the alert against procrastination – at least the palaeontology from a fragment of verse by Bert Leston Taylor, a *Chicago Tribune* columnist, which I stuck in my science scrapbook at St Mary's Road Central School:

> *Behold the mighty dinosaur*
> *Famous in prehistoric lore,*
> *You will observe by these remains*
> *The creature had two sets of brains –*

One in his head (the usual place),
The other in his spinal base.
Thus he could reason 'A priori'
As well as 'A posteriori.'
If something slipped his forward mind
'Twas rescued by the one behind.
For he could think, without congestion,
Upon both sides of every question.
Oh, gaze upon this model beast;
Defunct ten million years at least.

In my own pondering, I was not beholden to any party line. I did not have to duck a decision or temporize for fear of offending friends of the ownership or its commercial interests. When the Thomson Organisation was bidding for licences for North Sea Oil exploration, I ran reports damaging to all the bidders accompanied by an editorial saying the government's terms were too generous. To Thomson's abiding credit, I did not hear a word of complaint.

I published an Insight exposé of CIA involvement in elections in Guyana the day before a Thomson team met the Guyanese government to sell a television station. They were asked to leave the country forthwith. Something similar happened with a Thomson venture in South Africa. This sounds as if I was seeking confrontation with my own company. I wasn't. I knew about the oil licences, but I didn't know of the activities in Guyana and South Africa. Even if I had, I would not have felt obliged to delay or suppress the reports: independence from the commercial life of a very large conglomerate had been a condition of appointment. It was honoured both ways. Denis Hamilton, as editor in chief of Times Newspapers, did once have occasion to tell me he thought a business news report I published on the rigs of oil companies in the North Sea had been malicious and unfair, but that wasn't censorship: it was a professional judgement by a distinguished colleague – and he was, I fear, right. It was a reminder of the vigilance to be exercised in maintaining our standards. The press is not noticeably different from other institutions in an aptitude for closing ranks under attack; it

was important for me not to let our powerful esprit de corps protect error.

In short, there was no hidden agenda in our deliberations. But
that didn't make it easier. It made some of the decisions harder. I had
no boss I could turn to or blame. Fact checking was the least of it.
All the facts might check out, but that did not mean we should publish something as it stood. Have we put it in context? What are the
foreseeable consequences of publication and of non-publication?
With contentious material, I made a point of testing it on various
people, sometimes in groups but aware of the group dynamics. Is the
one who has not joined in silent because he is scared to disagree with
a peer group? I tried to cultivate suspicion of myself.

My emotional mindset was publish and be damned, so how could
I offset that with reason? I was acutely aware that I was making decisions in a social context where my colleagues subconsciously shared
my assumption that publication was ipso facto good, suppression
bad. There were issues where the weight of opinion in the office was
so evenly balanced in logic – and emotional force – I felt I had
become the editor of a paper called the *Daily Dilemma*. The rise of
full-scale terrorism in Northern Ireland from 1971, for example,
called for excruciatingly difficult judgements:

Should we talk with terrorists?

Should we seek and accept interviews if a condition is not to disclose
the identity or whereabouts of someone wanted by the authorities?

If someone has information which could save lives, what measures
are justified to get it out of him? Ill-treatment, threats, cruelty, torture? If you know about these practices, should you keep quiet?

Should we suppress everything which might conceivably make
things worse? In the violently paranoid state of Northern Ireland
there was always the risk of endangering someone's life.

Which comes first, truth or patriotism? As citizens protected by
the rule of law in a civilized society, are editors obliged to be loyal
first to the guardian state? President John Kennedy, after the Bay of
Pigs fiasco in 1961, put it this way: 'Every newspaper now asks itself
with respect to every story: Is it news? All I suggest is that you add
the question "Is it in the interests of national security?"'

And if other media distort the facts – as they have done consistently in America as well as Britain – how much time and space shall we spend correcting them?

The editor's decision is final in the sense that the story goes to press as approved. But that is all that is final. As I will relate, a decision is never without repercussions. What I decided about Bloody Sunday in 1972, the British Army's shooting of thirteen unarmed civilians in Derry, was still being challenged thirty-five years later, not by the government but by one of our star reporters.

In the newsroom one summer Friday in 1975, the news editor, Magnus Linklater, seeking a decision, thrust folios of copy into my hand. 'You'd better read this from Chris Ryder. I've questioned him. Pretty amazing.' Ryder was our plump young staffman, a native of Belfast who still lived there; he was distinguished by his rolling Belfast accent and cheerful determination to ignore warnings from the extremists of both sides in the conflict. In the early days of the Troubles the IRA, dedicated to achieving a socialist united Ireland, were welcomed as defenders in the Catholic areas under siege by mobs. Since then, Ryder had reported, the Catholic community had become progressively more disillusioned by random violence and intimidation from the 'Provos' – gunmen of the Provisional IRA who split from the 'Official' IRA.

Ryder had broken the news that three Provo women dressed as nuns had been foiled in attempting to rob a big Irish bank, but after the manager was contacted by the Provos at his home, the bank was so scared it paid up anyway. Ryder's newest report in my hand was that a number of Provo activists were operating 'a new element in urban terrorism'. It was said that behind the front of the Andersonstown Co-operative Society and the political organization Sinn Fein, the Provos were using force and fraud to secure community control by creating monopolies for themselves in construction work and taxi services. It was also said that they had set up a chain of highly lucrative drinking clubs.

James Evans, our lawyer, came over to read the piece. It was, he said, actionable, but since the Provisionals were an illegal terrorist organization it was highly unlikely the two men named would sue. One of them, however, was a spokesman for Sinn Fein, and if they did sue, we'd have to be sure we could prove that Sinn Fein was inextricably linked with the IRA. The courts in Belfast, he said, were as exacting in their standards as mainland courts. 'It's up to you, Harry.'

That was decision No. 1: play safe and not publish or risk it? I risked it and published two reports by Ryder, in August 1975 and August 1976. A full six months passed before a libel claim was served on me on behalf of the two men we'd named, Seamus Loughran, the Sinn Fein spokesman, and Gerald Maguire, who'd been interned. They alleged they'd been maliciously and falsely defamed.

At that time, local and national news organizations were regularly settling libel claims by people who'd been interned and who'd argued that any mention of them in this context was defamation since detention without trial was not a judicial process and no criminal conviction had resulted. So I had a second decision to make: Should we do as everyone else did?

Making our defence more challenging was the fact that jurors and witnesses were regularly terrorized by the IRA. One witness to a terrorist attack had been killed. All criminal and terrorist cases had to be tried by a single judge and no jurors. So taking our case to civil trial before a jury where jurors and witnesses might be intimidated was a big risk. Was it worth it? After all, the costs of paying compensation were likely to be much less than the monetary costs of fighting.

But that was only one consideration. It had been my decision to publish. Either I had confidence in the reporting then, or I hadn't. If I hadn't, I'd been reckless; and if I had been satisfied with the reporting, I surely had a duty to stand by the reporter who'd exposed himself to harm. Retreat would be a rebuke to one reporter, but it would also stain the integrity of all our reporting. Furthermore, it would be a betrayal of those who were willing to testify or sit as jurors. A newspaper operated under the assumption that the rule of law prevailed: how could we undermine it? 'Accept service' I told our lawyers.

Two years later, in October 1979, I was summoned to appear in

Belfast in the Queen's Bench Division of the High Court of Northern Ireland. In preparing our defence, we were going to have to call on the police and expert witnesses; the police accepted that, the Northern Ireland Office (NIO) did not. The court assisted us by ruling that the NIO, for the first time, would have to give evidence – evidence critical to our proving our case.

I'd got used to testifying in the Law Courts in the Strand in years of suits brought against the *Sunday Times*. This experience was very different. It was nightmare time in the province. More than 200 IRA prisoners were on 'dirty protest', smearing excrement in their cells in a campaign to regain political status, culminating in hunger strikes. Killings had been trending down for years, but in March an IRA splinter group had blown up Airey Neave, the Conservative MP, as he drove out of the House of Commons parking space. On the morning of 27 August, the IRA murdered Lord Mountbatten on a little fishing expedition in Sligo, and with him his fourteen-year-old grandson, a local fifteen-year-old boy, and 84-year-old Lady Brabourne. In the afternoon of the same day two concealed bombs in Warrenpoint, County Down, killed eighteen men of the Second Parachute Regiment, the regiment's biggest loss since their sacrifices holding the bridge at Arnhem in the Second World War, and the single most disastrous day in Ireland for the security forces.

It was a bleak wet morning with poor visibility when I was met at the airport by two detectives armed with pistols and sub-machine guns to assure my safe passage to the fortified courthouse. By then a staggering nearly 2,000 had died in the Troubles in Northern Ireland: in proportion to population it was as if a small English town the size of Darlington had been wiped off the map. The streets of terraced houses were like those I'd grown up among in Manchester – seeing a solitary man running along with a greyhound, I had a flash memory of my Dad's betting days – but desolation was the adjective that came to mind. Even in the blitz our Newton Heath wartime streets did not have the foreboding that hung like a fog over Belfast. Where there was colour, murals and graffiti painted on the walls of a gable end, the message was death to the other side. Every pub in the city had armed guards, gunmen of both sides having found it

tempting to burst open the doors and spray with automatic fire whoever was having a drink. There were distant sirens in the city, but the
noise in my imagination was the wailing lament and rifle shots of the
frequent funerals, the sobs of the widows.

No imagination was required to bend double in the car when one
of my escorts shouted urgently: 'Get down! Get down!' and the
driver did a quick U-turn. They'd taken a wrong street. In parts of
the city the security forces feared to run into a trap, a roadblock in
front and sinister cars moving in behind. When we got safely to the
fortified courthouse and awaited admission, my bodyguard was kind
enough to point out two heavy-set men on the other side of the ante-
room. 'They're the ones,' he said, 'we've got to watch for you.' It
was good to find two experienced staffers, David Blundy and Phil
Jacobson, waiting in the courthouse. They'd had armed escorts; so
had the other witnesses. Ryder, who'd been assigned two bodyguards
for the duration of the case, arrived in an armoured Land Rover that
varied its route every day. As the trial went on, this protection business became curiouser and curiouser. At one point, a lookout 'dicker'
(spy) of one of the more violent Loyalist groups was identified in the
public gallery, so the police ended up having also to protect the IRA
people who showed up in court.

I took the witness stand, facing a jury of three men and four women
and Mr Justice Murray. I had a hard time from Mr Michael Lavery
QC, the lawyer for the men we'd written about. We were conducting
a vendetta, weren't we? Didn't we realize these men were providing
the community with jobs? Hadn't we invented the story about his
clients, because I was in business to sell newspapers and make money
for myself or my employees? The *Belfast Telegraph* recorded:

> Mr Lavery: Are you making the case that the plaintiffs and the
>   Andersonstown Co-operative were . . . part of robbery, fraud
>   and protection rackets?
> Mr Evans: Yes. I would stand by every word in the two articles.

Ryder testified for three days, threatened with imprisonment for
contempt of court if he refused to reveal all his sources. The lanky

and deceptively casual young Blundy, who made us all laugh with his gift for puncturing egos (including mine), said under cross-examination that he had spoken with one of the defendants when writing earlier reports about the IRA, identifying him then only as 'an IRA source'. Lavery pounced. 'So you're willing now to betray a source in the witness box?' Blundy replied that of course he'd protect the anonymity of a source, but if the source brought a lawsuit and threatened to kill one of his colleagues – Ryder – might not that immunity be regarded as questionable?

The lowering atmosphere of Belfast must have affected me. That night back in London, as I walked from the office towards an apartment, a man shuffled towards me and asked if I'd show him the way to Tottenham Court Road. His theatrical Irish accent made me jump out of my skin. In my nervy state, I told Scotland Yard that night. By morning, I'd calmed down but they insisted I went along to examine mug shots.

At the end of October the jury considered the evidence for a full day. When they returned in the afternoon, they accepted the thrust of our case, dismissing the libel claim by the two men; the Andersonstown Co-op was awarded a token £200 damages. Loughran, who'd played a prominent part in the proceedings, was eventually relieved of his public duties as Sinn Fein spokesman on 'health grounds'. One of Ryder's sources clarified this: 'It is more to do with his future health than his present health.'

The whole experience reinforced my admiration for our reporters and my sadness at the miserable existence of the people of Northern Ireland. Life there was indeed brutish and nasty. The paramilitaries, but especially the IRA, didn't much care who died. The IRA incinerated men and women at a happy get-together of the Irish Collie Club at La Mon House Hotel in Castlereagh. The Protestant 'Shankill Butchers' gang led by a cutthroat psychopath abducted and slaughtered thirty Catholics picked at random. Loyalist members of the outlawed Ulster Volunteer Force ambushed and machine-gunned the popular Miami show band, a mix of Catholics and Protestants, returning to Belfast from a Catholic dance hall gig at Banbridge, County Down. In the Poppy Day massacre at Enniskillen an IRA splinter group detonated a bomb to kill people gathered together at the cenotaph in Enniskillen to remember the victims of all conflicts. And then the bombings came to London by the score and the terrorists almost succeeded in murdering Mrs Thatcher.

Was it an inevitable tragedy? I've endlessly run over in my mind how journalism might have made a difference after I took over the paper in 1967.

Ever since the British government had partitioned Ireland in 1921, separating an independent Republic of twenty-six counties in the South from a province of six British counties in the North, the people had been divided by faith and by flag as much as Shiites and Sunnis by religion in Iraq. In the Northern six counties, loosely called Ulster, Protestants formed more than half of the 1.5 million population, while the South was Catholic. The Protestant Unionists ('Orangemen') passionately saw themselves as British, loyal to the Crown and the Union Jack. They had their own Parliament in Stormont just outside Belfast with a large degree of self-rule and they used it to suppress the Catholic minority, keeping them out of the best jobs and housing.

The Protestants were fearful of losing their cultural and political identity as their majority shrank against the faster-growing Catholic population. They were always on the alert for subversion by Irish Republican Army revolutionaries who regarded themselves as the true repository of the Irish identity and sought to force the six counties into the Republic to the South (though that, too, they regarded as an illegitimate state). The Republican dream of 'one Ireland' under the Tricolour flag was anathema to the Loyalists. They saw no poetry in the terrible beauty attending the violent birth of the Republic. The modern reality of 'one Ireland' for them was a poor priest-ridden state where Gaelic was the national language, where they would lose the benefits of the British welfare state and where their personal liberties would be compromised by the ordinances of the Roman Catholic Church. The 'special position' of the Church was then enshrined in the constitution and aggressively enforced. Divorce and the sale of contraceptives were banned; it had a plan for maternity care thrown out in 1951; and it controlled the schools, though the Irish constitution did not recognize an endowed religion. So the Protestant ('Proud to be Prod') Unionists rigged elections, controlled the Royal Ulster Constabulary (RUC) and could call up B Special part-time reservists; they maintained an omnipresent threat of violence.

The Catholics in the North developed a burning sense of resentment and frustration – but in turn they fuelled Protestant anxieties by insisting on their separate Church schools and by continuing to talk of a united Ireland. 'They are no more willing to renounce it,' our special correspondent John Whale was to write, 'than they are to renounce transubstantiation.' The constitution of the Republic of Ireland, moreover, still laid claim to the whole of the island.

But the Irish calamity is not unique. The seeds of disaster there were comparable to those sown in Iraq, comparable to the earlier desegregation traumas in the Deep South, comparable to the illusions of the Vietnam War. Having observed all of these episodes, I have insufficient reserves of humility to suppress the conviction that you can't beat honest first-hand newspaper reporting – when you can get it. Governments may know a lot more about our lives than we care to contemplate, but frequently they know less about the world than we presume. They are captive to preconceptions, electoral concerns, political affiliations, special interests and bureaucratic hierarchies that filter 'truth'. Government just cannot govern well without reliable independent reporting and criticism. No intelligence system, no bureaucracy, can offer the information provided by free competitive reporting; the cleverest agents of the secret police state are inferior to the plodding reporter of the democracy.

To Fleet Street, for many years, and its readers, Ulster was about as riveting as Ecuador. I'd taken no interest in the province myself when I edited the *Northern Echo*; in fact, I knew next to nothing about it. But the *Sunday Times* was very early in its reporting. In July 1966, when I'd just become managing editor, I didn't expect much when I read an item on the news schedule: Queen's visit to Belfast. But the reporter assigned the story was Belfast-born Cal McCrystal, who'd been beaten up covering the riots of October 1964, when a Belfast Republican club provocatively displayed the Irish Tricolour. His feature before the Queen's visit was so much more than the usual backgrounder. It was an authoritative depiction of the Protestant majority's crude apparatus of political and religious oppression, concluding that the real dilemma for the new Labour Prime Minister, Harold Wilson, was whether to allow the province to work out its own bizarre destiny or 'use reserve power to bring elementary social justice to Ulster'. McCrystal's report appeared as the paper's main feature that week and we headlined it 'John Bull's Political Slum'. In his study *How the Troubles Came to Northern Ireland,* the academic Peter Rose describes it as 'one of the very few articles in the British press during those years which made a genuine attempt to warn mainland Britain of the consequences of the failure to tackle Catholic grievances'.

I expected the feature would produce the same reaction in the Labour government as it did in me: a sense that political reforms were urgently necessary. That didn't happen. The report was immediately denounced by Stormont as biased. This made more impression on the British government than our first-hand report, because the government took its advice from the Home Office in London – which in turn took its cue from Stormont.

The pity was that this would have been a perfect time for the British government to change direction. The hard men of the Irish Republican Army trying to blast the two Irelands into one had faded; their successors, a left-wing leadership based in Dublin, opted for Marxist pamphlets and polemics rather than bombs; their agitation for a socialist workers' state implicitly recognized partition. (Happily, this lost them Irish-American funding that had always fomented violence.) The old IRA hands in the North grumbled at this pacifism, but leadership had moved principally to a new generation of educated middle-class Catholics who wanted to 'take the gun out of Irish politics'. They were building a civil rights movement that did not insist on Irish unification and was open to Protestants as well as Catholics. Even those of them who still yearned for a united Ireland, the constitutional nationalists, nonetheless set out to win social justice within the province by peaceful persuasion modelled on Martin Luther King's movement rather than by the violent over-throw of the state. The Marxist-Leninist Roy Johnston, a computer specialist, described it as trying 'to salvage the basic Enlightenment republican democratic tradition from various overlays of Catholic nationalism, Fenian conspiracies and quasi-Stalinist centralism which have infested it'.

This new peaceful coalition was the window of opportunity. In Britain, the Conservative – and Unionist – government had given way to Labour, there was a reformist Prime Minister in Belfast, Terence O'Neill, and the Catholic leaders best represented by Derry's visionary John Hume had entirely reasonable demands ('one man, one vote, removal of gerrymandered boundaries, allocation of public housing on a points system based on need'). Editorially, we sup-ported O'Neill in his struggle with the Loyalist hard-liners, and Hume in his antipathy to the bigotry of Catholic Ireland, but the haunting question in my mind is how much difference would have been made at this time by even more insistent advocacy on our part for Britain to impose its will to meet Catholic grievances, coupled with extended reporting of the kind I'd urged on the American press over treatment of the blacks in the South.

As excuse I can offer only that Northern Ireland was just one developing story. We had to rush teams to cover Israel's Six Day War, we had reporters in the midst of America's never-ending war in Vietnam, in the civil war in Nigeria and in the anarchy of the Congo. The Soviet Union and China were on the brink of a border war, and the world's first democracy was taken over by a bunch of fascist colonels. But these excuses are not good enough; news is always at an editor's throat.

It was at the end of 1968, after violent clashes between the Royal Ulster Constabulary and civil rights marchers, that I committed us to continuous serious coverage. To explore the roadblocks to reform, I hired the political correspondent of Independent Television News, John Whale, the scholarly son of an Anglican Canon; his book *The Half-Shut Eye* impressed me with its perceptions of how limited a medium television was for documenting the undercurrents in a

society. That needed context and fine print, and television is preoccupied with immediacy and images.

To monitor what was happening on the streets, I set up a rolling
team from the newsroom (two weeks in Northern Ireland, one week
off) and also ran reports by Chris Ryder, Murray Sayle and David
Holden, who wrote a graphic account of being roughly handled in a
Protestant demonstration. The chief reporter I recruited from the
Sunday Telegraph was its chief investigator Tony Geraghty, who'd
made a name for himself on the *Guardian*; he could not be typecast
by either side. He was a British subject and an Irish citizen – and a
veteran of the British Paras (later to serve as a military liaison officer
with the US forces in the Gulf War).

Geraghty's reporting convinced him that the 'pusillanimous'
Labour government was making a tragic error acquiescing in
Stormont's approval of provocative Loyalist marches in the
summer of 1969. He was right. The more radical elements of the
civil rights movement, students in the People's Democracy organization, staged a counter-march in Derry; police brutally attacked it
in the Battle of the Bogside; that was followed by wolf packs of
Catholic youths in the Falls Road area of Belfast hurling rocks and
petrol bombs at police stations. The RUC drove armoured cars into
the rioters and Protestant mobs firebombed Catholic homes. Ten
civilians and four RUC men were killed by gunfire on the night of
14–15 August. The uneasy but viable mixture of peace and gradual
reform was broken, and for good as it turned out. When the
Labour government in August 1969 sent in the British Army, it
would have been wiser at the same time to impose direct rule from
Westminster, instead of assigning the soldiers to work as common
law constables with the distrusted RUC: the ancient fault lines
remained.

Still, there was no excuse for the gross misrepresentation in
American media of the peacekeepers as an invading 'army of occupation'. Caught up in retailing Irish tribal folklore, local TV stations
in the US and the more thoughtless popular press quite ignored that
Ulster was constitutionally as much a part of Britain as Massachusetts
was of the United States; that without the Army there'd be civil war

in which the Catholics would suffer most; and that the democratic Republic of Ireland also regarded the IRA as a menace to its own democracy.

We were supportive of the soldiers caught between warring parties, but our reporting soon ran into difficulties with the Army. Geraghty happened to be on the spot when a brigadier jumped out of a staff car and strode alone and unescorted into the 'no-go' dangerously tense Falls Road where the Catholics, surrounded by 60,000 Loyalists, had barricaded themselves against mobs. 'I'm going to see Father Murphy and these Citizens Defence chappies,' said the brigadier. He'd no objection to Geraghty tagging along to the door of the vestry of St Peter's Pro-Cathedral.

The brigadier would say nothing when he came out. But among the emerging Central Citizens Defence Committee (CCDC) delegates, Geraghty recognized their chairman as a habitué of the Long Bar. He was Jimmy Sullivan, a 37-year-old leader of the IRA in the Lower Falls area. 'We've got this back of the envelope treaty with the British military,' he told Geraghty, showing him the understanding that the CCDC would open the no-go areas within three days, in return for the Army and local vigilantes looking after security to the exclusion of the distrusted RUC.

It was news, but it was news that could have consequences. The Loyalists might hate the Army talking to anyone with an IRA connection. Still, I told myself, it was also a tribute to the Army's diplomatic skills. They were going to get the barricades down and they were talking to the only people capable of persuading the community it would be safe to do so. So I published. The Loyalists rioted in protest at the idea of anyone talking to the IRA. The day after Geraghty's report, our sister paper *The Times*, briefed by Whitehall, knocked the report: 'Diligent investigations by journalists have failed to reveal that the IRA is now nothing much more than a slogan out of the past.' An Army brigadier, who was Director of Public Relations, came to my office to protest against Geraghty's 'inventive' reporting. This puzzled Geraghty. He wrote to me: 'How could what every dog in the street in Belfast knows is true be denied in London 90 minutes' air time away?'

The answer was that Belfast was then 300 years away from the Ministry of Defence and the Army. They were just not as well-informed as the reporter. General Ian Freeland, who'd been in charge for only two months, and was incensed by our report, told me later: 'The Army did not know at that stage who were current members of the IRA.' They should have if police and Army intelligence had done their homework. The Civil Rights Association opened its doors to anyone. Five days after I had received the indignant brigadier, the Scottish judge Lord Cameron issued his report on the disturbances of the previous autumn. It confirmed Geraghty's assertion that the IRA had become involved in the uneasy coalition forming the civil rights movement, though not yet as gunmen. They had virtually no firearms then to defend the Catholic areas and some graffiti around the Lower Falls in Belfast read: 'IRA = I Ran Away'. What had been political heresy on Sunday morning was by Friday a judicially tested fact. Cameron's report, reinforcing Geraghty's observations, should have led to the Army and police recognizing the weakness of their intelligence and alerted everyone to the terrible risk that defence of the Catholic ghettoes against mobs might fall to a resurgent IRA. The old equation loomed: fear − trust = IRA.

The dragon's teeth had been sown. Irish-American dollars, denied to the constitutional nationalists, started to flow again to bombers and shooters. As an admirer of American journalism, I was appalled by reports of what was being broadcast on local television in Boston, New York, Chicago and Philadelphia. They gave time to IRA front men who, without challenge, retailed propaganda and incitement. ('Violence is the only thing left . . . The only language the British ever understand is violence . . . The only real criminals in this matter are the English.') In the bars along Second Avenue in New York, near the *Sunday Times* office at 42nd Street, I was often approached to give dollars to Noraid, a charity supposedly raising money for the families of slain or imprisoned IRA men. The *Chicago Tribune* nailed the lie: 'The money bankrolls the sort of sub-humans who can pack six-inch nails around a bomb and put it in a place where women and children and tourists will gather.'

American audiences generally were given no idea of the truth that the killing was mainly the work of paramilitaries, not the security forces. Those who died as the result of Army and police intervention in the end numbered fewer than half those killed by nationalist and Loyalist paramilitaries. And of the paramilitaries, the well-armed IRA killed at twice the rate of the Loyalists.

Seeing how distorted reporting could become stiffened my resolve to keep ours as straight as possible. In view of the risks our reporters were accepting, I was resentful of the reactions in Westminster and Whitehall, which became more dismissive when Edward Heath and the Conservatives assumed power in June 1970. Basically, they consistently ignored our warnings of increased disenchantment within the Catholic community, creating a sea in which guerrillas could swim; the imposition of a curfew during the weekend of 3–4 July had a decisively adverse effect on Catholic sentiment. Against the fervent advice of a perceptive civil servant in Stormont, the government allowed Orangemen to march and bloodshed followed; Catholic homes were searched for guns while the Protestants were allowed licensed weapons. Junior Army officers in Belfast did soon realize that military actions had to accompany notable visible improvements for the community, but their superiors saw it as their mission to submit upbeat reports to London. It was what London preferred to hear.

There was much the same scenario in the war in Iraq. Not wanting to be accused of defeatism, the senior commanders shrank from conveying bad news to Washington as the insurgency gained strength – and Vice President Cheney accused reporters who conveyed the unpalatable truth of being lazy, foolish, cowardly and unpatriotic.

All the reporting we were doing was fair and first-hand, and television's brave cameramen were routinely bringing the horrors into the living rooms. But it was not possible to understand Northern Ireland by focusing on the latest outrage. Violence is always sure of space on television and in the press. Political change, being more subtle and dull, is frequently neglected until it explodes into 'inexplicable' violence.

We devoted hours to discussing what constructive suggestions we might offer on the editorial page, based on the reporting; and we organized seminars of leading figures.

There were degrees of emphasis among the group in the weekly editorial conference deciding the paper's policy, but we agreed on pressing reforms harder while recognizing that the Provos were using the civil rights movement as a cover for armed insurrection, just as the Loyalists had long feared. We assailed Democratic Congressmen in the US for appearing to condone violence; we were unsparing in criticism of a major speech by Senator Edward Kennedy drawing a parallel between Ulster and Vietnam: 'It is in most respects of a piece with the rest of his ill-researched, ill-considered and destructive speech.'

The most important consequence of tying the comment to the reporting was our conviction that Westminster would make a catastrophic mistake if it started interning people without trial but simply on suspicion. We could see the problem. The bullet-riddled bodies were there, but nobody would admit to seeing a burst of automatic fire at a group on a street corner. Court convictions were difficult to get because witnesses were frightened. Still, we felt that the crude and random measure of internment would do great damage. In March 1971 we wrote of internment: 'If it were done on a large enough scale, it would arouse more Catholic viciousness than it allayed.' And again in August 1971: 'Internment would worsen the army's chief problem which is mass Catholic hostility. More important it would carry the security forces beyond the frontier of what is ordinarily considered tolerable in a civilised society.'

Again, the government listened to Stormont, cheered on by sections of the press in Britain which had frankly done far less on-the-ground reporting than we had. In retrospect I suppose I could have started a personal lobbying campaign, but we were writing what we knew and I was mindful of H. L. Mencken's alert: 'Reporters come in as newspaper men trained to get the news; they end as tin-horn statesmen full of dark secrets and unable to write the truth if they tried.'

Three hundred and forty-two Catholic men were 'lifted' in very rough raids on houses on 9 August 1971. We were the only newspaper to come out against it; in various political encounters I was made to feel I was letting the side down, but internment was a disaster. Intelligence had been too weak to capture the most dangerous men. By November, 908 were imprisoned, many guilty of nothing more than where they lived; by December, 1,576 had been arrested and 934 released. Not a single Protestant gunman was arrested. The key Provos escaped. The advocates of internment defended it as an emergency measure following the deaths of 27 people in the first eight months of 1971, and 91 bombings in July. It had the opposite effect. In the rest of the year, more than 140 died and bombings went to over 100. In the four months from April to July, 1971, four soldiers were killed, no policemen and four civilians. In the four months after interment, 30 soldiers were killed, 11 members of the RUC and the Ulster Defence Regiment, and 73 civilians.

It was no pleasure at all to be vindicated. It was infuriating. The British public was bewildered. It was like coming into a movie halfway through. How had we got into this mess in the first place? Nothing made sense. How could Catholic women who'd come out to give cups of tea to soldiers in 1969 now be on the streets shouting to the tune of Auld Lang Syne: 'Go home, you bums, go home'? How did the Army's velvet glove develop, in August 1971, into the iron fist of internment? The monster of sectarian violence, we wrote, was well out of the cage, the issue no longer civil rights or even jobs and houses, but whether the state should exist and who should have the power and how it should be defended, an issue on which the wild men on both sides had sworn for forty years, frequently in blood, they would never back down.

Bruce Page made the inspired suggestion that Insight should be given the time and resources for a major historical reconstruction of the origins of the crisis that he would supervise. The editor of Insight was now John Barry, the disconcertingly omniscient baby-faced reporter who'd done well on Philby. He took himself off to the province with four reporters and for three months they engaged in questioning hundreds, retracing what each of them had personally experienced and done: Catholics and Protestants, householders and activists, generals and IRA leaders, politicians and civil servants, newspaper observers in the North and Dublin, lawyers and academics. 'It's proving absurdly easy to get everyone to talk,' Barry wrote me. 'I think it's because nobody has ever asked them to look back.'

Insight's report, with help from Whale and Geraghty, tracked the origins of the crisis from partition to the first stirrings of the civil rights protests and the rebirth of the IRA. I thought I was up to speed on Northern Ireland, but I read it in November 1971 with a mounting sense of shock. It was like rewinding the tape on a terrible crime. It had been an unjust society, but here step by step one could see how it began to descend into murderous chaos and why; and why the reel was still unwinding. It was heartbreaking to read of the misperceptions, peaceful protest failing and degenerating, old prejudices hardening, decent people feeling betrayed, so that the men with guns came to prevail. Westminster had insisted that the IRA was just a small bunch of thugs and troublemakers who could soon be defeated. There was an idea in parts of the press that it was all got up by communist infiltrators. 'The present turmoil in Ulster,' the *Daily Mail* said, 'has been conceived on Maoist–Castroist–Trotskyist lines.'

The Insight portrait of a disintegrating society, on the contrary, demonstrated that the province faced a crisis of governance for which no solution could emerge from military action, for all the innumerable acts of forbearance and individual courage by soldiers assigned to policing. The real base of terrorism was not a correspondence course from the Tupamaros, but profound Catholic distress and disillusion in the North and tenacious Catholic sympathy in the South. 'Too long a sacrifice,' wrote W. B. Yeats, 'can make a stone of the heart.' The people who had refused to face Catholic disillusion had only prolonged the agony.

Initially, I'd cleared two full pages for the report. I was on the stone as trays of type arrived a couple of hours before press time. It was clear there was too much metal, not enough space – and still more copy was landing on the printers' desk. It was all too good to cut so I cleared still more space. And still the copy arrived. I gambled on writing an announcement that this was a two-part series. It transpired we had more than enough to justify that impromptu decision.

The team's 50,000 words, carefully edited by Hall and Page, occupied eight pages in the end, the longest news report the paper had ever published. I ran 'Perspective on Ulster' over two weeks in November 1971. It wasn't just long, however, one of those lengthy newspaper series we mentally categorize as too important to read. Thanks to the skill of the writers and editors, it was a gripping fast-paced narrative, taking the reader into the minds of the competing characters, all acting for what they thought best and together producing the worst.

There was an enormous and typically extreme reaction. The newspaper was lauded by some for 'saving Ireland from insanity' when in reality we could only have hoped to accelerate a political debate. Alternatively, the reporters were accused of 'doing the dirty work of the IRA'.

There was an important news fallout from our commitment to writing an accelerated history of the troubles. Insight's researcher in Belfast, Parin Janmohamed, made the rounds of Catholic lawyers who were trying to represent some of the men seized in the internment swoops by the police and the Army. The lawyers were too frightened to say much, but in one of the offices she induced a lawyer to give her half a dozen handwritten statements smuggled out of prison. They laid out what internees claimed had happened to them but also recounted the alleged experiences of a few others. These latter allegations were second-hand, but dramatic: they told of men under interrogation being hooded, made to stand spread-eagled for hours, and deprived of sleep. She went back to Insight's hotel headquarters saying: 'You won't believe what I've just been told.' And from under her donkey jacket she produced the smuggled statements.

According to one of them, written by a Michael Farrell of People's Democracy, he'd been forced to run barefoot over a path of broken bricks at Girdwood Barracks. Barry hired a small plane to fly over Girdwood to see if the basic layout corresponded with the statements. It did, but the brick path story didn't sound credible. Insight asked the Army. A path of broken bricks? Nonsense. Irish fantasies.

Barry talked his way into a Catholic convent which had grounds adjoining the barracks. He climbed a tree to see over the wall and there, facing him, was a long path of broken bricks, the foundations for a concrete path still to be laid. He remembers clambering down, thinking: 'Oh, my God, what's been going on here?'

The brick path meant Farrell's allegation might be true, but it was not solid evidence. Insight was also told of Alsatians snapping at the internees as they ran over the bricks. Farrell's statement said one of the dogs had taken a bite out of the sleeve of his jacket. Barry persuaded Farrell's wife to get the jacket from prison. One sleeve was ripped. He took it to a forensic chemist. Yes, he reported, there were saliva stains around the tear, though he could not be absolutely sure they were canine.

Barry was convinced Farrell was telling the truth, but he was baffled by talk of hooding, wall-standing and deprivation of sleep at somewhere other than Girdwood. All the internees had been roughly treated, but if the statements were to be believed a few had been subjected to five techniques that became known as highly coercive interrogation (HCI): covering the prisoner's head with an opaque cloth with no ventilation (hooding); standing a prisoner against a wall, hands raised with fingertips to the wall, for as long as twenty hours; subjecting him to high-pitched 'white' noise; depriving him of all but bread and water; and depriving him of sleep.

These practices potentially transgressed the Geneva Convention barring cruel and degrading treatment. But how to check the facts? Nobody on the team had ever heard of anything like this before. In December 1971 the IRA had staged a great jamboree of a press conference in Dublin, putting on show three IRA men who'd escaped from jail in Ulster and claimed they'd been tortured with lighted cigarettes and needles in their bones. Photographs of defaced limbs flashed across the nation's television screens. The *Guardian* front-paged the story: IRA Men Show Wounds.

These horrific details of burning and bone scraping were, as it happens, without foundation. On 19 December 1971 Lewis Chester, a former Insight editor, documented the falsity of it all in a way far more effective than official denials. He was able to do it because for some time he'd been investigating on the ground, and by hard work uncovered some apparently genuine allegations of ill treatment under interrogation. Comparing these earlier statements and doctors' reports on the IRA men, Chester demonstrated the December 1971 allegations were fiction.

How did newspapers and television press correct their earlier acceptance of the false stories? They didn't. Of the papers which had splashed the original story, only the *Guardian* bothered with a follow-up, but it was brief and relegated to the back page (*The Times* had played the original story much more cautiously). And on television, there was silence.

We'd learned to be very wary of IRA propaganda, always playing the victim card, but Barry thought of someone who could help us on the nature of the techniques allegedly being used. An SAS man we'll call 'Mike' had spent hours telling Insight of his adventures in the Yemen in 1965 running a British/Israeli/Saudi covert campaign against Egyptian troops intervening in a civil war there. Suddenly one day Mike got scared he might be identified and asked Insight to drop the whole story. They did. Back in London from Belfast they took him to their favourite watering hole, the Bunghole at the bottom of Hatton Gardens. He felt he owed them one, so in the tiny glassed-in private cubicle which was Insight's home away from home he said: 'Sure, those are the interrogation techniques taught at Ashford.' He was referring to the Army Intelligence headquarters and opened up a bit more to say the five techniques were designed to induce sensory deprivation and disorientation and Ulster was the first time they were tried out for real. They were seen as a more humane alternative to the electrodes used for interrogation in other countries, but they'd been originally developed, I learned, as resistance training for Special Forces personnel and RAF aircrews who might be captured, particularly by Warsaw Pact countries.

No one with a grievance understates it, but it wasn't conceivable that the wretched internees could have known enough to make it all up. The question then was whether the interrogations had taken place somewhere Insight could check, if not Girdwood. The victims had been taken up in helicopters and flown, they were told, to the mainland. We wasted a week checking bases in Britain. One of the reporters thought to make friends with an air controller who said yes, the copters had indeed flown eastwards but had then turned round and landed back in Northern Ireland at the Palace military barracks, Holywood. But how could we substantiate this? Another reporter pointed out that 'Mike' had said doctors had to be present at these interrogations. The doctors must have been housed somewhere, so Insight combed the hotels around the base. Bingo – they found a chatty receptionist who told them about all those nice young Brit military medical men who'd stayed there for two weeks – at just the right time. The reporter checked names and dates against the register. They tallied.

At about the same time, and quite independently, John Whale came back to the office from Stormont to write a report incorporating a remark by a Northern Ireland Cabinet Minister: 'Those fellows are singing like birds . . .' I didn't have what CBS and the *New Yorker* had with Abu Ghraib prison – photographic documentation. I had to make up my mind on the basis of the interviews, but we now had a multiplicity of statements of ill-treatment tending to corroborate one another in substance, and yet made by men who could not all have coordinated their stories. I was satisfied it all added up to a prima facie case.

The next question was whether there was a public interest argument against publication. I knew it would embroil the paper in still more controversy between those who would declare it unthinkable Britain would do such a thing and those who felt that nothing was too harsh for the internees. I shared the repugnance for the unspeakable cruelties of the IRA. It was an evil enemy, its methods indiscriminately vicious; there could be nothing but admiration for the skill and bravery of the soldiers who disarmed its murderous explosive devices. Introducing the 'Perspective on Ulster' series, arguing that Ulster as then constituted had no future, we ran this editorial indictment:

The IRA is a wholly damnable and despicable body, made up of men who pervert and ravage Ireland's energies in pursuit of an

ideal which is irrelevant to the country's real needs. Their tactics
of indiscriminate and brutal slaughter are proof of a heartless-
ness which the noblest cause could not condone.

But further issues were raised. The first was that there was far from
any certainty the men in prison were members of the IRA or guilty
of any crime. The operation was too haphazard. The second was
that our report might incite retaliation. But one of the ethical philosophies I'd absorbed at Durham was Immanuel Kant's maxim that one
should act as if the principle one followed would become a universal law. And it seemed to me that condoning cruelty by keeping silent,
for whatever reason, was immoral. So I ran the Insight–Whale report
on the front page, albeit with just a modest single-column headline,
'How Ulster Internees Are Made to Talk'.

We were roundly condemned. A group of Tory MPs came angrily
to my office to say what I'd done was close to treason. The establishment mouthpiece the *Sunday Telegraph*, which had done very
little front-line reporting, fuelled the fire. The line of argument
seemed to be that if the British Army was doing something it must be
right, and even if it was wrong it must be supported. *Crossbow*, the
influential magazine of the Bow Group of younger Conservatives,
caricatured me sinisterly reading the *Sunday Times* with the headline
'Army Atrocity'. When I entered a reception one evening, the dila-
tory Home Secretary, Reginald Maudling, called out: 'Here comes
the editor of the IRA Gazette.'

This was rich. We'd been unequivocal in expressing our detestation; we had exposed the IRA torture story the rest of the press had
retailed and never corrected; we'd prominently featured the sufferings of the victims of bomb outrages; and we'd depicted the lonely
ordeals of Army patrols.

To his credit, Prime Minister Edward Heath appointed Sir Edmund
Compton to head a three-man inquiry into our report. We were
vindicated. Of eleven internees questioned in depth, Sir Edmunds's
report said: 'We consider that the following constitute physical ill
treatment: posture on the wall, hooding, noise, deprivation of sleep,
diet of bread and water. On the Girdwood bricks [12 names], we

conclude that the men concerned may have suffered some measure of unintended hardship.'

Subsequently, on a complaint by the Irish Republic, the European Court of Human Rights found the five techniques used were 'cruel, inhuman and degrading'. It stopped short of calling them torture, but the British government gave a 'solemn undertaking' they would never be used again.

In five years of reporting Ulster, everyone involved had been acutely sensitive that we'd gone out on a limb with every story that did not regurgitate the conventional wisdom. What happened on Bloody Sunday, 30 January 1972, tested our rigour.

In the space of twenty minutes in Londonderry, a company of British paratroopers fired 107 high-velocity bullets that killed thirteen unarmed Catholics and wounded fourteen. The event was immediately overlaid by propaganda from both sides, and as I write thirty-six years later has still not been resolved. The Bogsiders were outraged. They believed a massacre had been planned. The British government immediately insisted that the paratroopers, sent into the confines of the Bogside to arrest violent rioters, had been fired on by IRA gunmen – and fired on first.

Controversy has persisted on what I did about Bloody Sunday. Put baldly, why did the editor of the *Sunday Times* fail to publish an immediate article on the shootings? Was it because the writers 'diverged from the official line', as the *London Review of Books* phrased it? Did I 'help to bury the evidence' that the British Army planned the shooting in advance, as alleged in 1998 by James Ledbetter in New York's *Village Voice*.

It is true I did not publish an article by two *Sunday Times* reporters. The reasons were different from the one implied.

Immediately, when I heard of the shooting that Sunday evening, I reached out for John Barry, the chief author of our reconstruction 'Perspective on Ulster'. He was on a bizarre holiday, riding a camel deep in the Sahara with the Tunisian anti-drug patrols. I got hold of Murray Sayle and asked him to leave at once for Derry. He'd covered Northern Ireland extensively, beginning in 1965, and in particular the riots that followed the internments in August 1971. The newsroom assigned two reporters, Derek Humphry and Peter Pringle, who had contacts in Londonderry.

Sayle is a legend in journalism, an unmistakable buccaneering figure with a large broken nose acquired in graduating from Sydney University, and a spellbinding retailer of stories. His hilarious novel *A Crooked Sixpence* recounts his time as a vice reporter on the *People* newspaper, exposing prostitution rings when editor Sam Campbell's instructions were that the reporters offered sex for money should watch the lady disrobe, then 'make an excuse and leave'. For the *Sunday Times* Murray had climbed Everest, sailed the Atlantic, reported in the battlegrounds of Vietnam, Israel, Czechoslovakia, Jordan (Black September), Bangladesh and anywhere else that a foreign editor had needed a reporter who could talk his way through a brick wall.

Murray was the principal author of the report that reached our office on Thursday afternoon. Before I had a chance to read it, both Page and Hall, the responsible editors, came in, very concerned. 'You can't publish Murray's piece.' Why not? Page was especially vehement. He said the piece implied that an unprovoked Army had plotted the killings, a serious charge we should publish if it could be substantiated, but this piece did not do that. The sources had not been subjected to enough scrutiny. The findings were inconsistent. There were too many 'internal contradictions'. It just did not meet the *Sunday Times* standards. It would damage the credibility established by years of work on Ulster.

I said I would read the piece and consider all their objections. It is generally a good rule not to let head office second-guess the man in the field, and Sayle was revered – but Page and Hall had investigated and edited many contentious stories. They were zealous guardians of the paper's unimpeachable investigative record, neither beholden to the other. The idea that either of them would toe 'an official line' is ludicrous; the very idea of an official line would simply rouse their hostility.

Reading the piece, I noted it said right at the start that not a single shot had been fired at the soldiers, then later quoted one Official IRA

man saying he did fire a shot from a .38 pistol, then quoted Gilles
Peress, the French Magnum photographer who brought back devastating pictures, saying he heard two pistol shots near Free Derry
corner when there were no paratroopers there. This inconsistency
wasn't confronted. I could see the reporters had worked hard. The
background to the whole tragedy was lucid. The tumultuous scene in
Derry was vividly depicted, assisted by a graphic street map of the
action by John Butterworth. But it bothered me. As research, it was
probably as good a job as anyone could do in four days, but it went
beyond quoting witnesses. It tried to reconstruct a chaotic, fast-
moving scene, reconcile conflicting stories, and reach conclusions.
That is an objective I would normally applaud – I am critical of
reporting restricted to reciting 'he said, she said' – but there just
wasn't the evidence in the copy I had. My immediate thought then
was whether we could preserve the bones of the reporting while editing for internal consistency and dismantling the shaky hypothesis.

At this point James Evans made an appearance. We called him
The Enabler because, uncharacteristic of press lawyers, he liked to
find a way to justify publication. He'd come in to support Hall and
Page. The evidence wasn't good enough.

Before I had time to invite Page and Hall to discuss what we might
do, the news desk rang to say the government had appointed Lord
Widgery to conduct a judicial inquiry. This complicated matters. The
whole question of whether or not to publish would be moot if the
Lord Chief Justice decided that the rule of contempt of court applied.
I telephoned the Lord Chief Justice. I thought he might not take the
call – judges in Britain don't jump to the telephone for pressmen –
but I got through. I said we had done a great deal of interviewing
and proposed to publish this Sunday. We also had compelling photographs. I'd told him I presumed contempt would not apply since
nobody had yet been accused.

It would be an exaggeration to say he was aghast, but he made it
very clear it would be 'unhelpful' to publish anything and yes, he
would apply the rules of contempt. I told him that we would continue our own vigorous inquiries. I withheld the Sayle–Humphry
article, but that week I took the chance of publishing the shocking

photographs by Gilles Peress of unarmed men being shot. They represented photojournalism of the highest order so I gave them prominence. I ran an article setting out the questions Widgery would have to answer. 'One remarkable circumstance,' we noted, 'is that the government chose first to announce what the facts of the matter in its own view were, and then to set up the inquiry afterwards.'

At the same time, I gave the Sayle article back to Hall and Page, asked them to make use of the reporting, but get John Barry off his camel and without delay set in train our own parallel inquiry. 'You have to be ready as soon as Widgery reports,' I told them.

'It was the most intense period of our lives,' remembers John Barry, who led his team into the Bogside. 'We camped out at the City Hotel fleapit' (later blown up). Insight interviewed 250 witnesses, including members of the IRA. It was essential to hear what they had to say; those who assert you can never 'talk to the enemy' are more interested in party-line propaganda than the difficult business of weighing evidence.

In April 1972, eleven weeks after the shootings, Lord Chief Justice Widgery issued his report. He judged some of the paratrooper firing had 'bordered on the reckless' but he basically exonerated the Army of any premeditated plot to kill. But the report was not the whitewash the members of the Catholic community immediately said it was. It demolished the rash initial statement by the Minister of State for Defence that the paras were in Londonderry as a precaution, not (as Widgery found) as an arrest force. Widgery confirmed that one of the thirteen people killed was an unarmed man shot from behind while crawling; that four other men were killed by shots fired without justification; that an excessive number of rounds was fired; that grounds for identifying targets were nebulous; and that all this happened in a battalion operation not clearly authorized at brigade level, discountenanced by the police and launched at a time when other methods of keeping order were succeeding.

Insight was ready. They had amassed 500 photographs from all the sources that day, laboriously sorted these into sequence and from them identified the witnesses who had been present at critical moments. Then they had tracked these people down and questioned them. They tried, above all, not to create a seamless narrative when there wasn't one. Nobody in the Army, press, television, rioters, politicians, could offer a single perspective on a kaleidoscope of images where a second of life was an eternity. We laid out what we knew, made clear what we didn't know.

Insight's four-page report was critical of Widgery. It differed from him on his certainty that the Army had fired only in response to IRA fire – but nor did it endorse the Sayle–Humphry conclusion that not a single shot had been fired by the IRA. 'The Provisionals admit to a burst of machine gun fire from the area of the Bogside Inn which is recorded by the army after 4.40. It is certain that they fired other shots. Eye witness accounts vary from none to 50 but witnesses agree all shots were fired after 4.30 [when the army ceased fire]'. The vicious assaults of the more reckless rioters were acknowledged, but the government was faulted for authorizing an attempt to scoop them up using heavily armed paratroopers. Militarily it went wrong in plan and operation; soldiers did shoot at obviously unarmed civilians. We added the rider that while the paratroopers' response was out of proportion, it had to be remembered that of the 100-odd involved, the vast majority of soldiers, under great stress, did not fire, let alone kill anyone.

Through the intervening years, Bloody Sunday has remained an open wound. In 1992, in the small Irish magazine *Fingerpoint*, which covers the community in Derry, Murray Sayle was reported as saying: 'I don't blame Harold Evans for not publishing the story.' He reiterated this in a series of emails with the editor Peter Baker, but added: 'Publication might have saved much subsequent bloodshed.'

Here I part company with him. The original article, with its errors and shaky imputations, was likely to inflame feelings still more, rather than do justice to all those involved. The complexity of Bloody Sunday is exemplified by the fact that the tribunal of inquiry set up by Prime Minister Tony Blair under Lord Saville began sitting in 1998 with the power of subpoena, had by 2007 taken evidence under oath from 900 people, including the Prime Minister at the time, Edward Heath, and by 2008 had still not reported.

Among the Insight group, John Barry, Phil Jacobson and Peter Pringle were summoned to testify, as were Sayle, Geraghty and I. (Pringle and Jacobson have also written a well-researched book, *Those Are Real Bullets: Bloody Sunday, Derry, 1972*.) The entire Insight archive on Bloody Sunday, including their notebooks at the time, Murray Sayle's rejected article and my memos, had been volunteered to the Commission of Inquiry (before it asked for them) by the *Sunday Times* management after I had left, surprisingly without consulting any of us as to the sensitivity of sources. They were a mother lode of material because they included scores of statements taken in the immediate aftermath of the event, before either side – Army or community – had had time to concert its version of events, especially valuable since Insight's previous work in Ireland meant that they were able to question people, for example IRA men, who would talk to nobody else. There was no other comparable single source.

I was and remain proud of our Bloody Sunday reporting. We revised the articles we'd published as 'Perspective on Ulster', corrected the inevitable errors, and extended the reports as a paperback book called simply *Ulster*. It was a bestseller, which paid for the costs of the reporting, because to minds numbed with the cruelties it made some kind of sense out of the insanities. The main characters were portrayed as rather more than cardboard cutouts, but succinctly, and each step on the road to Armageddon made maddeningly explicable from that point of view. It was one of the most important initiatives I ever undertook and made me more ambitious for that kind of contextual journalism. It was possible only because of the skill and integrity of reporters willing to subordinate their individual egos in a collective effort to present as truthful an account as they could, informed by narrative energy but untainted by preconception.

The United Kingdom government, the British Army, the Provisional IRA and certain Protestant activists continued to take positions they thought points of principle. Through the Anglo-Irish agreement of 1985, and the Good Friday Agreement of 1998, the rate of wanton

death declined with appalling slowness. Only the IRA was not willing to stop. Yet gradually after the event, intelligence successes on the
IRA side could be seen to have fallen further and further behind
those on the British side. John Hume worked hard to convince Gerry
Adams, leader of Sinn Fein, the political wing of the IRA, that there
was yet another historic opportunity for peace. In 2001, on a side
wind after the destruction of the World Trade Center, American
money for IRA causes ceased to flow. Another change at last brought
Protestant firebrand Ian Paisley and the IRA's Gerry Adams into a
kind of fellowship.

Such understanding as the two ageing enemies have pieced
together, they could have enjoyed at any time in the previous thirty-
five years following the tripartite 1973 Sunningdale power-sharing
agreement between the British and Irish governments and Northern
Ireland's leaders.

Millions of words have been written about 'The Northern Ireland
Question', but just four lines of verse by the poet Desmond Egan
have stayed in my mind as an expression of the tragic futility of all
the hate:

> *two wee girls*
> *were playing tig near a car . . .*
> *how many counties would you say*
> *are worth their scattered fingers?*

19

SHOWDOWNS

I opened the description of my *Sunday Times* years with a photograph on my wall of an editorial conference. I close with another photograph that is seared into my consciousness: a lightly bearded tall man in a Russian fur hat, deeply tanned in midwinter and wearing dark sunglasses. He is exultantly linking arms with a group of others outside our offices in Gray's Inn Road in 1980; in the foreground is a coffin labelled 'Sunday Times'.

The man is Reg Brady, a communist 'father of the chapel' in the pressroom. In more prosaic terminology that's a trade union shop steward, in his case representing the unskilled casual workers who helped to man the basement presses. His key achievement was to shut down the *Sunday Times* for a year and pave the way for its acquisition by Rupert Murdoch. It was not a solo effort. Brady's fellow unionist, a clerk who was father of the clerical chapel, Barry Fitzpatrick, had a hand in it; so did the members of another union chapel, the 100 or so machine minders in the pressroom, led by a squat, tight-lipped man called Vic Dunn. They were perpetually fighting with Brady's members about pay differentials and who-did-what, arguments that held up the production of the newspaper. These were of graver concern than the multitude of demarcation sensitivities I found on first arriving in Fleet Street; every item of work was the jealous preserve of one union or another. If I hung up a picture myself, unplugged a reading light or changed a light bulb on my desk, I was told the heavens would fall. 'Good job nobody saw you do that,' said the administrative editor. 'We might have had a work stoppage.'

Was he serious? I'd laughed like everyone else at the farcical antics of Peter Sellers playing Fred Kite the shop steward in the vintage 1959 film comedy *I'm All Right, Jack*, but thought of it as confined to the Midlands car industry. Our relatively small workplace at the *Northern Echo* in Darlington had been nothing like that, apart from the traditional prohibition against a journalist touching metal type in the composing room. At the *Sunday Times*, I was pleased to see one secretary reading a novel every day. I simply preferred she did it in her own time rather than the office, but every effort to move this studiously redundant young woman to work at typewriter and telephone or some other form of hard labour was regarded by Barry Fitzpatrick as the Rape of the Sabine Women.

It would be fair to say that we in management did not excel in guerrilla warfare at the *Sunday Times*. It escalated in the economic squalls of the 1970s and we became increasingly exasperated. The ink had not dried on an agreement before one or other of the chapels broke it. Fitzpatrick, a fluent, nattily dressed clerk in his thirties, had a genius for ceaseless negotiation stimulated by management's expectation that his members would do the work (mainly processing advertising) they were paid for. Brady had a different wheeze. He and his union had insisted that 540 casual workers were needed to get the paper out. Only half of the 540 actually bothered to show up at all on Saturdays, but 540 pay packets were collected and signed for every week. Managements throughout Fleet Street closed a blind eye to this 'old Spanish custom', but our labour editor, Eric Jacobs, was willing to venture into the basement with a flashlight. He discovered the Spanish custom was so engrained that, apparently, we had working in the *Sunday Times* pressroom none other than M. Mouse of Sunset Boulevard, Hollywood, and one week, big joke, another payment receipt bore the name of Marmaduke Hussey, the managing director of Times Newspapers. We were tensed for a work stoppage when I published this story, but Brady and his merry men took it in their stride, sure that nobody would dare to do anything about it. They reckoned without the tax authorities, who were gratifyingly curious and eventually reported that in Fleet Street more than 50 per cent of the pay packets in newspaper pressrooms were drawn under fraudulently false names.

Corruption was only one goblin in the serial nightmare. Wildcat stoppages and downright sabotage were others. If management demurred over some new demand, the pressroom chapels damaged production; a favourite dodge was to accidentally leave chewing gum on a reel of newsprint in the presses, producing a paper break and time-consuming rethreading. Thousands of copies failed to reach readers. In 1978, the *Sunday Times* was unable to fulfil all the orders on nine occasions; we became known as the 'Sunday Sometimes'. The importance of the news itself made no difference. In July 1977, the European Commission of Human Rights report included as an appendix our long-suppressed draft article on the thalidomide children. The news came from Strasbourg at noon on Friday. The machine minders chose this occasion of editorial triumph to ramp up a running battle with management on the number of minders required to print the 72-page paper. The run began with only eight of the nine presses we needed. We fell badly behind.

It was line management's job to sort this out. I was on the phone every hour. They answered my entreaties by trying again to reason with the minders. I didn't want to complicate the lives of these duty managers – the stress of dealing with the crews undoubtedly led to the heart attack that felled the director in charge – but at midnight, as anger overtook despair, I invited Vic Dunn and his chapel committee to my office to tell them of the significance of the thalidomide article. I beseeched them to work normally and argue later. I thought I'd persuaded them that extortion on this issue would be immoral. Their response was to persist with their inaction, losing us 540,000 copies, one third of the print.

Much more comprehensible to me than such bloody-mindedness in pressroom and clerical was a collision of tradition and technology. I was an early addict of the computer. In 1954, as a science reporter,

I was introduced at Britain's National Physical Laboratory to code-breaker Alan Turing's Automatic Computing Engine (ACE) which, wondrously then, informed the waiting world what day my birthday would be twenty-five years hence. I must have been one of the first British newsmen to use a touch screen and video stylus, in 1973, on a visit to innovators along Boston's Route 128. I came back from a tour of American newspapers to enthuse about the computer for typesetting and for research.

Management didn't need any urging to adopt computer-assisted typesetting. A number of my editorial colleagues did. They were troubled that acceptance of the computer would take jobs away from the Linotype operators who set the type for stories and classified advertising and the 'comps' who assembled the type into pages. We had long bonded with these men. Some of them joined editorial for a friendly post-production beer in the Blue Lion. The comps were cheerful allies in the weekly battle to meet press times, loyal to the paper, disgusted by the anarchy in the pressroom. Having helped to set my RAF newspaper by hand, and written about typography, I was still in love with the whole romance of hot metal, and appreciated the pleasure they took in their jealous craftsmanship. I spoke their language. I thought we could work out a civilized transition that, by attrition and retraining, would keep the comps at work in the company.

It would be more costly, but such an arrangement would be equitable – and it was essential for the future of the *Sunday Times*. As a text-heavy newspaper, access to the computer would save millions in money and hours of time. When every minute counted, it was ridiculous for journalists to type at the clunky keyboard of a typewriter, manually returning the carriage, and then have the same keystrokes duplicated by a typesetter – a typesetter who had no use for a facility the computer offered of an accurate word count or the ability to transpose paragraphs without starting to type all over again. Moreover, as an investigative newspaper I was eager for us to embrace computers for basic research (though even my untutored enthusiasm underestimated quite how valuable it would be).

In a negotiation with the printers' union, we proposed a phased introduction over several years with the men most affected guaranteed employment for life. The adroitly charming anarchist of the Far Left of the Labour government, Tony Benn, referred to this as an attempt to impose our wishes by force. Our own workers might well have been amenable, but the national union leaders rejected every inducement out of hand, fearful that what we did would set a precedent for the whole industry. We got nowhere in endless negotiations, so for three years the computers we'd optimistically purchased lay unused under dustsheets, ominously referred to as 'The New Technology'. By 1979, nobody in Fleet Street had been able to introduce computers and display screens (then unappealingly called VD units for visual display), though they were in all the American newsrooms I visited.

These are only glimpses of the obduracy that undermined the success of the *Sunday Times*. I was depressed and, frankly, bewildered by it all. Why couldn't the wreckers, as I saw them, realize they were hazarding the whole ship? I had the conceit that I could make contact with working men of my dad's generation. In my no doubt sentimental reflections, they seemed to me to exemplify the cliché of 'solid working-class values', preserving their natural dignity as they struggled through the bad times to keep their families together, proud of being able to do 'an honest day's work', noticeably distancing themselves from the 'slackers' and 'scroungers' among them.

Perhaps I was so disappointed because I was nostalgic for the mythic North of my childhood which began to vanish when close-knit *Coronation Street* neighbourhoods with terraced homes and corner shops and pubs were replaced by drably anonymous housing estates where the 'telly' glowed every evening, inciting acquisitive envies. In the 'bad old days' people were poorer, they were more or less stuck in the place where they were born and grew up, but there was comfort in being rooted in a community and recognized within it as a good neighbour. The wartime spirit of solidarity had been very real, but it had evaporated along with the British Empire and the pride and affection for its glory that everybody felt but was not willing to admit. Dean Acheson kept saying in the 1960s that Britain had lost an empire and had yet to find a role, and as a people we seemed to have lost one identity and were struggling to find another. The class divisions had faded, we assured ourselves, and we'd had reformist Labour governments, but the positions of power and privilege were still predominantly occupied by Oxbridge as they had been for a few centuries. What would George Orwell make of it all?

Whatever historians have to say about our disintegrating society, cut adrift from its traditional moorings, I cannot blame anyone else for the personal stresses I felt in these years. In the crises of the 1970s I created a crisis of my own. After twenty years of a serene marriage to Enid, moving from Durham to Manchester to Darlington and to London and raising three children together, I fell in love with a young woman half my age. Torn by the pull of a magnetic North and a magnetic South, I inflicted great pain on others, my own pain the least of it.

Tina Brown came into my life through her writing. The late Pat Kavanagh, the literary agent (who was later married to the novelist Julian Barnes), sent me some clippings from the *New Statesman* magazine. She urged me to think about commissioning features from the writer who was about to graduate in English studies at Oxford. 'She's very young, won a place at Oxford when she was 16, but has a wicked eye.' I put the articles in my briefcase; they got buried under other submissions and manuscripts from agents pitching book serials for the Review Front. I didn't get round to the necessary archaeology until some two weeks later. One of the Tina Brown clippings was a description of the stab-in-the-back gossip fest at a *Private Eye* lunch in Soho to which she'd been invited by the literary critic Auberon Waugh, who'd admired her contributions to the Oxford university magazine. The Cabinet Minister Richard Crossman was the guest of honour, i.e. he was in the hacks' hot seat where victims were goaded to sing for their supper with confidences the *Eye* would wittily betray in the next issue. This Ms Brown's column about the lunch was hilarious. I'd normally have passed it to Ian Jack, the editor of our Look feature page in what used to be the women's section, but feeling guilty at my delay in reading the submission I got on the phone at once to her to say how much I enjoyed her writing and I would like her to come in to meet Mr Jack.

'So pleased you liked my columns,' she said. 'But sorry, not today, my husband has friends coming round for dinner.'

Wait a minute! Married before she'd even left Oxford? Wasn't that carrying precocity too far?

She went on to ask how it was that I'd come across her writing in a Spanish magazine. It transpired that the Tina Brown I was talking to was known to her husband as Tina, but she was Bettina Brown, indeed a sharp writer but Tina Brown's mother. The husband whose dinner party took priority over the needs of the *Sunday Times* was a celebrated Pinewood film producer, George Brown.

Duly fricasseed by Ian Jack for her lack of provincial training, the correct Tina Brown was nonetheless given a few trial freelance assignments by the paper and the colour magazine. Her entry was apparently eased by the fact, which I hadn't realized, that she was known to the critics at the *Sunday Times*. They'd named her as the winner of the paper's annual student drama contest for her play *Under the Bamboo Tree*, a comic ménage à trois. A year or so into her freelance work, I heard she was going to America to write a new play. She asked if anyone could give her introductions, and I said I'd drop a note to induce my new friend S. J. Perelman to see her. I'd published a few pieces by Perelman, the resident wit at the *New Yorker* who had authored a couple of scripts for the Marx Brothers, and the screenplay for *Around the World in Eighty Days*. The result two months later was a cross letter from Perelman:

I don't know why I am being cordial to a man who wrote me way back on November 1st that a beautiful blonde playwright (who had won your drama award) was coming here and would phone me. The only blonde I have seen around here is a Polish maid with fat thighs and no chest who persistently spills ammonia on my suede shoes. This can't be the woman you meant, Harry, or else you have a low opinion of me as a judge of feminine sexuality. Was Tina real or merely the product of an erotic opium dream?

He forgave me when they did meet and they became soul mates.

Late in 1974 when I was in New York myself, I agreed to listen to some feature ideas Tina had, but I ran late returning to the Regency Hotel where I had arranged a dinner meeting of Insight reporters and the New York office manager. We were in the middle of our investigation of a scandal, the deaths of 346 people in the world's most fatal air crash, near Paris, caused by a DC-10 airliner shedding in flight a cargo door known to be defective. I'd been summoned to a court in California to press our claim for access to secret company documents and, preoccupied by our discussions, I forgot Tina Brown was still waiting. My meeting ran way beyond dinner so I suggested she write me a memo I promised to read when I got back to London. We corresponded about her work, and then about newspapers and literature and life, and so our relationship began. I fell in love by post.

It was absurd. She was twenty-five years younger and courted by the likes of the enfant terrible Martin Amis and, I discovered, our own dashing star reporter David Blundy. When it became clear to her how much I was attracted, she gave up freelance reporting for my paper so that there could be no question that any success she gained might be attributed to having caught the boss's eye. She moved to write features for the rival *Sunday Telegraph* and won the Catherine Pakenham Award as Young Woman Journalist of the Year.

My infatuation, I told myself, was a typical mid-life crisis, get over it. But I couldn't. Sporadic panicky 'goodbye and good luck' separations, initiated by both of us with resolve and good intentions, failed to last. One crazy night, when she was in Spain with her parents, I got on my BMW bike and raced to the airport for the last plane to Malaga, realizing upon landing after midnight that I hadn't bothered to find out precisely where in somewhere called San Pedro di Alcantara Mr and Mrs Brown lived. Nor did my Spanish phrase book help me with, 'Do you know where I can find the Englishman who came to Spain before the civil war, made films out of Pinewood, speaks Catalan and has a young blonde daughter about five foot six?'

I was ashamed that I had begun a secret life, separated from Enid. I took a company flat next door to the *Sunday Times* office, ostensibly to be close to work. The habit of quick decision-making didn't travel a couple of doors from the office to the company flat. I could disentangle the complications in deciding whether and how to take on the government over publication of the Crossman diaries, but I couldn't sort out my life. For two whole horribly fraught years, I preferred to park my conscience while I wrestled with nerve-racking events at the paper.

Tina was deeply conflicted, too, about her association with a married man. She kept trying to withdraw, but the bond we had, professional and personal, was too deep to break. I was the older, supposedly more responsible one, but the thought of living without her completely paralysed me. I moved from the large bleak company apartment to the tiny flat she rented in Bloomsbury. If she was in town and not on assignment for the *Sunday Telegraph*, we'd walk to nearby Charlotte Street in Soho to our favourite Greek restaurant, oblivious of everything about us. I was enraptured by her and her innocent integrity and wit; she was as tormented as me by what was happening to us, simultaneously rejoicing and regretting.

When we escaped London together we retreated to the safe haven of both our childhood summers – the English seaside. By the mid-1970s, people who wanted to bake in the sun had fled by the million on package tours to the Costa del Sol, so there was an almost ethereal, seductively solitary air around the uncrowded British resorts, with their half-empty, windswept Victorian piers and timeless boarding houses advertising 'Vacancy' in the front windows, and the once intimidating grand hotels, too imposing for their own good.

On Sundays, after the week of work, I'd collect Tina on the pillion of my bike and we'd scout the coast for romantic hideaways. We'd hole up in some boarding house with a pile of books and magazines, eat at the baked-beans-on-toast cafés, scramble among the rocks for shells, walk the downs atop the cliffs at Beachy Head. In Hastings one morning a downpour forced us to retreat to a smoke-filled pub where we sat with the locals watching the Queen's silver jubilee celebration on television as the rain fell. On an excursion to the Irish coast at Connemara, we impractically considered buying a boathouse where we could disappear from the real world. One magical

Sunday exploring the coast of West Sussex we found a little house with a For Sale sign at Angmering-on-Sea, where the sea lapped right up to the back garden, and dreamed of buying it if one day we could afford it.

Meanwhile, at the *Sunday Times*, we were not alone in our industrial miseries. Waves of strikes crashed into and over the remaining sea-walls, culminating in the 1979 chaos of the 'winter of discontent'. In two months 30 million working days were lost. I saw pickets blocking cancer victims arriving for treatment at St Thomas' hospital across the river from where I lived. Going to a restaurant through Leicester Square I walked past high piles of uncollected rotting garbage that got it called Fester Square. The National Union of Journalists, pursuing a wage claim, made a mockery of years of press protests against secretive local authorities by actually asking council officers to deprive people of news about gas leaks, fires, building plans, rent and rates. It was like asking Sweeney Todd for a close shave.

The Thomson Organisation sanctioned a dramatic bid to start anew. They offered to invest millions of pounds to buy out obstructive practices and overmanning, but the chapels and their unions didn't want a brave new world. Every proposal was rejected. As a result, the paper was shut down in November 1978, a temporary break, we all thought, until negotiations resumed.

I drank the cup of bitterness many times over as I walked through the silence of a dead composing room, shrouded Linotypes and darkened offices. Gathering dust in my pending tray was a scoop of world importance. Anthony Mascarenhas, the man who'd exposed the genocide in East Pakistan, detected that Pakistan was well on the road to possessing a nuclear bomb – and he pointed the finger at the then unknown Dr Abdul Qadeer Khan, whose thefts of blueprints from a European facility were to enable Pakistan to become the first nuclear power in the Muslim world. Khan, wrote Mascarenhas, didn't stop there. He supplied both Iran and Libya with centrifuge components and information. As the weeks of suspension turned into months, I gave approval for Mascarenhas to send his report to the Australian magazine *Eight Days*, started in Sydney by former *Sunday Times* executive Colin Chapman. Trading a world scoop of historical importance killed any lingering feelings I had of conciliating the unions.

We were suspended for a full year, but even when agreement was reached to restart, the recidivists in the pressroom worked their mischief again, and the comps' national leaders reneged on the computer deal we'd worked out together.

I've never forgiven the print unions for what they did. Kenneth Thomson, Roy's son and then head of the company, was deeply wounded. Ken was a kindly, somewhat absent-minded man with a gentle sense of humour who thought the best of everyone he met. In Canada, where he lived, he was not Lord Thomson – 'call me Ken' – and never took his father's seat in the House of Lords. He delegated the management of Times Newspapers to a London board, but he took pride in the newspapers as his father did. The *Times* journalists had been paid normal salaries for a year of not working. The strike they called for more money soon after returning was the last straw, a betrayal of the Thomson family who had spent millions to save *The Times*. Thomson sadly concluded he could do no more. 'I promised Dad I'd keep *The Times* going, Harold, but this is too much.' He put both papers up for sale. I led a management buy-out bid for the *Sunday Times*, but Thomson's London management, and Denis Hamilton too, thought Rupert Murdoch had a better chance of dealing with the unions.

I'd encountered Murdoch often enough to appreciate the delusiveness of his charm. He was a chameleon, who could switch from good humour to menace. I'd heard every jolly swagman's yarn which placed him somewhere between Ned Kelly and Citizen Kane. I'd been at seminars on newspaper ethics where he was a caged lion, glowering his contempt for the do-gooders and sappy academics. I often agreed with him. Once, expressing admiration of the *Sunday Times* investigations, he'd joked that I should take over the *Village Voice* and teach the journalists the meaning of responsibility. My friend the Australian editor Graham Perkins had declined to work for Murdoch but thought that within the hard exterior of the riverboat gambler there might still be found the lost idealist of the 'Red Rupert' of his Oxford days. I didn't think that but, after the years of hand-wringing at our board meetings, I did find his buccaneering can-do style very refreshing. 'Sure,' he laughed, 'we'll sort out the unions. We're going to print the *Sunday Times* in two sections Friday and Saturday, and go up in size.' Music to my ears.

The journalists felt badly let down by the Thomson management. They didn't trust Murdoch. The Australians associated with the paper were especially vehement that he had fired every editor who'd stood up to him, that he would have no respect for the paper's cherished independence nor any promises made. But when the *Sunday Times* journalists' chapel came to vote at the end of a passionate debate (which as management I could not attend) it voted against a court action to force a reference back to the Monopolies Commission. Many of them feared that a breakdown would mean the end of the sister paper *The Times*. Fourteen favouring legal action, members of the so-called Gravediggers Club, printed a T-shirt bearing the cry: 'Don't Blame Us. We Voted Against'.

The Thomson Organisation and Parliament had asked Murdoch for guarantees that the tradition of editorial independence of both papers would continue to be protected in two ways: by the appointment to the board of independent national directors and by five guarantees of editorial freedom. Murdoch – of course – readily promised that editors would control the political policy of their papers; they would have freedom within agreed annual budgets; they would not be subject to instruction from either the proprietor or management on the selection and balance of news and opinion; instructions to journalists would be given only by their editor; and any future sale of the titles would require the agreement of a majority of the independent national directors.

It was on the basis of these guarantees, and only because of them, that I accepted Murdoch's invitation to edit *The Times* on 17 February 1981, giving up the job that had given me such fulfilment and pride at the *Sunday Times* and my power base as a defender of press freedom. My ambition got the better of my judgement. I guess the bitter experience with the unions had made me eager for a new start. I hadn't been enchanted either by the furtiveness of the Thomson London management during the sale. Still, it was wrenching to leave my friends at the *Sunday Times*; it had been a partnership sustained by a conviction everyone shared: we were doing something worthwhile in bringing the public early intelligence they'd not get anywhere else and associating it with the highest levels of cultural commentary we could achieve. It was a community of shared values. Not political values but the values of purposeful, honest journalism. Selecting and promoting people of excellence who shared the ideals, and whom I could trust to live by them in a collaborative enterprise, had been one of my principal tasks as editor.

Despite the difficulties we had with the national leaders of the print unions, I retained an affection, too, for the printers who worked with us. On my last Saturday evening putting the front page to bed, I was touched that the comps' farewell was an honour rare for someone not a member of their union (it originated when an apprentice was recognized as a fully qualified journeyman). They banged me out, which meant that everyone on the floor seized whatever piece of metal was to hand and hammered away, creating a tremendous noise as I waved goodbye holding my last page proof. The photographers later ended a more sedate dinner given by the company by hoisting me on their shoulders. A week later at *The Times*, on my first night as editor, the comps accorded me the privilege of pushing the front page into the foundry, a pleasant welcome that was not a harbinger of things to come elsewhere in the building.

In my first six months at *The Times*, Murdoch was an electric presence, vivid and amusing, direct and fast in his decisions, and a good ally against the old guard, as I worked to sharpen the paper's news values while retaining every element of its traditional coverage of Parliament, the law, obituaries and the arts. I had his enthusiasm for a thorough overhaul – 'Go to it, Harry' – making headlines more readable and letting photographs breathe. He overruled the squeaks from his advertising director when I swept classified advertising off the back page for an irreverent Parliamentary sketch and an information service. I brought in new political writers and started a new tabloid-sized arts section.

Twenty-one days into my editorship I was at dinner with Tina at Langan's Brasserie just off Piccadilly on the night President Reagan was shot. I left the dinner table in a tearing hurry to oversee our coverage, calling for the most detailed narrative, a separate report on the gunman, another on the violent history attendant upon American presidents, and a third on the character of the next-in-line Vice President George Herbert Walker Bush. There was argument around the picture desk about which of three near-simultaneous photographs should be used – one of the President looking towards the shooter, one of him being hit, and another of him being bundled into a car. This was an unusual true sequence and to choose just one or use three images that were too small would be to miss an opportunity. I schemed all three running down the page across six columns. Finally, I ruled that the whole front page would be given to all the Reagan elements and for other news created a second 'front page' in the normal *Times* style. We developed the same approach for other late-breaking news: the Columbia shuttle, Israel's bombing raid on Iraq's nuclear reactor at Osirak, the assassination of Sadat, riots in London and Liverpool.

The Reagan front page was a departure from the traditional *Times* style as dramatic as the event, and I'm still proud of it today. There were mutterings of course from some of the old guard I had dislodged from positions they had come to think of as tenure. But readers responded in the thousands. Circulation stopped falling. News Corporation's 1981 annual report said that the 'exciting' editorial changes had the 'extremely gratifying' result of increasing the paper's circulation from 276,000 to more than 300,000.

My difficulties with Rupert really began in the autumn of 1981 as the economy showed little sign of recovery from a recession. Mrs Thatcher's government was facing a catastrophic fall in popularity. We supported her editorially on any number of issues, including her determination to curb excessive pay demands by the Civil Service, but I was critical of her reliance on monetary policy in a recession and disappointed that she seemed unwilling to tackle the abuses of the trade unions as she'd promised. (She made up for that later.) At the same time, we were unsparing in documenting the disintegration and spiritual collapse of the opposing Labour party. We identified the virtually unknown left-wing activists who were conspiring to win control of the leadership by changes in the party constitution and with that gave fair weather to the rise of the Social Democratic party. However, it soon enough became obvious that nothing less than unquestioning backing of Mrs Thatcher on every issue would satisfy Rupert.

His managing director, Gerald Long, wrote me a stream of memos asking me to downplay or suppress news that was bad for the government. In the spring the Chancellor of the Exchequer had said the recession was over and recovery would begin in the early summer. It didn't. Six months later the Central Statistical Office released figures showing that output had fallen for the sixth successive quarter. Gerald Long stood amazed at our temerity in printing a summary of this official report. Did I not understand that if the government said the recession was over, it was over? As far as I was concerned his rebuke was a red rag to a bull. I was not going to let anyone in management tell me to fix the news. (Output fell by 2.2 per cent in 1981.)

The warfare with Long escalated through the winter of 1981–2, with Murdoch himself giving instructions to editorial writers, and continually ducking the pledge to give me a budget. Of course, this came in handy later for the fiction that I had exceeded non-existent limits. In fact, by this time he'd blithely broken all the editorial pledges. Stories mysteriously appeared that I was thinking of resigning or being asked to resign. Murdoch denied them all. On 10 February 1982, hours after I'd been named Editor of the Year in the Granada press awards, he issued a statement saying there were absolutely no plans to replace Harold Evans whose outstanding qualities, etc. The reality was that on two occasion early in March he went to the national directors to ask them to dismiss me and install a new editor. They refused both times. They told him that if he himself dismissed me, I had a right of appeal to them and no pressure should be brought on me.

It was a dark time, and then came news I'd long dreaded. Since Dad had received his gold watch (and his miserable pension) for fifty years on the railway, he and Mum had lived very happily in a bungalow by the seaside in Prestatyn, North Wales. Into his eighties, he rode his bike to the Post Office and bowling green. He played football with his visiting grandchildren, cajoling my first son Mike to shoot with both feet and eat his crusts. In summers he put on his glossy peaked cap for a return to railway work, giving rides to children on a miniature steam train on Rhyl promenade; he took it as seriously as he had driving mainline expresses. Mum and Dad lived close to an unpretentious golf club and Dad liked to walk to it through the sand hills for a game of darts and, of course, for the oxygen of his days, conversation about the world.

He'd been a staunch trade unionist all his life, and on the Labour left, but he had a dim view of the irresponsibility that had come to pass for trade unionism. I have his diaries, an entry of his activities every day, written in a hand far more legible than mine, and notebooks of the arithmetic for the family budget (July 2: 'Good news railway pension increased by 40 pence a month from 7.23 to 7.63'), and every Sunday, I am touched to see, he had recorded the length of the suspension at the *Sunday Times*. The big highlight of their retirement was to cross the Atlantic twice to stay with my brother Peter and his wife Dorothy in Ontario. They took the dome-car train – naturally – to make the 2,400 mile journey to the Rockies and beyond to Vancouver, giving Dad a good excuse to wear a cowboy hat and ride in the canyons of his imagination.

Then the inescapable day arrived. Dad had recovered from the heart attack he'd had while visiting Tina and me in Kent and had resumed normal life in Prestatyn. Now a year later, when I was editing *The Times*, word came that he had suffered a stroke and was in a coma in hospital in Prestatyn. He was in his eighty-second year.

All the sons had kept in close touch with Mum and Dad, Fred especially, since John was in distant parts on Foreign Office work and Peter had emigrated to work for an insurance company in Canada. We were all told Dad would be in a coma indefinitely and we were discouraged from visiting: he would not be able to see or hear anyone or speak. In about the third week, though, Enid went to the hospital; my parents were fond of her and she of them. She was surprised to find him sitting upright in a chair by the bed. She asked him to nod if he could hear anyone. She thought he did. All four sons hastened to Prestatyn: Peter from Canada, John from Hong Kong, Fred from Gloucester and me from London. Mum was too ill to be with us. We stood by his bedside and one by one spoke to him to say we were all together again for the first time in many years. We thought we detected a responsive flutter of an eyelid.

Dad died forty-eight hours later. His friends said: 'He was waiting for his four sons,' and I think he was. We buried him on the hill of Bluebell Wood cemetery overlooking the sea at Prestatyn, and two months later Mum, broken-hearted, joined him there. I couldn't for many years bear to open the diaries of their good last years together.

On Tuesday, 9 March 1982, upon return from my father's funeral, when I was supervising the newspaper's Budget edition, Murdoch suddenly summoned me to his office. He leaned forward in his chair, took off his glasses, and stared at me. 'I want your resignation today.' I was astonished at how calm I was: it was rather like the out-of-body sensation I had the time I was mugged in New York and seemed to contemplate my own experience from Cloud Nine. I noticed how red was the rim of his left eye, the thickness of the black hair on the back of his hands. 'You cannot have my resignation,' I heard myself saying. 'I refuse.' I asked what criticisms he had of the paper. 'Oh, you've done a good job with the paper, sure. We haven't signed your contract, you know [I didn't] . . . but we'll honour it.' And then he veered. 'You've said I put pressure on you. I haven't put any pressure on you. I've always made it clear political policy is yours to decide.' In the midst of these exchanges, his voice wavered. He began to say how much harder it was for him than me. No need for me to worry. I'd get lots of jobs. He had wondered if I'd take a job in News International, but guessed I would refuse. He guessed right.

I broke off these exchanges, which had gone on for some twenty minutes. I said I had to get back to the Budget edition, but as I left, saying he did not have my resignation, I asked who he would have had in mind as a successor. It was then I learned he'd suborned my deputy Douglas-Home. 'Can't bring in another outsider at this stage,' said Murdoch. 'He'll be all right for the time being.'

Back in my office, I confronted Douglas-Home. Eton and the Royal Scots Greys, the second son of the second son of the 13th Earl of Home, 'Charlie' was a member of the *Times* old guard par excellence. I'd only appointed him as a gesture to that faction. He'd been most ardent in expressing his determination to stand with me in preserving the paper from managerial interference, so I asked him how he could have conspired for my job. He replied: 'I would do anything to edit *The Times*. Wouldn't you?' Saying 'No, I wouldn't do anything to edit *The Times*' seemed wan in the glare of his ambition. Accustomed to having a loyal and supportive deputy at the *Sunday Times*, I'd underestimated how much Douglas-Home longed for the validation of being anointed leader of the 'top people's paper'.

I was now glad that I had kept in touch with the four key original national directors out of the six (two others were Murdoch appointees). They assured me of their votes if I wanted to stay on, but I now had to envisage what that would mean. Nothing in my experience compared to the atmosphere of intrigue, fear and spite inflicted on the paper by Murdoch's lieutenants. I was confident I could stand up to the bully boys, but why should I give any more of my time and energies to an enterprise where every man feared another's hand? I was certainly not going to dilute, still less forsake, a lifetime commitment to journalism free of political manipulation. I got madder and madder. I spent a morning discussing tactics in a meeting with my chief ally among the national directors, the burly Lord (Alf) Robens, another Manchester man (and formerly in charge of Britain's nationalized coal mines). He expressed contempt for Murdoch and his methods, a reference to a ploy by which Murdoch had attempted to move the titles out of Times Newspapers without consulting the national directors as required. Robens affirmed my feeling: 'You'll be in a lunatic asylum at the end of six months the way they go on in that place.' On his advice, I went back to the paper and continued editing and writing.

Murdoch had gone to New York, but his henchmen told the press I'd resigned, when I had not. They proffered statements praising my record. I was not about to comply with this pretence, so I took my time and continued with my conferences. After a week, besieged outside my house by TV cameramen and reporters, and only when my lawyers were satisfied with the terms, I resigned on ITN's *News at Ten*, citing 'the differences between me and Mr Murdoch'.

It was 15 March. Only later did I recognize the significance of the date. One of the Shakespeare passages my father knew well and liked to declaim was: 'Beware the Ides of March.'

Two and a half decades later in the US, when Murdoch's appetite for newspapers led him to acquire the *Wall Street Journal*, I could not restrain a mirthless laugh on reading that the controversial sale in 2008 was hedged about with guarantees enforceable by a well-remunerated troika of the good and wise. This illustrious tribunal very shortly afterwards had the pleasure of reading that the editor had resigned without their knowing, still less approving. Still, I have to say that Murdoch's capacity for risk and innovation is proving better for this fine newspaper than the lacklustre Dow Jones management and those Bancroft family members who sold it to him.

Frankly, I now agree with Murdoch that editorial guarantees are not worth the paper they are written on. At Times Newspapers, their invention enabled an air of respectability to be given to an unnecessary and hazardous extension of monopoly power, and they suggested that *The Times* tradition had been maintained when behind the fake ivy it could so easily be plundered. Much as I appreciated the stalwart support of the independent national directors, in reality outsiders are incapable of monitoring the daily turmoil of a newspaper. This has nothing to do with their theoretical powers, and increasing or entrenching them would make no difference. Arbitration is impossible on the innumerable issues which may arise at warp speed every day between editor and management. Moreover, any intervention on editorial matters inevitably hazards the future relationship between complaining editor and resentful proprietor.

That relationship has to be based on trust and mutual respect. I recognize that the proprietor who imposes a political policy and fires a recalcitrant editor can invoke his right to do what he will with his property. He is the one risking his capital. In the case of Times

Newspapers, however, the situation was different – Murdoch had unequivocally forsworn that right when he signed the guarantees to Parliament.

Today I have no residual emotional hostility toward him. On the contrary, I have found many things to admire: his managerial effectiveness, his long love affair with newspapers, his courage in challenging the big three television networks in the US with a fourth, and altogether in pitting his nerve and vision against timid conventional wisdom. And there was one issue where he proved positively heroic.

In my efforts at a staff buy-out in 1981, the print unions at Times Newspapers had let it be known they preferred Rupert Murdoch to the other bidders for the titles. 'We can work with Rupert,' a general secretary told me. ('You mean *not* work,' I rejoined.) The unions took Murdoch's shilling – and five years after he bought the papers he put them to the sword. It was an equitable sequel. Under the guise of starting a new evening paper at Wapping, in Docklands, he secretly gave bargaining rights to the sensible electricians' union and reached an agreement with them for journalists and clerks to access computerized typesetting. He installed colour presses capable of printing both the *Sunday Times* and *Times* and his other major titles, the *News of the World* and *Sun,* then on 24 January 1986, in an astonishing commando operation no less remarkable because it was planned in total secrecy without leaks, he overnight switched production of Times Newspapers from the battlefield of Gray's Inn Road to a new barricaded plant at Wapping, wrapped in looped barbed wire.

Six thousand members of all the unions went on strike and plunged the journalists on the two papers and supplements into a crisis of conscience. A few refused to cross a picket line. Two foreign correspondents who did, David Blundy and Jon Swain, said it was like being back in Beirut or Belfast, escorted by an armoured car on the day they went through the barricades. People in all departments who wished to go on working assembled at secret pick-up points that changed daily; they were collected in coaches with metal grids at the windows. On Saturdays thousands of flying pickets greeted them, rocking the coaches going in, the politer ones shouting 'Judas,' 'Effing scab' etc., and trying to stop the trucks going out. Only the presence of mounted police prevented the violence from getting out of hand. As it was, hundreds were injured and 1,000 people were arrested.

At the height of the siege of Wapping, as it came to be known, a British television company called me in Washington where I was now working to ask if I'd appear on a programme about it. On the morning of the show, they explained the line-up.

'We have so and so defending Murdoch and you and someone else attacking him.'

'Wait a minute,' I said. 'You've got this all wrong. Murdoch is right. What he's doing is long overdue.'

There was a pause. 'We'll get back to you.' An hour later, they did. 'Sorry, we have to drop you. Hope you understand. You don't fit the scenario.'

But Murdoch did. The old script of endless warfare on Fleet Street that always ended with a management whimper was being rewritten. The siege of Wapping lasted a full year, but not an issue of any of the papers printed there failed to come out. I didn't have any doubt where I stood. Murdoch and his managers had struck a redemptive blow for the freedom of the press. We in the old management that cared so much for responsible journalism had failed and he'd succeeded. Wapping was brave in concept and brilliant in execution. What was achieved there made it possible for other newspapers to follow. Not only that, it opened the way for new publications to begin. The *Independent* newspaper was nourished at birth by this victory (staffed in part by a diaspora from the *Sunday Times*). For that, every British newspaperman is in his debt. The carnivore, as Murdoch aptly put it, liberated the herbivores.

20

MY NEWFOUNDLAND

American lives, said F. Scott Fitzgerald, have no second act. I beg to differ. At least this Englishman had a second act in America – and for that I have to thank America, and Rupert Murdoch too. If he hadn't given me a shove I wouldn't have enjoyed twenty-five exuberant years exploring new frontiers. And America produced a marvellous convergence in my life with Tina.

In 1968, when Ben Bradlee took over the editorship of the *Washington Post*, I'd been editing the *Sunday Times* for a year, so we'd got together to compare notes and we became friends. Later on, the timing in our personal lives was the same. He'd fallen in love and made a second marriage with his paper's intrepid and glamorous young Style writer, Sally Quinn. I'd been amicably divorced for some time from Enid (and preserved an affectionate friendship that has endured to this day). Bradlee thought I was being much too slow about popping the question to Tina, which I was, largely because I feared she wouldn't say yes. 'What are you waiting for, Evans? She'll get away!'

I seized a moment on a short vacation we took at Chatham Bars Inn on Cape Cod in August 1981. She was under the weather, so I said it would be prudent to have a blood test, without mentioning that a blood test was required for marriage. Sweetly, she fell for it.

Then I popped the question. With our joint legendary impatience, we decided to do it immediately. I called my co-conspirator Bradlee and he suggested a perfect site for a Brown–Evans civil wedding at the end of that week. The Bradlees had just finished restoring the near-derelict Grey Gardens, a shingled beauty of a house near Georgica Pond in East Hampton on the Atlantic coast that had been the fabled retreat of Phelan and Edith Bouvier Beale, uncle and aunt of Jacqueline Kennedy Onassis. At a day's notice, a number of close friends managed to make it to Grey Gardens – Tony Holden, the former *Sunday Times* Atticus who'd become *The Times* features editor; Mortimer Zuckerman, the real estate tycoon with whom I'd first become friends when he came to London two years back to ask me to edit his first media acquisition, *The Atlantic*; the journalist Marie Brenner, the critic John Heilpern, the essayist Nora Ephron, and the *Sunday Times* New York correspondent David Blundy, with his daughter Anna, who was maid of honour.

Bradlee was best man. He hid a tape recorder in the bushes so that Handel could join us as Tony Holden walked the bride through the bougainvillaea, and the presiding judge pronounced us man and wife. After champagne and cake, we drove into Manhattan for a honeymoon, all of one night at the Algonquin. In a simultaneous moment of panic at what we'd done, we exchanged promises that we could part at any time simply by returning a signed piece of paper. The next day Tina had to go back to her job in London editing *Tatler* magazine, and before going home I had to meet Henry Kissinger at the Rockefeller family estate in the Pocantico hills of New York State where I was editing a second volume of his White House years.

Two years later we were back in America for good.

I still don't know quite how it happened. Not long after I'd left *The Times* I was invited to be a visiting professor for a term at Duke University, North Carolina. It was all I needed to gamble on the promise of a new life: Mr Micawber's instinct that something would turn up under the big blue skies. At least, I thought, I'd escape having to answer people asking whether I was 'all right' as if I'd just been let out of Broadmoor and seeing the mix of disappointment and

incredulity on the faces as I explained that no, I wasn't bitter about
The Times. And the new Mrs Harold Evans (not that she ever called
herself that) was ready to cut loose, too, having resigned from *Tatler*
a year after its acquisition by Condé Nast magazines. Besides, over
the years I'd made a number of friends in New York, Washington,
Rochester and St Petersburg, who might, at the end of the Duke
term, point us in the direction of gainful employment.

The immediate plan was for Tina to do a course on American
literature at Duke while I took an alarmingly bright group of law
and politics students into the thickets of the First Amendment and
the vicissitudes of English law. On the way to the United States, we
paused in Barbados for a Christmas break. A phone call from New
York to the beach cottage disrupted our vacation. The legendary
editorial director of American Condé Nast, the grey fox Alexander
Liberman ('tsar of all the Russias'), was on the line asking if Tina would
come right away to meet him and his chairman S. I. (Si) Newhouse,
Jr. They'd relaunched the great Frank Crowninshield magazine of the
Twenties, *Vanity Fair*, and after ten issues and two editors it was
sinking fast amidst media ridicule and advertising collapse.

Tina flew to New York for lunch and returned to Barbados two
days later in a state of anxious excitement. She'd been invited to
move to New York immediately to take over as editor in chief of
Vanity Fair. It would mean a commuter marriage, since I was committed to Duke for six months.

Of course, I urged her to do it. She could take a rain check on
Melville, Hawthorne and James; they'd still be there, but *Vanity Fair*
might not. New York, though, did take a bit of getting used to as
a resident rather than a visitor. Our first apartment was a beginners'
blunder, a sublet in a glass tower on Third Avenue, midtown. We found
the agent through the Yellow Pages, paid the five thousand bucks
cash deposit into his Homburg hat and faithfully followed his instruction to use assumed names for entry. We never saw him again. The
apartment itself had so much furniture that if you tried to walk across
the living room quickly you risked being precipitated against the glass
walls, and no doubt through them if you had attained sufficient velocity. I opened a closet and out fell half a ton of pornography.

Tina speedily found another apartment, on Central Park South, while I was teaching in Duke. It was a romantic, touristy address, its ritizness an attraction for a better class of cockroach. It was another disaster. For a start, on my first visit the doorman wouldn't let me in. 'But Tina Brown,' I told him, 'is my wife and that's my apartment.'

'Sir, Mr Brown is already up there.'

So he was: Tina's father. Not long afterwards we fled to a two-bedroom rental at 300 East 56 Street in time for the birth of George.

We soon realized that New Yorkers don't muck up their kitchens by doing breakfast. We got into the habit of walking down Second Avenue and trying every restaurant, bar and diner, moving from Irish to Italian joints, from the tolerable to the smart to the intolerable in the space of six blocks. Within a very short time the New York vortex kicked in. When you are in the outer edges you can swim quite happily in cool waters, but as you get closer you get sucked into a level of activity that is calculated to drive you crazy. There was a *New Yorker* cartoon that caught it perfectly: man on the phone saying, 'How's Wednesday? No? A week the following Thursday? Or the Wednesday after that? No? How's *Never* for you?'

It was exciting, and very eighties. The city was a temple of conspicuous consumption – people liked arriving at the Plaza in stretch limos – but it was disconcerting to see white-collar drug transactions in Midtown and around the magnificent Public Library on Fifth Avenue. The intellectual excitement of competing in the media capital was high, though, and America seemed on top of the world. It was like going to dinner with some wonderful person and looking underneath the table and finding mouse droppings. Years later, when New York had become the safest city in the country, we were to find our way to a ground floor co-op apartment at Sutton Place with a small ivied garden and from that seclusion gradually learned how to adapt to Manhattan's throbbing and very proximate cultural life.

Twelve months on from our move to the US the young woman whose prose style I'd admired had become the toast of New York in saving and recreating *Vanity Fair*. David English, the editor of the *Daily Mail*, wrote a droll article about how the James Bond of

British journalism, as he was pleased to call me, had become a wistful shadow of a successful wife. The gossip columnist Liz Smith referred to me as Mr Harold Brown. But I was thrilled for Tina. I admired her bravery and rejoiced in her success. She'd supported me in the traumas at *The Times* and I'd supported her as she tried to find her way in her first editorship at *Tatler*. And within no time at all after Duke I was running hard myself, in charge of a distinguished publishing house, the Atlantic Monthly Press, with offices in Boston and New York, while at the same time I was editorial director of *U.S. News & World Report* in Washington, back at the throbbing heart of news. I rented a tiny house on N Street in Georgetown, former slave quarters for the big houses: a few doors down the street Ben and Sally lived in a glorious mansion with gardens and tennis court where occasionally I was Ben's doubles partner trying to put a couple of senators in their place. At weekends I scurried back to be with Tina in our New York apartment.

Even now, I marvel at the thrilling speed of the changes in our lives, for the better. I'd been back to America many times since my first taste of the country in 1956, travelling through forty states in the golden Eisenhower years. I remained as fascinated by its opportunities and contradictions, attracted by its openness and freedoms, appalled by racial discrimination, excited by the ideal of the American dream of individual fulfilment through equal opportunity, intrigued by how a society so thrusting and ambitious could protect civilized values. No doubt I romanticized my first experience in the fifties, maybe actuated a little then by envy that while in 1949 I was trying to find a crack in the Norman walls preserving higher education for the elite in Britain, millions of American ex-servicemen were going straight to college on Roosevelt's GI Bill. I thought America had a franchise on the future and I wanted to be part of it.

I could not get over how fast Tina and I were welcomed and absorbed into American life in 1983. We were each warmly received even by colleagues in journalism who saw plum jobs go to a couple of foreigners. We told ourselves that the reception was no better than Ben Bradlee and Sally Quinn would have been given had they arrived in London in similar circumstances, but who were we kidding? I doubt that Fleet Street in the eighties would ever have accepted inter-lopers in the way America embraced us two expats.

For me to be entrusted with the editorial conduct of both a book company and a news magazine, so soon after arriving in America, was a curiosity. It happened because of Mort Zuckerman's appetite for public affairs. He had barely appointed me editor in chief of the Atlantic Monthly Press, at the end of my Duke stint, than he bought *U.S. News & World Report* and urgently wanted its poten-tial developed as the most serious of the three competing news magazines – its rivals being *Time* and *Newsweek*. The magazine had a circulation of more than 2 million and was well plugged in to Washington politics. This time, after Murdoch, I was more cautious: Zuckerman had a reputation of being mercurial.

There was an early test of Zuckerman's commitment to the mag-azine's integrity. I wrote an editorial identifying the blatantly false statistics used in advertisements by the powerful lobby the National Rifle Association (NRA) to justify a Bill that would make it easier for criminals, drug dealers and lunatics to get hold of guns. The new chief executive of the magazine dropped by my office. This was Fred Drasner, Zuckerman's business partner, a lawyer new to publishing. He was known as 'Firestorm Fred' for his passion to incinerate anyone and anything that stood in his way. 'Whaddya written this week, Harry?' I told him. The embers glowed: 'Hey you can't do that, I just sold the NRA $30,000 of ads.'

I'd no time to debate. I had to catch the train to New York for a meeting at the Atlantic Monthly Press where my associate publisher, Walter Weintz, was in the throes of publishing an art scoop, the sketchbooks of Pablo Picasso. That afternoon, I got a message from the equable David Gergen, whom we'd recently appointed as the *U.S. News* editor. Would I mind writing another editorial in a hurry? I imagined David's hair was still smouldering. I told him I would mind and, no, I wouldn't write another editorial. On the Monday when I picked up the magazine, my NRA editorial was there as I wrote it. Zuckerman had overruled Drasner (who lost his deal).

Rather impertinently, I told my boss Zuckerman he'd completed his apprenticeship as an owner in record time; indeed, throughout he remained steadfast on all the issues of principle that counted and proved immensely well informed. In 1984 he was the first mainstream journalist to dare to comment on the growth of the new black underclass; he was at one with Nobel laureate Paul Krugman in warning that the 2005 housing bubble would burst with attendant financial dangers.

I had things to learn myself. I put a lot of effort into writing editorials for the magazine, acutely aware I was a foreigner, but what most surprised me, after so many years immersed in Americana, was that there were concealed differences between English English and American English. I was deflated early on to be told by a colleague that the editorial I'd written on terrorism was 'quite good'. Pray, I asked, in what way was it deficient? 'Oh, none at all. It really was *quite* good.' It dawned on me that while 'quite' was a qualifier in English usage meaning 'not very', it was an intensifier in American usage.

Re-entering big-time journalism – interviewing President Reagan and getting hold of the smuggled letters of Soviet dissident Andrei Sakharov – was exhilarating. I could hardly believe my luck as I walked on crisp fall mornings from N Street across the bridge and into the *U.S. News* office. I did the round of diplomatic lunches and receptions, taking time out to swim at the Watergate complex and run a few miles along the Georgetown canal, but I spent most of my life in the office engaged on an extensive study of the magazine's strengths and weaknesses. In the early months I worked on a redesign undertaken by Edwin Taylor, who'd transformed the *Sunday Times* and *The Times*. While our former colleagues in London were still chained to typewriters, the considerable British talent for innovative design stupidly wasted, we worked at *U.S. News* at the cutting edge of modern technology. I had unfettered access to the computer for writing and editing and seeing the pages we laid out. I got sad and angry when I heard from my friends in Britain how they were still impeded in their daily lives by demarcation rules and by prejudices of the kind I'd come across from the old guard resistant to changes in *The Times*, comfortable in their assumptions of superiority. In an atmosphere like that, it becomes not worth the aggravation to risk making changes, so a company, and eventually a nation, stultifies.

I'd expected the attitude to change to be different in an American organization, maybe not always for the good. What I find altogether liberating is to be anonymous in the United States, by which I mean to work in a country where you can be who you are instead of being immediately typed by your accent, or where you were educated or what class you are from. I discovered anyone can reinvent themselves in America, probably more easily than anywhere else because of the scale of the country and the attitudes. You are allowed to fail or suffer a firing without being cast into outer darkness. I cheered the American business leader Mark Gumz, the president of Olympus, who said: 'Success comes from failure and acting upon this knowledge.'

For all the satisfaction of working at the Atlantic Monthly Press and *U.S. News*, after some two years of daily absence from Tina, and the constant travel, I was ready to move when I got a call from Si Newhouse, who opened by saying he'd gone crazy. He'd persuaded himself he should start a travel magazine and was I interested? Some of my friends thought it was me who'd gone crazy. The refrain was: 'Why on earth would you leave the sharp end of journalism for a travel magazine of all things?' But I did and I'd say to everyone who loses a job in mid-life not to get stuck in who you were.

Reinvention as the editor of a monthly glossy was enormous fun. I was given a quiet room next door to the main Condé Nast building to ensure that the new boy wouldn't be distracted by the high-stepping models strutting into the offices of *Vogue*, *Glamour* and *Vanity Fair*. All I had to begin with was a no-nonsense silver-haired secretary and a few blank sheets of paper on which I could scribble headlines and layouts for miracle marriages of subjects, writers and photographers for hypothetical stories I'd like to read: ask Robert Hughes to describe the joys of Barcelona, send Christopher Buckley up the Amazon, invite Mimi Sheraton to assess the cuisine on a round-the-world flight. In any event, travel journalism was ripe for a revolution.

There was no shortage of information in bulk. Travel was a

marketplace with a million hawkers. It was bewildering enough to choose among the honest vendors, but there were also travel journals tied to the travel business and travel writers who took free trips and portrayed the Never Never Land where all headwaiters bowed. There were guidebooks that did not reveal they had taken baksheesh. Still in my mind was an incident at the *Sunday Times*. One of the reporters fell sick on a cruise, a misery he shared with several hundred others, but he hesitated to write the story because he'd been on a freebie. Thereafter, in my budget at the paper I always provided for us to pay our own way and Si Newhouse agreed *Condé Nast Traveler*, too, should invest in honesty. I compressed our philosophy in the slogan 'Truth in Travel'.

I recruited a young staff eager to make waves, but spiced with a few seasoned executives who could coax fine, cultivated writers and adventurous photographers. I wanted to combine enjoyable writing and photography with a passion for the environment, not yet a fashionable subject, and harder-edged journalism. I enlisted the tenacious Clive Irving, the *Sunday Times* managing editor before me who'd come to the States to make films and forgot to go home. We carried out prodigious research to identify the safest and worst airlines. Oh, you'll never get away with that, I was told by the cognoscenti in the trade. Such no-holds-barred reporting would lose us every hope of attracting advertising. The prophecies were soon borne out. One month in a small news item we advised people with breathing problems of the risks of air pollution in Mexico City. An advertising agency angrily cancelled all its business because we'd printed an item 'unsuitable for a travel magazine'. I published the protest and defended our policy – with a reaction better than we could have dreamt. The agency was then itself denounced by the travel industry and the whole of a Madison Avenue sensitive about its image. They all signed on for truth in travel.

Condé Nast Traveler took off, an instant success that thrives today in America and Britain.

In my fifth year at *Traveler*, Alberto Vitale, the hard-charging chief executive of the Newhouse book companies, barrelled into the office 'to look around a magazine operation', then surprised me by saying that the visit was only a cover for his real purpose. Once inside my private office, he shut the door and asked: 'Would you like to run a publishing house?' He'd only just taken over Random House, the largest trade publisher in the United States comprising three major houses: Random House ('little Random'), Knopf and Crown. With Newhouse's approval, he was inviting me to be president and publisher of Random House trade; I'd also have Times Books and Villard imprints in my portfolio. It was an interesting challenge, one I hadn't expected at the age of sixty-one. My passion for books had been unbounded since filing book jackets for Mum's little lending library and haunting Failsworth public library, but it was also an opportunity to return to journalism of the scale of the *Sunday Times*.

I knew a lot about the writing and editing of books, and by now I knew most of the formidable publishers in New York. As a visitor from London looking for good books we might acquire for serialization in the *Sunday Times*, I'd been impressed by the authority of Sam Vaughan at Doubleday, whom the great and the good invariably chose as their publisher; by Phyllis Grann's dominance of fiction blockbusters; by the determination of Dick Snyder at Simon and Schuster, who'd more recently beaten me off when, as the apprentice editor in chief of the Atlantic Monthly Press, I'd flung everything we had into trying to secure the memoirs of Reagan's indiscreet budget director, David Stockman ('None of us really understands what's going on with all these numbers'). Snyder could also call on the editorial flair of Michael Korda, who strolled into meetings wearing jodhpurs and riding boots and found time to write bestsellers of his own.

Militating against any anxiety I might have was the artillery of Random House, its editors in 'little Random'. In publishing, the editors are key. They acquire (with the publisher's approval), they nurture the author from conception to line-editing, caring for every word. My job as publisher was to judge the merit and value of manuscripts editors wished to acquire, to do some acquiring and editing of my own, and to ensure the viability of the house. I had no doubt I could work happily with the editors. They treasured literature; they saw themselves, with justification, as defenders of American cultural values and feared the corporatism to which the industry was apt to succumb. I heard of a bureaucrat put in charge of a new imprint who in his first cost-cutting exercise complained, 'What's that fellow doing in the company? Whenever I pass his office, he's always just reading.'

Three of the editors I'd be working with were renowned. Jason Epstein, Joe Fox and Bob Loomis had a hundred years' experience between them. Epstein was perhaps the most creative force in the history of modern publishing, always seeking new frontiers. At twenty-two, fresh from Columbia, he'd invented the groundbreaking trade paperback as a format for quality books – distinct from the pocket-sized softcover mass-market books – a profitable format that everyone imitated; he'd been a co-founder of the *New York Review of Books*; and a participant in the founding in 1979 of the Library of America series of classics seeded by state dollars. He had an omnivorous appetite intellectually and in the kitchen. You never knew whether his next disquisition would be on the virtues of St Thomas Aquinas or a properly prepared artichoke. He was also, it has to be said, captain of the praetorian guard of pessimists, so I discounted his warning, when I called him, that the job of publisher had become 'impossible'. More challenging was that at Random House I'd be responsible for a $100-million business habituated to its own way of doing things.

Vitale was pleased, inordinately pleased, when I said I'd like him to take me through their system for managing the nuts and bolts of profit and loss predictions, printing, binding, warehousing and selling into stores. I'd stumbled on someone as didactic as I was. He was an immigrant himself, a former Olivetti executive impervious to doubt, his preference for order and certainty expressed in his smart buttoned-up double-breasted suits and his handwritten notes ALWAYS IN BIG CAPITAL LETTERS. But he appreciated books and he kept his promise that I'd have pretty much a free hand as the custodian of a pantheon of the greatest American writers. (I took over as president and publisher of Random House at the start of November 1990.)

Every author, said one of the founders of the house, is a son of a bitch. It was not a considered judgement. Horace Liverwright had just had a cup of hot coffee flung in his face by Theodore Dreiser.

But as the author of seven books myself, I was instinctively on the author's side. I knew the angst provoked by contemplation of the first resoundingly empty page, the tension waiting to hear from the publisher, the feeling that once the manuscript is delivered you might as well have died and have done with it. Writing a book, as our prized novelist E. L. Doctorow put it, is 'a lot like driving a car at night. You never see further than your headlights but you can make the whole trip that way.' To which I'd add that the editor marks the route with signposts and is always at hand with a jack and spare tyre. I took an oath of office that we'd be swift in our responses to authors and agents, and that we'd repay the mental exertions of the writer by putting real promotional muscle into letting everyone know there was something very much worth reading here.

The galaxy of writers in the history of Random House was stunning – William Faulkner, Eugene O'Neill, Theodore Dreiser, John O'Hara, Ayn Rand, Upton Sinclair, James Joyce, Robert Penn Warren, W. H. Auden, Truman Capote, Jane Jacobs, Daniel J. Boorstin, and Dr Seuss of *Cat in the Hat* fame. Some of the greats were still with us – William Styron, James Salter, Shelby Foote, Pete Dexter, Robert Ludlum, Mario Puzo, Dave Barry, Norman Mailer, James Michener, Gore Vidal, Maya Angelou, David Halberstam, John Richardson, Hunter S. Thompson and the aforementioned Doctorow.

Styron hadn't written much lately. Early on Tina asked me to accompany her to join a psychiatrist friend's table at a dinner benefit for medical research. Styron was there, persuaded to speak for the first time about the reasons he'd not been able to write. He spoke of his struggles to overcome a long depression (in the years before it was understood what medication might do). It was moving to hear him. Tina right away went over to his table to persuade him that if he wrote an article for *Vanity Fair* describing his experience he would help so many others who felt isolated and ashamed. He did. Inspired by Milton's *Paradise Lost*, Tina wrote the headline 'Darkness Visible'. Styron then felt encouraged to write a book under that title, and we published it at Random House, where it rode the bestseller list for many weeks.

Clearly we had to find new authors of similar eminence, marrying their literary excellence with a number of commercial blockbusters, without managing to shed the authors we had. I was sorry to lose one writer within a few weeks of taking over. Rupert Murdoch withdrew his memoirs. Pity. I'd have done a good job for him.

Gore Vidal was unhappy about Jason Epstein's initial read of a new novel – 'concoction' Jason called it. I flew to Miami to see Vidal and express our undying loyalty (soon justified by a magnificent collection of his essays, *United States*, which won the National Book Award). In my eagerness to expound on how great it was to have both Vidal and Norman Mailer in the same house, I had to reverse course in mid-flow when I remembered that the two never missed a chance to beat up on each other.

Front-list fortunes are notoriously unpredictable. I had to grow a reliable back list of steady sellers we could count on for income when new acquisitions didn't realize our hopes. It makes sense to read the DNA of an institution; Tina had done it on taking over *Vanity Fair* (and would do so again at the *New Yorker* in 1992). The original animating spirit of Random House was Bennett Cerf. He'd died in 1971, but I listened to him. His ebullience came over loud and clear on a tape his son Christopher Cerf dug up from the archives, in which Bennett had recorded how he'd been assisted by the womanizing habits of the owner of the Modern Library of inexpensive classics, Horace Liverwright, in 1925. Liverwright, having agreed to sell to Cerf, was hesitating to sign when a cuckolded husband arrived in the office with murder in his heart. Liverwright escaped the wages of sin this time, but intimations of his own mortality induced him to sign the agreement. Cerf built on the Modern Library to publish regular books 'at random'.

I was delighted at the end of my first week as president when Vitale called to say he'd like to amble down and talk about the Modern Library. He appeared in my office with Sonny Mehta, the subtle, reflective and quietly competitive publishing legend at Knopf. The proposal was that they'd help me out by relieving me of the Modern Library to combine it with the Everyman's Library Knopf had just acquired.

Thanks but no thanks, Alberto and Sonny. The Modern Library was dear to my heart; I remembered my astonishment, as a Harkness

Fellow skimping to get by, that for less than the cost of breakfast I could buy its volumes of Gibbon's *Decline and Fall of the Roman Empire*.

Jason had misgivings about my enthusiasm, but I'd already begun an evaluation of the list, looking for other great works we might acquire, and I'd scouted new members for a Modern Library board. Most of all, I was impatient to begin a phenomenal project originally inspired at the *Sunday Times* by Godfrey Smith. He'd suggested we identify the best 100 novels in the English language in the twentieth century, and feature them, with biographies and photographs, in the colour magazine he edited. I'd planned to accompany the launch of the series with an inexpensive reissue of every title by arrangement with all the original publishers. We were halfway there when I prepared to leave to edit *The Times*. At a handover meeting with the new management team Murdoch had installed at the *Sunday Times*, I proudly presented the great books package. Rarely have I been more swiftly deflated. No, thanks, Harry, they said, one of them adding genially: 'Fuck literature!'

So I brought the orphaned project to Random House. Discussing which novelist should make the cut and who should not was at once an education and an entertainment, closeted with a committee that included Edmund Morris, Daniel J. Boorstin, Shelby Foote, John Richardson, A. S. Byatt, Arthur Schlesinger, Jr and Gore Vidal. I could claim to have read most of the preliminary list; they seemed to have read everything twice and the divisions of opinion were arresting. 'Edith Wharton? Never! *Ulysses*? Unreadable!' The project was simpler than it had been in London. Random House already owned a good proportion of the copyrights of the fancied titles; for the rest, the publishers who held the copyrights joined in the fun. We told them we had no intention of ranking the list other than alphabetically. The renovated Modern Library itself became the backbone of a profitable back list again, and I'm pleased to be still on its board.

I'd worried that working with editors preoccupied with their manuscripts might give me a sense of desolation compared with the hurly-burly of the newsrooms and the incessant changes on a monthly glossy. I'd been in the job just over two months when it became clear the coalition armies President George Herbert Walker Bush had assembled would use force to eject Saddam Hussein from Kuwait. I fretted that any one of the three news magazines would be gearing up to produce special issues or books if and when war came. What was to stop me producing an instant illustrated history? Well, I didn't have an art department that could interrupt its normal work, I didn't have the staff to acquire hundreds of photographs or the space to display them, and I didn't have the writers and editors on tap as a newspaper does. In short, nothing compared to flinging an army into the desert against a dug-in enemy armed to the teeth.

Vitale, exemplifying the American can-do spirit, swiftly organized printing and distribution, and pledged 50 per cent of the net sales revenue to the Gulf Crisis Fund of the American Red Cross. I induced Ray Cave, the former editor of *Time* magazine, and his wife Pat Ryan, a former editor of *Life*, to acquire and lay out photographs in a war room I secured at Condé Nast; I commissioned the foreign editor of *The Economist* in London, Peter David, to write 35,000 words; deployed *Traveler*'s John Grimwade on a warfront graphic; and then went to the Pentagon to describe our package to the chief of the armed services, General Colin Powell, in the hope he'd write a prologue. (He was tickled that I could, on command, recite my number in the Royal Air Force.)

The ground war began on 24 February 1991. It was over in 100 hours. I'd thought the coalition armies would give us more time. Still, the picture pages were pretty well laid out, Powell's prologue was in, the dust jacket was at the printers and Grimwade was finishing his 3-D graphic of the battlefront. All we lacked was the text. That was in London. It was a magical experience in those days to put the phone down on David writing away at *The Economist* in St James's Street, walk from the Random House offices on Third Avenue to our Condé Nast war room on Madison, and find that the 35,000 words had got there before me, transmitted from David's computer to ours; not only that, it was already in the pages with Ray Cave's headlines.

Triumph in the Desert, published on Memorial Day, was a success as the first illustrated history of the Gulf War in colour. I was well placed to secure Powell's life story two years later on his retirement as chairman of the joint chiefs of staff. The bidding war for the American hero was hot. It was my first experience of an auction where you started with six zeros and the only question was the number you put in front of them. Vitale calculated that a $5 million bid would be viable and would probably succeed. I recalled Duff Cooper's observation that the United States are more subject than any other country to inundation by great waves of conviction. 'What elsewhere might be called a craze becomes there a creed.' The creed in 1995 was that Powell would run for President in 1996 and would win. From my conversations with Powell and his wife Alma, I guessed all the speculation was froth; my fascination was less with his political future than with his past: how did he get where he did, this Harlem-born soldier destined to be chief of staff who came home as a wounded Vietnam vet in the sixties and was refused service at a hamburger joint in Alabama?

Si was always ready to back his publishers, so we all took a deep breath and bid again when our original $5 million was topped by someone else. Not yet scarred by bidding wars that got out of hand and ended in disaster, I was keen to go higher: the scar in the cultural memory of Random House was called John Grisham, lost to another house for the sake of a final $25,000. But here we were talking hundreds of thousands of dollars, maybe a million or more. We ended up bidding another $1.5 million. We were into David Stockman territory ('all those numbers'), our bid an act of faith really by Si, Vitale and me. It really was our final throw. We were outbid again – but Powell ended the craziness. He stopped the bidding and we were told he would come to us. We hired the author Joe Persico to help and I edited the manuscript with a promising junior called Jon Karp, but it was very much Powell's book: he is a natural storyteller. The only difficulty we had was settling on a title. After another session with the marketing department, I recoiled from the favoured *My American Dream* and typed up a note to Powell I still have:

I have come up with a title that everyone here likes a lot. Let it brew with you and Joe and we'll pick up when I get back:

Colin Powell
My American Journey
An autobiography

I think it is better than My American Dream because it avoids
the MLK connections. It is more active, more of an adventure
and less of an introspection. And it has been quite an adventurous journey – the boy from the south Bronx who made
something of his life and something that is redolent of America
and opportunity. And again it is a journey that is not complete.
It is a cool title, not thrusting but with a quiet emphasis.

It was one of the more remarkable experiences of my life to travel
with Powell on part of his thunderously popular multi-city whirl-
wind book tour. President Clinton was worried Powell might
threaten his chances of a second term; nobody knew what party affil-
iation Powell might have. Thousands lined up around three or four
blocks in every city, buying the book and urging him to go for the
White House. He'd sign three or four thousand books, wisecracking
with the customers in line, and then cheerfully set off to the next city
for more of the same. When we were well and truly launched, I was
touched to receive from Powell a framed copy of the title memo I'd
sent him. Typically gracious, he'd written across the bottom in red
ink: 'Harry, You were right, as usual. God Bless.' Happily, in good
time the red ink vanished from our accounts. My American Journey
was a fabulous number-one bestseller; it kept selling in paperback
and in a few years our faith was amply rewarded.

There is no way of removing the risk from publishing. It is easy to
forget, in the excitement of an auction, that you and your rivals
might all be wrong. Maybe the big name is just a big name. And how
do you calculate the price you will pay for an author with no track
record at all – in fact, no name at all? I had no idea who the author
was who sent a bunch of typewritten pages to the agent Kathy
Robbins. She gave them to me in a brown paper carrier bag over
breakfast at the Waldorf in 1992 with the warning that if I liked
what I read I was not to try to discern or guess the identity of the

author, nor ever, ever suggest that the characters were based on real people, and I had the pages exclusively for the weekend provided I coughed up $250,000. The manuscript, entitled 'Primary Colors', was a compelling fiction of the turmoil and intrigue of a Governor seeking the presidential nomination. Wild horses would never drag from me the admission that I thought it bore a marked resemblance to the primaries in 1992 which ended in the nomination of Governor Bill Clinton, with a war room whose colourful director liked to talk to women about 'walking the snake'.

On the Monday, when I said snap to *Primary Colors*, Kathy and the unknown writer insisted they wanted it published under a pseudonym. I wasn't keen on promoting a bogus name, then I remembered what a fuss there had been in Britain in the sixties during Harold Macmillan's premiership when *The Times* published a series of caustic political articles by Anonymous. So Anonymous became the author of the carrier-bag pages that became *Primary Colors* that became a runaway bestseller and a Mike Nichols movie starring John Travolta.

The speculation on who might be the author of a No. 1 bestseller 'who dares not speak his (or her) name' became a media craze. Nobody believed me when I said I didn't know. It was true. I was guessing like everyone else. We might never have known but for an unusual lapse among the sales force. Rather than let them have galley proofs, we'd distributed a few numbered copies of the edited manuscript. They were instructed to return them, but after publication one landed up for sale in an antiquarian bookstore and David Streitfeld of the *Washington Post* bought it, did some detective work on the handwriting, and announced that Anonymous was Joe Klein, a *Newsweek* political writer. The death of Anonymous was regretted by all concerned.

I considered the manuscript of *Primary Colors* well worth the investment, but never dared to hope it would bring in millions of dollars as it did. Why didn't we just publish profitable titles like that? It's a nonsense question but that doesn't stop it being asked (with movies, too). The truth is nobody can predict with certainty; it is the whole list year in and year out that, with back list, determines the fortunes of a house – with the important proviso that the publisher's sacred duty is to find the right market for each author.

We didn't have to do much to let people know General Powell had written his life story, but we had a duty by some means or other to find the right audience for non-fiction books that would never make a headline, books by new authors that might not command review space, books of all kinds whose budgets did not justify advertising monies, and books by foreign authors who would not be available for television. And we had to be quick about it, bearing in mind the dictum of publisher Howard Kaminsky that 'new books last in the stores about as long as milk takes to turn into yoghurt'.

I'd inherited excellent people in publicity and marketing (overseen by the imperturbable Walter Weintz, who seemed not to have had enough punishment at the Atlantic Monthly Press), but typically they were overstretched. I augmented their efforts with a literary magazine called *At Random*, collating interviews, photographs and articles all about our authors; it was edited by Helen Morris whose interview with Martin Scorsese led to marriage and a Scorsese–Morris daughter. I created a special events department of four people headed by an inventive marketer I poached from BBC America named Jonathan Marder. I was apprehensive about his idea that Random House should, every month, invite the public to a literary breakfast panel at Barneys store on Madison Avenue, open to authors from all publishing houses. We'd record the proceedings for national radio distribution and I would moderate the discussion from a platform surrounded by people munching bagels. I didn't expect many busy New Yorkers to turn up at an ungodly hour to listen to authors debate the legitimacy of Truman Capote's technique writing *In Cold Blood* or the reality behind science fiction, but the city has a concentration of book lovers and they packed the place every month. You could pretty well guarantee that if we were discussing the life and novels of a late-lamented author there'd be someone in the audience with intimate knowledge of his working methods and moods. One morning Brendan Gill of the *New Yorker* intervened to explain how John O'Hara became the 'master of the fancied slight', furiously ending his association with the magazine.

And if the topic was movies based on a book, there'd be someone at a breakfast table who had directed, starred, cast, written the script, composed the music or sued the studio. Director Michael Winner's adaptation of Chandler's *The Big Sleep* got even more arresting when we learned from Sarah Miles of the mayhem on the set.

Marder was the magic man who pulled rabbits out of the hat. On the collapse of the Soviet Union, I commissioned a researcher to go to Moscow to collect photographs they'd suppressed over the years. *The Russian Century*, as I called it, needed a venue for an exhibition. Marder came into my office: 'Do you want the good or the bad news first?' The bad was that the Russians had run out of money for redecorating the beautiful beaux arts Consulate building where he'd hoped we could stage an exhibition. The good was that Marder had raced around New York and persuaded designers and stores to finish the redecoration for free, a generous gesture that produced an appreciative front-page arts feature in the *New York Times*, a crowded exhibition, a good sale, and an over-close embrace for me from the redoubtable wife of the Consul General.

Gerald Posner had been working for years with his editor, Bob Loomis, on a book called *Case Closed*, about the assassination of President Kennedy. There had been some creditable attempts to penetrate the mysteries, but they'd been overlain in the public imagination by thirty years of conspiracy stories. Posner's manuscript proved these were paranoid garbage. I was impressed by his assembly of incontrovertible medical, ballistics and scientific evidence proving that there was no gunman on the grassy knoll; Lee Harvey Oswald was the lone rifleman firing three shots over eight seconds. Everywhere around town when I mentioned we had a sensation, I got the same response, 'Not another Kennedy book! Give us a break!' Bookstore buyers had the same response. How could we make people pay attention when the sensation was that there was no sensation? Clearly, we had a big marketing problem.

This was a profoundly important book. The ever-prudent Loomis had let a few academics and journalists of invincible integrity have sight of the manuscript. Tom Wicker, the veteran political reporter and columnist of the *New York Times*, was seized by its significance. Posner's work, he said, could do much to restore faith in government and in democracy, because it demolished the insidious insinuations that the highest officials of the US government had been involved in their President's murder. I became so exasperated I quite lost my temper over lunch with a publisher from London when I was told yet again the public had passed the point of satiation on the death of Kennedy. 'We're naming the guilty men!' I cried out. The editor sat up. 'You mean the men behind the killing? Wow, that is something!' No, I said, the guilty men are all those who ignored the evidence and misled the world.

I was grateful to the publisher. He'd provoked me into a spur-of-the-moment response that might solve the marketing problem. On the napkin I roughed the outline of an advertising campaign, leading off with a big 'GUILTY' splashed across photographs of the principal propagators of conspiracy. We made that the overture to the campaign, backed up by a special *U.S. News & World Report* pre-publication issue. The result was spectacular. It was not only a huge bestseller but a blast of cold air on the fetid distortions; it was a contribution to a nation's sanity and faith in its institutions. The conspiracy industry, of course, saw our book and ad campaign as another conspiracy. I was warned we'd be sued, and we were. But we won every time in court.

There were times when my enthusiasm betrayed me. I was convinced that we had a literary and commercial masterpiece in Jonathan Harr's book *A Civil Action*, telling of the fight by a small law firm to recover damages from a polluter suspected of afflicting children with leukaemia. It was so riveting I'd stayed reading on the plane to a sales conference and barely escaped being carried to the next destination. My absorption in the book induced me to sign off on a weak jacket (which the author liked) and we made little of an endorsement by John Grisham. The book was a flop, but I was convinced that people would be sorry to miss it, and I felt that we bore the blame, so I did something many thought a waste of money. I relaunched the book in hardback with a new jacket and invested still more on publicity. It worked, as it should have done first time if I had not made an assumption treacherous in publishing: that it was so good it would sell itself.

Given the inescapable uncertainties, we needed more sure-fire authors who would regularly sell into the top of the bestseller list – easier to achieve in fiction, where an author might produce every second year, whereas a serious non-fiction author like Robert Caro on Lyndon Johnson or Robert Massie on the First World War might need five years or more. Even a list of hugely popular novelists provides no assurance of profitability: blockbuster authors just secure larger advances. The one-off celebrity book is clearly desirable if it is of quality and you judge it will repay its advance and cover the un-predictable losses on other books. So I pursued and promoted celebrity books that I judged might be worth the risk. It was moving to go to the hospital where the unbelievably brave Christopher Reeve (Superman) lay paralysed from a fall while show jumping and hear him, between breaths from a tube, say he'd like to tell his story. It was a success. Kate Medina listened to the way CBS anchor Tom Brokaw talked, decided he was a natural author and signed up *The Greatest Generation*, a runaway bestseller.

But you could never tell. My attempt to secure the memoirs of Marlon Brando and the sequel was more bizarre. I heard he made a habit of humiliating publishers who flocked to his Beverly Hills hill-top retreat with open chequebooks. He satisfied himself that they were all East Coast phonies by inviting them to express their enthu-siasm by going down on their knees in front of him. I was ready for that. When the call came for me to make the trip to Hollywood, I planned to tell him that declining to kneel was not a mark of disre-spect but a recognition of physics: a skiing injury, I'd say, meant I'd never be able to get up again and he'd have a problem disposing of the body.

For me he had a different test. After a restaurant dinner where he accused me of being a CIA agent, and asked what music I planned to die to, we went back to his house for several hours of erratic con-versation. He flitted from topic to topic – the American Indian, the genius of Dr Salk, diet, Israel, blood pressure, the proximity of American history, the horror of living in New York ... When we finally got round to the book, he said: 'I know how to write an interesting story, get the people in. I know this is necessary.' Then he gave me a hard stare. 'What you hear about me is nonsense. I don't want to hurt anyone when I write. There are things I will not put in. I will not write about the night at the White House with John Kennedy when I could have fucked the first lady in the darkened kitchen, something I thought about when she became the widow in weeds.' (Could this shocker be true? I did check and found that he'd indeed been at dinner with the Kennedys in the White House a few months before the assassination.) At midnight, when I tried to get away, standing by a limo in the moonlight, he demanded I there and then give him a sample of my handwriting to deduce whether I was lying about the CIA.

On the next visit, when he met me with a kimono draped over his 300 pounds, we played chess all afternoon as he beautifully intoned his favourite passages of Shakespeare. Eventually, we sealed our understanding sitting in his fiendishly hot sauna into the early hours. Perhaps he calculated I was about to expire in the heat, but he finally relaxed enough to talk about his son's killing of his sister's boyfriend in the house we were in. The book he wrote with Robert Lindley (*Songs My Mother Taught Me*), edited by Joe Fox, was highly readable, but getting Brando to promote it was a nightmare and a farce. (He suggested we made a film in which he would dress as a woman and I would unmask him during an interview.) I winced as I watched the interview he finally organized himself with Larry King on CNN. King allowed him to go off on various wild riffs, ending with Brando kissing him on the lips. It was the kiss of death for my hopes, stopping the book dead in its tracks in its rise on the bestseller list.

Brando's brooding menace was theatrical. The sense of physical menace was palpable when I got smuggled into a Miami jailhouse. I was in a cell with General Manuel Noriega, the deposed dictator of Panama and alleged torturer, who'd intimated to a go-between that he was ready to spill on the involvement of US agencies in drug smuggling. The next day back in New York, entirely on impulse for fact checking, I called an author who'd written on Panama. 'I knew you were going to call,' he said. 'How come?' 'A friend in the CIA told me.' Since I'd decided to go to Miami only at the last minute and told nobody, and since I'd called the author without warning, this was spooky. I suppose the prison cell was bugged, so I was glad I'd told Noriega he was hated in America and peppered my questions with assertions that Uncle Sam would never lie. When we published Noriega, a number of worrywarts asked how could we when he'd been convicted. This provoked me into my earnest worst. Did they know the meaning of publish? It meant *to make known*. Were we publishers intent on 'making known' whether we liked the subject or not, or were we in the business of not making known? In short, were we censors? Bennett Cerf found Ayn Rand and Whittaker Chambers politically repugnant, but he published them.

The thought police were active again in 1993 when Richard Nixon asked me to edit a book he was writing as a foreign policy manifesto for America. I didn't hesitate for a second. Even his critics – count me among them – conceded that he had an original approach. His manuscript tackled the key questions of the day: Should we punish China for its abuses of human rights? Was it wise for America to stay aloof from the genocide in Bosnia? Was it cowardice or prudence for the United States, confronted by a handful of thugs, to back away from its mission to restore democracy in Haiti?

I'd go to Nixon's house in New Jersey with my editorial observations, and he'd invite me to stay for lunch with him and his astute assistant Monica Crowley (later author of *Nixon off the Record*). In our meetings, he was not the Nixon of the tapes, no growls at criticism, all expletives deleted. He was never less than intriguing, his forefinger stabbing, the melancholy folds in his face uncreasing, his slow voice deepening as he expounded on the spiritual crisis – a spiritual deficit – he saw facing America, manifesting itself in crime, race relations, and what he called 'the corrosive culture of entitlement, one of the greatest threats to our fiscal health'.

What he loved talking about most of all was American history. It was uncanny that he should segue from some foreign confrontation in the day's headlines into an analysis of Woodrow Wilson, when he couldn't have known (could he?) that this was the point I'd reached in writing my political history of the second hundred years of the Republic, *The American Century*. On another visit, I asked if he didn't think Eisenhower had made a mistake not taking Prague in May 1945 and thereby letting the Russians occupy the city. He made it very clear that he did. 'It sealed Czechoslovakia's fate.' All these lunch meetings ended with the same ritual. He'd sign the label on the fine bottle we'd consumed. I should have asked for a full bottle. Nixon completed *Beyond Peace* in February, but he asked me to hold it up until he'd returned from Moscow and briefed President Clinton on Russia. In April we agreed on the jacket and final text – he was receptive to all my pencil marks – then a few days later he suffered a stroke. At Random House, we were already on a crash publishing schedule, then went into a crash-crash schedule to get the book to him in hospital as his family wished. He was too impatient to reorder the next world. He died on 22 April, four days after his stroke.

His daughter Julie Nixon Eisenhower invited me to join the 2,000 friends and former opponents at the funeral in the sunshine at Yorba Linda, his boyhood home where the house his father built still stood. Officially, it was a state funeral. The representatives of eighty nations sat in chairs in the garden. A military band played 'Hail to the Chief' as the flag-draped coffin was carried to a plinth in front of us, four jets flew overhead, and a twenty-one-gun salute followed. For all that, the occasion had the feel and quiet dignity of a family gathering, its mood caught in the deep bass voice of Henry Kissinger. The presence of the five living presidents – Carter, Reagan, Ford, Bush and Clinton – symbolized, Kissinger suggested, that Nixon's long and sometimes bitter journey had ended in reconciliation. 'He achieved greatly and he suffered deeply.'

For most businesses there is only one balance sheet. For a publishing house there are two: the numerical and the cultural. Over a number of books and over a period of time, the numerical balance sheet, which is a complex of factors, has to be positive unless one has a patron, a Medici, an Emperor Franz I . . . But I became convinced that the purpose of an imprint, or publishing house, cannot merely be defined in terms of numbers, no more than the purpose of architecture can be defined by the arithmetic of quantity surveying. The house had first to be defined by its cultural balance sheet, by the creativity of its writers and its editors striving to enlighten and entertain. The identity of the house may not matter to the casual book-buyer but it does to authors, their agents, and buyers of subsidiary rights like Hollywood: several of our books were made into movies.

My experience in newspapers and magazines had persuaded me that provided we were not reckless, quality would produce a viable numerical balance sheet, whereas the simple notion of following the numbers wherever they might lead – the tyranny of numbers! – would diffuse rather than enhance the purpose of the enterprise. It was gratifying to see the policy vindicated year after year in the bestseller lists: our titles were on the *New York Times* list for an aggregate of 173 weeks in 1992, 117 in 1993, 156 in 1994 and 205 in 1995. There were commercial as well as cultural benefits to establishing our watermark. When we sought to sign Jimmy Buffett, the music star who was a bestselling commercial fiction writer, his agent directed him to Putnam. He came to us, despite a bid several hundred thousand dollars more than ours, because he wanted to be in the same house as William Styron, Norman Mailer and Gore Vidal.

Throughout Random House and our imprints (Times Books and Villard), we sought to establish our identity by publishing books of intellectual merit, literary merit and journalistic authority. To this end we signed the novelists and storytellers John Irving, John Berendt, Robert Harris, Anna Quindlen, Alan Furst, Christopher Buckley, Barbara Taylor Bradford, Marc Salzman, Ethan Canin, Caleb Carr. In public affairs and biography, Roy Jenkins, Henry Louis Gates, Carl Sagan, Jeffrey Toobin, Clive James, Lewis Lapham, Sy Hersh, David Remnick, Robert K. Massie, Gail Sheehy, Ron Chernow, Paul Kennedy. And in the arts, Richard Avedon, Adam Gopnik, Alexander Liberman and John Richardson.

But the perils of the publishing business are illustrated by one year, 1993, when we had no fewer than eight of the twelve books on the American Library Association list of the year's best books.

Wanting to demonstrate that quality pays, I asked my finance director to tell me their final profit. He came in with a long face. 'Sorry, Harry, you lost $370,000 on those eight.' I asked him to check the results from the twenty-one titles of ours in the *New York Times* editors' pick of the year's most notable books. He looked even more miserable. 'No good. You lost $698,000 on those.' Then he gave me the big smile he'd been holding back: 'But they are all still selling – and on two other titles alone you made a profit approaching $2 million.'

If you fancy yourself as a publisher, try guessing which four of these eight books in the Library selections were viable in the year of publication. They were *Preparing for the Twenty-first Century* (Paul Kennedy); *A Tidewater Morning* (William Styron); *United States* (Gore Vidal); *Fraud* (Anita Brookner); *Dead Man Walking* (Sister Helen Prejean); *FDR: Into the Storm* (Kenneth Davis); *Lenin's Tomb* (David Remnick) and *Selected Stories* (Mavis Gallant). Out of respect for the authors, I'll not give the details, but it has never to be forgotten that good books have a long life. Jason Epstein always said, when beating down opposition in-house to one of his many brilliant titles, 'This book will be read long after we're all gone.'

In 1994 we had a submission by a young first-time writer, not long out of university, whose contract with another house had been withdrawn for failure to deliver on time. Unpromising? Well, thanks to the alertness and judgment of a young Random House editor, Henry Ferris, at Peter Osnos' Times Books imprint, and the superb quality of the writing when I took a look, we judged the book worth an advance of $40,000. It was entitled *Dreams from My Father* by a community organizer called Barack Obama. Fourteen years later, Tina met him on the eve of his presidential inauguration and remarked: 'My husband is proud to have signed the contract for your book.'

He gave that wide radiant smile: 'Worth a lot more now!'

A young boy walks on a beach with his father. This time it is not Rhyl in 1940, it is Quogue in 1998 at Long Island's Hamptons, and

I am the father. The boy is my son George, he's twelve, as I was on Rhyl beach, and his mother is Tina. His younger sister Isabel was born just as I took over Random House. Tina, meanwhile, had reached the pinnacle of her profession, accepting Si Newhouse's invitation to move from the now profitable *Vanity Fair* to edit the *New Yorker*.

She worked very hard at the *New Yorker* (and then six years later at her *Talk* magazine start-up, killed by the advertising collapse after 9/11), while still being devoted to George, who'd been born prematurely, and to Isabel. In work, Tina and I remained the mutual support team we'd always been in editing and writing at all levels. I'd taught her layouts at *Tatler* and advised on the *New Yorker* design, and she'd taught me about glossy magazines and covers when I started *Condé Nast Traveler*. We enjoyed life in New York, finally settling in a ground-floor apartment in Sutton Place with a garden – and a ping-pong table. Fifty years after playing in the English Open championships, I came across the American who'd won, Marty Reisman (a.k.a. The Needle), so I installed a table in the basement and a group of us find it therapeutic to whack the celluloid ball. Reisman is still unbeatable.

As George and Isabel grew up, Tina and I split the evening engagements in New York so that there was always one of us at home. The division of family duties between Tina and me, entailing our separate attendances at functions, caused New York tongues to wag. It passed us by. We were living an American idyll: work in Manhattan, and at weekends we'd at last found our seaside dream, an old house on a beach on Long Island, twenty miles from where we'd been married in 1981.

The American predilection for the car is such that we had been regarded by some of our friends as English eccentrics when we took our first summer foray by train from the city, looking for somewhere to rent away from the heat. Of course I love trains for my own special reasons, and Tina does too. We took the Long Island Railroad out, relaxing for two hours in the parlour car while a man in a straw boater served cold beer and the engineer sounded the whistle through the dreary suburban crossings and then joyously into the rolling pine barrens. At the end of a disappointing day in squally rain inspecting exorbitant glitzed-up beach huts in Westhampton, the letting agent drove us to nearby Quogue, a secluded seaside village of quiet lawns and white picket fences – a community of WASP-y literary folk rather than the high rollers of East Hampton and Southampton. The seashore road was flooded by a tidal surge in the inland waterway and the agent turned us round to go back. 'You wouldn't want to see that house, anyway,' she said, 'it's very old-fashioned.' Our hearts leapt. 'Yes, yes, show us right away.'

The house on Dune Road, set down amid beach plum and dune grass, turned out to be a grey clapboard beach cottage with dormer windows. Built in 1928, and shielded from the ocean by a great double dune, it had survived the great hurricane of 1938. Every stick of furniture and ornament dated from the same period in the 1930s. Little card tables were set for a game of bridge like a scene from Agatha Christie. Framed on one wall was the original owner's share certificate dated 1937 for the Siscoe Gold Mines.

We took it of course. This was the dream seeded in those secluded spots at Angmering-on-Sea and Connemara when we first fell in love. In our house on the dunes, we lived the sepia print of an American summer, cocooned in a time warp while Tina edited her *New Yorker* articles and I absorbed myself in American history and wrote and illustrated the story of the nation's ascent from 1889 to 1989: *The American Century*. It became a bestseller and I followed it with *They Made America*, a history of innovation over two centuries made into a four-part PBS television series. The old iron stove broiled local flounder pretty well, the ancient radio wafted in a narrative of baseball from somewhere, and every day for a morning dip the sun showed up promptly.

Twenty summers later, having saved up to buy the old house, we're still there with George, now twenty-three, and Isabel, nineteen, neither impressed that we can't tell them about the mysterious Siscoe gold mine. We retain our friendships and links with Britain. Enid came to Quogue for the wedding of our second daughter, Kate, who's settled in America. Our son Mike worked in Los Angeles as a photographer and then in New York and later London as a specialist

in computer printing. Ruth managed London bookshops. I am proud
of them all.

Tina and I now have dual citizenship; I became an American citizen
in 1993 and Tina seven years later. When we can, we cross the
Atlantic to Britain by sailing on a Cunard *Queen Mary 2* transatlantic liner, a nostalgic journey for me since I returned to Britain in
1957 on the original *Queen Mary*. Around the time of 9/11, our
daughter Isabel, then eleven, was asked at school whether she was
English or American. She said she was 'Amerikish'. Some months
after 9/11, her homework for a class in Greek mythology was to
make a Pandora's box. We asked her what she'd put in it. She
showed us an empty plate for hunger, a Tylenol bottle for disease, a
cracked mirror for vanity, a chocolate for greed. And there was a
tiny coloured drawing she had made of the Stars and Stripes.

'And that?' we asked.

'Hope,' she said.

I often think of that today. I flew into America on the wings of
hope and it has not let me down. When I walk on the beach worrying what to put in this memoir and what to leave out, I hear the
distant long soft whistle of the locomotive rattling through the
Hamptons, I see my father on his footplate, and I think of my own
journey from the steam age of newspapers to digital delivery and all
the people I was privileged to work with in journalism and publishing. At the beginning, I never conceived this memoir as a valediction
to a vanishing world. Now I hear so much about the imminent end
of newspapers, it's a relief on a morning in New York to find I can
still walk to the corner newsstand for a bunch of them, meaningful
stories on paper produced by what the web world calls 'human
agents' rather than a bunch of bloodless algorithms. In fact, I'm not
alone. In the United States, there are another 49,999,999 people similarly engaged. Fifty million read a daily in the US, ten million in
Britain.

Yet even as I have been writing this memoir several major
American newspapers have closed and famous titles have gone into
bankruptcy. I am pained for the men and women who dedicated

themselves to work they saw, rightly, as essential to a functioning democracy. My hopeful nature makes me believe that we are in a period of transition at the end of which we will see a perfect marriage of the Web and the traditional newspaper with its dedication to discovery, its careful calibration of news values and its eclectic mix. Technology will deliver a digital newspaper to our homes over the Internet and we'll be able to choose to read it online and print it out in tabloid format too. (Disclosure: in 2008, Tina founded and edits a comprehensive and exciting website, www.thedailybeast.com, that I call up every morning).

In fact, the necessary worrying about what is happening to newspapers and their staffs tends to obscure the fantastic utilities of the Web. Internet journalism sites have immense potential, not just for their speed but for increasing our comprehension and enjoyment. Hyperlinks open a panorama of global sources. We, the sceptical or curious readers, can explore primary documents quoted. We can replay the sensation at a political rally caught by a spectator and posted to YouTube. We can keep track of a hurricane from a weather centre, watch the new theatrical star the critics are acclaiming. We can be sure that misstatement and tendentious entries will be stung to death by a thousand blogging bees. The question is not whether Internet journalism will be dominant, but whether it will maintain the quality of the best print journalism. In the end, it is not the delivery system that counts. It is what it delivers. There has never been such access to knowledge in all its forms. What we have to find is a way to sustain truth-seeking. If we evolve the right financial model, we will enter a golden age of journalism.

I was exceptionally lucky to practise my craft for so long in the creatively free atmosphere cultivated by the Thomson and Newhouse families and the Westminster Press and the *Guardian* and the *Manchester Evening News* – and for that matter William Hobson Andrews – Mr Will – with his milk can and impossible questions in Ashton-under-Lyne:

How many words, Evans, in a memoir?

Enough!

Acknowledgements

What are your sources? Are they sound? Why don't you name them? The questions I've answered as a reporter and asked as an editor now demand answers from an author.

Well, I'm glad you asked. It's an opportunity to acknowledge my considerable debts. When I set out to follow my paper trail through the labyrinths of memory, I had the sometimes enigmatic diaries I'd kept over the years in Pitman's shorthand I could still read; I had school reports, wartime ration books, letters, photographs, articles, transcripts of radio and television programmes I'd been involved in; I had years of my newspaper files I cherished; and I had innumerable notes. I learned early, when challenged on a story, that if you wanted to survive as a journalist, you never threw away anything (and it works if you have a researcher as good as Jolene Lescio). Still, knowing that memory plays tricks, especially on sequence, I became an intruder on other people's tranquillity, ransacking their recollections to affirm or amend my own.

My premier debt is to my younger brother Fred, curator of family folklore, who wrestled me to the ground on various things I'd got wrong in family history (just a bit!), as he used to wrestle me in boyhood. Fred was my guide when I revisited our haunts in Manchester and North Wales; I thank his widow Christine for her forbearance when I took time from Fred. My brothers Peter and John helped to recreate those vanished times. Alf Morris – sorry, Lord Morris of Wythenshawe – told me something about my life I didn't know, that as a schoolboy I was known in the neighbourhood as 'Posh' Evans; Derek Kinrade's book of Alf's ascent from Newton Heath to Labour minister and the House of Lords (*Alf*) is a fine social history of Northern working-class life.

My knowledge of my father's working life was much enriched by the recollections of Ken Law, his fireman mate on many an adventure on the footplate of steam locomotives. To check my memories of my start in newspapers, I revisited the town of Ashton-under-Lyne and the library at Stalybridge and I thank the librarians. It was an exercise powerfully assisted by Derek Rigby, who graduated from carrying Mr W. H. Andrews' milk can to making headlines as an enterprising reporter. My two closest *Ashton Reporter* pals, all in our early teens when we met, Eric Marsden and Frank Keeble, reassured me that various eccentricities I remembered really did happen; our Weegee, Charlie Sutcliffe, scoured his photo library to my benefit. As for my years in the Royal Air Force, yanked out of Ashton, it's all in that Lubyanka Ministry of Aviation Records Office at Innsworth if anyone cares to check, and they'll have a record, too, of another airman, Peter Spaull of South Wirral. He heard me on the BBC's *Desert Island Discs* and touched down out of the blue to testify to the fun of producing the *Empire Flying School Review*; he volunteered the information that my tapping him to write film reviews and gossip items eventually led to him covering music and arts for BBC radio and a column in the *Liverpool Daily Post*. *Per ardua ad astra.*

My diaries at Durham University reflect my joy in meeting Enid Parker and I am grateful for the assiduity she brought to checking the details of those days and our years of married life. It was delightful recreating the glow of those years with her and with Derek and Daphne Holbrook, Roy Arnold, Brian and Shirley Scrivener, John ('Lofty') Morland and Keith Nodding. Durham meant a lot to all of us, and to the others reminiscing in Castle reunions: John Perkins, John Hollier, Bill Burdus, John Bridges, Lou Hamer, Edgar Jones, Geoff Pulling, Ridley Coats, Roy McKenzie, Eric Thompson and Chuck Metcalfe. The Master of University College, Professor Maurice Tucker, went out of his way to assist.

I was lucky that amid the paper storms at the *Manchester Evening News*, when my diaries went blank for days, I had a colleague from those times possessed of total recall, Duncan Measor; I thank Duncan and his wife Marjorie. I did find it stimulating to retrace steps when I could, and a visit to the *Manchester Evening News* offices was most rewarding. I thank the *Evening News* editor Paul Horrocks and his resolute assistant Lisa Brealey, chief executive Mark Dodson, deputy editor Maria McGeoghan, Tom Waghorn and the reporters, subs and photographers I interrupted on their way to a deadline. Bob Corfield's film on the paper's centenary caught the atmosphere well. Andy Harvie, the news editor in my time, was helpful as was Jane Futrell, the daughter of Denys, and Tony Watson, editor in chief of the Press Association. On this visit to Manchester I had the big benefit of the hospitality and knowledge of school chum Peter Charlton, the official historian of Newton Heath, and his wife Lillian. My friend Barrie Heads, one of the redoubtable producers of Granada Television in its early glory days in Manchester, was kind enough to let me read his hilarious television memoir before its publication. I am sorry that I failed his high standards of pronunciation.

Absolutely indispensable from the *Northern Echo* onwards was Joan Thomas, my first-ever secretary who later joined me in London. I'd not have been able to reach so many who shared the excitements without Joan's indefatigable resource in tracking people I'd lost touch with. Michael Morrissey, the paper's first news editor, and David Spark, the assistant editor, were extraordinarily generous with their time. Ken Hooper was helpful in retracing our cervical cancer investigation. I also thank the current editor Peter Barron, Peter Ridley, Ray Robertson and that kid photographer of the rock stars Ian Wright, who grew up to be a celebrity in his world. Don Berry, like Joan Thomas, came from Darlington to the *Sunday Times*, in his case via the *Rochester (NY) Times-Union*, and brought his super-powered sub's black pencil with him. I thank him for his wry observations.

I could fill a telephone directory with all the people who made the *Sunday Times* what it was in my fourteen years of editing (not forgetting the late Mike Randall, Peter Harland, Peter Sullivan, Jack Lambert, Steve Brodie, Malcolm Crawford, Peter Roberts and Tony Bambridge). We were a community, sharing our passions for journalism, and I am forever indebted to them all for their skill, courage and companionship. It's wonderful that I was able to talk with the head printer, George Darker, who is nearing a hundred years of age, despite the stresses to which we subjected him. I can only make a particular mention here of those *Sunday Times* individuals who failed to evade my long arm when I sought to test my recollections and records on theirs, chief among them, John Barry, Godfrey Smith, Bruce Page, Godfrey Hodgson, Phillip Knightley, Paul Eddy, Peter Gillman, Elaine Potter, Edwin Taylor, Cal McCrystal, Tony Holden, Keith Richardson, Tony Rennell, Magnus Linklater, Peter Pringle, Philip Jacobson, Tony Dawe, Colin Chapman, Michael Ward, Parin Janmohamed, Charles Raw, Lewis Chester, Frank Giles, Helena Cobban, Michael Jones,

George Darby, Don McCullin, James Evans and Anthony Whitaker, along with the recently much-mourned Hugo Young, John Whale and Peter Wilsher. Yvonne Mascarenhas, the widow of the brave Anthony, told me the story of her escape from Pakistan which Anthony had kept to himself. Clive Irving, creator of the early Insight pages, filled in the gaps in my knowledge and understanding of those days before I joined the paper. For images, but also recollections, I drew freely on the skill and energies of photographers Bryan Wharton (who acted as informal photo editor), Sally Soames, Michael Ward, Peter Dunne, Mark Ellidge and Ian Berry. The collage on the endpapers is the work of New York's Kate Reilly whose good temper matches her skill. Gerald Scarfe's brilliantly pointed caricatures and pungent wit enlivened my *Sunday Times* years and I am indebted to him for permission to incorporate in the collage his drawing celebrating the paper's award of the European gold medal.

My review of our Northern Ireland work owes much to John Barry, the former Insight editor (now with *Newsweek*), who challenged and enriched my account – though responsible for nothing that invites criticism – and with him the intrepid Chris Ryder. My chapter 'Death in Cairo' owes a great deal to Eddy and Gillman, who never gave up on the story. I very much appreciate how Scotland Yard was ready, as the saying goes, to assist us in our inquiries. I am indebted to the cooperation of Sir Ian Blair, then Metropolitan Commissioner of Police at Scotland Yard, and of Commander Simon Foy, head of homicide, Inspector Graham Jenkins and former detectives Ray Small and Tony Comben.

For their readiness to help, I must also acknowledge Jan Morris, David Holden's friend; Sy Hersh at the *New Yorker*; Steve Emerson at the Investigative Project on Terrorism in Washington DC; Roger Louis, director of British Studies at the University of Texas at Austin; Professor Allen Weinstein, the ninth archivist of the United States; and Williams and Connolly DC, notably in the person of Bob Barnett.

My Paper Chase – which is what it truly was – might never have been finished on time (well, only a year or two off) without the needling by my agent and friend Ed Victor. Cindy Quillinan, my assistant, has survived the vicissitudes of my book and television series on innovation, and crested the waves of producing manuscript Mark XI with uncanny calm. Geoff Shandler, editor in chief at Little, Brown, New York, whose original idea it was to divert me from recording other people's history to my own, proved to have reservoirs of patience as deep as his editorial judgement. At that crucial moment in the life of a book when an author is wondering whether to turn tail and run, I was vastly encouraged by Michael Korda who has vibrant memories of his own of those years in Britain and life in the RAF.

For publication in Britain, it was a distinct pleasure to arouse the interest of Ursula Mackenzie, chief executive of Little, Brown, whom I'd admired for many years, and of her publishing director Richard Beswick. Vivien Redman and Steve Cox managed the transatlantic arrangements with impressive élan. Elizabeth Dobson, proofreading, had a quiverful of queries that were most helpful.

I was most fortunate of all that John Heilpern, who grew up in Manchester and was a star on the *Sunday Times*' rival, the *Observer*, took an early interest in what I might do to retrieve those vanished times – his phrase. A brilliant biographer and theatre critic himself, he urged me not to skimp on my early life and family and in many a conversation he enabled me to retrieve the half-remembered and cherish it anew. His critical overview of the manuscript was invaluable and I will always be grateful to him.

Throughout, from that daunting first blank page, during periods of uncertainty and distractions, I was sustained by the discerning eye, professional skill and loving support of my gifted wife Tina. My driving fear was of disappointing her and my driving hope is that our children George and Isabel will regard the memoir as some compensation for those days in the present when I was lost in the past.

Bibliography

Principal *Sunday Times* Books

The Zinoviev Letter by Lewis Chester, Stephen Fay and Hugo Young (Heinemann, 1967). How the famous 'Red letter', which helped to defeat Ramsay Macdonald's Labour Government, was forged by White Russians and circulated by Conservative Central Office with Secret Service help.

Philby, The Spy Who Betrayed a Generation by Bruce Page, David Leitch and Phillip Knightley, with an introduction by John le Carré (Deutsch, 1968).

An American Melodrama by Lewis Chester, Godfrey Hodgson and Bruce Page (Deutsch, 1969). History of the US Presidential election of 1968, during which Richard Nixon was elected and Robert Kennedy murdered.

Journey to Tranquility by Hugo Young, Bryan Silcock and Peter Dunn (Cape, 1969). History of man's assault on the Moon.

The Secret Lives of Lawrence of Arabia by Colin Simpson and Phillip Knightley (Nelson, 1969). Documentation of Lawrence's sado-masochism and unsuspected role in Middle East politics.

The Strange Voyage of Donald Crowhurst by Nicholas Tomalin and Ron Hall (Hodder, 1970). The mystery of lone sailor Donald Crowhurst, who vanished from his trimaran during the *Sunday Times* single-handed non-stop race around the world.

The Pound in Your Pocket by Peter Wilsher (Cassell, 1970). Century of Sterling 1870–1970.

Do You Sincerely Want To Be Rich? by Charles Raw, Bruce Page and Godfrey Hodgson (Deutsch, 1971). Subtitled 'Bernard Cornfeld and IOS, An International Swindle'. Investigation of the rise of Investors Overseas Services (IOS) and its creator, Bernie Cornfeld, how it operated as an 'offshore' company responsible to the law of no single nation and what it did with the £1,000 million entrusted to it by a million savers.

Hoax by Lewis Chester, Stephen Fay and Magnus Linklater (Deutsch, 1972). The forgery and retailing of Howard Hughes's autobiography by Irving.

Ulster by the *Sunday Times* Insight Team (Deutsch and Penguin, 1972). Results of four months of inquiry into the origins of the troubles.

The Thalidomide Children and the Law, the *Sunday Times* (Deutsch, 1973). Documents and texts.

Watergate by Lewis Chester, Stephen Aris, Cal McCrystal and William Shawcross (Deutsch, 1973).

Nicholas Tomalin Reporting (Deutsch, 1975). Ron Hall introduces reporting by his colleague and friend, killed on duty for the *Sunday Times* on the Golan front October 1973.

The Yom Kippur War by the Insight Team (Deutsch, 1975). Sequel to *Sunday Times* book *Insight on the Middle East War*, published in 1974.

The Exploding Cities by Peter Wilsher and Rosemary Righter (Deutsch, 1975). Foreword by Barbara Ward. Stimulated by *Sunday Times* conference with United Nations Fund for Population Activities at Oxford University.

Insight on Portugal (Deutsch, 1975). Portugal's return to democracy.

On Giant's Shoulders by Marjorie Wallace and Michael Robson (Times Books, 1976). The story of thalidomide victim Terry Wiles.

Death of Venice by Stephen Fay and Phillip Knightley (Deutsch, 1975). Investigation of threat to the survival of Venice.

The Crossman Affair by Hugo Young (Cape, 1976).

Destination Disaster by Paul Eddy, Elaine Potter and Bruce Page (Hart-Davis, MacGibbon, 1976). Investigation of Paris DC-10 crash.

Slater Walker by Charles Raw (Deutsch, 1977). Jim Slater tried to prevent publication of Charles Raw's four-year investigation, which concluded that in all its various forms Slater Walker was really about one thing, the manipulation of share prices.

The Abuse of Power by James Margach (W. H. Allen, 1978). The war between Downing Street and the media from Lloyd George to Callaghan by veteran *Sunday Times* political correspondent.

The Fall of the House of Beaverbrook by Lewis Chester and Jonathan Fenby (Deutsch, 1979). How Trafalgar House acquired the *Daily Express*, *Evening Standard* and *Sunday Express*.

Jeremy Thorpe: A Secret Life by Lewis Chester, Magnus Linklater and David May (Deutsch and Fontana, 1979).

Suffer the Children by the Insight Team (Deutsch, 1979). Thalidomide story.

Siege! by the Insight Team (Hamlyn, 1980). How the SAS rescued hostages at the Iranian Embassy, London, 1980.

Stop Press by Eric Jacobs (Deutsch, 1980). The inside story of the year of the suspension of Times Newspapers 1978–9.

The Vestey Affair by Phillip Knightley (Macdonald, 1981).

Of special interest

Lawsuit by Stuart M. Speiser (Horizon Press, New York, 1980). Lawyer in the DC-10 case opens his files on celebrated cases.

General References

Alterman, Eric. 'Out of Print: The Death and Life of the American Newspaper.' *The New Yorker*. 31 March 2008. http://www.newyorker.com/reporting/2008/03/31/080331fa_fact_alterman

Bacon, Robert William. *Britain's Economic Problem: Too Few Producers*. London: Macmillan, 1978.

Barnett, Steven. 'Future of the Printed Word: The Press; Reasons to be Cheerful.' *British Journalism Review* 17.1 (March 2006): 7–14.

Bayley, Edwin R. *Joe McCarthy and the Press*. Madison, Wisconsin: University of Wisconsin Press, 1981.

Behr, Edward. *Anyone Here Been Raped and Speaks English*. London: New English Library, 1982.

Bell, J. Bowyer. *The Irish Troubles: A Generation of Violence, 1967–1992*. New York: St Martin's Press, 1993.

Benn, Tony, and Ruth Winstone. *Conflicts of Interest: Diaries 1977–80*. London: Hutchinson, 1990.

Blundy, David, and Anthony Holden. *The Last Paragraph: The Journalism of David Blundy*. London: Heinemann, 1990.

Boyd, Ruth. *Stanley Devon: News Photographer*. England: D. Harrison, 1995.

Braddon, Russell. *Thomson of Fleet*. London: Collins, 1965.

Brandon, Piers. *The Life and Death of the Press Barons*. London: Secker, 1982.

Briggs, Susan. *The Home Front: War Years in Britain, 1939–1945*. New York: American Heritage, 1975.

Brown, Anthony Cave. *Treason in the Blood: H. St John Philby, Kim Philby, and the Spy Case of the Century*. Boston: Houghton Mifflin, 1994.

Brown, Derek. 'Future of the Printed Word: Cyberspace; Joe Blog's Turn.' *British Journalism Review* 17.1 (March 2006): 15–19.

Butler, David, and Anne Sloman. *British Political Facts 1900–1975*. London: Macmillan, 1975.

'The Changing Newsroom.' Journalism.org. 21 July 2008. Pew Research Center's Project for Excellence in Journalism. <http://journalism.org/node/11961>

Coleridge, Nicholas. *Paper Tigers: The Latest, Greatest Newspaper Tycoons and How They Won the World*. London: Heinemann, 1993.

Compton, Edmund. *Report of the Enquiry into Allegations against the Security Forces of Physical Brutality in Northern Ireland Arising Out of Events on the 9th August, 1971*. London: HMSO, 1971.

Coogan, Tim Pat. *Michael Collins: A Biography*. London: Hutchinson, 1990.

Coogan, Tim Pat. *The Troubles: Ireland's Ordeal and the Search for Peace*. New York: Palgrave, 2002.

Cottle, Simon. 'Reporting the Troubles in Northern Ireland: Paradigms and Media Propaganda.' *Critical Studies in Mass Communication*: CSMC: a publication of the Speech Communication Association 14.3 (1997): 283–296.

Crossman, R. H. S. *Secretary of State for Social Services*. Vol. III of *The Diaries of a Cabinet Minister*. London: Hamish Hamilton, 1975.

Cudlipp, Hugh. *The Prerogative of the Harlot: Press Barons & Power*. London: Bodley Head, 1980.

Cuozzo, Steven. *It's Alive: How America's Oldest Newspaper Cheated Death and Why it Matters*. New York: Times Books, 1996.

Davies, Nick. *Flat Earth News: An Award-Winning Reporter Exposes Falsehood, Distortion, and Propaganda in the Global Media*. London: Chatto & Windus, 2008.

Deakin, James. *Straight Stuff: The Reporters, the White House and the Truth*. New York: William Morrow, 1984.

Dean, Joseph. *Hatred, Ridicule or Contempt: A Book of Libel Cases*. London: Constable and Company, 1953.

Donoughue, Bernard. *The Heat of the Kitchen*. London: Politico's, 2003.

Donoughue, Bernard. *Downing Street Diary: With Harold Wilson in No. 10*. London: Jonathan Cape, 2005.

East, P. D. *The Magnolia Jungle: The Life, Times and Education of a Southern Editor*. New York: Simon and Schuster, 1960.

Eckley, Grace. *Maiden Tribute: A Life of W. T. Stead*. Philadelphia: Xlibris, 2007.

Edwards, Robert. *Goodbye Fleet Street*. Sevenoaks: Coronet, 1989.

Edwards, Ruth Dudley. *Newspapermen: Hugh Cudlipp, Cecil Harmsworth King and the Glory Days of Fleet Street*. London: Pimlico, 2004.

Egerton, John. *Speak Now Against the Day: The Generation Before the Civil Rights Movement in the South*. New York: A. Knopf, 1994.

Elliott, Geoffrey. *I Spy: The Secret Life of a British Agent*. London: St Ermin's Press, 1999.

Evans, Harold. 'The Suez Crisis: A Study in Press Performance.' (MA thesis, University of Durham, 1965).

Evans, Harold. Introduction *Don McCullin* by Don McCullin. London: Jonathan Cape, 2001.

Evans, Harold. Foreword to *Killing the Messenger: Report of the Global Inquiry by the International News Safety Institute into the Protection of Journalists*. Brussels, Belgium: International News Safety Institute, 2007.

Friendly, Fred W. *The Good Guys, The Bad Guys and the First Amendment: Free Speech vs. Fairness in Broadcasting*. New York: Random House, 1976.

Friendly, Fred W. *Minnesota Rag: The Dramatic Story of the Landmark Supreme Court Case That Gave New Meaning to the Freedom of the Press*. New York: Random House, 1981.

Geraghty, Tony. *The Irish War: The Military History of a Domestic Conflict*. London: HarperCollins, 2000.

Giles, Frank. *Sundry Times*. London: John Murray 1986.

Giussani, Vanessa. *The UK Clean Air Act 1956: An Empirical Investigation*. Centre for Social and Economic Research on the Global Environment, 1994.

Glover, Stephen. *Paper Dreams*. London: Jonathan Cape, 1993.

Goff, Peter, and Barbara Trionfi, eds. *The Kosovo News and Propaganda War*. Vienna: International Press Institute, 1999.

Greenhill, Denis. *More by Accident*. York: Wilton 65, 1992.

Greenslade, Roy. *Press Gang: How Newspapers Make Profits from Propaganda*. London: Pan Books, 2004.

Grundy, Bill. *The Press Inside Out*. London: W. H. Allen, 1976.

Haines, Joe. *The Politics of Power*. Sevenoaks: Coronet, 1977.

Hamilton, Denis. 'The Sunday Times.' *Punch Magazine*. 23 December 1964: 944–947.

Hamilton, Denis. *Editor-in-Chief: The Fleet Street Memoirs of Sir Denis Hamilton*. London: Hamish Hamilton, 1989.

Hampton, Henry, Steve Fayer and Sarah Flynn. *Voices of Freedom: An Oral History of the Civil Rights Movement from the 1950s through the 1980s*. New York: Bantam Books, 1990.

Harris, Geoffrey, and David Spark. *Practical Newspaper Reporting*. London: William Heinemann, 1966.

Hattersley, Roy. *Fifty Years On: A Prejudiced History of Britain Since the War*. London: Little, Brown & Co., 1997.

Heads, Barrie. *Medium Close Up*. Unpublished manuscript.

Hennessy, Peter. *Having It So Good: Britain in the Fifties*. London: Allen Lane, 2006.

Herd, Harold. *The March of Journalism, The Story of the British Press from 1622 to the Present Day*. London: George Allen and Unwin, 1952.

Hetherington, Alastair. *Guardian Years*. London: Chatto & Windus, 1981.

Hilty, James W. *Robert Kennedy: Brother Protector*. Philadelphia PA: Temple University Press, 1997.

Hobsbawm, Julia, ed. *Where the Truth Lies: Trust and Morality in PR and Journalism*. London: Atlantic Books, 2006.

Hobson, Harold, Phillip Knightley and Leonard Russell. *Pearl of Days*. London: Hamish Hamilton, 1972.

Hodgson, Godfrey. *America in Our Time*. Garden City, NY: Doubleday, 1976.

Hoggart, Richard. *The Uses of Literacy: Aspects of Working-Class Life with Special Reference to Publications and Entertainments*. Harmondsworth: Penguin Books, 1958.

Holden, Anthony. *Of Presidents, Prime Ministers, and Princes: A Decade in Fleet Street*. London: Weidenfeld and Nicolson, 1984.

Hooper, David. *Official Secrets: The Use and Abuse of the Act.* London: Martin Secker & Warburg, 1987.

Howard, Anthony. *Crossman: The Pursuit of Power.* London: Pimlico, 1991.

Isaacs, Jeremy. *Storm Over 4.* London: Weidenfeld and Nicolson, 1989.

Jack, Ian. *Before the Oil Ran Out: Britain 1977–86.* London: Secker & Warburg, 1987.

Jackson, Brian. *Working Class Community: Some General Notions Raised by a Series of Studies in Northern England.* London: Routledge & Kegan Paul, 1968.

Jacobs, Eric. *Stop Press: The Inside Story of the Times Dispute.* London: Deutsch, 1980.

Jenkins, Roy. *A Life at the Centre.* London: Macmillan, 1991.

Jenkins, Simon. *Newspapers.* London: Faber and Faber, 1979.

Jenkins, Simon. *Thatcher and Sons: A Revolution in Three Acts.* London: Penguin, 2007.

Keen, Andrew. *The Cult of the Amateur: How Today's Internet is Killing Our Culture.* London: Nicholas Brealey, 2007.

Kennedy, Ludovic. *10 Rillington Place.* London: Panther Books, 1972.

Kennedy, Robert F. *The Enemy Within.* New York and Evanston: Harper & Row Publishers, 1960.

Kingston, Shane. 'Terrorism, the Media and the Northern Ireland Conflict.' *Studies in Conflict and Terrorism* 18.3 (July/September 1995): 203–231.

Knightley, Phillip. *A Hack's Progress.* London: Jonathan Cape, 1997.

Knightley, Phillip. *The First Casualty: The War Correspondent as Hero and Myth-Maker from the Crimea to Kosovo.* London: Prion, 2000.

Kovach, Bill, and Tom Rosenstiel. *Warp Speed: America in the Age of Mixed Media. A Century Foundation Report.* New York: Century Foundation Press, 1999.

Kovach, Bill, and Tom Rosenstiel. *The Elements of Journalism: What Newspeople Should Know and the Public Should Expect.* New York: Three Rivers Press, 2007.

Kurtz, Howard. *Media Circus: The Trouble with America's Newspapers.* New York: Random House, 1993.

Lapping, Brian, ed. *The Bounds of Freedom: A Series of Six Granada Television Programmes in Which Top Level Communicators Show How They Respond to Moments of Crisis – How They Decide What Gets Published, What Doesn't and Why.* London: Constable in collaboration with Granada Television, 1980.

Leapman, Michael. *Barefaced Cheek*. London: Hodder and Stoughton, 1983.

Leigh, David. *The Frontiers of Secrecy: Closed Government in Britain*. London: Junction Books, 1980.

Lennon, Peter. *Foreign Correspondent: Paris in the Sixties*. London: Picador, 1994.

Lloyd, Chris. *Attacking the Devil: 130 Years of The Northern Echo*. Darlington: Northern Echo, 1999.

Lords, Walter. *A Night to Remember: The Classic Account of the Final Hours of the Titanic*. New York: Henry Holt, 2005.

Madigan, Charles M., ed. *-30- The Collapse of the Great American Newspaper*. Chicago: Ivan R. Dee, 2007.

Mansfield, F. J., and Denis Weaver. *Mansfield's Complete Journalist: A Study of the Principles and Practice of Newspaper-making*. London: Pitman, 1962.

Marr, Andrew. 'Future of the Printed Word: A Changing Culture; Brave New World.' *British Journalism Review* 17.1 (March 2006): 29–34.

McLuhan, Marshall. *Understanding Media: The Extensions of Man*. London: Abacus, 1973.

Meyer, Philip. *The Vanishing Newspaper: Saving Journalism in the Information Age*. Columbia: University of Missouri Press, 2004.

Morton, J. B. *Beachcomber: The Works of J. B. Morton*. London: A. Wheaton & Company, 1974.

Nasaw, David. *The Chief: The Life of William Randolph Hearst*. Boston: Houghton Mifflin, 2000.

Neil, Andrew. *Full Disclosure*. London: Macmillan, 1996.

Orwell, George. *The Road to Wigan Pier*. London: Victor Gollancz, 1937.

Orwell, Sonia, and Ian Angus, eds. My *Country Right or Left: 1940–1943*. Vol. II of *The Collected Essays, Journalism and Letters of George Orwell*. Boston: David R. Godine, 2000.

Page, Bruce. 'Future of the Printed Word: The Dangers; It's the Media that Needs Protecting.' *British Journalism Review* 17.1 (March 2006): 20–28.

Page, Bruce, David Leitch and Phillip Knightley. *The Philby Conspiracy*. Toronto: Fontana Books, 1968.

Pimlott, Ben. *Harold Wilson*. London: HarperCollins, 1992.

Polsgrove, Carol. *Divided Minds: Intellectuals and the Civil Rights Movement*. New York: W. W. Norton & Co., 2001.

Powledge, Fred. *Free at Last? The Civil Rights Movement and the People Who Made It*. New York: HarperPerennial, 1992.

Prevett, J. H. 'Actuarial Assessment of Damages: The Thalidomide Case I.' *Modern Law Review* 35.2 (March 1972): 140–155.

Prevett, J. H. 'Actuarial Assessment of Damages: The Thalidomide Case II.' *Modern Law Review* 35.3 (May 1972): 256–267.

Prichard, Peter. *The Making of McPaper: The Inside Story of the USA Today*. Kansas City: Andrews, McMeel & Parker, 1987.

Pringle, Peter, and Philip Jacobson. *Those Are Real Bullets: Bloody Sunday, Derry, 1972*. London: Fourth Estate, 2000.

Righter, Rosemary. *Whose News?: Politics, the Press and the Third World*. London: Burnett Books, 1978.

Roberts, Gene and Hank Klibanoff. *The Race Beat: The Press, The Civil Rights Struggle and the Awakening of a Nation*. New York; Vintage Books, 2007.

Rose, Peter. *How the Troubles Came to Northern Ireland*. New York: St Martin's Press in association with the Institute of Contemporary British History, 2000.

Rose, Richard. 'On the Priorities of Citizenship in the Deep South and Northern Ireland.' *The Journal of Politics* 38.2 (May 1976): 247–291. JSTOR www.jstor.org (2 April 2008)

'Rover Boys Rewarded.' *Time Magazine*. 8 April 1957 <http://www.time.com/time/magazine/article/0,9171,809365-1,00.html>

Sampson, Anthony. *The Changing Anatomy of Britain*. London: Hodder and Stoughton, 1981.

'Scandal in Portland.' *Time Magazine*. 4 June 1956 <http://www.time.com/time/magazine/article/0,9171,866980,00.html>

Schama, Simon. *A History of Britain 3. The Fate of Empire 1776–2000*. London: BBC Worldwide, 2004.

Sebag-Montefiore, Hugh. *Dunkirk: Fight to the Last Man*. Cambridge, Mass: Harvard University Press, 2006.

Shepard, Richard F. *The Paper's Papers: A Reporter's Journey Through the Archives of The New York Times*. New York: Times Books, 1996.

Smartt, Ursula. *Media Law for Journalists*. London: Sage Publications, 2006.

Smith, Richard Norton. *The Colonel: The Life and Legend of Robert R. McCormick, 1880–1955*. Boston: Houghton Mifflin Company, 1997.

Smith, Zay N., and Pamela Zekman. *The Mirage*. New York: Random House, 1979.

Spark, David. *Investigative Reporting: A Study in Technique*. Oxford: Focal, 1999.

'The State of the News Media 2008.' 17 March 2008. Project for Excellence in Journalism. <http://www.stateofthenewsmedia.com/2008/>

Steiger, Paul E. 'Read All About It: How Newspapers Got into Such a Fix, And Where They Go From Here.' *The Wall Street Journal*. 29 December 2007. <http://online.wsj.com/article/SB119888825411356705.html?mod=hpp_us_pageone>

Swanberg, W. A. *Citizen Hearst: A Biography of William Randolph Hearst*. New York: Scribner, 1961.

Swanberg, W. A. *Pulitzer*. New York: Scribner, 1967.

Thomson, Roy Herbert. *After I Was Sixty: A Chapter of Autobiography*. London: Hamish Hamilton, 1975.

Trevor-Roper, H. R. *The Philby Affair: Espionage, Treason, and Secret Services*. London: Kimber, 1968.

Walker, Martin. *Powers of the Press*. London: Quartet, 1982.

Waterhouse, Robert. *The Other Fleet Street: How Manchester Made Newspapers National*. Altrincham: First Edition Limited, 2004.

Waugh, Evelyn. *Scoop: A Novel about Journalists*. Harmondsworth: Penguin Books, 1976.

Weatherby, W. J. *Breaking the Silence: The Negro Struggle in the U.S.A.* New York: Penguin, 1965.

Wendt, Lloyd. *Chicago Tribune: The Rise of a Great American Newspaper*. Chicago: Rand McNally, 1979.

Whale, John. *The Half-Shut Eye: Television & Politics in Britain and America*. London: Macmillan, 1969.

Wilkinson, Brenda. *The Civil Rights Movement: An Illustrated History*. New York: Crescent Books, 1997.

Williams, Francis. *The Right to Know: The Rise of the World Press*. Harlow: Longmans, 1969.

Winchester, Simon. '13 Killed as Paratroops Break Riot.' *Guardian*. 31 January 1972. 5 April 2008. <http://www.guardian.co.uk/uk/1972/jan/31/bloodysunday.northernireland>

Wincour, Jack, ed. *The Story of the Titanic: As Told by its Survivors*. New York: Dover Publications, 1960.

Young, Hugo. *The Crossman Affair*. London: Hamish Hamilton, 1976.

Young, Hugo. 'Rupert Murdoch and the *Sunday Times*: A Lamp Goes Out.' *Political Quarterly* 55.4 (October 1984): 382–390.

Young, Hugo. *One of Us: A Biography of Margaret Thatcher*. London: Macmillan, 1989.

Young, Hugo. *The Hugo Young Papers, Thirty Years of British Politics Off the Record*, ed. by Ion Trewin with forewords by Harold Evans and Alan Rusbridger, Allen Lane, Penguin Books, London, 2008.

Index